D1610635

Critical Moments

Fintan O'Toole on Modern Irish Theatre

Critical Moments

Fintan O'Toole on Modern Irish Theatre

Edited by Julia Furay and Redmond O'Hanlon

With an Afterword by Fintan O'Toole

Carysfort Press

A Carysfort Press Book

Critical Moments | Fintan O'Toole on Modern Irish Theatre
Edited by Julia Furay and Redmond O'Hanlon

First published in Ireland in 2003 as a paperback original by
Carysfort Press, 58 Woodfield, Scholarstown Road
Dublin 16, Ireland

Typeset by Carysfort Press
Cover design by Alan Bennis

Printed and bound by Leinster Leader Ltd
18/19 South Main Street, Naas, Co. Kildare, Ireland

the arts
council
schomhairle
ealaíon

Contents

Contents

Contents

Acknowledgements

Redmond O'Hanlon and Julia Furay would like to thank Eamonn Jordan, who has been an ideal and patient mentor as well as an expert resource. Dan Farrelly and Lilian Chambers at Carysfort Press have also been remarkable for supporting and funding this undertaking. Thanks, too, to the Arts Council for such continued support to the Press.

Julia is especially grateful to those who assisted in collecting the reviews, specifically Irene Stevenson at *The Irish Times* and the extraordinarily patient staff at both the National Library and Trinity College Library. She would also like to thank Lilian and Robert Chambers, and especially the uncommonly generous Trisha and Michael Geaney, for their hospitality during her numerous trips to Ireland.

Redmond would like to thank Hilary Gow and Katherine O'Hanlon for their help in transcribing the interviews.

Most of all, we thank Fintan O'Toole for his cooperation and for providing us with a richness of criticism we hope is fairly represented in this collection.

We gratefully acknowledge permission to reproduce work by Fintan O'Toole from the following sources: *In Dublin*, *The Irish Times*, *The Sunday Tribune*, the *New York Daily News*.

Julia Furay
Redmond O'Hanlon

Note on the Text

Apart from a few corrections (mainly typographical), all the reviews in this collection are reprinted exactly as originally published. While we have included most of the key works and notable authors in the contemporary canon, we have also reprinted reviews of lesser-known plays which either provoked particularly interesting criticism or seemed unjustly forgotten.

For the purposes of this volume we have decided that the phrase 'Modern Irish Theatre' should refer only to those new plays produced on or after 1953, the year which saw the premiere of *Waiting for Godot*. Undoubtedly this excludes many of the seminal productions of the last twenty years – Druid's *Playboy of the Western World* and the Gate's *Salomé* come to mind. Unfortunately, space constraints did not allow a broader definition.

Introduction

By Julia Furay

Like any piece of journalism, theatre criticism is a timely piece of prose. Once a show closes, your average theatre review of that performance is no longer alive and interactive, though it remains important as a historical document. Fintan O'Toole's criticism is particularly valuable in this respect: as historical documents they are exemplary.

To begin with, they are sharp, accurate first hand accounts of the Irish theatre. Throughout his career, O'Toole has combined the practical elements of a theatre review – description, summation and judgement – with expertise and intelligence. Not only that, but these reviews are also highly readable, funny and passionate. O'Toole, over a stretch of twenty-two years at five different publications, does more than simply document the progress of Irish theatre since 1980: he tells its story.

As an historical document, however, this work is extensive but necessarily incomplete. Obviously, editorial decisions have forced a focus on modern Irish drama alone, despite O'Toole's copious amounts of criticism on foreign texts, on reinterpretations of classics (both Irish and international), and on the many visiting companies to hit Dublin, particularly during the Theatre Festival. And of course, there are the reviews he did not write. Gaps occur due to his extended coverage of the Irish Beef Tribunal, his year as a literary adviser at the Abbey, and his three years spent as a critic at the *New York Daily News*.

Fortunately, the historical usefulness of a set of newspaper clippings is just one of the elements that make O'Toole's criticism invaluable. On one level, in fact, O'Toole's writings aren't historical documents at all. Because of his particular style and approach, O'Toole's work remains contemporary even as it becomes a historical document. His writings stay progressive for two major reasons, both of which come across as driving impulses in his overall criticism.

The first is that throughout his career O'Toole has continually searched for the ultimate meaning, intent or significance in a piece of drama. (O'Toole discusses this in depth in conversation with Redmond O'Hanlon later in this work.) His quest for meaning in every play means that he is unusually adept at dealing with the timeless and universal questions.

And yet his writings on these ageless issues maintain a strong sense of time. One example is emigration: the Irish attitude towards this has changed greatly. In examining such plays as *True Lines* and *Philadelphia, Here I Come!*, Fintan O'Toole looks at changes in perception towards the issue. It's this sort of close examination that continues to be important long after the play he reviewed has closed.

A second – and related – driving force in O'Toole's criticism is his penchant for putting plays into a larger framework. He is famous for placing much of the theatre he sees in a political context. This is true: O'Toole does indeed draw out the political aspects of a play as often as possible. However, O'Toole is just as anxious to place a play within its theatrical or societal context. With such a wealth of background information and width of perspective, the reviews become not just a discussion of one play at one moment in time, but of entire genres and currents of thought. For instance, he'll review a new Dermot Bolger comedy, *Blinded By the Light*, by discussing not only its place within the form of Irish comedy, but also writing at length about Irish comedy itself. Only after 500 words of discussion does he get around to reviewing the play at hand. And after seeing *Bat the Father, Rabbit the Son* a second time, he doesn't criticize it so much as attempt to pinpoint its place in the Irish tradition of dramas about fathers and sons. These pieces, more analysis than review, retain meaning and validity where many reviews would not.

This tendency is one of a number of traits that become more apparent when we survey O'Toole's reviews as a whole. Beyond what these reviews expose about Irish theatre past and present, O'Toole's criticism reveals much about Fintan O'Toole himself, and indeed, criticism as a whole.

Most obvious, of course, is that discussion and argument – not the description of the theatrical experience – is foremost in O'Toole's reviews. That is to say, his reviews do not just depict a theatrical experience by detailing what is happening on stage. Description is just one of many elements of O'Toole's argument, rather than a major force. For example, he will often refrain from describing the acting, unless he can link it to the core of the experience. Or, he will describe the direction by noting how well it brings out – or fails to bring out – the play's relationship to its larger context.

Also noticeable is that he is allowed the room to bring discussion to such a level. During his years at the *New York Daily News*, he was allowed just a few hundred words – sometimes as little as 300, even for a major new play – and his criticism suffered for it. The New York pieces, written for a less sophisticated readership, may be more concise, more quotable, but they lack the real relationship with the theatre that keeps his Irish criticism contemporary even years later. A 1998 piece of criticism for the *Daily News* becomes somehow more dated than a 1982 review for *In Dublin*.

O'Toole was never an overnight reviewer, so much of his writing became much more highly developed than would be the case for critics who have to write even more quickly. The Second Opinion pieces, written at *The Irish Times* beginning in 1988, are particularly noticeable in this respect: they featured the short and snappy style he later exploited in New York, but also included depth and elegance to boot. Nevertheless, all of the pieces in the book were written on a tight deadline, so the occasional lazy phrasing and intermittent use of journalistic catchphrases is not surprising. Ultimately, however, it's irrelevant – some amount of awkward or even turgid phrasing is probably built into the form of a journalistic theatre review, just as a degree of sentimentality is inherent in the musical theatre.

Another element that is perhaps intrinsic to all theatre criticism is that of savagery, found in reviews that are gleefully nasty (and usually hilarious). Fintan O'Toole is not, for the most part, a critic who has historically thrived on savagery, and he has never been cruelly dismissive. His negative reviews are wittily damning, not maliciously so (take his piece on Ira Levin's *Deathtrap*: 'The corpses may come to life but the production doesn't'). Generally, he explores the failures in a work with an intellectual eye, more inclined to explore the reasons for a play's failure by intellectual argument rather than savage dismissal.

The problem comes, then, not from malice or viciousness, but condescension. O'Toole has long been somewhat scornful towards naturalistic middle-class drama; he admits to preferring works that challenge forms and exhibit a visceral sense of danger. These are certainly valid inclinations. However, when it comes to reviewing middle-class drama, his criticism carries an air of disdain. He does not even approve of works that fit well into the form. In his 1994 review of Arthur Riordan's *Hidden Charges* he admits that it is deftly and wittily written, with a 'sharp, snazzy' production. Yet he cannot truly praise the play, because he finds the form in which the playwright has chosen to write objectionable: 'You can't write 1950s kitchen comedies about 1990s Ireland. […] Our reality is just too perverse and too elusive to fit into the discarded moulds of 40 years ago'.

The form then does not speak to O'Toole – which is perfectly acceptable. But it can cause problems for a writer as intent as he is on finding the deeper meaning in a drama. If a form – be it middle-class drama, agitprop, or even musical theatre – does not resonate to him, then it's difficult to accept his criticism as valid. O'Toole is so intent on finding the core of the apple that sometimes he doesn't notice that he's holding a peach.

And though he has admitted openly to certain prejudices, he couldn't tell the whole story. Only with the juxtaposition of these many years of reviews do we find more, unacknowledged prejudices. The sheer number of critical pieces on Passion Machine or Druid versus the relative paucity of writings on Billy

Roche, Corn Exchange or Loose Canon reveals much. True, critics need holidays just like everyone else, but O'Toole was careful not to miss Mercier, Hynes or McDonagh productions. The same can't be said of several other theatre figures.

Clearly O'Toole has his detractors. However, critics are human, and personal preferences are always going to be a factor. Even if there is bias or inaccurate perception, Fintan O'Toole's reviews are the most honest, concise and widely accepted initial reactions to drama in Ireland.

In conversation with Redmond O'Hanlon, O'Toole refers to Brian Friel's *Faith Healer* as being about 'the impossibility of narrative,' then reflects on Friel's bravery in 'confronting genuine cultural and political disarray'. Fintan O'Toole's subjective and incomplete but wide-ranging and deeply intelligent collection of criticism documented here parallels these comments. O'Toole has been consistently prepared to accept and examine unexpected shifts in the Irish theatre, to open up new paradigms and new ideas on the possibilities of drama itself. He has unfailingly endeavoured, as well, to weave the myriad developments during the last twenty years in Irish theatre into a larger tapestry, into a chronicle that we all can understand.

So much for the impossibility of narrative.

New Irish Drama

Island Protected by a Bridge of Glass, by Garry Hynes

Peacock Theatre
In Dublin, 26 June 1981

A week which saw two Irish plays new to Dublin offered a rare opportunity to assess the strengths and weaknesses of our modern drama. Both Garry Hynes and Liam Lynch revealed the problems of trying to find a theatrical form that is original and flexible enough to express new ideas. Druid's production of *Island Protected by a Bridge of Glass* (Peacock) offers almost as many solutions as *Krieg* (Project) creates problems.

Druid bring an astonishing arsenal of techniques to bear on their effort to represent all the complexities and shades of the sense of Irish nationhood which emerged for the first time in the sixteenth century. To grasp just how we have come to be as we are, Garry Hynes goes back to the genesis of the Irish political consciousness in the catastrophic downfall of feudal lords which must have seemed to the native Irish as the onslaught of the white man was to the American Indian, a massive upheaval of the universe. The fluid rush of disasters is solidified in the play through the mind of Gráineuáile and particularly through her fatal mixture of fascination and repulsion for the visitor of the plague, Queen Elizabeth.

The conception of the play depends centrally on the dramatic fusion of two opposed facets of Gráineuáile – the mythical queen symbolic of the nation who appears in romantic poetry and the actual woman at sea on the tides of history, vulnerable and spiritually uneasy. The realization of this conception is a triumph not only for Garry Hynes's mastery of technique and language but also for Marie Mullen's strength and depth as an actress.

Druid raid every available cupboard for the elements of the drama. Use is made of the sparse, rapid flow of language into space of Beckett (*Not I* comes particularly to mind at times), the comic representation of ideas by objects and caricatures of agitprop farce, the folk rhythms and stylized dance of Siamsa, mime and the marvellous music of De Danann. At times the imaginative simplicity of Garry Hynes's use of objects such as long sticks and black balls is startling and the energy created by the quick succession of forms and methods is irresistible. The concentration of all these elements is never confusing but there are times when the switch from one mood or device to another is so sudden as to draw attention to the technique rather than to the dramatic action, making for an occasional hollowness in the resonance of the words being spoken.

Above all *Island* succeeds because Garry Hynes has achieved a dramatic language which encompasses fully the poetry of speech, the rhythm of movement and the direct visual impact of physical objects. She has done so in such an original and essentially native way as to suggest that if there is to be a revitalization of Irish theatre it is most likely to be inspired by Druid.

Scenes from an Album, by William Trevor

Abbey Theatre
In Dublin, 4 September 1981

'The tradition of all the dead generations,' said Marx, 'weighs like a nightmare on the brain of the living.'

In the opening scene of William Trevor's *Scenes from an Album*, set in 1610, Eustace Malcolmson, founder of the Ulster line of his family, ignores a warning and, like the house of Atreus, his descendants are cursed forever. Still steaming from the slaughter, Malcolmson the triumphant Conquistador conjures a personal El Dorado from the ravaged and blighted land where he is to settle and plant his seed. Listening to Malcolmson's dream of a new beginning, Bryce, a lawyer, warns him that soldiers and theologians do not mix, that what is won by the sword must be retained by the sword. But the Malcolmsons ignore the logic of conquest believing themselves above the apparatus of bigotry which keeps the natives in their place, and for this sin they are condemned to slow drowning in the whirlpool of history.

Trevor keeps this opening scene firmly before us as the action moves into the twentieth century and Eustace Malcolmson's heirs and namesakes are successively destroyed by one or other of the warring camps and wasted by a 'weariness that will not go away'. As women are brought from England to continue the line, Trevor includes pointed references to them 'falling into a clergyman's arms'. But by now the theology itself has been reduced to crass bigotry, no longer capable of sustaining the Malcolmsons' dream.

The triumph of Trevor's impeccable sense of form – and of John Kavanagh's brilliance as an actor – is that there is still room and reason for a flash of hope. The final speech of the last Eustace Malcolmson is imbued with the belief that it is the very function of the doomed to cast a faint light on a better future. For that alone, this is a very important play.

The Silver Dollar Boys, by Neil Donnelly

Peacock Theatre
In Dublin, 16 October 1981

The new Irish playwrights have tended to see drama as a way of commenting on our society in which the drama is secondary to that comment. In Neil Donnelly's *The Silver Dollar Boys* (Peacock) it is made clear that the purpose of the play is to explain how Billy Wrafter, terrorist bank robber, came to be what he is. We are taken back to a Christian Brothers school in the mid-Sixties, where Billy and his mates Des, Boy and Lorenzo are in the melting pot of a good Christian education.

Neil Donnelly shows considerable dramatic skill and a fine comic touch in his recreation of the vicious absurdity of the classroom. Some of the dialogue, particularly Brother Duffy's explanation of the advantages of learning Irish and the heroism of the patriot dead, is deadly accurate and very funny. The characters of Billy, his friends and the Brothers are interesting and convincing. But having created them Neil Donnelly uses them only as fodder for a rather mechanical plot, all aimed at explaining Billy Wrafter. Ironically, in his anxiety to make a point about contemporary Ireland, he destroys the credibility of that explanation.

From what we see of Billy's evolution, his development into a bank robber, far from being the result of his education and upbringing, is largely a haphazard outcome of chance circumstances. He happens to be in a London bedsit where he meets two IRA bombers – one a junkie, the other an Elvis freak (the IRA would be far more likely to kneecap a junkie than have one as a member) and because he is afraid of the police he runs off with the bombers. It is not convincing. Dealing with the minutiae of a fixed period of life, Neil Donnelly can be very effective. When he tries to span the years in a few short scenes, he reduces his carefully created characters to cardboard cut-outs.

The Fabulous Journey of Mac Con Glin, by Sidney Bernard Smith

John Player Theatre
In Dublin, 16 October 1981

The Fabulous Journey of Mac Con Glin is not just a play, it is a demonstration of the capacities of theatre and of the difference between telling a story and acting out a drama. As a children's play it goes straight for the essentials, dropping all pretence that the actors are doing anything but creating an illusion out of nothing. Only the most simple props – sticks, masks, pieces of cloth – are used, but they are used directly, as an imaginative representation of the things they stand for. Though this kind of theatre should really be played in the round, reducing the distance between the audience and the actors, there is sufficient strength and vigour in this cast to break through the rigid arrangement of the John Player Theatre. The fact that we have actors with the skill and creativity to go back to the basics and produce exciting theatre is one of the most important revelations of the Festival so far.

The Informer, by Tom Murphy

Olympia Theatre
In Dublin, 30 October 1981

Liam O'Flaherty's novel *The Informer* is two stories in one: a ripping yarn of loyalty and betrayal, complete with a Perry Mason-style courtroom drama, and a psychological study of a man in the process of achieving a degree of self-awareness. In rewriting the novel as a stage play, Tom Murphy's interest was almost exclusively in the second of these stories and his main problem was to disengage it from the surrounding structure of romantic adventure. He has not fully succeeded in doing this and his failure is to some degree responsible for the unsatisfactory nature of the production.

Although it is an adaptation, it is more useful to consider *The Informer* as a new Murphy play, and in many ways as a continuation of his last work *The Blue Macushla*. Not only is the revolutionary gang of which Gypo Nolan is a member strongly reminiscent of the gangster-terrorists of *The Blue Macushla* but Gypo himself is interpreted by Murphy as another of the outsiders, the misfits who have always obsessed him. Add to this the melodramatic form of the play, the desire for a wide sweep of action and emotion, and it is clear that *The Informer* is continuous with Murphy's recent work.

There is no doubt that Murphy has carried through his conception of Gypo as one of life's eternal blow-ins with the clarity and thoroughness that we expect from a playwright of his stature. Gypo's journey from innocent animality through guilty self-knowledge and on to some form of tenuous forgiveness and reconciliation with the world echoes the themes of many of Murphy's major plays and is brilliantly realized by Liam Neeson in this production.

Neeson's Gypo is a creature of brutal ignorance, utterly at sea in the artificial world of the city. His movements are blunt and awkward, like a man trying to swim in a spacesuit. Without real friendship or love, belonging to nothing except a corrupt and vicious gang of self-appointed revolutionaries, he does not understand the meaning of loyalty or the stigma of betrayal. He sells his comrade to the police without any conception of what his action means to himself.

In a superbly contrived scene, Gypo listens while a pathetic evangelist preaches of the sin of betraying 'that other who dies for me'. Nothing is said, no confessions are declaimed, but Neeson chews the chips he is eating more slowly and deliberately. We can see the seed of thought being planted in his brain. It is the one moment in the play when the internal drama and the external fuse completely, and it is also the point in the adaptation where Murphy has strayed furthest from O'Flaherty.

It is a mark of Murphy's (and Neeson's) achievement with the character of Gypo that the sentimental melodrama of his death-scene could in fact have worked. The main reason why it doesn't is that Murphy, both as writer and director, has failed to make the necessary connections between Gypo and the teems of people amongst whom his drama is played out. His fellow revolutionaries, the family of his betrayed comrade, and the drinkers and prostitutes of Dublin never seem to really impinge on his world. As a result, when Gypo finally transcends his isolation, it does not carry the impact it should. In particular, since Frankie's mother, the instrument, through her forgiveness, of Gypo's reconciliation with the world, has never been developed as a dramatic force, her intervention at the end of the play has too much of the *deus ex machina* about it.

But more than anything else, what disrupts the form of Murphy's play is the entirely inadequate staging. With its broad canvas and multiplicity of scenes, it requires an almost cinematic treatment in terms of pace and seamlessness. The scene changes are so cumbersome, however, that each scene seems like a separate entity and the threads of Gypo's development are nearly lost in the confusion. Given the incomprehension that he has faced at the hands of other directors, it is entirely understandable that Murphy should have accepted the task of directing *The Informer* himself, and it says something for the poverty of our theatre that we do not seem to have the resources of skill to handle the work of such a major playwright. But Murphy's direction has followed the line of his singular interest in the character of Gypo to the detriment of the necessary interaction between the actors. Another director might have redressed that imbalance.

The Hidden Curriculum, by Graham Reid

Peacock Theatre
In Dublin, 30 April 1982

As the lights come up on Graham Reid's new play, *The Hidden Curriculum*, to the accompaniment of Alex Harvey's violent and lyrical song 'Anthem', two boys are standing on stage in front of a red brick terrace façade. Slowly, almost ritualistically, they throw mock punches and kicks at each other. Their gestures are a stylized form of violence, a simultaneous expression of aggression and of camaraderie. Before any words are spoken, Graham Reid's dramatic world has been established. It is a world somewhere between viciousness and familiarity, the world of the ghetto, where the only sense of community is that of a tribe at war.

The scene shifts to a school staff room in the heart of the same ghetto, and we soon realize that here there is also a sense of siege. The rules of conformity are subtler, but then when a more cynical member of staff, David Dunn, threatens to disturb the comfortable consensus, he is threatened in return. On the street and in the school, insecure communities impose their own discipline over those who break the rules.

As the play comes into focus, we begin to see two men who in very different ways break the rules, and two boys who are to be the instrument of their punishment. The men are Eric Alexander, a former loyalist paramilitary commander who has informed on his son, the murderer of four Catholics; and Tony Cairns, a naive middle-class teacher, beating the War Poets into the heads of kids who can barely read. The boys are Tom Allen and Bill Boyd, unemployed youngsters from shattered families, drawn inexorably into paramilitary violence.

Reid's machinery is complex, as the play moves in an almost cinematic sequence of scenes from the classroom to the street, from the staff room to Eric Alexander's house. The ultra-naturalistic sets leave nothing to the imagination – all is precise, clear and sharp. In the superb second act, the finest piece of dramatic writing that Reid has yet achieved, the various worlds intersect, as the two boys pay a visit to their old school and slowly reveal to their former teacher Tony Cairns the exact nature of the world he inhabits, dispelling his illusions about his former bright and promising pupil, Roy Alexander, multiple murderer.

Eric Alexander, the informer barricaded into his house against the threats of his former comrades, and Tony Cairns the innocent teacher partially emerging from behind the barricade of his ignorance are each an intolerable disturbance to their community. Cairns, who has no moral authority within the play, is defeated by his colleagues, resigning his post as head of the English Department in the school. Alexander, who has moral authority because of his action against his son, is allowed by Reid an equivocal victory. But it is a victory of violence – he has a gun, the boys who come to kill him are armed only with clubs. He wins because he refuses to surrender to the forces which crushed his son, because he does not kill those who would kill him. It is a bleak triumph, allowing for escape, not change.

Formally and intellectually, *The Hidden Curriculum* is Graham Reid's most ambitious and complex play to date. If the play as a whole seems somehow insufficient – and after the brilliant dialogue of the second act, the third act opts for a disappointingly discursive use of language – it is because it attempts so much.

Seán McCarthy's production is in every respect worth of the play, and Des Cave's performance as Cairns is quite excellent. The play is dramatically incomplete perhaps, but it is still theatre at its most challenging and engrossing.

Here are Ladies, by Siobhán McKenna et al.

Abbey Theatre
In Dublin, 11 June 1982

Here Are Ladies is a hotchpotch of extracts from poems, plays and novels by Stephens, O'Casey, Yeats, Synge, Shaw, Beckett, Lennox Robinson and Joyce. The individual extracts bear no relation to each other. Emotions are skimmed off the top of the works from which they come, like a cream bun without the bun. Everything, from O'Casey's Mrs Tancred to Joyce's Anna Livia Plurabelle, is melted down into the mush and gush of the McKenna style. None of the pieces, except perhaps the Molly Bloom monologue which ends the show, is treated on its own terms; everything is assimilated into the operatic vocal gestures which characterize her acting.

Ms McKenna's style is essentially a product of the nineteenth century, and it strongly reflects a notion of female acting that arose out of a male-dominated theatre and a male-dominated society. Male actors were expected to carry with them some kind of force, to suggest that they were capable of some kind of effective action. The great female actress was one who could express her suffering and give vent to great bursts of introspective emotion. In this school of acting, nothing succeeds like excess.

These particular talents which Siobhán McKenna has developed are especially unsuited to the enunciation of Joyce's language in *Finnegans Wake* and the Anna Livia Plurabelle episode is recited without any obvious interpretation of what is being said.

The best piece of the evening is the *Drama at Inish* extract from Lennox Robinson, where Ms McKenna parodies herself as a gushing actress. Unfortunately for the rest of the show, the parody and the performance come too close for comfort.

The Communication Cord, by Brian Friel

Riverside Theatre, Coleraine
In Dublin, 29 October 1982

From the very beginning of Brian Friel's new play *The Communication Cord*, which opens at the Gaiety next week, we are in a world that refuses to make sense. The play opens with Tim Gallagher (Stephen Rea) entering a restored thatched cottage through a door that is not closed while offstage the voice of his friend Jack McNelis (Gerard McSorley) shouts instructions on how to open it. Farce demands deception and confusion, and

Friel is concerned with engineering these elements into a general statement about the decay of language. Plot and theme must move in step. Tim, a junior lecturer in linguistics, is borrowing Jack's cottage for three hours so that he can pretend to his girlfriend's father, a politician of the 'comely maidens dancing on the village green' variety, that he owns the property and is responsible for its meticulous restoration. The initial step into deception leads with mechanical inevitability to a miasma of disintegrated identities and meaningless discourse.

Farce glories in shattering the sense of unity which we constantly attempt to create for ourselves. In this case, the unity shattered is the spurious unity with the romanticized past represented by Senator Donovan's antiquarian posturings. The cottage symbolizes a world which is close enough for those who have gathered in it to want to keep it at a distance, and far enough away for that distance to be created by nostalgia. This is indeed Hugh Leonard territory – the terrors and obsessions of upward social mobility. 'Everybody's grandmother was reared in a house like this,' claims Jack early on. Later Senator Donovan goes one better: 'I was born in a place like this'.

But although *The Communication Cord* is clearly written to amuse, the departure from Friel's obsessions as a playwright is only superficial. For at the heart of farce is the chaos of confused identities which exposes the vulnerability of people faced with a collapse in the normal rules of social intercourse, and it is the whole question of identity which has dominated Friel's work over two decades. Every single character in *The Communication Cord* is at some point confused with someone else or assumed to be what they are not.

Typically for Friel, the confusion is achieved through linguistic disruption. Tim, pretending to know what he is talking about when guiding the Senator around the cottage, is reduced to handing Donovan back his own statements as gibberish. Claire, Tim's former girlfriend, found unexpectedly to be in residence in the cottage, is forced to pretend she is French and understands hardly any English, while Jack decides to make an entrance disguised as a German. Finally, Donovan is forced to make a nonsense of his own outpourings of piety as he flees the cottage in absolute disgust and disarray.

On one level the play obviously operates in tandem with *Translations*. There is a real sense of loss compared to the richness of Ballybeg (where *The Communication Cord* is also set) in 1833, but there is also a strong element of parody of the earlier play. The delving into the historical derivation of names in *Translations* is mirrored here by Donovan's ludicrous attempts to explore the recesses of meaning contained in the names which Tim desperately invents for the locals. When Donovan spots Jack out swimming, Tim tells him that it is a local fisherman called 'Jack the God'. Donovan delightedly extols the beauties of the old way of naming which includes in the name both the man's profession and the local opinion of his merits.

In its use of language, *The Communication Cord* is a work of consummate cleverness and is at times, very, very funny. Stephen Rea's Tim Gallagher is an extraordinary comic creation, a simpering sleeveen, a twisted knot of incompetence constantly on the verge of mania but without the courage to take the plunge into unfettered lunacy. Not only is he incapable of verbal communication, but his body seems to curve back in on itself as he tries to ingratiate by making himself small. The rest of the cast revolves effectively around him, and Joe Dowling's production handles the convolutions of language with clarity and assurance.

Where the production falls short of the controlled hysteria of great farce, though, is in the handling of the physical objects. Friel's plot calls for the cottage to take on a malign life of its own, inflicting an almost intentional revenge on its usurpers. On stage, however, the fireplace which assaults Tim, the oil lamp which redoubles the confusion by going out at vital moments, the hitching post which humiliates the Senator (and should produce a wonderfully grotesque image of the debasement of Irish politics) and the roof which collapses on the whole affair, are dealt with unconvincingly and at times awkwardly.

Still, *The Communication Cord* is the funniest new Irish play for a very long time. It is a slight work, one that need not be taken too seriously and one that should not tempt the unwary into exaggerations, but it is very easy to enjoy. Above all it confirms

Friel's ability to wriggle out of formal and thematic straitjackets. To the pleasure of the comedy is added the enjoyment of watching a good escapologist.

The Golden Hair, by Mairéad Byrne

Project Theatre
In Dublin, 10 Dec 1982

The Golden Hair is too playful to be a play in the usual sense. Presented by a company called Animals Don't Tap Dance under the direction of David McKenna, it is not the enactment on stage of a piece of written literature. It is a creation rather than an interpretation. It involves us in a theatre whose sphere is physical and plastic, not psychological, and the language at work is a theatrical one which does not embody thought but actually makes us think. Mairéad Byrne's text is an important, indeed a defining, element but it remains an element. Just as central, and often more memorable, are the colours, gestures, sounds, above all the performances of the actors. In this production as in few other Irish shows I have seen, the actors make themselves (in Artaud's phrase) 'athletes of the heart'. Because so much of the theatre we see here is an attempt to convince us of the reality of the unnatural, with a series of extraordinary events crammed into a two-hour slice of life, its virtues tend to be cunning and cuteness. *The Golden Hair*, however, is conspicuous. Skills are paraded, words are stylized and ridiculed, the theatre is desecrated and desanitized. It has about it more than a touch of circus, a form of which one is reminded by the diaphanous cloth which hangs from the ceiling like a safety net. But the sense of sheer display, the succession of tricks, the raiding of cupboards as far apart as the ballet and the Flying Karamazov Brothers, are contained within a structure of remarkable lucidity and clarity.

The form of the piece is epic – it is a performance for Tristan and Iseult at the wedding of Iseult's maid Brangwen. But the frame which normally in epic theatre acts only as prologue and epilogue, here refuses to remain a frame. Towards the end it twists back on the play almost in the manner of a thriller like *Sleuth*. Within the grand game, other games of sexual relationship between men and women are played out. There are Samson and Delilah, a girl called Rose Lavery and a boy called Joe Cantillon, Adam and Eve, John the Baptist without Salomé, and Niamh of the Golden Hair without Oisín. Though largely about itself, *The Golden Hair* is also very much about the sexes.

The richness of ideas and the diversity of approaches behind and in the show, however, should not obscure the fact that it is solely and simply hugely enjoyable. It is as live as an electric eel and very funny. The dialogue is full of delicious wit and showy conceits. The costumes, particularly those for Mannix Flynn's dwarf and Tony Rodenko's fool, are superb. Donal Lunny's soundtrack is the best I have ever heard in the theatre. There is room for some inspired clowning, particularly from Jack Lynch, Mannix Flynn and Donal O'Kelly and the actors as a group reach moments of genuine enchantment. The lighting is inventive and the use of the theatre space constantly surprising. Above all there is none of the aura of self-congratulation which too often clings to theatrical experimentation. Things are done because they work, and they work because they give pleasure to the audience and the performers.

Its constant inventiveness, its immediacy and its sense of purpose make *The Golden Hair* a unique event in Irish theatre. Learning from the Brazilians and the Poles who have brought the qualities of magic to Dublin audiences, it creates two worlds upon the one stage and uses their juxtaposition to transform reality. In such alchemy is the power which lies at the heart of theatre.

Pledges and Promises, by Peter Sheridan

Project Arts Centre
In Dublin, 25 March 1983

The City Workshop's second production, *Pledges and Promises*, directed by Maggie Byrne and Peter Sheridan and scripted by Peter Sheridan from improvisations by the members of the Workshop, shows just how effective, theatrically and politically, this type of creation can be. *Pledges and Promises* is at once an accurate chronicle of Dublin's docklands, true not just to the surface form of its history but to the working people who lived in and off the docks area, and a strikingly original piece of living theatre. It is probably the most significant piece of political theatre created in Dublin since Arden and D'Arcy's *The Non-Stop Connolly Show* in 1975.

The structure of *Pledges and Promises* is looser, more fluid, than that of City Workshop's first play *The Kips, The Digs, The Village*. Risks can be taken with the narrative line because the skills of the performers have developed in the meantime to a point where they can as a company range about the stage without losing a sense of coherence. The production is intelligently built around the strengths of the company, in a way that would not be possible in any other method of working, mobilizing its resources in a way that is constantly exciting. The script is witty, poetic, vulgar and hard-edged, held together by a series of songs in which the actors are instantly welded together into a single voice.

The Great Hunger, by Tom Mac Intyre

Peacock Theatre, Dublin.
Sunday Tribune, 15 May 1983

The fear of the flesh which infected Ireland for so long affected our theatre just as much as it affected social life. A mistrust of the physical has given us a theatre that has always sought safety in words alone, ignoring the other senses and maintaining an anchor in things that can be understood verbally, abstractly. Tom Mac Intyre's version of Kavanagh's *The Great Hunger* heralds a theatre that can express what words can only suggest.

What Mac Intyre is expressing, though the medium of Kavanagh's imagery, is the sexual psyche of Irish manhood. Caught inescapably between desire and impotence, Patrick Maguire, the central figure of the poem, is the victim of the world's contradictions. The forces of life are abundantly present, but warped and twisted into deadening rituals. In the first half of the play, a frenzied dance of ecstasy is ordered under the gaze of the priest into a leaden procession. The image speaks powerfully of our history and our present.

The play is full of images that enter the mind and remain. Maguire looking backwards through his legs at passing women, a Mass at which the prayers are only the empty phrases of everyday conversation, Maguire taking up the collection at mass with a long-handled collection box that he holds like a spade, Maguire flinging stones at a wall and frantically dodging their ricochet.

As the play progresses, the images become similar, less obviously inventive, more and more heart-wrenching. If in the end it is grim, the bleakness is not achieved cheaply.

Traditions, though, are not reversed overnight, and the production does seem to lose its nerve at times. Director Patrick Mason seems not to have been prepared to cut off the anchor in naturalism. The result is that some of the acting clashes with the general intention of the piece. Vincent O'Neill's Priest and Conal Kearney's Tom Malone are played as full characters, rather than collections of characteristics. In this kind of theatre the actor's role is a bearer and creator of images, self-consciously and unapologetically artificial. Too often here the actors try to present the illusion of 'real' characters where none are present, and the result is blurring and confusing.

Tom Hickey, who plays Maguire and is in every sense the heart of the piece, is the glorious exception. He has always been an actor to speak with his body and here he is terrifyingly eloquent. His Maguire changes and grows old without really changing at all, and that is the tragedy which Hickey enacts.

Once you begin to trust your own reactions, to trust the language of the piece, *The Great Hunger* attains a remarkable clarity and strength. If it is not always true to itself, it does overall achieve its goals. With goals as high as Mac Intyre's, that is a very considerable achievement.

The Gigli Concert, by Tom Murphy

Abbey Theatre
Sunday Tribune, 2 October 1983

Tom Murphy has always taken risks, the risk of delving into the human psyche, the risk of putting fierce emotions to work on the stage, the risk of trying to transcend the ordinary. In *The Gigli*

Concert (Abbey) he stakes everything. At one point in the play, Godfrey Quigley, playing the millionaire client of the quack 'dynamatologist' J.P.W. King (Tom Hickey), demands that King 'sum up'. In many ways Tom Murphy is summing up here.

The risks pay off, the power of Murphy's striving matched for the first time in many years by performances of remarkable energy and depth from Tom Hickey and Godfrey Quigley. Hickey plays a pseudo-psychologist, a faith healer infected by the disease he is trying to cure. His movements are manic, hilarious, hyped-up. The hilarity, the frenetic mobility, almost, but not quite hide the desperate emptiness beneath. He ignores his emptiness until he comes face to face with the more obvious devastation of his client.

Quigley's character is a self-made millionaire for whom success is a nonsense. He longs to sing like Beniamino Gigli, to open his mouth and express his soul, to create a sound that might annihilate the world he refers to darkly as 'out there'. He is partly a helpless cripple crying for help, partly a terrible messenger from what to King is an unknown world, a world he has insulated himself from with his own illusions.

To resolve the complexity of this play into the crystal clarity which it needs ultimately to achieve, the audience must be allowed to participate in, to see and feel and understand two intangible elements. We must firstly be made to sense the slow breakdown of the barriers of identity between the two men, the mingling of personality as they descend to the absolute zero of hurt humanity, the common level of need which is all that they share.

The second essential element is that when Gigli's voice is used as an element of the theatrical action, it is used at the right moments to convince us of the existence of another dimension that creates a second world on the stage.

Both elements are here. Patrick Mason's production is structured around the music, reaching the crescendos and plunging to the low notes. And in spite of the physical contrast between the rooted Quigley and the active Hickey, there is ultimately an unspoken communion between them. The sands of reality shift imperceptibly through the three hours of the production, making the final leap into the magic possible. To achieve that leap is an astonishing triumph, possible only in a play of this length, with the time to unfold at its own pace.

The Gigli Concert is dense, complex and like all fundamental things, full of infinite riches. It is a celebration wrung out of desperation, a triumph forged from failure. The performance itself is a victory analogous to that which is achieved in the play. It is the best new play at the Abbey for at least a decade and has, in Tom Hickey's J.P.W. King, a performance that is among the best I have seen.

Horseman Pass By!, by Dan Magee

Dublin Theatre Festival
Sunday Tribune, 9 October 1983

What I had seen of Dan Magee's work before *Horseman Pass By!* (he had two short plays in last year's Festival), showed him working in a mould of experimentation, both in terms of the form of theatre and of its concerns. *Horseman*, though, is a largely naturalistic work, dealing with the family and social background of an IRA man in Belfast, an attempt to plumb the uncharted depths of killing, bigotry and ruthlessness. With such a theme it is, of course a political play. It is possible to write naturalistic political plays, but there is a limit to what can be done in them. Naturalism is very good for description, not so good for drawing conclusions from the description. You can state a number of political positions, but it is difficult to draw them together into a coherent point at the end. Problems like these led political playwrights to develop epic forms.

This is the central formal problem with *Horseman Pass By!*, a problem that inhibits the play but by no means destroys it. There is some really good writing here. Dan Magee not only has an eye for powerful and imaginative images, he has the ability to make those images dramatic, to root them in the action and the personality of his creations. The failings in the play are those of ambition, of a vibrant imagination straining at the bit of an inadequate form.

Whatever its outward forms, the play is not really of the well-made variety. It may have begun with a desire to express the motivations of Brendan, the hard-edged revolutionary with socialist as well as nationalist goals, but it clearly developed into a similar exploration of four other people as well – Harry Samson (on the surface a barroom bigot), Brendan's father Paddy (a man who has compromised to feed his family but will not compromise with his son's hatred), Brendan's mother, and the young recruit from next door, one of the new breed of IRA men, born into violence and determined to continue in it.

This constant shift of focus, the failure to concentrate on a single central figure damages the play in formal terms but makes it an infinitely better work than it might otherwise have been. If it is unsatisfactory, if the play ends in a Jacobean heap of corpses that leads nowhere, it is because Dan Magee's imaginative sympathy for his characters is bigger than the form he is working in.

When the characters begin to talk of what has happened to them, of how they have come to be as they are, a complex and terrifying picture of life under Stormont emerges. In one way it is the picture of working-class life anywhere on these islands in that period, but there is of course a much deeper, specifically Northern, dimension as well. The strength of the play is that when it comes to the reactions of the different characters to terrorism and to Brendan's perception of his mission, Magee refuses to load the dice. There is a fascination in the depths of the motivations. The characters are allowed to speak with a certain autonomy. But there is, ultimately, a real need for some sort of conclusion when dealing with questions like murder and political violence. It is ironic that a play which seeks to deal with violence at a complex and human level should reach its ending through an act of instinctive and reactive violence, blind and simple. There is no distancing at the end, nothing to be gained except a sense of futility. Dan Magee, though, is on this evidence a writer of real strength. When he finds forms to contain this strength he will be a writer of real importance.

Bust, by Peter Sheridan

Project Arts Centre
Sunday Tribune, 27 Nov 1983

Peter Sheridan spent the year 1980 working in the Liberties market selling electrical goods, thinking about where he wanted to go as a writer after the end of his involvement, along with his brother Jim, in the Project Arts Centre. He thought about working for one of the established theatres but found no enthusiasm for his ideas. Instead he chose a path which was to make him a central figure in the development of the City Workshop trilogy, (*The Kips, The Digs, The Village*; *Pledges and Promises*; and *A Hape A'Junk*) and has led to three other plays in two years. *Bust*, commissioned by the Dublin Youth Theatre, is a continuation of that work and reinforces the belief that a writer like Sheridan, working with non-professional actors on a script that relates to their lives, can add an important new dimension to Irish theatre.

One of the problems of youth theatre in this country has always been the lack of relevant texts to work from, texts which reflect the language and experience of young actors and thus give them a basis for genuine creativity. *Bust* answers that problem. For all its roughness and lack of formal nicety, it is thoroughly vindicated by performances of real depth, complexity and power. There is no sense in this production of young actors trying to ape their professional betters. What comes across is a strong sense of identity and an impressive degree of control. Anto Nolan plays the central character of Smack, a young man trying to assert control over his own life, firstly through violence then through conformity, and finally through the autistic individuality of drug addiction. There is no attempt at a comprehensive statement about 'the drug problem'. Instead there is an attempt to express the responses of one individual to himself and the people he encounters and to show how those responses end in addiction and isolation. We follow Smack, in an episodic and almost televisual production, from middle-class bootboy to bored soldier, to lethargic drug-dealer.

What holds this loose structure together is Anto Nolan's excellent performance. He manages to convey the dissipation of an undisciplined energy, an energy that finds no real goal and finally turns in on itself. The transition is effected with unbroken conviction and an absorbing fluency.

Bust works best in the scenes that involve male characters only – the bootboys on the street, the army barrack room, the gathering of drug dealers. The women have less well-written parts, mostly because they are associated with a domesticity which is peripheral to the thrust of the play. But the sense of relationship between the male characters, particularly Smack and Glucose (another fine performance from Larry Nolan) is very well achieved. This production gives the Dublin Youth Theatre an impressive base from which to build, and a clear direction in which to go. Together with the news that Peter Sheridan and Maggie Byrne, who jointly supervised the City Workshop project, will be artistic directors of a new Inner City theatre company to be established next year, *Bust* gives hope for a theatre that will get close to what is happening in Dublin now.

The Diamond Body, by Operating Theatre
Project Theatre
Sunday Tribune, 11 March 1984

There is no reason in the theatre why a man should not play the part of a woman or a woman that of a man. Theatre presents a pretence and many great performers have had an androgynous quality which allows them to expand the boundaries of their own personalities (Micheál MacLiammóir's great version of Lady Bracknell comes to mind). But when an actor plays a role of the opposite sex, there is a temptation to create the illusion of 'reality' by merely accentuating the most obvious stereotypical characteristics of the sex which is to be portrayed. In this way for instance, female impersonators present a hopelessly exaggerated and distorted version of femininity. In their pocket version of *Romeo and Juliet,* in which they play all the roles themselves, Derek Chapman and Deirdre Morris succumb to this temptation. In *The*

Diamond Body Olwen Fouéré, playing a character more male than female, does not.

The Diamond Body is a performance by Olwen Fouéré of a text by Aidan Mathews with music by Roger Doyle. The performance is everything: the text, though very well written, is relatively slight, while the music, again very effective, seldom rises above a narrative function in creating an ambience for the action. But all of the elements cohere in Olwen Fouéré's incredible performance, in her extraordinary feats of voice, movement and intellect.

The Diamond Body is located in the state of androgyny. It tells the story of a communal act of violence against Stephanos, the hermaphrodite owner of a gay disco on a Greek island. Olwen Fouéré invests this story with a controlled passion that gives it an unexpected force and moments of genuine terror and beauty. She plays a role that is a million miles away from any conventional notion of character. It is instead a composite and shifting portrayal of Stephanos himself and of his lover/companion. The tone of the performance is predominantly male, suggested in voice and movement, but it remains ambiguous and therefore fascinating. In concert with Roger Doyle's music and John Comiskey's rich and inventive lighting design, Olwen Fouéré achieves a pure theatricality that is rare indeed.

The Interrogation of Ambrose Fogarty, by Martin Lynch

Peacock Theatre
Sunday Tribune, 29 April 1984

In the last few years the Peacock has produced a large body of plays by writers like Neil Donnelly, Graham Reid and Bernard Farrell which have in various ways attempted to make a point about aspects of Irish society. In Belfast Martin Lynch has been doing a similar job with plays like *Dockers*, *The Interrogation of Ambrose Fogarty* and *Castles in the Air* at the Lyric. The first Dublin production of *The Interrogation of Ambrose Fogarty*, therefore sits easily at the Peacock conforming well to what is now virtually a house style. In spite of some infelicitous contradictions of approach, Lynch's tough, witty, convincing script loses nothing in its journey southwards.

One of the reasons for this is the appalling relevance of Ambrose Fogarty's story to the current debate on the Criminal Justice Bill, the play's sharp evocation of the climate of disorder which leads to a disregard for basic civil liberties. Like *The Quare Fellow* 20 years ago, which gathered much of its resonance from the emotional campaign against the death penalty, *The Interrogation of Ambrose Fogarty* benefits from the timeliness of the clash between an individual and a system of 'justice' which it enacts. It is, of course, only able to do so because it is so powerful, so compelling and so theatrical.

Lynch's central device is a superb one. We are introduced at the start of the play to two men from the same area arrested at the same time, one, the half-daft country and western club singer Willie Lagan, supposedly for involvement in a riot, the other, the tough, politically conscious Ambrose Fogarty for alleged bank robbery. The absurdity of Lagan's position, his patent harmlessness, not only allows for some very fine humorous writing but also throws an ironic light on the routine ritual of Ambrose's interrogation.

Ian McElhinney's Willie Lagan is a masterpiece of characterization, with an innocence that defies the hopelessly compromised humanity of the CID men who question him. But in a world like that of a West Belfast RUC station, innocence, in either the legal or the more general sense, is not enough. Ambrose is no innocent, though he has not committed the crime for which he is questioned. His ability to withstand, his mixture of hardness and common sense, sees him through the ordeal. Ultimately, it is the innocent, in this case Willy Lagan, who suffer most.

Paul Moore's production seems at times a little confused. In the central position of Lagan in the production, in the stylization of the violence, and in the use of soliloquy where Ambrose expresses his thoughts alone in the cell, there are elements which are decidedly non-naturalistic. But the rest of the production is almost televisual in verisimilitude. This contradiction at times creates a sense of unease, but it is for the most part overcome by some very fine performances. Maeliosa Stafford in the title role manages the switch from the private, worried man going through lists of famous football teams to keep his mind off the gnawing anxiety, to the blank, hard man of the interrogation room. Peadar Lamb, in the crucial scene where Ambrose is beaten up by the CID men, convincingly conveys the cold, unemotional rhythm of the experienced torturer going about his job. He is far more terrifying than any hysterical outburst of violence could be, and Paul Moore's handling of this scene has a physical assurance and sense of movement which is the main achievement of his direction.

The Interrogation of Ambrose Fogarty shows Martin Lynch to be a fine writer, though he does not yet seem to have matched its power in his subsequent work.

The Riot Act, by Tom Paulin and High Time, by Derek Mahon

Guildhall Theatre, Derry
Sunday Tribune, 23 Sept 1984

Though they are theatrically the starkest contrast imaginable, the two halves of Field Day's new production have a certain thematic coherence. If *The Riot Act*, based on Sophocles' *Antigone*, is essentially about the self-destructiveness of excessive severity, *High Time*, based on Molière's *The School for Husbands*, repeats as comedy what we have already seen as tragedy. But *High Time* gains considerably more from the association that *The Riot Act* does.

One play tells the story of an act of political self-destruction through the failure of Creon, ruler of war-torn Thebes, to temper law with justice. The other enacts the folly of a man who believes that he can win the love of his young ward by shutting her off from the world outside, destroying his chances by his own severity. One operates primarily in the political area but has a personal dimension. The other operates primarily in the personal area but has political resonances. But whereas this political dimension of *High Time* gains enormously by the fact that it comes after a political play, the lack of a personal element in *The*

Riot Act is cruelly underlined by the fact that it is followed by *High Time*.

The *Riot Act* puts the finger on one of the broader problems for the whole Field Day enterprise. By choosing to do a version of *Antigone*, Field Day cannot but have been drawn by the political resonances of the play in modern Ireland. The focus of the play is on the conflict of a woman, Antigone, who feels bound to perform an act, burying her dead brother, which is forbidden by the law, and the man who has made that law, her uncle Creon. The area where myths and modern realities meet is the territory Field Day has staked out for itself.

But just as Field Day has entered the political arena without stating all the political consequences of its stance, Tom Paulin's version of *Antigone* exploits the resonances of the classical text without clarifying them. It goes half way and ends up in something of a theatrical never-never land. For the sake of the modern resonances much of the theatricality of the original *Antigone* is lost. And there is no clear political passion to compensate.

The loss of theatricality is in relation to the figure of Creon, played by Stephen Rea. Rea's first speech is a brilliant parody of a Northern Ireland Office political functionary appealing for public support. It is enormously enjoyable to spot the Irish parallels and to smile. But it immediately draws the theatrical sting of the play. *Antigone* works as a play because we are also interested in Creon as a man, concerned with his dilemma and the way he tries to cope with it. Sophocles' Creon is a tragic hero as well as a villain. By satirizing him from the start, the drama of his conflict with Antigone is rendered impossible.

If Tom Paulin had chosen to carry through all of the political parallels, we could easily accept a Creon who was no more than a personification of a corrupt state. But he does not. As Creon's tragedy mounts, with the death of Antigone, his own son and his wife, we are expected to switch from satire to sympathy, an impossible transition. This basic contradiction robs *The Riot Act* of the kind of momentum it needs. It ends up full of fine moments – in much of Paulin's language and in the performances of Rea, Veronica Quilligan as Antigone, Des

McAleer as Tiresias and Ciaran Hinds as the chorus leader – but entirely unsatisfactory as a piece of theatre.

Stephen Rea's direction fails to impose the coherence that is missing, or the element of theatricality that is needed. There is little here besides talking heads and, however fine the talk, it is not in itself enough.

Whatever the problems of *The Riot Act*, *High Time* would not be such a resounding success without it. Stephen Rea, Creon in *The Riot Act*, plays Tom, the jealous guardian, in *High Time*, while Veronica Quilligan's Antigone is transmuted to Isabel, the over-protected ward. This by itself gives a different dimension to Derek Mahon's adaptation from Molière. It gives an unconscious sense of substance to a production that is a delight of lunacies, full of style and exuberance and riotous humour.

High Time is directed by Mark Long and Emil Wolk of The People Show and it is infused with their penchant for physical jerks and theatrical quirks. Their utterly artificial style is a kind of modern equivalent of the stylization that Molière himself would have employed, and their production is entirely in keeping with the playfulness of Mahon's brilliant translation. Mahon uses rhyme with a deft abandon, playing on the qualities of the verse itself, making language not just an instrument of the fun but a great running joke in itself.

Stephen Rea is an extraordinary comedian. His mixture of superb timing and physical assurance creates the kind of utter hilarity which the old silent movie comedians could manage. His character is at once entirely self-assured, confident that he is master of all he surveys, and utterly at sea, lost to the significance of everything that is going on around him. In this contradiction is the essence of comedy – the delight that the audience feels in knowing more than the character.

But *High Time* also has the hallmark of Field Day's productions – a sense of a company absolutely at one. Behind the anarchy there is an almost choreographed precision that goes straight for the laughs. It is a mark of the quality of the company playing that even such an extraordinary actor as Rea is not out on his own. And Mark Lambert's performance as a stumbling, falling down, running gag almost steals the show.

This is a brilliant comedy and production that makes the double-bill highly rewarding. It opens at the Gate Theatre in Dublin tomorrow night and then continues on a national tour.

Northern Star, by Stewart Parker

Lyric Theatre, Belfast
Sunday Tribune, 2 December 1984

There is no past tense in Irish history. The ideas by which we describe ourselves, Republicanism, Orangeism, Catholicism, and Protestantism, are still in the process of forming themselves, but still play a powerful role in the present. But equally those ideas do not necessarily mean the same thing now as they did when they originally became part of the political process on this island.

It is this shifting set of alliances between the past and the present which is at the heart of Stewart Parker's wry, tough-minded, funny new play *Northern Star*.

Centring on the intriguing figure of Henry Joy McCracken, the Presbyterian Ulsterman who entered history as a Republican martyr in a Catholic tradition, Parker considers the cruel joke which history has played on the North, turning the dream which inspired McCracken, the dream of a unity of the men of no property regardless of religion, into a force which was instrumental in creating the lines of division between the two tribes. The 1798 rising in Ulster, which McCracken led, served, by a cruel irony, to tie the Protestants more firmly to Britain in crushing the Croppies underfoot.

One of the reasons why *Northern Star* is such a fine play is that Parker manages to maintain a constant tension between the past – the events that McCracken was involved in – and the present – the audience in Belfast in 1984. The play is addressed to the citizens of Belfast and involves not so much the historical McCracken, as the images of McCracken which have come down to us through history. *Northern Star* is not a naturalistic narrative of McCracken's life but a theatrical entertainment that constantly reminds the audience that it is watching a performance in Belfast, in the present.

The setting of *Northern Star* is the semi-derelict labourer's cottage on Cavehill overlooking Belfast where McCracken spent his last night of freedom before the soldiers came to take him off and hang him. The set, by Joe Vanek, is half-realistic, reproducing the structure of the cottage, and half-stylized, with a painted sky and a gaudy moon. It achieves the same mix as the play itself – moving from the precise reproduction of 'facts' to sheer theatre.

McCracken imagines, as he awaits the death which he has little desire to avoid, the seven years of his political life, corresponding in Parker's theatrical scheme to the seven ages of man, from innocence to shame. Underlying his wry self-mockery is the awful fear that because he has fumbled the birth of the new Ireland by allowing his Jacobin uprising to become 'a Catholic riot' history will produce, from the same womb, terrible monsters. There is no need, for a Belfast audience, to spell out what the monsters are. The Catholic Defenders of 1798, whom McCracken led into his revolution of Reason, and the Orangemen whom he did not.

Parker insists on the theatricality of his view of McCracken, on the fact that what we see is happening *now* and not in 1798, by having each of his protagonist's seven ages played in a pastiche of a different Irish playwright – from Sheridan to Beckett, through Boucicault, O'Casey and Synge. The different styles fill in the passage of time between McCracken's day and ours, bringing the play towards the present as well as providing for a great deal of hilarity and avoiding the trap of making the audience vicariously share in McCracken's plight.

The great thing about *Northern Star* is that all of these devices contribute to the sheer entertainment value of the play rather than bogging it down in its own cleverness. Parker's touch here is wonderfully sure, allowing him to present history with complexity rather than heaviness, subtlety rather than obtuseness.

In the Lyric production, Parker's deftness is matched by Peter Farago's fluid and imaginative direction and his wryness is fully realized by Gerard McSorley's McCracken. The Lyric company, in fact, is at its best, with fine performances particularly from

Emer Gillespie and Marcella Riordan. Together they make
Northern Star the best new Irish play of 1984.

Observe the Sons of Ulster Marching Towards the Somme, by Frank McGuinness

Peacock Theatre
Sunday Tribune, 24 February 1985

Life on the brink of extermination has become at once starkly
simple and infinitely complex. The nuclear threat, the spectre of
collective annihilations, has made the issue of life and death
plainer than it has ever been. But the question of how to get out
from under that threat has forced us to see human motivation as
more complex, more entangled, than we have ever done before.

Two new Irish plays premiered last week try to find a path
through those complexities, while keeping an urgent eye on the
stark realities. Frank McGuinness's play *Observe the Sons of Ulster
Marching Towards the Somme* at the Peacock has the strength and
clarity of a great bell ringing, while Mairéad Byrne's *Safe Home* at
the Project manages only to obscure what should be clear as
crystal.

We have in Ireland been so concerned with our own corner of
madness, with the inward spiral of death that we call the national
question, that we often fail to see that question in the light of the
similar madnesses that have gripped the world in this century.

In *Observe the Sons of Ulster*, Frank McGuinness has found a
way of looking at the problem of the Protestant presence in
Ireland through wider and more universal events – those of the
First World War. The story of the men who walked towards the
German machine gun, their Orange sashes draped across their
shoulders, in defence of small nations, is a story that is of
immediate concern to modern Ireland while also sharing in a
wider international significance.

Frank McGuinness plumbs the Ulster Protestant mind and he
also exposes the nerve ends of a modern schizophrenia which
turns the love of home, tradition, and ancestral piety, into a
destructive passion half in love with death, a schizophrenia which
makes security a euphemism for chronic insecurity.

Observe the Sons of Ulster takes eight Ulster Protestant recruits to the British army, seven of them working class, one a suicidal maverick from the land-owning Unionists, and follows them on a path to predetermined destruction, from their first barracks to a spell of leave from the front, and back to the morning of their fatal offensive at the Somme.

Central to its effectiveness is its use of expressionist techniques. We are 'alienated' from the action by the fact that it is framed in the memory of the one survivor. There is no central character, no hero – the protagonist is the Protestant mind itself.

Patrick Mason's production makes superb use of these techniques. Mason uses a bare open stage, with only a huge banner of the Red Hand of Ulster as a backdrop. But his production dominates and inhabits that stage, making it a truly theatrical space where McGuinness's often ambiguous but never obscure language finds physical realization. It is the strength of both play and the production to be wonderfully concrete and yet not over-defined, not limited to a single time or a single meaning. The richness of the story is not lost in the ultimate clarity of the play.

The strongest points of the play are the quintessentially theatrical moments when a physical image, created from the interaction of things and human bodies, expresses all the emotional power of the story. Thus a Lambeg drum becomes the voice that speaks what one of the soldiers hardly dares to articulate; a suspended bridge at the back of the stage becomes a psychological combat zone and in a stunning scene towards the end of the play a re-enactment of the traditional Orange game of King Billy and King James fighting out the Battle of the Boyne on horseback becomes a portent of doom as powerful as those of Greek tragedy.

This kind of physical inventiveness draws much of its strength from the work that Patrick Mason has been doing at the Peacock with Tom Mac Intyre and marks the beginning of the rich influence of Mac Intyre's impulses, but the play also marks the re-introduction to Irish theatre of the neglected heritage of the later Sean O'Casey.

In its expressionism, its use of religious language, its concern with the First World War and its probing of the power of Protestantism, it takes up after more than 50 years some of the impulses that the Abbey rejected when it turned down *The Silver Tassie.*

Observe the Sons of Ulster is in some senses a beginning and in others a revival. It is an important play.

Baglady, by Frank McGuinness

Peacock Theatre
Sunday Tribune, 10 March 1985

Frank McGuinness's lunchtime play at the Peacock, *Baglady*, a one-woman show for Maureen Toal, is an important addition to the development of a fine playwright. McGuinness's first play at the Peacock, *Factory Girls*, had an all-woman cast and was largely an exploration of female togetherness. His current play *Observe the Sons of Ulster Marching Towards the Somme* explores maleness in the context of Ulster Protestantism and war. *Baglady* evokes the violation of a sense of gender, the destruction of a woman's sense of herself through an act of sexual violence, within the family. It is a complex and disconnected play that achieves a stark clarity through the strength of McGuinness's poetry and the measured construction of Maureen Toal's performance.

Baglady emphasizes the poetic nature of McGuinness's writing. Like *Observe the Sons of Ulster*, it moves forward and backwards in time, allowing past, present and future to haunt the stage. It is the images, verbal images of purity and defilement which drive the play. Blood and water, windows and doors, bridal dresses and soiled garments, colours red and white, are the protagonists.

Patrick Mason's production incorporates a physical imagery as a counterpoint to this verbal richness. The actress is on a bare stage, hemmed in by reflective glass borders on the floor, suggesting both the river that plays a large part in the story and the mirror held up to the woman's life. Her words are incarnated through a pack of playing cards with which she tells the future and through the chain that she carries around in her bag, a simple but devastating image of her life's inheritance. And it is in the physical imagery, the unspoken acts, that the possibility of her redemption lies. At the end she divests herself of her burden and places her baggage in the river with the command 'drown'. At a time when the Irish countryside is yielding up its secrets, *Baglady* is an exploration that reaches towards expiation.

Conversations on a Homecoming, by Tom Murphy

Druid Lane Theatre, Galway
Sunday Tribune, 21 April 1985

The people in Tom Murphy's plays look for somewhere to hide, for sanctuaries and places of refuge. Clinging on to their illusions, they try to clear a space for themselves, where they can avoid the realities that will eventually be forced on them.

Most of his plays have such places – the dance hall in *On the Outside*, England in *A Whistle in the Dark*, the forest in *The Morning After Optimism*, the church in *The Sanctuary Lamp*, the nightclub in *The Blue Macushla*, the 'dynamatologist's' office in *The Gigli Concert*.

Conversations on a Homecoming, a substantially rewritten version of *The White House*, a Murphy play from the early Seventies, deals with a failed attempt to construct a refuge and the bitter legacy of the illusions that lay behind the attempt.

The White House is a pub in a town in East Galway, presumably Tuam, where JJ Kilkelly, modelling himself on the myth of John F. Kennedy, tried in the early Sixties to construct a vague version of Camelot where art and culture and intelligence, swathed in Kennedy's pretentious rhetoric, would flourish amid the bigotry and crassness of small-town Ireland. Around him he gathered acolytes, the young men for whom he represented flight and hope. *Conversations on a Homecoming* is set in the pub on the arrival home of one of these men in the early Seventies, a decade after the disintegration of their dream. Their erstwhile hero JJ is on the batter in a pub that used to be 'the opposition'.

Conversations on a Homecoming expresses Murphy's concern with the search for refuge against the specific background of the social and cultural change which took place in Ireland during the Sixties.

The notion of refuge itself is seen to have undergone a change in that period. Tom, the most bitter and coherent of JJ's former acolytes recalls ironically that The White House was to be 'our refuge, the wellspring of hope'. Liam, another former member of the coterie, now the local auctioneer and gombeen-man refers to Ireland as the 'last refuge in Europe' for his kind of capitalism. The notion of refuge itself has been corrupted.

The play charts a process of disillusionment, as Michael (Paul Brennan) returns form America where he is an unsuccessful actor, still hanging onto an exalted notion of JJ's importance. Liam, who will inevitably take possession of The White House, represents the changing of Ireland during the Sixties and his anthem is a maudlin, absurd country and western song. He represents the new breed of 'sad-eyed inquisitors [...] sentimental fascists' who are taking control.

What was enacted in *The White House*, the original version of the play, is instead recalled in *Conversations on a Homecoming*. JJ's high-flown speeches, his clash with clerical authority, his impersonation of Kennedy, which make up the first half of *The White House*, are remembered in *Conversations* by Tom, remembered with a sense of irony and parody which adds a major dimension to the play. There is now a distance from events which would anyway seem absurd to an audience already disillusioned with the Sixties, and that distance adds a bitterness and a humour to the play.

That fundamental change in the play's structure places a huge emphasis on the character of Tom, played here by Seán McGinley. He is now the agent of remembrance of the past, and it is he who sets about a relentless demolition of Michael's illusions. Michael and Tom are spiritual brothers, one hard-bitten and cynical, the other full of illusions. They are two halves of one man, and in their coming together there is some kind of resolution. Tom kills Michael's illusions, and Michael is left alone at the end of the play, without his false dreams, but with the chance of some kind of bitter wholeness.

By concentrating the energy of the play into this relationship, and having JJ only as a haunting offstage presence, Murphy has created a better play and one that is more typical of his work as a whole. There is a retreat into a highly naturalistic style of theatre, into a play that is essentially pub talk, but that talk is made up of Murphy's extraordinary stage language, full of the kind of rigorous poetry that can carry the weight of emotion and ideas.

If there is a problem in what is generally a superb production by Garry Hynes, it is in the balance between McGinley's Tom and Brennan's Michael and in a certain lack of clarity in making them two halves of the one man.

McGinley's performance is brilliantly convincing, a stand-up show that catches the rhythms of Murphy's language and the right mixture of irony and desperation in the remembrance of JJ's speeches. But there is a certain flatness about Paul Brennan's Michael which fails to make it clear that he is the essence of the play, that the story which the play tells is about him.

But this lack of balance does not detract too much from the deep confidence and assurance of the production. There is a sense of conviction about the performances, particularly in Ray McBride's Liam, a beautifully judged mixture of brashness and aching insecurity, and Maeliosa Stafford's loping, amiable Junior.

Garry Hynes brings her tactile sense of the physical reality of the things on stage, the slap of spilled porter on the bare floor and the rising miasmas of cigarette smoke as the night descends towards revelation.

This sense of grimy physicality is nicely caught by a fine set designed by Frank Conway

As an overwhelmingly male play, *Conversations on a Homecoming* leads well into Murphy's new play for women, *Bailegangaire*, which Druid are to present in the autumn.

Rise Up Lovely Sweeney, by Tom Mac Intyre

Peacock Theatre
Sunday Tribune, 15 September 1985

Out on the borderlines, the critic's simple distinctions between success and failure begin to break down. Half way through Tom Mac Intyre's new play at the Peacock, *Rise Up Lovely Sweeney*, you think: 'This is either great stuff or rubbish'. By the end, you begin to feel that it's both. There are plays that are born onto the stage like sparrows' eggs, small, neat, perfectly formed and delivered with a self-satisfied cheep. There are others that explode like volcanoes, releasing a blaze of fire and a few tons of rubbish. *Rise Up Lovely Sweeney* is one of these, a dangerous and enlightening play whose burning core is often obscured by seemingly arbitrary distractions. It is not easily judged or summed up, but it burns with an unmistakable integrity and attempts a voyage that few in the modern theatre would venture.

Tom Mac Intyre's theatre draws on two main sources in modern drama. The first is Beckett's economy of language, the whittling away of words until they approach, as nearly as possible, silence. Mac Intyre's continuation of Beckett's approach was brought to mind last week by the coincidence of Chris O'Neill's performance in Beckett's *Krapp's Last Tape* at the Gaiety Dress Circle Bar, an accurate and entertaining performance of the play.

As well as the economy of language, *Krapp's Last Tape* shares with *Rise Up Lovely Sweeney* the same sense of memory and regret, the same sense of isolation, the same pining for a lost woman and a similar use of the devices of modern technology as part of the action. And the second source of Mac Intyre's theatre is contemporary American theatre dance, the trend towards a language of movement on the stage. In *Rise Up Lovely Sweeney*, these two impulses, the economy of verbal language and the use of a language of gesture and movement, seem to be working at times in opposite directions.

The irony of Mac Intyre's play, created with director Patrick Mason and actor Tom Hickey, is that while the dialogue uses words in a way which is as cryptic and as terse as a set of crossword clues, the visual language of movement and action is often profligate, arbitrary and anything but economical. While the words are precise and poetic, the visual images are jumbled and often incoherent, with a television screen competing for attention with the live action and a general air of fussiness preventing the formation of a single, stark image.

Again ironically, it is the narrative, the literal story of Sweeney rather than the images, which holds the piece together.

The story of Sweeney, the king who is driven mad and turned into a bird-man for his transgression against a saint, has had a particular meaning for our century and we can see it now as a precursor of the many images of man turned into animal which occur in modern writing from Kafka to Neil Jordan. It is thus ideal for the conflation of history which Mac Intyre attempts, bringing together an ancient and modern consciousness.

Mac Intyre's Sweeney, played by Tom Hickey, is a modern man on the run, seeking forgiveness for his violent deeds, pining for the women from whom his madness has separated him, seeking solace in nature, trying to evade at once the embrace of a repressive stage and the embrace of a medicine that seeks, not to heal, but to control his madness.

The play's political resonances are all drawn from contemporary Northern Ireland, its nightmarish quality a deliberate reflection of Irish reality. That reality is defined in images of threatening authoritarian power and a pervasive media consumerism.

Tom Hickey's Sweeney, like his Gaelic original, is placed in a military society. The play opens to the sound of helicopters and the search of tracker dogs for the escaped man. There is a literal story of the chase, of the gradual intertwining of the hunted man and his interrogator, played by Vincent O'Neill, until Sweeney becomes his own interrogator, questioning himself from the television screen.

But there is also a symbolic story, as Sweeney becomes a kind of representative historical Irishman, asking the question which the first stage Irishman (In Shakespeare's *Henry V*) asks: 'What is my nation?', seeking that elusive identity and finding an answer only in the whirl of history and nature: 'My nation is the howl, some say the whinge, I say the howl, but not the black howl'.

This story is told essentially through words, both in English and in Irish, and through the interplay of Hickey and O'Neill, who represent two faces of madness. Hickey's madness is shameless, calling out and crumpling up in pain and anger. O'Neill's is the madness of official terror, cold, sharp and blind as a knife.

The verbal images work cumulatively, by repetition, becoming clearer and more potent as they reach towards the end, taking on new meanings and deeper echoes. The visual images, on the other hand, largely fail to establish any kind of cumulative coherence, working on a hit-and-miss basis and often missing. The most potent visual images are the ones which are allowed to develop without the bombardment of the eyes and ears: the eating of watercress, the drinking of milk, the simple gestures between lovers. Too often, however, there is a sense of mere bustle, of actors and actions doing nothing other than adding to the impenetrability.

That so much of integrity should survive the seemingly arbitrary and indulgent play of some of the action is a mark of the seriousness and courage that lie at the heart of the piece. *Rise Up Lovely Sweeney* builds up to a shattering climax of images that represents a moment of extraordinary theatrical poetry. By laying bare a sickness in the Irish mind, a condition of schizophrenia and deep disturbance, Mac Intyre, Mason and Hickey have made it possible to touch on a nerve that it still raw, as they do at the end of this play. What they touch is a longing for wholeness and forgiveness. *Rise Up Lovely Sweeney* ultimately manages to suggest that, to lay aside the confusions it has created and to reach some kind of clarity. For that, it is worth sticking with.

I'll Go On, by Samuel Beckett

Gate Theatre
Sunday Tribune, 29 September 1985

Mathematics play a large part in Samuel Beckett's work as a whole, as they do in *I'll Go On*, Barry McGovern's one-man show based on Beckett's trilogy of novels, *Molloy, Malone Dies* and *The Unnameable* performed at the Gate. *Molloy/Malone*, the waning, world-weary hero, expends inordinate amounts of his declining mental energy in calculating his average number of farts per hour or the proper disposition of 16 stones in his four pockets. Beckett's language too has an algebraic quality about it, approaching but never reaching silence, as the numbers in calculus approach but never reach zero. *I'll Go On* captures that quality superbly.

The elements of the play complement each other beautifully. The texts are very well chosen by McGovern and Gerry Dukes. Robert Ballagh's set, lit by Rupert Murray manages to give at times an illusion of depth and space which shrinks and narrows in a different light to an oppressive claustrophobia. Colm Ó Briain's direction is stark and sharp without ever becoming static. And Barry McGovern's performance is a tour de force of Beckett acting.

Callers, by Graham Reid

Peacock Theatre
Sunday Tribune, 6 October 1985

Graham Reid is one writer who has not shirked the task of putting political murder and its consequences on stage. Writing out of a Belfast experience, he has consistently tried to root violence in the community from which it springs, exploring the intersection between personal, family relations, the daily intimate cruelties and the problems of endemic pathological aggression. Like almost everyone else, however, he has held back from exploring the mind and motivations of the killers. In *Callers*, his new play at the Peacock, he tries to fill that gap. It is a brave attempt but not a successful one.

Callers works by intercutting between a group of three Republican killers and the family of their intended victim, a member of the RUC. Reid's concern with the explosiveness of family life, explored most widely in his television trilogy, *Billy*, continues here.

The Millar family, the chosen victims of an act of violence whose motives are murky, is not an idyllic haven of normality set against the madness of the terrorists. David Millar, played with insight and conviction by Des Cave, is an often threatening presence, attempting to command his wife and daughter as he would a squadron of policemen, and suspected by his daughter of involvement in torture. Nor are Reid's terrorists the cold, calculating animals of the ritual denunciations. Their motives are complex. Here too, political violence is deeply imbued with personal emotions and private causes.

The problem, however, is that Reid's terrorists are too emotionally convoluted, too caught up in their personal angst to have any political force at all. The woman, played by Barbara Brennan, is convinced that their cause is doomed and is primarily involved because of her attraction to her comrade, O'Neill. He, for his part, is motivated by revenge, the Protestant son of a mixed marriage whose family was burnt out by his co-religionists. In trying to get beyond the stereotypes of the senseless killers, Reid has removed them from the political sphere altogether, making them into a pair of voyagers on some doomed existentialist journey. The result is unconvincing and at times turgid. Ben Barnes's production grapples awkwardly with the play's uneasy mixture of naturalism, black farce and self-contemplation. The dramatic climax, the shooting of David Millar, is exploded by the sudden flailing jump from one style to another and from one location to another.

The most effective dramatic device of the play, the rehearsal for the murder in a hall hired in the name of an amateur drama group, is not developed by Reid, and its chilling simplicity as a metaphor of the emotional emptiness at the heart of the play is lost in a welter of verbal agonizings. We are left with a confusing and poorly shaped piece, which for all its courageous intent clarifies nothing about the politics of murder.

Wasters, by Paul Mercier

SFX Theatre
Sunday Tribune, 1 December 1985

Twenty years ago the plays that tried to reflect the way life was lived in Ireland were about emigration, about the schizophrenia and the scars of being forced away from a place you love. Ideas of home, of family, of a native place, of a fixed and rooted world from which the hero was wrenched were powerful then. There was a mood of elegy as well as anger.

That mood has changed. The plays that try to reflect Ireland now allow for no nostalgia. Ireland is not a place from which one is forced into exile; it is now seen through the eyes of the returned emigrant, seen in all its stasis and hopelessness. Coming home is as painful as going away was 20 years ago.

Tom Murphy has already explored this theme in *Conversations on a Homecoming*. Now in *Wasters*, a major new play at the SFX in Dublin, Paul Mercier deals with another homecoming, this time to the waste ground of a corporation estate, where three young men and three young women gather to mark the return on holidays of one of their number, Bonzo, who has been working on a building site in Islington.

It is no nostalgic emigrant's return – nothing has stood still but nothing has changed. The past is gone but the present is no better and no worse. The characters of *Wasters* are the disenfranchised of Irish society and of Irish literature. Urban corporation housing estates have been around in Ireland since the Thirties. Brendan Behan lived in one, so did Christy Browne. But Behan set his writing mostly in the more 'literary' territory of declining Georgian Dublin; Browne set his in an unnamed and undefined urban landscape.

Only now in the work of the Finglas poets Michael O'Loughlin and Dermot Bolger is the voice of the estates being heard. Paul Mercier adds a very significant dramatic expression to that voice.

Wasters owes much to the kind of dramatic writing which emerged in Britain in the Sixties in the work of people like Edward Bond and Barrie Keeffe and in the wave of socially realistic television drama. But the language is new.

Paul Mercier, together with his six actors, has captured a densely woven texture of slang, vulgarity, metaphor and wisecrack that establishes the world of the corporation corral better than any amount of 'realistic' setting and design.

This is not the lilting, indulgent language of O'Casey's Dubliners, a language that functions as the only luxury in a sparse world, but a rapid, sneering, ironic speech that takes no literary prisoners.

Having a writer direct his own work can often be a mistake, but here it means that there is a seamless energy flowing between the text and the performances, a sense of pace and rhythm that is irresistible. From the moment the lights come up on the three lads in the field, we are drawn into their world.

The setting of *Wasters* on a literal wasteland is no mere signal for a descent into desperation. The six characters are hemmed in by a world of butter vouchers and petty crime and unemployment, but the bleakness is as much a punchbag for their shadow boxing as it is an inescapable fact of life.

They drink, they have sex, they play games, they dance. They act out fears and fantasies with a self-conscious sense of humour and absurdity. With the adult world hanging over them – in the shape of marriage, exile, and prison – they try to hold it at bay with the weapons of childhood.

The playing out of fantasies, led by Joycer, fast talking and feckless, allows the play to step far beyond straightforward naturalism and into an often superb theatricality. Joycer imagines himself as a victim striking back, imprisoned and making a bid for freedom.

The others humour him and themselves. The device allows the notion of freedom itself to arise naturally in the play, without a hint of forced moralizing or a tacked-on message. And the fact that it is all a self-conscious game means that there is a devastating undercutting of the fantasies at the end of each act of the play.

The great thing about *Wasters* is that it takes its setting and its working-class characters for granted – there is no sense of a writer using people as colour, no frantic pointing to the fact that these are not the usual characters of Irish theatre. Because of this it is entirely convincing.

This conviction comes through in every moment of the performances by Brendan Gleeson, Anto Nolan, Joe Savino, Charlotte Brady, Bríd Mhic Fhearaí and Ger Ryan. Savino in particular is on the way to being a marvellous actor. He has a physical command, a sense of gesture and attitude which are rare, and in the part of Joycer he is superb.

But he is by no means out on his own and the whole production provides the unusual spectacle of a group of actors who know exactly what they are doing and what they are saying all the time. They take a bare, black stage, without even a strong lighting design, and inhabit it.

Where Tom Murphy has given us a sense of the disillusion after the Sixties, Paul Mercier conveys the world of the children of the Seventies who never had any illusions. This is one of the best productions of 1985. See it.

Bailegangaire, by Tom Murphy

Druid Lane Theatre, Galway
Sunday Tribune, 8 December 1985

With his play *The Gigli Concert*, a story which Tom Murphy had been telling for nearly 25 years was finished. The leap beyond despair which his people had been seeking was accomplished. With his astonishing new play for the Druid company in Galway, *Bailegangaire*, a new story begins, a new search for love in the chaos of modern Ireland. The new departure is marked by the fact that, for the first time in Murphy's work, *Bailegangaire* is a play for women. The frenetic and often violent search of Murphy's men is replaced by a new note of yearning, of hoping for a new day.

Bailegangaire has the typical Murphy motifs of a journey into night and of a homecoming but they are turned to a new and deeply moving note.

The Ireland of the play is the Ireland of 1984, caught between one failed dream and another, the dream of a rural Gaelic idyll and that of a bright new industrial paradise. The setting is a thatched house in the West. The plaster saints in Frank Conway's fine design beam down on a turf fire; there is talk of a pony and trap, hair ribbons, and even the odd phrase of Irish. And there is, for that matter, Siobhán McKenna planted in a big bed in the middle of the stage.

But there is also the sound of motor cars on their way to the Japanese data-processing factory up the road, and talk of videos and carpeting the lounge. And the factory is closing down.

The old woman in the bed is a crazy crone. Her talk is dislocated, like a Christian Brother teaching Peig Sayers in a classroom in Tallaght. She rattles on like Peig, like Maurya in

Riders to the Sea, like something out of an Ó Conaire story. Her language is full of Gaelicisms and circumlocutions. She even utters an 'Ara, phwat!' straight out of Synge. But she has a story to tell, and until it is told, until it is finished, there can be no new beginning.

Her story, often funny and extravagant, is a formal seanchaí's tale, polished and embellished, about a laughing contest and the way Bailegangaire got its name. She and her two granddaughters, Mary and Dolly, know it by heart. They can break off and resume at any point.

But the tale is incomplete, full of dark hints of 'hatred, terror and desperation' that have not been made explicit. Until the tale dovetails with reality, until there is recognition of its meaning, the old woman and her two granddaughters are like a doomed household of Greek tragedy, cursed to repeat what cannot be expiated.

Dolly and Mary, though young and lucid, are just as dislocated as Mommo, the old woman. Dolly is at the mercy of a loveless marriage to a man who prefers to live in exile, away from her. Mary is stuck with the old woman, having given up her nursing career to come home and mind her.

She is sunk in a well of loneliness, looking not for thanks but for the recognition which the old woman refuses her. Her demand, as the night stretches out, that the story be finished once and for all, is a demand that things unsaid be said, that she herself, a woman unseen, be recognized.

Dolly and Mary are both literal orphans and orphans of God. The misfortune of the past has left them without parents, only Mommo. And Mommo tells a story of what her father said, about God leaving man and the earwigs, the only creatures without a function in nature, to their own devices.

God has long since abandoned the world of *Bailegangaire*, and the only salvation is in human compassion and hope. This is a play about women and the presiding deity is the Virgin Mary, the image of human suffering and overcoming.

That the story does get told, that the play does manage to convincingly attest to the power of human love, is due both to the extraordinary mastery of Murphy's language and to the fierce integrity and strength of Garry Hynes's production. Murphy's orchestration of sound and words into a richly-layered texture allows the play to work on many levels, as a social drama about two young women trying to look after an old one, as a devastating allegory of modern Ireland, as a riveting suspense story, and as a metaphysical work of great poetic beauty. The production, rigorously modulated and perfectly balanced from moment to moment, is sensitive to all of those levels without ever operating on only one of them.

Siobhán McKenna emerges in *Bailegangaire*, as she has not done in Ireland in recent years, as a great actress. Her grand style and the amazing range of her voice work here not as mere display but as a superbly disciplined and well-aimed performance. The scale of her style, the fact that Mother Ireland hovers in the background of her stage persona, is exactly right here, precisely because she is, in one dimension of Mommo, Mother Ireland. But it is not the Mother Ireland of long and noble suffering, weeping and wailing. It is a Mother Ireland who spits and urinates.

Siobhán McKenna here is foul, terrifying and insidious, as well as being somehow haunting and ultimately very moving. She makes herself at times physically very ugly, setting her face in a hard, mannish expression that will melt only when the moment of resolution is reached. It is a performance of rare stature.

But it is not given to her to finish the play. That is done by Marie Mullen's Mary, whose quiet, understated agony has acted all along as a careful counterpoint to Mommo's loquacity. That care and control mark every point of the production, making it a consummate piece of theatre.

There is talk in *Bailegangaire* of 'the field haunted by infants,' of the dead babies buried in the night. But the play ends with a new child that will be born and a new beginning that will be entered. At the end of a year haunted by dead infants in the fields, *Bailegangaire* offers an exorcism of that haunting, and an expiation of that buried guilt. It is theatre that reaches for life and will live. It is a new beginning for Murphy, and in a sense, for the rest of us.

Double Cross, by Thomas Kilroy

Guildhall Theatre, Derry
Sunday Tribune, 16 February 1986

Ideas have always sat uneasily in the Irish theatre. Plays which take it on themselves to interpret the world for us, to add to our understanding of politics and history, have generally been either ignored or travestied. The theatre of ideas needs styles of production which we are unused to. It demands more than straightforward stories about recognizable characters.

In a week where we have had three productions of plays concerned primarily with ideas, all of them Irish plays and two of them new Irish plays, it is clear that this kind of theatre is still extremely problematic for us. While Thomas Kilroy's new play for Field Day at the Guildhall in Derry, *Double Cross*, comes nearest to solving the problem, Patrick Mason's elegant production of Shaw's *Heartbreak House* at the Gate suffers from uncertainty about how to handle Shaw's ideas, and Aodhan Madden's *Sensations* at the Peacock never finds a form to contain its passionate convictions.

Kilroy's *Double Cross* is an audaciously intellectual play, full of challenging and complex ideas about the psychological relationship between the colonizer and the colonized. It is essentially a dramatization of what Field Day director Seamus Deane has called the fictive nature of Irish politics – the way in which we invent political identities in much the same way as a writer invents characters. Field Day has been committed to the notion of seeing language as politics, ever since its founding work, Brian Friel's *Translations*.

Double Cross goes a good deal further and takes politics as art. Focusing on the figures of two Irishmen who 're-invented' themselves, Brendan Bracken, who became Minister for Information in Churchill's wartime cabinet, and William Joyce who became Lord Haw Haw, broadcasting Nazi propaganda while remaining loyal to an exaggerated notion of Britishness, *Double Cross* looks at politics as an artistic invention.

Joyce and Bracken were not just two Jesuit-educated Irishmen passing themselves off as English: they were also both propagandists. They lived in a world where identities and allegiances were up for grabs, where truth was something you made up from a compound of lies. Joyce's Lord Haw Haw, in the second act of the play, uses his knowledge of a single insignificant fact, that a particular town clock is showing the wrong time, to build up a sense of fear in his listeners. Both he and Bracken, in Kilroy's vision, do the same thing all the time, using their command of the minor details to set the imaginations of their audience running, making people think that they are so much more than they really are. They are both actors.

What Kilroy does in *Double Cross* is to make concrete and particular the general notions at work in Genet's *The Maids* about the way in which servants ape their masters. The play is full of the same sense of role-playing. We see Bracken's sexual relationship with an upper-class English lady in which he needs her to dress up as a boy scout before he can become sexually aroused. He is fixated on a role-playing game. Similarly Joyce, an inadequate and obsessive man in his personal relationship with his wife, comes alive, becomes a whole and rounded personality full of power and arrogance, only when he is in front of his radio microphone.

Of the two men, Joyce is the more interesting and Kilroy concentrates on him in the second half of the play in which most of the conclusions are reached. Whereas Bracken is 'a red haired golliwog wearing indifferent suits', an Irishman who has decided to be a member of the English ruling class, Joyce has gone a step further to accomplish the real double-cross. Having invented himself as an Englishman – indeed, a super-Englishman, fetishing the purity of the race and the symbols of its authority – he achieves his apothesis by becoming an English traitor. With a delicious irony, his life ends with a triumphant declaration of this Englishness by the judge at the Old Bailey who rules that he can be hanged for treason even though he is not a British citizen. In punishing him, his England claims him as its own.

Bracken and Joyce do not meet in the play, but Kilroy brings them into constant contact through Joyce's radio broadcasts and through the use of a film backdrop in which each appears to haunt the other. Joyce's politics follow Walter Benjamin's definition of fascism as the eruption of aesthetics into politics, the desire to invent the world as on ordered, symmetrical work of art.

The fascination of the play lies in the fact that Joyce is ultimately more sympathetic than Bracken, seeing through, as he does, Bracken's adoption of the trappings of privilege and seeking instead the realities of power. Bracken is an egoist, Joyce a twisted visionary.

A play which teems with so many ideas cannot be presented in straightforwardly naturalistic terms, and neither Kilroy nor director Jim Sheridan attempts to do so. The style is open and expressionistic, moving rapidly from one short scene to the next, with narrators, actors in a succession of different roles, and a sparse functional set.

There is, however, a sense that the style has not been completely mastered – some of the narrative passages come across awkwardly as desperate grappling-hooks between one scene and the next; the use of film becomes repetitious and undramatic and the elements of this style sit uneasily with the more conventional scenes between Joyce, his wife and his wife's lover. These problems are by no means crippling, but they do hold back the power of the drama.

They are overshadowed, however, by the magnificent playing of Stephen Rea as both Bracken and Joyce. His transformation from the nervous, watchful arrogance of Bracken to the haunting, melancholic mania of Joyce is masterly, and his acting avoids completely any spurious attempt at psychological explanation or 'characterization' of either man, which would be completely out of place in a play like this. Rea is always compelling and convincing and makes the play work even when it shouldn't.

Richard Howard displays an extraordinary versatility in his many roles, always capable and at times, both in the hilarious monologue of Lord Castlerosse and as Margaret Joyce's lover, Erich, inspired. Kate O'Toole is not as versatile, and it is difficult at time to distinguish her different roles, but she does have strength and presence.

Double Cross, then, is not a finished masterwork, but is certainly a play to be seen, an experiment with ideas in the theatre which takes bold risks and pulls most of them off.

Studs, by Paul Mercier
SFX Centre
Sunday Tribune, 13 April 1986

Plays are supposed to have heroes, individuals caught in one dilemma or another. In Paul Mercier's new play at the SFX Centre, *Studs*, the hero is not an individual but a football team. The concern is not so much with individual psychology as with the collective hopes, dreams and fantasies of a whole class. There are moments when the action focuses briefly on a particular individual, but essentially it is the team that moves, speaks and acts.

There is nothing like this in Irish theatre. Yet again, Paul Mercier and his Passion Machine company are breaking new ground and doing it with style, sharpness and a huge dose of entertainment.

Mercier's work has always been concerned with working-class fantasies. In *Drowning* the vehicle for fantasy was rock music; in *Studs* it is sport, the dream of being a hero, of ending all the humiliation, of winning. He gives us a local soccer team on a working-class suburban estate, a collection of losers whose only chance of winning lies in what they can do collectively. We see them only in their football gear, so that they are undifferentiated by any personal costume, and all of the action takes place either on the football pitch or in the dressing room.

Which is not to say that the world outside does not impinge. On the contrary, it is crucial. The team captain looks forward to their next match because his boss is on the opposing side and it is the one chance he gets to kick him back. For the backward goalie, winning a match is the only chance of gaining the respect of his father and brothers.

For each member of the team, the football field is the territory where they can play out their lives. It is their home ground.

The story of *Studs* looks like something straight out of *Roy of the Rovers*. We meet the team when they are nothing but a bunch of messers, playing as individuals, bickering in the dressing room. A strange man appears offering to be their manager, and is accepted out of perversity and derision. He brings them to book and bends them to his will. They call him Moses – he will lead them to the promised land.

It is a story which runs close to John Godber's popular English rugby league play *Up 'n' Under*, but it is infinitely better. For whereas *Up 'n' Under* follows a comic-strip plot of fantasy success, *Studs* turns the fantasy into a harsh bitter enactment of the reality of being a loser. It subverts the comic-strip story and creates a collective portrait of the urban dispossessed.

It does so, however, with humour, energy and panache. The harsh language of the Dublin working class is combined with constant, dynamic action, as the football matches are played out with wit and invention. Words and movements come fast and furious, from a cast that has been welded together by Mercier's direction into a single, fluid entity.

The whirling pace of the first half is dropped for a while in the second, giving space for more pointed probing of what is going on. The confidence and assurance of the fine cast allow for this change of pace, their convention never slipping, their sense of being part of the team never being marred by individual histrionics.

Studs is a play which manages to encompass a real sense of modern urban life in Ireland and to probe the success ethic of the Eighties with perspicacity and toughness. But it works firstly as a piece of theatrical entertainment, accessible, playful and funny. It uses the pace and excitement of television, the medium best known to the audience it is aimed at, without sacrificing the essentials of theatre.

With *Studs* following on *Wasters* and *Drowning*, Paul Mercier's two previous shows at the SFX, it is possible to say that something new has arrived in Irish theatre: a completely urban playwright. Mercier's Dublin has no nostalgic tenement communities, no fine Georgian houses to remind us of the glories of the past. It has, in fact, no past at all, only a continuous present of frustration and survival and odd flights into a fantasized future.

The new Dublin and the new generation that has grown up in it is being, finally, enfranchised in the Irish theatre. It is about time.

Ourselves Alone, by Anne Devlin

John Player Theatre
Sunday Tribune, 5 October 1986

Northern Ireland may be as British as Finchley, but it is apparently not British enough for English audiences to be able to stomach it on its own terms. In a number of recent plays about the North which have had their first productions in London, such as Ron Hutchinson's *Rat in the Skull*, the authors have contrived to bring in English characters, as if, without them, we Paddies could not be 'relevant' enough to an English audience. Anne Devlin's *Ourselves Alone* (John Player Theatre) from the Royal Court in London, suffers from the same problem.

For a very good opening stretch of the play, the focus is clearly on three Andersonstown women, each tied by family or by conviction to the Provisional movement. The writing is sharp and convincing, the portrayals, by Sylvestra Le Touzel, Fiona Victory and Aingeal Grehan, excellent. Then, enter an Englishman, an Oxbridge type who wants to get involved in the struggle for obscure personal reasons to do with his improbable marriage to a Derry woman.

There is a long scene in which he is interrogated and in which he reveals his psyche. You keep thinking: 'What is this man doing here? What function has he other than one of drawing an English audience into the play?' After that, it is impossible to believe a word of what is going on. It gradually becomes clear that this is a play which could just as easily be set in Hampstead, about the problems that women have with men only here flavoured with the thrilling tang of terrorism. It is well written, beautifully produced, beautifully acted, and utterly false.

Cromwell, by Brendan Kennelly

Damer Theatre
Sunday Tribune, 14 December 1986

For a theatre which is supposed to have its roots in poetry, the speaking of verse has always been a problem for the Irish stage. The founding father of the Irish theatre, Yeats himself, discovered this too late.

Having begun by insisting that the way to speak poetry on the stage was to stand stock still and enunciate, Yeats came to understand that poetry in the theatre is just as much a matter of movement and gesture as it is of words.

By the time he made his discovery, the Abbey had got so used to taking his earlier advice that it was literally unable to do his later plays. Together with his verse plays, he retreated to the sitting rooms of Merrion Square to a select audience and a rarefied atmosphere.

Theatre Unlimited's version of Brendan Kennelly's massive poem *Cromwell*, playing in private performances in Trinity last week but opening to the public in the Damer after Christmas, is a joyous reunion of word and gesture, putting poetry back into its proper theatrical context.

Where much of modern technical experiment comes close to abandoning words altogether, Theatre Unlimited's *Cromwell* is in fact very wordy, giving weight and reverence to the poetry, the metre, and the rhyme. It is not afraid of the density of verbal language and is at times content to luxuriate in it.

But, and this is where it is both original and exciting, it surrounds the words with rich theatrical imagery, recreating the poem for the theatre rather than merely adapting it to the stage.

The transition from the printed page to the stage is not as illogical as 'adaptations' almost always are. For one thing *Cromwell* the poem is already quite dramatic, full of direct speech and internal dialogue.

The poem is also populated by figures who approach the status of characters, chief among them Buffún, the archetypal Irishman who dreams the nightmare of Irish history and Cromwell himself, present both as a historical figure with his own biography and as a phantasmagoric focus of a nation's spite, hatred and self-disgust. The poem shifts between interlaced layers of Buffún's life; the Cromwellian slaughter in Ireland; and a mocking Night of the Living Dead in which history is conflated into a single continuous present of absurd contradictions and ludicrous bathos.

Maciek Reszczynski's production for Theatre Unlimited preserves this effect of three different layers intermingling, but makes it physical and real on the stage. On the surface of the playing area there is a sloped construction which is both Buffún's bed and psychic battleground.

From below the surface, the nightmare figures emerge, come into the half-light and disappear again. Purely as a technical achievement of complex staging this is impressive, but its effect goes way beyond the technical.

In order to stage the poem and preserve its spirit, it is necessary to break the sense of chronological time, of one thing following another in a relationship of cause and effect. This is more difficult on stage than it is on the printed page, because on stage we see things precisely in their ordained order whereas on paper we ourselves determine the sequence and duration of our reading.

But Reszczynski manages, with his Jack-in-the-box effects of people appearing and disappearing, and with a delicate sense of rhythm, to remove the action from the realm of normal time and impose connections which go backwards and forwards from one image at the start to another at the end and back to one somewhere in the middle.

We are not tempted to understand this as anything other than a collection of images suggesting both the viciousness and the buffoonery of history.

Reszczynski's images are in the best tradition of the Poor Theatre, depending for their effect not on elaborate and awesome spectacle, but on simplicity and directness. The acting of the fine young company is unadorned and strictly controlled, marked always by confidence and a sense of purpose.

The discipline of their movements pays off at the end with an image that is unforgettable in its clarity and directness. This is the kind of simplicity which results from refinement and concentration and it is wonderful to see it on the Irish stage.

Brownbread, by Roddy Doyle

SFX Centre
Sunday Tribune, 20 September 1987

Starting a play with the kidnapping of a bishop is a risky business: the chances are that there's nowhere to go but downhill. As the lights come up on Roddy Doyle's new play *Brownbread* at the SFX Centre, three young fellas are about to bustle Bishop Fergus Tracey, abducted while on Confirmation duty in the wilds of Barrytown, into the bedroom of a corporation house.

The sight of a bishop in full regalia stumbling over the threshold of a bedroom with cutesy Woolworth's pictures on the wall is about as arresting an opening as can be imagined, but you can't help wondering whether everything else isn't bound to be an anti-climax.

Two hours later, after an unsuccessful assault by the Special Branch, an invasion of Dollymount by the US Marines, and a satellite linkup with Ronald Reagan, such doubts have been pummelled into submission. *Brownbread* is a panic.

In one sense the humour of *Brownbread* belongs to the kind of zaniness pioneered on television by Monty Python and transferred to the stage by groups like the Natural Theatre of Bath. *Brownbread* has the most unlikely plot since Shakespeare wrote *Cymbeline* and it does roll along with a Pythonesque absurdity. But, particularly on stage, that kind of determined zaniness tends to fall flat very quickly.

Once you've grasped the fact that the logic of the piece is that there is no logic, there's not much more to it. The absurdity of *Brownbread* works dramatically, however, because it is built on a base of authenticity, a robust and supple recapturing of the speech and mannerisms of the working-class suburbs of Dublin.

There have been various attempts to write about the aimlessness and lack of direction of the young unemployed, attempts which almost invariably end up merely reproducing the boredom which they intend to describe. *Brownbread*, on the other hand, dramatizes aimlessness by giving us three characters Ao, Donkey and John who completely lack motivation. Good comedy is not concerned with establishing the motives of its characters, and the three kidnappers essentially have no idea why they abducted the bishop, what they want to achieve, or how they are going to get out of the situation.

This supreme fecklessness is set against a world of authority – from the church to parents, to the guards, to Ronald Reagan – which is stupid, incompetent and completely crazy. Ao, Donkey and John may be off the wall but the people who are supposed to be in charge aren't exactly models of purpose and decision either.

Anyone who has read Roddy Doyle's recent novel, *The Commitments*, will have a good idea of his grasp of the language and humour of the people he is writing about. Berts Folan, Lawrence Lowry and Stephen Dunne could not be better as the three lads, acting together like life-long mates, slagging and undercutting each other, bringing into play all of the sharpness and the vulnerability that are needed.

Nor is Doyle's dialogue confined to the argot of Kilbarrack. His rural guards and his rednecked marines are also hilariously accurate in the idiosyncrasies of their speech.

The confidence of the dialogue is not always matched by the construction of the play, and there are times in the second half when it seems to wander off course. Paul Mercier's tight, fast production minimizes the damage, however. It is smartly paced without being manic, and it brings out the best of the humour by playing it with as much normality as can be mustered in such a situation. With a plot of such glorious wildness, there is a temptation to exaggerate and caricature everything, but the play is much the better for maintaining the impression of all of this being just slightly weirder than real life.

Aside from the three kidnappers, there are also really funny performances from Charlie O'Neill as a rural garda, a television interviewer, and an American private, and from Brendan Gleeson as Ao's Da ('Give back that bishop'.) Pat Kenny, Dave Fanning and Charlie Bird do passable impressions of themselves on tape. It all adds up to a show that has to be seen to be disbelieved.

Pentecost, by Stewart Parker

Guildhall Theatre, Derry
Sunday Tribune, 27 September 1987

'A future? In a place like this?' The question asked in the midst of
the 1974 Ulster Workers' Council strike by one of a group of
four spiritual refugees who have gathered in a terraced house in
East Belfast, is the one which is central to Stewart Parker's new
play *Pentecost*, this year's offering from Field Day, which opened
at the Guildhall, Derry, last week. Parker is concerned with the
search for transcendence, looking for a way in which the iron
laws of time and place can be convincingly escaped. In spite of
much splendid writing, terrific performances and a beautifully
modulated production by Patrick Mason, he doesn't quite
manage to find it.

Though its characters are from both Catholic and Protestant
backgrounds, the territory of the play is literally and imaginatively
Protestant. Militant Protestantism, with the Bible in one hand
and the pick-axe handle in the other, has taken control of the
city.

There is a state of siege: the gas lights are replaced with
candles, the food supply dwindles to a giant bag of muesli
brought across the Irish Sea by the Anglified Peter who hates
Belfast but cannot stay away from it, in this, its hour of darkness.

And the play itself becomes more and more evangelical,
building towards the image of being 'born again', using the
language of the Bible with an intensity and fervour that belongs
only to the Protestant tradition.

Not only does Parker, in *Pentecost* as elsewhere, use passages
from the Bible as his emotional touchtone, his other themes are
insistently Puritan. Everywhere in the play is the Puritan division
between the mind and the body, spirituality on the one side and
sexuality on the other.

Lenny Harrigan, the feckless musician who has inherited the
house in which the action is set, remembers an idyll in which he
saw a naked woman singing a hymn and a group of nuns
frolicking in the sea. It is his ideal of the spirit and the body in
harmony. But it is based on a strict division between the two

which Parker finds hard to overcome and which remains problematic for the play.

The basic image of the play is that of death and resurrection. It begins in the aftermath of the death of old Lily Mathews, who has left Lenny the house. Lily continues to haunt the house and she in turn talks of her husband as having come back from the dead when he returned from the First World War.

Then we learn that Lenny and his ex-wife Marian, who comes to take over the house, have lost a child five years previously and that that infant is also haunting them. Ruth, Marian's friend who takes refuge from a vicious policeman husband, has suffered repeated miscarriages. And in the course of the play, yet another baby, Lily's, comes to haunt the house. The images are powerful, but you begin to feel that they are being hammered home with too much insistence.

Lily, both in her haunting of Marian and in Marian's reading of her diaries and searching among her things, becomes an embodiment of Protestant history in this century in Belfast. We are exposed to a life of suffering, guilt, denial, strength, and the play's most successful intermingling of the personal and the political, Lily's insistence that through her personal trials 'I never surrendered, not one inch,' makes her an incarnation of the embattled mentality of her entire community.

All of this is built up with a confidence, wit and conviction that make the first half, and most of the second half, absorbing and entertaining. Parker has the gift of being able to turn a sharply epigrammatic line without losing a sense of authentic speech.

But this very authenticity carries its own problems for a play like this. Having convinced us of the reality of these people and of the time and place in which they live, Parker then has to try to leap beyond realism into some kind of metaphor of transcendence. That leap has to be credible on the level of the real political world which he has delineated so sharply. And it isn't.

We have been led to expect some kind of apocalyptic deliverance at the end of the play. What we get is an evangelical sermon on the 'Christ in ourselves' as the source of change. The problem is that this Pentecostal image works only on the level of words. Change is evoked verbally, it doesn't happen on stage. What we end up with is the notion that if we were all nicer people the troubles would go away. Nothing in the play gives us much reason to believe that.

It is to the great credit of the actors, particularly of Eileen Pollock as Marian, who delivers the sermon, that they manage to make this last 20 minutes of the play even somewhat believable. They do so by underplaying the lines, relying on the crispness and sureness of touch which Patrick Mason's production has throughout.

The performances are of a very high calibre, Stephen Rea both funny and moving as Lenny, Eileen Pollock superbly able to express emotion without emotionalism, Barbara Adair a perfectly judged Lily and Paula Hamilton and Jonathan Kent precise and convincing as Ruth and Peter.

This degree of quality makes the play worth seeing on its voyage round Ireland, however much it fails to meet the expectations which it creates for itself.

Somewhere Over the Balcony, by Marie Jones

Peacock Theatre
Sunday Tribune, 3 January 1988

Somewhere Over the Balcony at the Peacock is a picture of life in the Divis Flats in Belfast presented by the Northern company Charabanc. More like a revue than a play it is Theatre of the Absurd in which the absurdity is all too real. In Marie Jones's vision, the women who hang over the balconies of the flats don't feel like they are being watched all the time. They *are* being watched all the time: the army has an observation post on the tower block opposite. Life is stranger than drama.

Somewhere Over the Balcony manages to make something funny and entertaining out of life in Divis, without sentimentalizing or making a skit of that life, in a somewhat similar fashion to the way in which Roddy Doyle dealt with Kilbarrack in *Brownbread*. Like *Brownbread*, there is a madcap excess of incident: a siege of a church by the British Army; joy riders in a Saracen armoured car;

a tortoise called Starsky in a helicopter; a baby being born to a bride in the middle of a wedding ceremony; a demented nun trying to seize a child. The pity is that all of this is talked about rather than acted out, that everything remains essentially at the level of reported speech.

Peter Sheridan's production, however, is carried by tough and spiky performances from Marie Jones, Eleanor Methven and Carol Scanlan who are all wonderfully direct and skilful. Their rollicking energy makes for a sharp and captivating show.

Exit Entrance, by Aidan Mathews

Peacock Theatre
Sunday Tribune, 7 February 1988

In his new play at the Peacock, *Exit Entrance*, Aidan Mathews erects fierce obstacles for himself to overcome, making it all the more remarkable that in the end, the very end, he manages to do so. Some of the obstacles are the necessary result of an adventurous and inventive dramatic method in which a rigidly static first half exists, not for itself, but as a slow-release capsule infusing its resonances into a much more theatrical second half. Other obstacles are less necessary and considerably more irritating: the frequent silliness of the characters, the air of an etiolated upper-class world, the feeling of preciousness that sometimes descends on events.

In his previous plays, *The Diamond Body* and *The Antigone*, Mathews has shown a powerful attraction to both the classical Greek world and to the Greek islands themselves and both are important to *Exit Entrance*, providing much of the imagery and fleshing out the yearning of its characters. Each half of the play gives us a Helen and a Charles and each is full of classical learning and memories of Greece. In *Exit* the couple is middle-aged and on the brink of suicide, eking out their last hours with word games, reminiscences in which they try to recapture a lost life and a lost son through the evocative power of speech. In *Entrance*, a young Helen and Charles, who are at the same time separate people and a reincarnation of the older couple, imagine their future through the same words and images.

Both couples are 'people like us', people who write better in rooms with high ceilings, people who think that 'any fool knows' the Greek word for pity, people who sprinkle their speech with Italian and French words and are much given to Greek and Latin quotations, people who look 'wistful', people who used to model gloves. They are also people who have a haughty disdain for ordinary humanity: what seems to be impelling the first Charles and Helen towards suicide is the thought of common people coming to visit them in hospital when they are old and sick. All of this would be preposterous were it not for the wit and the restraint with which Mathews rescues it. As it is, though, it comes pretty close to making you give up on the play.

Exit Entrance in fact is a triumph of form over content. It is not so much that there is any extraordinary revelation in the course of the play, rather that its shape becomes increasingly beautiful as the filigree of correspondences between the first half and the second is traced. *Entrance* moves from the extreme stasis of *Exit* (in which Joan O'Hara as Helen is never allowed to leave her chair) towards a kind of ritualistic movement that is more and more theatrical. It is like looking at a portrait of someone you don't like and being forced to admire the delicacy of the brushstrokes, the perfection of the symmetry, the boldness of the execution. In its last moments the play achieves through its form the kind of concentration and richness that all theatre seeks.

It is helped immeasurably by an impeccably poised production from Ben Barnes. The performances from Joan O'Hara and Denys Hawthorne in the first half, and from Ingrid Craigie and Malcolm Douglas in the second are as decorous and dignified as they need to be, while Ms O'Hara manages to convey an emotional turbulence as well.

Sea Urchins, by Aodhan Madden

Project Theatre
Sunday Tribune, 14 August 1988

A new Western company, Sligo's very enterprising Acorn, reaches new and impressive heights with Aodhan Madden's *Sea Urchins* at the Project. Acorn has pursued a brave policy of commissioning new plays to suit its young actors, and it pays off handsomely with *Sea Urchins* which is Madden's best play since *The Midnight Door* four years ago. Des Braiden's production is also the best that Madden has had since then – tough, clear, well designed and very well acted.

Though it changes the location and many of the details, *Sea Urchins* is inspired by the notorious Fairview Park murder in Dublin some years ago, a 'queer-bashing' episode whose perpetrators were bound over to keep the peace. It is not – and this is its great strength – the kind of social drama-documentary that this would imply. Madden has the murder and the subsequent verdict but he is more concerned with an inner exploration of the condition of marginality, social and sexual, in contemporary Ireland, and his method is loose, largely non-naturalistic and sometimes bordering on the poetic.

The theme of marginality is a familiar one in Madden's work but *Sea Urchins* is set on Dun Laoghaire pier and the sea breeze blows away much of the stale smell of old greasepaint that has clung to some of his less successful plays. There is a freedom about the dialogue and the form of the play which is new and which allows for a much greater clarity of purpose. Particularly in the case of his central character Huey, Madden is concerned to explore the borders between yearning and actuality, fantasy and reality, desire and denial, shifting between a relative naturalism and an expressionistic use of monologue.

Acorn's performances are equal to the intent. Declan Croghan's violent self-contempt as Huey is always gripping, and Paul Kennedy's edgy, unsettling Squint has just the right mixture of hysteria and vulnerability. Gerry Marshall, Aoife Lawless and Conor Clarke as the other members of the gang also turn in performances of force and integrity. *Sea Urchins* is an important step forward both for Acorn and for Aodhan Madden. It makes it all the more important that Acorn's future should be secured and that its development should be allowed to continue.

Boss Grady's Boys, by Sebastian Barry

Peacock Theatre
Sunday Tribune, 28 August 1988

Ostensibly, Sebastian Barry's brilliant new play at the Peacock, *Boss Grady's Boys*, inhabits something of the same world as *The Righteous are Bold*, the world of dying Irish hill-farms, but though essentially a poetic piece it is much more sharply aware of history and change and the psychological complexities of real people.

Beautifully theatrical and taking a liberty with the use of language which it seldom abuses, *Boss Grady's Boys* is at the same time marvellously clear in its placing of its two central characters, Mick and Josey, the ageing 'boys' of the title, against the background of the death of a way of life.

In content, *Boss Grady's Boys* could be described as a cross between *The Great Hunger* and *Of Mice and Men*, evoking both the tyranny of land and family in sexually frustrated Irish rural bachelorhood and the movingly detailed relationship between a simple man and his younger, more clear-sighted brother. But Barry, though his writing is genuinely elegiac, is not concerned to mourn an idealized past.

The mythology of Josey, the older, 'simple' brother is not Fionn and the Fianna but the Marx Brothers, Fred Astaire, Maurice Chevalier and the cowboy pictures.

Barry keeps a miraculous balance between ironic absurdity and unrestrained yearning, between Mick and Josey's comic awareness of their own situation and the love and pity which underlie that awareness. We have, for instance, in Mick's evocation of Michael Collins, one of the most complete invokings of the hopes and failures of the War of Independence in Irish literature:

> That we wouldn't have to stand on the roadside and watch the cars go by with creatures in them from outer space, plastic and cushions and clothes, another Ireland altogether, people who would mock our talk. [...] That we could be men of our country was all my wish, that we might have a country that would nurture us, a spirit to get us up the road and out of the rain. How is it that after every change and adjustment I still

stand here in the same rain on the same mud, with the same sun laughing at me?

Simultaneously we have Josey's memory of Groucho singing *Hail, Hail Freedonia*.

Boss Grady's Boys, though, doesn't work entirely through its verbal evocations, powerful though they are. It is a superbly theatrical piece, already indistinguishable from the hauntingly resonant performances of Jim Norton and Éamon Kelly in the title roles.

Kelly's achievement is comparable in some respects to that of Siobhán McKenna in *Bailegangaire*, for he uses his own theatrical image, that of the archetypal Irish countryman, to devastating effect. Kelly takes the storyteller from his own one-man shows, and tilts him at an angle. Instead of naturalistic detail, he goes for something that is at once highly familiar and stunningly unnatural.

He pitches his voice to a high, singing tone, makes his movements like those of a marionette manipulated by a slightly drunken puppeteer, creating the effect of an oddness that comes not from being dim-witted but from being at odds with the world.

Kelly's performance is matched and deeply enriched by Jim Norton's Mick. Norton is the centre of gravity of the play, deep and echoing like a well. It is to speak very highly indeed of Caroline FitzGerald's superbly sensitive and imaginative production to say that it places and contains two such wonderful performances. *Boss Grady's Boys* has an emotional integrity, a theatrical fluidity and a sense of humanity that are rare and very special.

Carthaginians, by Frank McGuinness

Peacock Theatre
The Irish Times, 1 October 1988

The first week of the Dublin Theatre Festival has been a case, not so much of bread and circuses, as of meat and circuses, much of the meat coming from relatively unheralded home-produced shows and most of the carnival atmosphere from the generally lightweight imports. The substance of the Festival so far is that it has produced three significant new Irish plays. The exuberance that one associates with a festival has been most obvious in shows that fall outside of what used to be called the legitimate theatre, shows like Circus Oz or Nickelodeon's madcap *Did You See That?*

The nice thing, though, is that these two poles are not as far apart as they might seem. [...] Even Frank McGuinness's new play *Carthaginians*, continuing at the Peacock, a dense, richly woven work probing the state of the Northern Catholic soul, is not as far from popular entertainment as it might seem. The whole texture of *Carthaginians*, in fact is made up of varying forms of popular expression. Melodrama, jokes, quizzes, stories, songs, football chants and school poems make up a very large proportion of the dialogue.

In creating seven working-class Derry Catholics, gathered for a vigil in a cemetery on foot of a vision that the dead will rise, McGuinness needs to achieve a particular kind of realism – a realism that is credible and that is yet capable of bearing the brunt of visions, dreams, incantations. By using as his chosen language those parts of popular speech which are most formal, most self-conscious, he meets this need brilliantly.

Carthaginians is in a way an extended pun, making use of the ambiguity of the phrase, 'We'll rise again', a phrase which is at once a well-worn nationalist political slogan and a mystical vision of the Resurrection, to allow him to explore the area that lies between the political and the mystical. To put it another way, *Carthaginians* explores the double meaning of the term 'Catholic' in the North, both as an expression of a political community whose most traumatic common crises, Bloody Sunday and the H-Block strikes, are the touchstones of the play, and as a source of religious imagery, of ideas of salvation and resurrection.

As so often in McGuinness's work, the area where the political and the personal meet is sexuality. The play is more concerned with sexual borders than with political ones. Dido, the play's presiding spirit, a kind of Puck in pink flares, is as camp as Butlin's. In his wonderfully funny burlesque play-within-a-play,

The Burning Balaclava, which ends the first half, the men become women and the women men.

Later, more sombrely and disturbingly, one of the women, Greta, recalls her fears that at the onset of puberty she was turning into a man. In his sexual imagery McGuinness dramatizes both the desire to break through the borders, to elude rigid definitions of who you are and where you belong, and the terror of doing so. And this, of course, however obliquely, is a political metaphor.

What McGuinness finds in his probing of the Catholic psyche is not always palatable. He gives us a Catholic mind that is wounded certainly (Bloody Sunday) but that has also come to define itself by its wounds, to revel in them and hide behind them (H-Block), just as Greta holds up her heroin-scarred arms as a badge of identity. The play mixes its visionary desire to absolve and to bless with a call for truth and clarity.

This interweaving of the political, the visionary and the sexual makes *Carthaginians* at times a difficult and elusive play. But it is also desperately funny and wonderfully flowing, achieving its final leap beyond the dark with astonishing skill. And all of this is superbly realized in Sarah Pia Anderson's direction which achieves at times an almost sculptural stillness, at others a headlong rhythm that can be exhilarating.

Bat the Father, Rabbit the Son, by Donal O'Kelly

Mansion House
The Irish Times, 1 October 1988

Donal O'Kelly's extraordinary *Bat the Father, Rabbit the Son*, which finishes tonight at the Mansion House and of which he is both author and sole performer, is also steeped in the whole idea of storytelling. It is at times like one of those word games where the contestant has to take a given idea and talk nonstop for a defined period, only this game is conducted at an amazingly high level of imagination and invention.

It is a feat not just of prodigious eloquence, but of vivid recreation and reminiscence. Rabbit, the crabbed haulage contractor, and his hapless assistant Keogh set out on an imaginative odyssey in search of Rabbit's father. What follows is a freewheeling set of episodic adventures, excursions, diversions, tangents and ramblings. Such is the brilliance of much of the writing and the power of the performance, that were it not for some lapses and misjudgements in the second half of the play, *Bat the Father, Rabbit the Son* would be a masterpiece.

O'Kelly's great achievement is to take us with such utter conviction into Rabbit's mad mixture of memory and desire, his tyrannical yearnings and helpless sense of loss. He creates the momentum of the voyage, making Rabbit's story, with its yawning gulf between the father's days in the Citizen Army and the son's sordid acquisitiveness, into an oblique history of modern Ireland.

That momentum is sustained for a very long time until, well into the second half, it is broken by a loss of inspiration in the writing and a sudden, awkwardly knowing nudge-and-wink approach to the audience which marks a failure of nerve and a desperate turn towards stand-up comedy. Worse still, when the momentum is regained in a stunning closing section it is again squandered in a dreadful ending.

These are the things which cry out for the hand of the director, Declan Hughes, but the hand is withheld. As it stands, *Bat the Father, Rabbit the Son* is a remarkable piece of theatre: what it could be, though, is something unique and wonderful.

Departed, by Joe O'Byrne

Lombard Street Theatre
The Irish Times, 1 October 1988

Directed by the author himself, the style of *Departed* is much closer to Co-Motion's version of *Song of the White Man's Burden* than to Joe O'Byrne's previous play *Gerrup!* and is infinitely more successful as a result. Co-Motion's great strength lies in the integration of music, movement and words and in the confident utilization of space. *Departed* makes the most of these assets to stretch a historical canvas of the Land War across the yawing spaces of Lombard Street. The result is impressive and effective.

The play itself is sometimes too close to Boucicault and has a few too many purple passages, but it also moves very skilfully between private griefs and public campaigns with a very finely honed sense of dramatic structure to keep the diverse elements in a coherent and unified whole. Most importantly it is the basis for a rigorous and disciplined ensemble performance of a kind that is still rare in the Irish theatre.

Torchlight and Laser Beams, by Christopher Nolan and Michael Scott

Gaiety Theatre
The Irish Times, 8 October 1988

Michael Scott's adventurous collaboration with Christopher Nolan, *Torchlight and Laser Beams*, based on Nolan's poetry and prose, attempts perhaps the most difficult marriage of all, that of the internal and the external. Nolan's writing is an inner voice, a form of speech that often bears little relationship to everyday language. It is the voice of silence, a voice in which each word bears an enormous weight of effort and meaning. His language, particularly that of his early poems, is explosive, violent – a language in which the outburst itself and not some external point of reference is the meaning. To put that language on the stage, to try to find equivalents for it in gesture and movement, is a formidable task. Michael Scott doesn't always pull it off, but when he does the result is remarkable.

There are, inevitably, times when the battering-ram force of Nolan's language overpowers the movements of the actors. There are times when the language is too dense to be spoken and needs to be read. There are also, ironically, times when the need to find theatrical action distracts from the grace of the language. Nolan's elegant, lyrical description of the killing and preparation of a Christmas turkey from *Under the Eye of the Clock*, for instance, is robbed of its sense of summoning up something out of thin air by the literal presence of a turkey being dismembered by Catherine Byrne.

But when the outward action and the inner words come together, as they do when the theatrical images are neither too literal nor too heavily symbolic, then something very special is created. To enumerate these images here would be to rob them of their surprise, but there are three sequences in particular that electrify the stage.

Home, by Paul Mercier
SFX Centre
The Irish Times, 19 November 1988

Paul Mercier's latest play *Home* which finishes a highly successful run at the SFX in Dublin tonight, marks a new stage in the development not only of his own work, but of the whole style of theatre which we have come to associate with Passion Machine. It is not that it is a better play than *Wasters* or *Studs* and indeed in some respects it is a much more conservative piece of theatre than his extraordinary trilogy which was presented in just 12 months between November, 1985, and November, 1986. There is no great experimentation or formal development in *Home* and in fact it has unexpected echoes of the boulevard theatre of Neil Simon or Alan Ayckbourn. But it is nonetheless a logical and necessary step forward in his writing. It is also great fun.

What has characterized the work of Passion Machine more than anything else has been on the one hand its resolutely urban setting and on the other its lack of heroes, of central characters around whom the action might revolve. From *Wasters* onwards, the heroes have been groups, groups of young working-class Dubliners in the case of Mercier and of Roddy Doyle's *Brownbread*, groups of workers in the same job in the plays of Brendan Gleeson and Aidan Parkinson. The plays have been about the way people relate to each other and the world around them rather than about their inner psychology. They have worked incredibly well, constituting the most important movement in the Irish theatre of the 1980s.

But this approach has also, of course, had its limits. It has been difficult for Passion Machine style to contain groups of characters who are not essentially homogenous. Aidan Parkinson's *Going Places*, for instance, tried to incorporate a wider group of characters, both in age and background, and discovered the difficulties of doing so within the Passion Machine style. Now, with *Home*, Paul Mercier confronts the same problem. The play focuses rather more on one character than any of his work since *Drowning*, but it remains essentially about a group. This time, however, the group is shifting, transitory, deliberately ill defined. In terms of age range and geographical background it is vastly more varied than anything he has done before.

Even though it takes place indoors (to an extent that no other Passion Machine play ever has) and begins with a young man from Westmeath setting up home in a Dublin bedsit, *Home* is not a private domestic drama. Most of the action still takes place in public spaces – hallways, passageways, stairways, the shared back yard. Far from being a private sanctuary, Michael's bedsit is constantly invaded by his neighbours and much of the play's humour is in its running joke on the whole idea of domestic privacy. On the surface surprisingly close to the well-made play, *Home* is really more of a send-up of it. *Juno and the Paycock* on speed.

In its loose, episodic plot, *Home* is like a year's episodes of *Neighbours* crammed into two hours of comedy. Friendships are made, neighbours squabble, couples split up and reunite, a possible love affair for Michael flickers and is snuffed out before it begins. Both as writer and director, Mercier shows tremendous skill in keeping this whirl of characters spinning, balancing farce and realism, pathos and parody.

The best of the humour is physical and visual, and it is possible only because Passion Machine has now developed something close to a resident company whose strengths are in comic timing and physical fooling-around. Brendan Gleeson in particular has developed into a superb comedian, able to evoke laughter without opening his mouth, but Gerard Byrne, Berts Folan, Liam Carney, Eamonn Hunt and Mick Nolan also play together superbly. It is one of the great strengths of Mercier's dual role as writer and director that the plays and the players have evolved together, the plays both drawing on and developing the skills of the actors.

For all that, though, *Home* remains a decidedly transitional play. Mercier may have left behind for the moment a rich vein of his work, but there is a sense that he has not yet arrived where he wants to go, to a more inclusive dramatic vision. In *Home* the dramatic dice are still loaded in favour of the young, single, male and urban. Michael, the culchie, is essentially a sap. Valentine, his builder friend, also from the country, is a living throwback to the Irish navvy of the Fifties. And, more significantly, the one older couple with a child who feature in the play are an awkward problem. Mercier hedges his bets with them, at times showing their pain and desperation, at others treating them as objects of fun, in the end simply banishing them, to the unrelieved glee and relief of the other characters and, one suspects, the author.

Paul Mercier and Passion Machine have achieved an incredible amount in the four years of their existence, breaking so much new ground in terms of both subject matter and audience that Irish theatre without them is already unthinkable. But precisely because their style is so much based on playfulness, openness and innovation, they, of all companies, cannot afford to stand still or repeat themselves. Everything they have done in the past two years shows that they understand this, that they know their scope must always be widening. *Home* is a part of that process.

Una Pooka, by Michael Harding

Peacock Theatre
The Irish Times, 29 April 1989

It has always seemed to me interesting that in Ireland 'hysterical' and 'funny' are synonymous. We recognize somehow that humour and madness are close allies. We laugh to release the hysterical tensions of what can be, at times, a very, very strange society. Michael Harding's play at the Peacock, *Una Pooka*, plays on this double meaning of 'hysterical'. It is stark raving funny, uproariously mad. Its laughter is often that of the madwoman in the attic. Its humour is pitched at a higher and higher level of lunacy until it becomes, like white noise, disorienting and disturbing.

It is a mark of just how strange our society is that this play is happening at all. It is happening in the Irish national theatre just

10 years after the visit of Pope John Paul II, a visit which most sane commentators told us would profoundly shape the destiny of this nation for decades to come. And here we all are 10 years later, with full houses of ordinary Irish people, many of whom must have been in the Phoenix Park that day, joining in the fun of a play which turns those events on their head, turns them into a bizarre carnival, a backdrop to a parade of the Irish psyche from the Kerry Babies to the Moving Statues.

The fact of the play itself reminds us of how unformed this society still is – so unformed, indeed, that nothing, not even a papal visit, can have a lasting and continuing effect. If everything in history is enacted twice, the first time seriously and the second time as farce, then Harding shows the gap between the seriousness and the farce in Ireland to be frighteningly narrow.

What is fascinating about *Una Pooka* is that Harding is searching for a form to match this unformed society. He gives us a play that is badly behaved, unruly and unreal, but whose very unruliness seems exactly appropriate to what he is after. The apparent lack of form is not an artistic failure but an artistic success, an apt response to the mood which he is articulating. Not surprisingly in this kind of enterprise, there are byways that don't seem worth following, and for myself I found parts of the second half to be over-elaborated and at times a bit tedious, but in general he carries the whole thing off with wonderful confidence and clarity.

Harding's first play, *Strawboys*, seen at the Peacock in 1987, placed him, both in its uses of imagistic forms and in its drumlin country intonations, in the Mac Intyre school as the only real follower of the Mac Intyre/Hickey/Mason experiments that began with *The Great Hunger*. The thing about that series of plays is that it went very far indeed in liberating the Irish theatre, in opening up new avenues, but that, particularly after its last manifestation, *Snow White*, it badly needed to be brought back into contact with some kind of social reality, some kind of shared language and shared experience. In *Una Pooka* Michael Harding and Patrick Mason do precisely this.

They use the freedom of form and image gained from the Mac Intyre series and bring it into contact with what can only be called the state of the nation. The formal dexterity is amazing, Harding juggling with everything from Glenroe to Dario Fo, mixing farce, social realism, psychological thriller and metaphysical meditation and only rarely and momentarily dropping one of the balls. And Patrick Mason's free-flowing, pure and uncluttered use of stage and space realizes this superbly, managing to be firmly rooted but never literal-minded, sure of its ground but never grounded.

It is terrific to see what this does for actors. The potential for *Una Pooka* to be an unholy mess in performance must have been enormous. It makes contradictory demands on actors, asking them on the one hand to inhabit an apparently naturalistic stage world, building performances that are conventionally motivated and accurate in time and place. And at the same time it asks them to slip through those performances, to distort them to just the right degree, to tilt them at an angle to reality.

What this production shows is that actors can do the most difficult things so long as they really know what they are up to, so long as both the writer and director have given them a clear enough vision of what it is they want to achieve. Contrary to the popular wisdom, acting isn't primarily about emotion – it is primarily about the vision from which the emotion springs. This cast, and in particular Barry McGovern and Seán McGinley, carries through that vision superbly.

On a broader scale, that sort of vision is exactly what the Abbey as an institution needs. *Una Pooka* may be timely in coming 10 years after the papal visit, but it is all the more timely for the Abbey itself, showing that it can still do the business of producing risky and challenging work with considerable aplomb. In the Peacock at least, something is very much alive and kicking where it hurts.

Where it hurts in Ireland is still in that solar plexus that lies between the higher mental regions of religion and the lower physical ones of sex. This is the region at which *Una Pooka* aims its blow and in this it carries through in a more direct way many of the probings of the Irish psyche begun by Mac Intyre. That psyche is murky and the play sometimes gets stuck in that murk, throwing up caricatures of the domineering mammy and the alcoholic daddy and the dried-up ageing virgin. But the form is chosen to contain such caricatures – there is just enough farce in it to allow for caricature, not enough to make the caricatures comfortable and innocuous.

Harding uses farce as a handrail for a descent into the cellars of the Irish psyche, cellars inhabited by ludicrous and embarrassing monsters, as well as by dark and violent ones. The humour keeps his footing firm on the steps, allowing him to approach things that would otherwise be clichés and that have been protected from scrutiny precisely by being clichés which no writer wants to touch with a bargepole. Harding has found a fresh and original way of approaching things that we tend to shy away from, as much from boredom as from fear. It's a real achievement, carried through with style.

Wild Harvest, by Ken Bourke

Druid Theatre, Galway
The Irish Times, 10 June 1989

The lads are still hanging around. In the late Fifties and early Sixties, the last period in which emigration was gnawing away at our souls, Irish theatre was full of the lads, agonizing about going or staying, talking their way onto the cattle boats. Pouring out their scorn and bitterness at a country that couldn't find a way to keep them. But back then, the lads had charm. Brian Friel's Gar O'Donnell or Tom Murphy's John Joe Moran could still entertain us with their sharp-tongued fantasies, their lovable yearning for acceptance. Now, in Ken Bourke's remarkable first play at Druid in Galway, *Wild Harvest*, the lads have returned shorn of their charm. Like forgotten milk on a hidden shelf, they have turned sour and acrid and nasty.

One of the strangest, most unhealthy things about the return of mass emigration is the way that it distorts the whole sense of what it is to be a parent and what it is to be a child. The parents who emigrated and returned are forced to see themselves in their children, as those children again take the emigration trail. The children are forced to see their parents in themselves as they begin again what their parents were supposed to have finished with. The parents' past becomes the children's present; the children's future is the parents' past. The whole sense of living in one's own time, of being oneself and not someone else, is shattered.

This is the territory of *Wild Harvest*, a play in which father and son are not allowed to be father and son, in which the past, a past of claustrophobia and emigration, of Larry Taggart being 'squeezed out' of his Cavan farm, is relived in the present. Larry plays Claudius to young Colm's Hamlet, with Larry's wife Kay as Gertrude. And indeed the *Hamlet* parallels are everywhere – in Colm as the young, usurped heir whose enervated gloom is unsettling everything, in Colm's obsession with their dead parents, in the incestuous competition between brothers for the sexual favours of the same woman. But the importance of these parallels lies in one thing only: the way that *Wild Harvest* tries for, and largely achieves, the sense that one ingrown family where the categories of father and son, of brother and husband, are breaking down, mirrors the stunted, festering state of a nation.

Ken Bourke's central perception in *Wild Harvest* is that by putting together the older generation of returned emigrant with the present generation of young people, you get something painful and terrible but very powerful: a tragic sense of the way unfinished business refuses to go away, and comes back with a malign and ineluctable force. In the play, nothing new – specifically a family of their own for Larry and Kay – can be started until the past is acknowledged and put to rest. And that, because the past is alive and kicking where it hurts, is precisely what cannot happen.

What really makes the play work, though, is the way it gives an image, not just of individuals, but of two generations. Colm's friends – the lads – form a disparate but coherent group, imbued with the malicious innocence of young men in a gang. They are respectable in their yearnings – a job, property, a nice girl – and unrespectable in the violence, competitiveness and cruelty that mark their response to the knowledge that those yearnings cannot be fulfilled. In their clothes, their language, their manners, they are of the post-television age. But unknowingly, in, for example, the ruthless competition of the brothers Finbar and

Donie, they are acting out the same drama as Larry's generation did.

We can see that their future is the older generation's past. Bourke gives us images of the life of that older generation, of the digs and the building sites and the drink, and merges them with the images of the younger men's lives. The sense of entrapment which flows from this is both powerful and awful.

The play's final image, of Larry and Colm locked like drowning men in a terrible embrace, is perhaps the most disturbing and shocking that contemporary Irish theatre has to offer of contemporary Ireland. And the achievement of that image as something utterly convincing and not in the slightest over-the-top or meretricious is a result of careful and inspired work in both the acting and the direction.

Andy Hinds's production is superb and in this instance I have a better idea than usual of just how superb it is. Reading plays for a Listowel Writers' Week competition, I saw an earlier draft of *Wild Harvest*. At that stage, it was impressive, with something hot burning at its core, but it also had weaknesses which made it somewhat diffuse. Under Hinds's direction it has been reshaped and largely rewritten, lifting it onto a whole new level. It has been stripped down to its essentials on the one hand and broadened out, given more points of reference to the world at large, on the other. There is a clarity, a fluidity and a metaphoric power about it now which was not there before.

The same clarity is there in the performances. A young cast, almost entirely new to Druid, is placed around a towering performance from company veteran Mick Lally. Lally has an astonishing ability to pace a performance, to plant things almost unnoticed in the early stages, so that when they emerge later on we know that they are not coming from nowhere. Here, his performance is quiet and smouldering before it becomes almost unbearably fierce. And that kind of sureness and control allows the younger actors – Frank McCusker, J.D. Kelleher, Robert Taylor, Tim Loane and Frankie McCafferty – to be equally confident about what they are doing and to come across with striking assurance.

What Druid have done with *Wild Harvest* is a model of how new writers deserve to be treated by the Irish theatre. It's not just having the guts to risk the play in the first place. It's the fact that a play that might have seemed an interesting beginning comes out as an accomplished achievement. Passion is tempered with purpose, savagery with shape, to produce a play which cuts all the way to the bone.

King of the Castle, by Eugene McCabe

Abbey Theatre
The Irish Times, 15 July 1989

In Garry Hynes's style of directing plays, things tend to be conspicuous by their absence. Of the two great influences on her approach to theatre, one is music, the building of a drama in a symphonic way, through patterns, echoes, movements, counterpoints. But the other is Beckett, the way that Beckett has of making something central by making it almost, but not quite, absent. In Beckett movement is crucial because there is so little movement, humanity is vital because it is almost gone.

The way that Garry Hynes directs plays is often to go against the grain of the play's nature. If the play is metaphoric, if it is a parable or a fable – as in her productions of *The Playboy of the Western World* or *The Wood of the Whispering* or *Bailegangaire* – then she will root it in a kind of dirty realism. You remember the muck from *The Playboy*, the boiled sweets from *The Wood of the Whispering*, the jar of Sudocream from *Bailegangaire*, even though none of those plays could be described in any narrow sense as realistic.

Conversely, where a play is concerned with the flesh, with the body, with sex, she will almost empty it of the physical and tangible. In directing Ford's *'Tis Pity She's a Whore* or Congreve's *The Man of Mode*, plays that reek of carnality and desire, she placed them in an almost empty space, handled them with a rigorous restraint, made them, in a formal sense, almost abstract. If a play is a metaphor for the state of the nation, she will rub its nose in the grime of physical reality. If it is channeling currents of instinctive and physical desire, she will make it metaphoric. She works by setting up a dialectic between the play and the production, a clash between what we hear and what we see; and out of that clash comes the power of drama.

Such a way of working is bold and risky, but it is not to be confused with that of the director who tyrannizes and colonizes a play, pulls it out of shape and tries to make it say what it does not want to say. For what Garry Hynes does is to concentrate our attention on the core of a play by surrounding that core with things that are different. Just as the eye is drawn to the flaw in a pattern, just as a small hill on a flat plain seems much larger than it would if it were surrounded by mountains, so the energies that break through from a surround of bleakness and restraint are what we are immediately struck by in many Hynes productions.

This is very much the case with her production of Eugene McCabe's *King of the Castle* at the Abbey. The play itself belongs to the second kind mentioned above, the kind where the sexual and the physical are uppermost. It is not that *King of the Castle* is about sex in a simple sense, even though what initially drew outraged attention to it was its sexual frankness, the story it tells of an ageing and wealthy farmer who hires a traveling labourer to sire a child on his young and unhappy wife. Sex and reproduction are the physical embodiments of the desire to acquire; the need to have a child is the expression of the need to have everything that a man can have so that his neighbours will no longer have a hold over him. But sex is the currency of the play, the language into which everything else – greed, history, the rise of the self-made man – is translated.

Scober MacAdam, the ageing farmer in question, is the figure who identifies the play as a product of the Sixties, for his quest is the quest of the Ireland of his time: to drag yourself up from nothing, to vanquish the servile past, to be beholden to no one for anything. His tragedy is that he has no children and that this failure keeps him in thrall to the small farmers and labourers he is trying to rise above, for the meanest of them who has children of his own has something to sneer at Scober about. He has worked for independence, but his plight makes him dependent on two people: on Tressa, his young wife, and on Lynch, the labourer on whom he settles as the instrument for solving his problems.

Scober believes that he can buy his way out of anything, but his needs give him a dependency he cannot buy off.

In all of this, Scober is a typical figure of the plays of this period, trying to escape the past but entangled in it. What makes *King of the Castle* so remarkably distinctive, though, is the extent to which this basic story is entwined with something much less specifically of its time, with the dark wars of men and women, with the body and its secrets: blood and sweat and fertility.

What triggers the action of the play is not just the time of Irish history that it occupies but the time of the year and the time of the month. It is as important to the action of the play that it takes place in Tressa's fertile period as it is that it takes place in the Sixties, as important that it takes place at harvest time as that it takes place in a country on the move. The social is one dimension of the play – and it is granted its place in Garry Hynes's production – but the bodily and the seasonal are just as important and it is their more abstract and mysterious rhythms which are played at the centre.

What Garry Hynes does is to take this play which is so bound up with the natural and to emphasize its artifice. The setting by Wendy Shea is abstract to the point of being almost geometric, leading the eye to a central point where the action is seen as though at the end of a tunnel, making it distant, framed, cold. The scenes are arranged as paintings or sculptures are arranged, making us always aware of their own formality, so that the first scene reminds us of one of those paintings of haymaking that used to be so popular, the second of the The Last Supper, and so on.

Movements are wary and restrained, the individuality of the body is hidden in uniform clothing. Nothing draws attention to the physical and the sexual until and unless the play demands that attention. People are arranged like statues, as if the stone of their hills had invaded their bones. But the effect of this is to emphasize rather than to deny the instinctive physical urges that hold the play together, for when the physical – naked flesh, the lunge of desire, the frantic movements of copulation – is let loose, it is all the more shocking for having been so completely submerged.

The risk in this approach is that it involves so much slowness, restraint and austerity. But the slowness never descends into boredom, because of the richness and precision of the acting of Ruth McCabe, Brendan Gleeson, John Kavanagh and Patrick Laffan in particular. Here, too, there is a musical formality, with the voices arranged in duets and the dense, tight language treated almost as poetry, the words spoken as much for their sound as their sense – to such an extent that at times the process is taken too far and the meaning is inaudible. But there is so much going on that you never mistake the slowness for stagnation; you always feel that the drama is in motion. Only Ewan Hooper's lack of ease with the role of Scober, the fact that he does not manifest the sense of being rooted in this place which Scober talks about so much, breaks the unity of the mood.

This is, though, an immensely impressive production, rich in words and images, unflinching in its gaze, relentless in its dissection of cruelty and above all true to the vision of a remarkable and darkly potent play.

Blood Guilty, by Antoine Ó Flatharta

Peacock Theatre
The Irish Times, 2 September 1989

Irish acting in recent years has been a late-flowering plant. Time and again, the freshest actors have been the oldest ones. […] An actor who is very much a part of this tendency in the Irish theatre is John Cowley, who gives a splendid performance in Antoine Ó Flatharta's short play *Blood Guilty*, which finishes its turn at the Peacock tonight along with Neil Donnelly's *Goodbye Carraroe*. Whereas Tom Hickey escaped from *The Riordans* with relative ease and speed, it is only in the past two or three years that John Cowley has fully emerged from the shadow of Tom Riordan. Even as the rural paterfamilias in *The Riordans* there was more than a touch of blackness about the persona which he projected. It is this black side which he used to such effect in *The Gentle Island* and which is again at the heart of his performance in *Blood Guilty*.

The play is a tough but subtle piece, using the spate of attacks on old people in rural Ireland a few summers ago as the starting point for a conflict of mutually uncomprehending generations in which the young are doomed to repeat what they cannot understand. Cowley plays the more dominant of two old men living in remote rural Ireland whose home is invaded by two young urban men on the watch for something to steal. Cowley is at the pivotal point of the drama as the man whose own unthinking cruelty to his blind brother is reflected back on him by the two brothers who come to steal his money.

While the style of the play is intimate, its intention is clearly public, offering as it does an image of Ireland as two entrapped generations, the old and the young, tormenting each other out of fear and anger, unaware of their own cruelty to those closest to them – their brothers. There are touches of Pinter in the menace of the banal, in the way that victims and tormentors are interchangeable, but the aim is not absurdity. Ó Flatharta is after an image of the state of the nation. It is Cowley who bears the burden of this imagery and bears it with both strength and suppleness.

Such a role could easily become rhetorical, a series of set-piece speeches. Much of the dialogue that Cowley has to speak is declamatory almost to the point of being expressionist, of addressing the audience to state a position rather than addressing the other characters. It needs an actor of real strength to carry it off and Cowley rises to the challenge. He has the sort of vocal range that doesn't have to measure emotional intensity by the volume of the voice nor passion by the highest pitch of scream. Cowley can express extremes of anger and even madness in a low, staccato voice, bringing the rhetoric of the speeches down to a recognizable earth, rooting them all the time in character and situation. The quiet frenzy of his performance is much more effective than any amount of emotional pyrotechnics would be, much closer to what real madness might look and sound like.

The strengths of Caroline FitzGerald's production are in the acting, the weaknesses in the more peripheral but nevertheless important areas of staging. The play is very well acted and works because of it. It might have worked even better had there been less concern with realistic detail, less fussing with doors and lights, and more freedom for the actors to move in space in a way that would avoid the sense which sometimes descends of being at the recording of a radio play. Still, this is a fine piece of work.

The Trial of Esther Waters, The, by Mary-Elizabeth Burke-Kennedy

John Player Theatre
The Irish Times, 30 September 1989

Mary-Elizabeth Burke-Kennedy's *The Trial of Esther Waters*, which finishes its run at the John Player Theatre tonight, is confident, clear and perfectly able to match style to content. It's a style that she has been perfecting over many years and through a number of different companies, culminating in Storytellers, which has brought her particular method of narrative theatre to new heights. She borrows both from literary sources (*The Trial of Esther Waters* is based on the George Moore novel) and from epic theatre, but blends the borrowings into something that is both original and sure of itself.

Esther Waters is a classically Victorian story and therefore, with Victorian values in the ascendant, a timely one. Burke-Kennedy's version puts the emphasis on the role of chance in a society where luck, fate, accidents of birth and fortune, are what governs the lives of such as Esther, a domestic servant who conceives a child out of wedlock and decides to keep it. She makes Esther almost into an English Victorian version of Brecht's Grusha from *The Caucasian Chalk Circle*, a woman whose love for a child impels her onto a journey through a cruel and unjust world, exposing along the way the manner in which that world works. Kate Thompson's Esther captures this questing, open instinctual nature extremely well.

The strength of the Storytellers' style is that it is very well suited to taking a story from one and showing its relevance to another, without being preachy or unsubtle. *Esther Waters* isn't transferred into contemporary England or contemporary Ireland, but neither is it left in a naturalistically-conceived Victorian world. The fluidity of the style, the fact that it is so obviously telling a story and not presenting a slice of life, bolstered greatly by Robert Armstrong's inventive and wittily stylized set, allows for something in between, a realm of theatre that is of a particular time but not confined to it.

The only problem is with the sentimental and somewhat fantastical happy ending which pulls some of the play's teeth and robs it of much of its social bite. But this doesn't stop it from being a really absorbing and impressively precise piece of theatre, universally well acted by a cast of actors who always give the impression of knowing exactly what they are doing.

The Lament for Arthur Cleary, by Dermot Bolger

Project Theatre
The Irish Times, 30 September 1989

The most impressive Irish show so far in the Festival, though, has been Dermot Bolger's first play *The Lament for Arthur Cleary*, which is now touring suburban community venues after its run at the Project. It is both, in David Byrne's wonderful production for Wet Paint, theatrically rich, and socially powerful, saying more about the way that Dublin has developed and changed in the last decade than a hundred treatises. Out of an eclectic mix of theatrical elements — a comedy of modern manners, social realism, masks, music (Gerard Grennell's hauntingly understated score), voice-over, flashback, poetry — it constructs the kind of all-embracing language which is needed if the strange, almost unreal, atmosphere of modern Dublin is to be articulated.

There is a kind of quiet mastery about Byrne's approach which never degenerates into showing off, which never appears to be using its arsenal of techniques for their own sake. The theatrical invention always seems to grow out of, rather than being imposed on, the dramatic situation, as the action moves from sharp and funny social observation to a nightmarish metaphysical thriller, from Alan Bleasdale to the Flann O'Brien of *The Third Policeman* and the Sartre of *No Exit*, from love to terror. The story is simple — Arthur Cleary's return from the life of the gastarbeiter on the continent to a Dublin whose new

viciousness he does not understand, the fatal innocence that will
lead to his death – but it takes on the voyage into the dark heart
of a city where Irish theatre has seldom been before.

La Corbière, by Anne Hartigan

Project Theatre
The Irish Times, 7 October 1989

Anne Hartigan's new play at the Project, *La Corbière*, is almost
equally minimal, but to much profound effect. It tells its story –
the drowning of a boatload of French prostitutes off the coast of
Jersey, where they had been brought for the use of the Nazi
soldiers – through constructing a soundscape made up of single
words or phrases, linked through association but always with an
ear for meaning as well as sound. There is no dialogue as such,
but the intricate word play builds a strong sense of oppression, of
the women as flotsam and jetsam tossed on the unruly wills of
men.

What it doesn't do often enough in Cathy Leeney's inventive
but limited production is to build a real sense of physical and
musical presence. The actors remain constrained, achieving the
discipline and precision that are needed, but are not really
allowed to express much individuality, either in the range of
voices or in the range of movement. It remains, nevertheless,
consistently absorbing and genuinely humane, a lament for loss
that is also a tribute to what is not lost but lives on.

War, by Roddy Doyle

Olympia Theatre
The Irish Times, 21 October 1989

There is a very strange moment in Roddy Doyle's play *War*
which this week transferred to the Olympia from Passion
Machine's home base at the SFX. We are well into the second
half, and the crack is ninety. We are building up towards the
climax of the epic pub quiz war between George and his arch-
rival Bertie. Everything has been funny, even the disasters and
the agonies, the fights and the nervous breakdowns. Suddenly,

we are in George's house, in the kitchen. A row develops between George and his wife Briget, a row in which George is the aggressor, picking on his wife, making little of her, moving in on her, coming very close to striking her, forcing her to run out saying: 'You're not going to bully me'. George says: 'I just did'.

The centre of the comedy, the character we have looked to for most of the laughs, has started to act like a real bastard. How does the audience react? The answer, last Wednesday night anyway, is that many of them laughed. They though it was funny when George said: 'I'll kill yeh: I'll split your fuckin' head for yeh'. They thought the 'I just did' answer was witty. They liked it when she said she was leaving and he put some money in her bag for her bus fare. Not all of the audience, by any means, but certainly a significant number reacted like this. And why wouldn't they? An audience is trained by what it sees on stage, and this audience has been trained to laugh at whatever George says.

What's interesting about this moment is that it sums up the difficulties of the very delicate balance that Passion Machine is trying to maintain. For all the right reasons – reasons of political perspective and the way you see the function of the theatre in a society – they want, need, a large audience, an audience that includes large numbers of people who wouldn't normally be seen dead in a theatre. The way to get that audience is through humour. But what happens when the laughing has to stop, when what you want to show is the negative, violent, even brutal side of working-class life as well as the funny, warm, zany side?

The scene with George and Briget in the kitchen is crucial to the quality of *War* as a play, a very important part of the whole strain of realism in the play that makes it much more than a funny, witty piece of entertainment. Doyle is interested in the cost of the trivial pursuits – not in any portentous or angst-ridden way, but presumably, because Passion Machine is interested in showing people to themselves, in exposing tensions rather than ignoring them. But that scene doesn't work on stage, and its failure isn't something accidental.

It's not to do with performances that just aren't up to it: both Brendan Gleeson and Caroline Rothwell, who play the roles, are terrific. And it's not a failure on the part of the audience – they see what they have been led to expect. The failure of that scene is to do with quite deliberate choices that have been made in the production, choices which we can see clearly because the text of the play has been published by Passion Machine. It differs from what we see on stage in two significant respects.

The first of these might seem like a technical point, but it is crucial to the audience's experience of the play. It is to do with the set, with the way space is used. In the published version of the play, the intention is to have the stage split between two playing areas – the pub where the quiz is held, and Briget's kitchen. The important point is that these two places are to be present at once. While the crack is going on in the pub, we are to see Briget at home in the kitchen, doing the crossword, reading the *Evening Herald*, being bored. The device is simple but important – it allows for irony, allows the action and the humour to be contrasted with something which gives it a perspective, gives the audience a constant sense of unease to underlie the laughter.

What happens in the actual production is something quite different. Both playing areas are used, but not simultaneously. For most of the play, the entire stage is occupied by the pub set. When the kitchen is needed, a part of the pub set revolves and the kitchen swings in. It is literally subsumed into the pub. Put crudely, the arena of laughter (the pub) subsumes and dominates the arena of irony, of boredom, of pain (the kitchen). So when George and Briget fight in the kitchen, it is literally something that is swung into the play from nowhere rather than a constant thread of the play coming to life. No wonder the audience doesn't know how to react.

The second point is rather more direct and less subtle. In the published version, the play ends in a complex way with three things going on. One is the expected comic crescendo, with George and the lads winning their war and heading off in jubilation. The second, equally pleasant, is the rendezvous of Leo the barman with Angela, who has been lusting after him throughout the play. All very nice and comfortable. But then we go to Briget in her kitchen. She is waiting, looking at the door, wondering what state George is going to be in when he comes home. Is he going to threaten her again? She is an isolated, frightened woman. The last line of the play is hers: 'Please God, he didn't lose again. Please'.

On stage, though, we have the lads winning their war, we have Leo and Angela all set up, and then we have the curtain. No isolation, no fear, no perspective on the comedy. It changes the whole nature of the play, provides a nice, warm conclusion and in the process makes nonsense of the earlier scene between George and Briget, whose whole point is that it leads towards this closing line. It also makes the play in a significant sense untrue.

What I'm not doing here is accusing Passion Machine of selling out or backing off. A company which has shown such enormous integrity in getting where it's got, which has taken so many risks and so few soft options in the last five years, deserves better than that. If the company was primarily interested in commercial success, it wouldn't have presented ten new Irish plays on an Arts Council subsidy totalling less than £90,000 over the whole five years. What I am saying is that in this instance the company's two main aims – to present contemporary Irish life and to attract a large audience – have come into a certain conflict with each other, and it's a conflict that's resolved in ways that leaves *War* as a very funny, very entertaining, but significantly poorer piece of theatre.

The problems are the problems of success, of a company that has done what it set out to do against all odds and logic: to create a new audience for theatre in Dublin. Having created that audience, having extended itself into the enormous financial risks and huge theatrical rewards of the large audience that a venue like the Olympia can provide, the company has got to a point where the consequences of failure are much greater than they should ever be if good theatre is to survive. It needs to take back the most important right for anyone in the theatre to have: the right to fail, to lose the fear of losing its audience by upsetting it.

Blinded by the Light, by Dermot Bolger

Peacock Theatre
The Irish Times, 10 March 1990

Out of a new society comes a new comedy, Ireland is a changing place and what makes us laugh in the theatre is also different. Comedy is largely about incongruity – the wrong things in the wrong places are funny – and Irish society now is full of almost nothing but incongruities, the religious and the profane, the traditional and the modern, the cool sophistication and the red-necked cuteness, all mingling together in one gloriously promiscuous ruck.

Atavistic gunmen watch themselves on satellite channels, priests lust after Dolly Parton's breasts, mountainy men who have never been to Dublin spend half their year in Queens or the Bronx, dopeheads tune in to Father Michael Cleary on the radio. In modern Ireland, the real and the surreal are on first name terms, and Irish dramatists are beginning to tap into the comic flow of it all.

Like so much else that seemed new and exciting and permanently achieved in the Sixties and Seventies, one form of theatrical comedy, farce, proved ephemeral. Farce quite suddenly became available to Irish dramatists in the 1960s because a self-conscious urban middle class also became available and wanted to see itself both satirized and confirmed.

It was Hugh Leonard's achievement to bring the form to fruition in Ireland, but what is remarkable is that he himself wrote few farces and had no real successors. Brian Friel's *The Communication Cord* was a self-conscious aberration, a counter-blast to his own work. Bernard Farrell's attempts to develop and continue the form stalled. Like everything else that came out of that period, Irish farce lost its way and its meaning.

The new comedy is also urban, but it resists the machine-like precision of farce and goes for something necessarily crazier, rougher, more concerned with throwing up apparently random and surreal juxtapositions. Its energy is manic rather than calculated. It is largely a product of Dublin's working-class suburbs, with the work of Paul Mercier, Roddy Doyle, Brendan

Gleeson, and now, with *Blinded by the Light* at the Peacock, Dermot Bolger.

But the same spirit is present in other quarters, too, in the first half of Michael Harding's *Una Pooka* or in Frank McGuinness's *Ladybag* plays. In all of this comedy, television and the movies are a big presence, with adaptations of television forms, movie parodies, voices coming from televisions on the stage. It is the jumbled-up world of modern media, the crazed clash of images which we now live in, that gives these plays their language, it is Ireland and its contradictions that gives them their matter.

New forms, of course, don't emerge fully grown and the new comedy is still searching for a technique to match its sensibility. It is interesting that both *Blinded by the Light* and an earlier play, Paul Mercier's *Home* skip back a few generations beyond the Sixties in search of a form, to Sean O'Casey of all people. The flatland these plays inhabit is a modernized version of O'Casey's tenements. Their dramatic structures, too, recall O'Casey, with doors that keep opening, rooms that keep getting invaded, privacies that are constantly denied. This skipping back can create a tension between the form and the content, and in *Blinded by the Light* it certainly does.

The play can properly be described as hysterically funny, its wild humour being always on the brink of dementia. It is in many ways a parable of the referenda years of the 1980s, the years in which the notion of private conscience became impossible, the years of the undermining of that wonderful right defined by the American Supreme Court as 'the right to be left alone'. The play's hero, Mick, is a Dublin Canute, trying to staunch the flow of the sea as it pours across the threshold of his bedsit in the form of Mormons, Legionaries of Mary, interfering landlords and would-be friends. The surrealism mounts to such a height that both Mick and we are unsure of how much is reality and how much hallucination, since in the play's Ireland the difference is negligible.

The comedy is freewheeling, absurd, associative. It is like the scenes in Flann O'Brien's *At Swim-Two-Birds* where the different plots – realistic, mythological, scatological – come together in bizarre conversations of the deaf, where everyone is talking and no one is listening. And this is handled with immense skill and wit by an author whose taste in bad taste is impeccable. The play operates on the basis that by being offensive to everyone you are really offensive to no one, and it gets away with it. It zigzags between theatre of the absurd and kitchen comedy, between farce and social realism, in ways that are always highly entertaining.

The main problem is that all of this madness is encased in a theatrical form that is sometimes too static and flat to allow it to flow freely. This has partly to do with the play itself, but more to do with Caroline FitzGerald's solid but insufficiently loopy production.

The production tends to exaggerate rather than diminish the play's naturalistic form, using a fussily ugly set full of naturalistic detail rather than the freer, more abstract use of space that might allow the play to breathe more easily. The advantage of the detail is that it supports performances which are even and precise, the disadvantage is that it works against what Donal O'Kelly is trying to do in his central performance as Mick.

O'Kelly's Mick is somewhat reminiscent of his own *Rabbit* character from his recent plays: a mixture of conventional characterization with edgy, expressive and far from naturalistic gestures and ticks. And this is much more than just an actor transferring tricks from one performance into the other. It is also the right thing to do here, picking up on the surrealism of the play and trying to construct a performance that is equally strange and angular. But it doesn't really connect with the rest of the performances, so that it seems at times like something from another play altogether.

Dancing at Lughnasa, by Brian Friel

Abbey Theatre
The Irish Times, 28 April 1990

Words and their relationship to real things dominated Brian Friel's work of the late 1970s and the 1980s. Words as invented stories in *Faith Healer*; words as the contours within which a civilization can be imprisoned and doomed in *Translations*; words as the foundation of 'the entire social order' in *The Communication Cord*; words as a way of making the past into an acceptable fiction in *Making History*.

Irish theatre has always exulted in the verbal, always regarded words as a playground. Friel, however, started to see them as a jigsaw puzzle, a set of arbitrary bits and pieces which, when arranged, made up a tragic picture of people, identities, civilizations crumbling. Words ceased to be an unconscious joy and became a terrible burden.

Now, with Friel's new play at the Abbey, *Dancing at Lughnasa*, the burden is lifted. In Patrick Mason's magnificently realized production the play's great moments are wordless, beyond language. There is a dance in the first act, a few minutes in which the five sisters at the heart of the play abandon themselves to the joy and terror of wild music from the wireless, that is one of the most articulate, most genuinely eloquent scenes in modern Irish theatre — even though, or rather because, its only sounds are music, animal yelps and the frantic thudding of feet on wood.

Dancing at Lughnasa is a release, but it is also a return. It is a return in two senses, in the sense that Friel always rakes over old coals and, astonishingly, finds the breath to re-ignite them, and in another, more important sense. In the first sense the play returns to scenes of previous Friel plays — *Living Quarters* and *Translations* in particular.

But these echoes are less important than the other, more fundamental, sense of return which *Dancing at Lughnasa* carries with it, the reason that the play is appropriately housed at the Abbey rather than with Friel's own Derry-based company, Field Day. For, to put it crudely, *Dancing at Lughnasa* is a Southern play rather than a Northern one. The essential tensions are the ones with which Friel's work as a playwright began over 30 years ago: the tensions of Southern society modernizing itself, the clash between a traditional culture and a modern, industrial one. The escape from language in the play is also the escape from the concerns with colonialism, with cultural domination, with the Northern questions which have dominated Friel's work since *Translations*. And where this is not the case, where those concerns linger and the escape is not achieved, the play is at its weakest.

The play is narrated (with a superbly ironic sense of resignation and enchantment in Gerard McSorley's performance) by Michael, the son of Chris and Gerry. His opening monologue describes a dramatic clash of tradition and modernity: a new radio in the house and the pagan Feast of Lughnasa. The play's moment is the moment 'the Industrial Revolution finally caught up with Ballybeg', when the income that sustains two of the sisters, Rose and Aggie, dries up as their home-made gloves are replaced by the products of a new factory. What undermines the sisters as a family unit is that they are caught between this dramatic modernization and an equally extreme embodiment of tradition. Father Jack returns from Africa not as a missionary of white civilization but as a priest disgraced for having 'gone native', having given himself over to an old world of ceremony and ritual and ancient wisdom. The sisters are at the junction of these two conflicting forces and are destroyed by the conflict.

The articulation of this clash is breathtakingly skilful. Friel the magician plays such tricks with time that August 1936 becomes every time and no time. The adult Michael is also a child. The sisters' future is made known to us before their past has been fully played out. The spirits which haunt the play are both those of a long-lost Ireland of pagan tradition and those of the 1990 Irish in London's cardboard city. The play's tragedy, the tragedy of 'things changing too quickly', of control slipping away, is not one that draws only from the past, but also from the present, from what Ireland is and how it happened to become that way.

This tension is the pumping heart of the play, giving rich blood to the masterly characterizations of the five sisters. And when the play moves away from it, in the two male characters, Father Jack and Gerry Evans, it becomes much less convincing and much less dramatic. Both characters represent a layer of politics in the play which is never fully integrated and rooted. Gerry's decision to go and join the International Brigade remains extraneous and also gives the play a historical specificity which weakens its magical, universal quality. And, much more seriously, Father Jack is an uncomfortable mixture of whimsicality on the one hand, and a metaphorical version of a Field Day pamphlet on the other.

The connection between Ireland and Africa as colonized traditional societies which Father Jack's immersion in African custom posits, whatever its intellectual merits, is never really embodied in the kind of ritual expression which the play keeps promising. When the long-promised ceremony materializes it turns out to be whimsical, an exchange of hats. And Barry McGovern's playing of Jack as an existential eccentric, while it is carried off well, actually accentuates the difficulty. A priest who was recognizably a part of this family, and yet deeply African in his ways, would be more shocking and more dramatically effective.

This is merely to say that the play is a flawed wonder. It accounts for a certain feeling of anti-climax in the second act after an astonishing first act, since Jack and Gerry become more prominent in the second act, breaking the spell that the five sisters between them create. But there are also bravery and beauty in the second act. The bravery is in the resort to prophecy, in the making real of the sense of omens which is present throughout the play, as broken mirrors and single magpies give way to the stark and terrible facts of what will happen to these women. Here, there is another return: to Friel the short story writer, to narrative usurping drama in bold and courageous ways.

And the beauty is in the often breathtaking conjunction of words and movement and visual images. Never before in Friel have visual elements been so central – dances, ceremonial gestures, painted images – but never at the expense of the lyrical power which Friel can summon with words, of the deceptively easy cadences of speech which cover but do not hide deep and inescapable emotions. The reaching beyond language is not a disavowal of language but an immense enrichment of it.

It is absolutely essential to this achievement that there should be no sense at all of a disjunction between 'the play' and 'the production', no possibility of thinking of it as a collection of words brought to life by the movements and voices of the actors. Words and movements must be continuous, a part of the same language. And this is completely true of Patrick Mason's direction, Joe Vanek's dazzling design, and Terry John Bates's choreography. The performances of the five women – Anita Reeves, Frances Tomelty, Bríd Brennan, Catherine Byrne and Bríd Ní Neachtain – are simply great. They are absolutely individual and absolutely together.

From the first few moments you could not possibly confuse one with the other, so distinctive and richly characterized are they, and yet, by the end of the play the ultimate terror is thinking of them apart from each other. The emotional weight of the play depends on us feeling that something we would ordinarily take to be completely normal – the break-up of a family – should come to seem immensely painful, to be accepted by us as a kind of doom. And the coherence of these five women together is great enough to utterly convince us of this, to makes us feel their dissolution as a death.

Dancing at Lughnasa is full of the life of the tribe, its rituals and its regrets. In the 1980s, Brian Friel, with plays like *Translations* and *Making History*, tried to speak for his tribe. The rich paradox of *Dancing at Lughnasa* is that it is a farewell to that tribal role, full of both the pain and the liberation of a departure. It is a joyous abdication and a sorrowful exile. It moves into a new language, the language of the dance in which the yelp of despair and the rhythm of release are heard together.

Watching it, I was reminded of the end of Seamus Heaney's *Station Island*, the voice he hears urging him to stay away from the 'subject people stuff' and 'keep at a tangent', to 'fill the element with signatures of your own frequency, echo soundings, searches, probes, allurements ...'. The soundings Friel makes here are in a new and more liberated theatrical language; the frequency he tunes into picks up many musics on many wavelengths. The note of sadness in the leavetaking is counterpointed by the enormous excitement of the journey, a journey anyone with an ear for the music of humanity will want to accompany him on.

Siege of Derry Pageant, by Andy Hinds and Shaun Davey

Guildhall, Derry
The Irish Times, 12 May 1990

The Protestants got the power; the Catholics got all the good tunes. Victory soon petrifies into triumphalism – it is politically pleasing, aesthetically anodyne. Defeat, on the other hand, springs eternal, it flows sweetly in this vale of tears, brimming with poetry and lamentation.

The Protestants won the Siege of Derry and got a few hollow notes on a Lambeg drum to remember it by. The Catholics lost the Siege of Limerick and got 'Marbhna Luimní' ('Limerick's Lamentation'), one of the most beautiful musical laments ever written. In the third movement of his *Relief of Derry Symphony*, premiered last weekend at Derry's extraordinary pageant to commemorate the 300th anniversary of the Siege, Shaun Davey sets out to write a Protestant counterpart to 'Marbhna Luimní', to compose a slow air for Liam Óg O'Flynn's uileann pipes that will unite a Catholic sensibility with a Protestant icon. In the community play that followed, Andy Hinds sets out to bring the losers' sense of poetry, of tragedy, of yearning, to bear on the winners' understanding of their triumph. Together, these events and the culminating fireworks from Theatre of Fire constitute a cultural achievement of luminous generosity.

The pageant as a whole represents a genuine intermingling of traditions, not in the bland Kenwood Chef style of peace and love, but in a much more profound and significant confrontation of past and present. And this coming together of two streams is embodied in the form of the event by the brilliantly conceived mingling of words and music. Davey's rich and often beautiful symphony sounds the keynote for the play and the fireworks display, the image that haunts the wonderful song sung by Rita Connolly in the third movement – the image of the white horse that the famine-wracked defenders of the city believed they saw in the sky each night – provides the culmination of the play and the most beautiful part of the pyrotechnics. There is a sense that what cannot be said can be sung and this song is magnificently eloquent.

This kind of traffic from music into theatre, though, is matched by a similar movement in the other direction. Davey's symphony is itself highly theatrical. It has a plot – the narrative of the Siege, entrances and exits, pipers approaching and then entering the auditorium – and a dramatic sense of space – trumpeters at the back of the hall echoing those on stage, pipers heard in the distance, then closer and closer. The outdoor play and the indoor symphony have a symbolic relationship to the whole mood of the event. First, with the symphony, the audience is inside the Guildhall, under siege from the approaching pipe band. Then, after the symphony, the audience spills out onto the street, and finds itself literally outside the city walls, no longer under siege but out in the open. The sense of being hemmed in is turned into the sense of an outpouring, a physical representation of the mood of the event itself.

Andy Hinds's play (he is both writer and director) is then performed by 60 local actors and two local choirs. To the left, over a stage of ramps, platforms and steps brilliantly designed by Francis O'Connor, King James sits grumpily under a rain cloud that opens on him with the occasional downpour. At the back, high above the action, is the Sun King, Louis. The twist is that the kings are children. Hinds draws on the forms of Greek tragedy for his play, and the kings are like spoilt little gods, playing dice with the real people below.

These real people are, primarily, a family recently arrived from England and thrust into the heat of the conflict, their personal story coming to stand for the grand themes of guilt, betrayal, suffering and forgiveness which Hinds weaves into the drama. Around them are two other families, one Protestant and rich, the other that of a Catholic blacksmith and his daughter. Everything that happens, the atrocities, the defiance, bigotry, the heroism and, above all, in Hinds's vision of things, the sheer tragedy of people caught up in history and set against each other by forces outside of their control, happens through these people.

Sometimes, inevitably, this doesn't work. The need to go in close to people's lives and dilemmas isn't always compatible with the demands of a huge outdoor spectacle, with a wide, open stage, a faltering sound system and an onslaught of inescapable rain. But what is much more significant is the extent to which it does work, the way in which these personal dilemmas can become big images. The central image of a family cut off from itself, part of it forever doomed to be in England, part in Ireland, is both a convincingly-told story about a number of individuals, and a powerful symbolic embodiment of the Protestant dilemma. The conflict of a Catholic blacksmith and a Protestant over the tools of their trade is both simple and extremely effective. The singing of a Protestant hymn and a Gaelic air by two children in turn is similarly expressive. And the ultimate, intermingled deaths of the Catholic blacksmith and the Protestant blacksmith's son is perfectly led up to and achieved.

But this terrible culmination is not the end. The play finishes with a ritual of hope. Rita Connolly sings 'The White Horse'. It is taken up by a choir of children and then by a choir of adults. A real white horse, led by a girl dressed like Athene appearing at the end of a Greek tragedy to herald forgiveness, comes in, followed by a parade of local children carrying glowing white lanterns. They lead the way to the waterfront where, in the distance, a massive white horse is illuminated against the sky and the fireworks begin, like the outpouring of anarchic pleasure that always followed a Greek tragedy. This, indeed, is the nearest any of us will ever get to what those Greek plays must have been like, the sense of the religious and the political merging, the sense of a city celebrating and lamenting its own founding events, the public enactment of terror and forgiveness.

If anyone still doubts the importance of art in the real world, its ability to articulate desires and despairs that cannot be expressed in language other than that of metaphor, then the Siege of Derry Pageant was an utterly convincing answer to the doubts.

The Sinking of the Titanic, by Joe O'Byrne

SFX Centre
The Irish Times, 6 October 1990

The Sinking of the Titanic [...] is a remarkable feat of theatrical storytelling. It works on a big scale, both in terms of numbers on the stage and of forms used: mime, dance, dialogue, song, straight narrative, music, design and lighting all go into its melting pot. It brings together many of the things that the Co-Motion company has been developing over the last five years: the cabaret style of *Cabaret/Kabarett*, the sportlike movement of *Song of the White Man's Burden*, the historical narrative of *Departed*. And because it is a culmination of sorts, it is wonderfully confident, disciplined and resourceful, taking over the sometimes cavernous spaces of the SFX with considerable panache.

The strange thing, though, is that this storytelling works so well, because the story itself is something of a cliché, and because the play avoids the matter of Ireland which makes straight narrative so difficult. The story of the Titanic has become clichéd, its status as the archetypal disaster unaffected by the fact that there have been, from both a moral and a numerical point of view, much worse mass drownings since. (A German liner was torpedoed in 1945 with the loss of five times the number of lives lost in the Titanic, and boating disasters in India and Pakistan regularly claim hundreds of brown-skinned, faraway people.)

Poor Beast in the Rain, by Billy Roche

Andrews Lane Theatre
The Irish Times, 13 October 1990

The feeling that the lack of scale and the obscurity of much of the work from Irish playwrights in the Festival is more than just coincidental but has to do with the difficult and slippery nature of modern Irish reality is one that is confirmed by watching Billy Roche's *Poor Beast in the Rain* at Andrews Lane. The striking thing is that Roche does manage to create a clear, coherent, well-made play, only because he goes back to the themes and forms of 20 years ago. If some of the other plays could be short stories, this one could be a small-town drama from the Ireland of the early 1960s. The set itself acknowledges this: for a play which takes place in 'the present', Bláithín Sheerin's design goes to a lot of trouble to make the Wexford bookie's shop in which all the action happens into a shrine to the past, with the Sacred Heart and John F. Kennedy bestowing their sweet smiles on all below. Even the fact that the action depends on the notion that Wexford has a hurling team capable of winning an All-Ireland points us back into the distant decades.

The play's story is the conventional one of the return of the old tearaway from exile, its form the conventional one of naturalism. Within these confines, it is a very enjoyable piece, warm, witty and compassionate. Roche writes good dialogue, handles anguish without self-indulgence and sifts through 'the ranks of the left-behind' with a steady hand and a keen eye. He has a kind of hard-bitten melancholia that is distinctive, allowing him to show paralysis without paralysing his play. And, of course, there is a logic to this return to the world of the early Tom Murphy or John B. Keane: the emigration which was the hallmark of that world *has* returned.

The play, though, does depend on certain values that also belong to those times: on the notion that a young man would be devastated by the fact that his loved one might have slept with someone else in the past; on the pure heroism of hurling; on the belief that what really wild lads do is run away and join the circus. It is somewhat weakened by this sense of having a foot in two different worlds, of being able to achieve its well-made form only because it also avoids aspects of its own time and harks back to a time when well-made plays came out of a stable society.

The Cure at Troy, by Seamus Heaney

Abbey Theatre
The Irish Times, 10 November 1990

A poet of our times taking on a Greek classic play, as Seamus Heaney does with Sophocles's *Philoctetes* for the Field Day production *The Cure at Troy* – currently at the Abbey before continuing its extensive national tour – is going back to the roots of a fundamental contradiction in the relationship of poetry to theatre. Greek plays grew out of choral poetry, which in turn grew out of tribal rituals.

Epic poetry, on the other hand, the kind of non-dramatic verse which is closest to our notion of poetry as something different from theatre and ritual, grew out of the military aristocracy rather than the common actions of the tribe. The epics are concerned with the doings of the military caste.

'After the battle was over,' as George Thomson put it, 'tired but contented, the warriors forgot their fatigue as they listened to a lay, chanted by one of themselves, or later by a minstrel, in honour of their victory. The function of these lays was not to prepare for action, like that of choral poetry, but to relax after action, and therefore they were less tense, less concentrated, less sacral'. The modern poet going back to a Greek play is trying to return to a poetry that is not relaxed and reflective, but tense, concentrated, sacral, and, above all public rather than elitist. It is a return to poetry as a rite of the tribe rather than a form of relaxation.

All of this makes particular sense in relation to Seamus Heaney's career, a career which can be seen as a succession of reluctant acceptances and wistful shunnings of the role of tribal shaman, of the idea of the poet as the voice of the tribe. A sequence like 'Station Island,' for instance, ends with Heaney giving himself permission to 'swim/out on your own and fill the element/with signatures on your own frequency,' to leave aside 'all that subject people stuff'. But its very form, its movement towards dramatic dialogue and choral poetry, contradicts this, and points towards the continuance of the public, sacral impulse.

Heaney the shaman and Heaney the private poet are in constant struggle with each other, and in *The Cure at Troy* it is Heaney the shaman who is uppermost. The story of Philoctetes, the great archer marooned on the island of Lemnos by the Greek army advancing on Troy because of his offensively pustulant wound and then cajoled back ten years later to win the war for them, is a story about the conflicting demands of individual hurt and collective loyalty. The important thing about the story in relation to Heaney is that the collective demands win out in the end. And there is no attempt to hide the fact that the story is used as a metaphor for the North now, for the struggle between the desire to hold on to your wounds and the need to forgive and be healed.

This is made most obvious by the Chorus which speaks new lines of Heaney's that link the action to the suffering of the North and the role of the poet caught between what is and what should be. It is less obviously but just as importantly connected to Ireland by the relationship of *The Cure at Troy* to Heaney's superb version of an Irish legend, that of Mad Sweeney, published as *Sweeney Astray*.

Philoctetes, cursed, maddened, abandoned, exposed to the bittersweet tang of nature, fallen from grace, is another Sweeney. And Heaney's pen responds best to the Greek material when this connection is clearest, when his language is probing into Philoctetes's exposure, his nostalgia for his home landscape, his sense of melting into the natural elements of Lemnos as Sweeney melts into Glen Bolcam.

What this means is that most of the energy and brilliance and sympathy of Heaney's writing goes to Philoctetes himself. It is a superb piece, not of characterization, but of poetic embodiment. And it is taken to the limits of its considerable richness in a great performance by Des McAleer, a magnificent striking of the balance between the visceral and the elemental on the one hand and the stylized expression of an abstract force on the other.

McAleer does what a play that is word-heavy needs its actors to do: he uses his whole body rather than just his mouth, shows us a body wracked and wrecked, but also transfused with currents of pain, as it is, intensely alive. There is no misplaced sense of Philoctetes as a naturalistic character but there is full measure of suffering humanity, of physical reality that might have been lost in the welter of words. This alone makes the play always compelling.

On the other hand, though, these Greek plays as drama depend on the interaction of two competing and equally strong forces, and the forces in conflict with Philoctetes in *The Cure at Troy* are not as intensely engaged by his imagination as they need to be. Odysseus the cynical politician (unintended parallels with contemporary events in his justification for politicians lying raised laughs among the audience on the opening night) and Neoptolemus, the innocent tool of his manoeuvrings, are never given an engaging language on which to build. Consequently, the performances of Seamus Moran and Seán Rocks in the roles are far too small-scale and unpoetic to give us the sense of a real clash at work, and the direction of Stephen Rea and Bob Crowley gives them little to work with in terms of movement or gesture or stylization which might provide a physical compensation for the relative lack of linguistic excitement.

The problem, I think, is this: as a drama of language, *The Cure at Troy* depends on a dramatic shift from the savage and brutal language of the tribe to the lyrical language of vision and healing. Those versions of the Greek plays which work best find a way of creating a rhythmic, violent, tribal language for the utterances of the chorus and of the tribal leaders.

Tony Harrison's alliterative percussive Anglo-Saxon English in his version of *The Oresteia* gets this sense of things superbly. And you need this language so that the private lyricism of those at odds with the tribe can be in real dramatic conflict with it.

Heaney's version of Sophocles is closer to the downbeat, sometimes even throwaway style of Robert Lowell's *Oresteia* than it is to Harrison's. It is splendid in its handling of the lyrical visions, intensely moving in its imagining of healing and love. But it is too informal in its handling of the violent tribal language to give this lyricism its full dramatic, as opposed to simply linguistic, effect. It is clearly the work of a great writer, but not the work of a great writer attuned fully to the theatre in the way that, for instance, Yeats's versions of Sophocles are.

These are weaknesses in a compelling and fascinating piece, not fatal flaws. If the direction is sometimes too loose for the necessary sense of ritual to be achieved, this is not the case with Bob Crowley's brilliant design, which not only does with consummate skill the job of opening up a range of playing areas, but also creates a remarkable number of visual variations within a coherent set of patterns. The parallels with the North are properly inexact (Philoctetes, for instance, can be read as both the Protestants and the Catholics) so that the mythic and metaphoric force of the play is not reduced. At the same time, its pointed appeal to those on both sides 'shining with self-regard like polished stones' is eloquent, humane and full of the generosity of a very large mind at work.

The Holy Ground and In High Germany, by Dermot Bolger

Gate Theatre
The Irish Times, 17 November 1990

Sport and theatre have the same roots. The Olympic games and Greek tragedy, which we would now think of as opposites – one a popular entertainment, the other the highest of high art – began in the same old rituals. Games like soccer and modern European theatre can both trace themselves back to the riotous assemblies of the mediaeval carnival. Shakespeare uses the word 'sport' in ways which included everything from formal games to sexual play, to a sense of the world very like that of Greek tragedy: 'As flies to wanton boys are we to gods,/They kill us for their sport'.

There's a connection down there in the history of theatre, a connection to sport as ritual, as communal gathering, as a sort of game-playing, but it is one that was long lost. It comes up in good circus, where the performer is both athlete and actor, and in Brecht's notion of wanting the member of the theatre audience to feel like a spectator at a sporting event, but basically the end of the nineteenth century put a stop to most of it: the masses would have their football matches, the people of taste would have their theatre. Funny forms like ice-skating, where sport and ballet combine, are dismissed as vulgar, mostly because they undermine comfortable distinctions.

Still, efforts to bring sport back within the theatre walls have been going on in the British and Irish theatres for the last 20 years. A soccer play, like 7:84's *The Game's a Bogey* which was performed here in the mid-1970s, opened up ideas which have been developed through plays like John Godber's *Up 'n' Under* and, in Ireland, Paul Mercier's *Studs*. Co-Motion has been interested in the notion of actors as athletes. And Dermot Bolger's two plays at the Gate, under the general title *The*

Tramway End actually use soccer as a metaphor for Ireland as a whole.

The limitations of the pieces – Pat Leavy performing *The Holy Ground* about a woman's life with an embittered right-wing Catholic, and Stephen Brennan in *In High Germany* about an Irish fan in Germany for the European championships but going home, not to Ireland, but to his German wife in Hamburg – is that the metaphor is purely verbal. Both pieces are small-scale monologues. Things are narrated rather than enacted. Soccer acts as an image rather than an inspiration to the action. For all, though, the sense of sport as a kind of pure joy, as a way in which people give significance to their lives, is richly attained in the language and the performances.

The remarkable thing about the two plays is that they are so short, so slight, and yet manage to at least touch on so many things that we haven't heard about in the Irish theatre of the last few years: the abortion referendum, SPUC, contraception, emigration, soccer, train stations, green cards, youngfellas smoking dope in bedsits, civil servants going home for the weekends. That these are not huge epic works and yet manage to sketch in a whole history of the Republic of Ireland in the last 40 years, to mention so many things we haven't heard mentioned on Irish stages, is in one way a shocking reminder of how shy our theatre has been about trying to make something of our recent and desultory history. If they did nothing else, the plays would be interesting simply for going into this uncharted territory.

The plays do, however, many other things. They are linked both by the metaphor of soccer and by themes of internal and external exile. Monica in *The Holy Ground* and Eoin in *In High Germany* both understand soccer as an image of togetherness, Monica because the early days when she used to go to matches with her husband Miles are the only happy ones she has to recall, Eoin because the arrival in Germany of 'the lads' from Dublin affords a fleeting pretence that everything is as it was in his Dublin days. And in both cases, this image of togetherness is really an image of isolation. The need for those golden moments on the terraces arises out of the reality of being sundered and scattered, she divided from her husband, who didn't speak to her for the 20 years up to his death, he divided from his country and forced to realize that the only Ireland he really belongs to is that gathered temporarily on the slopes of a foreign stadium.

Bolger's impulse in both plays is not primarily one of debunking faith and nation. Monica's most bitter complaint is that her husband's religious mania stole her Christ from her. Eoin's harshest realization is that all his life other people have been trying to define his Ireland for him. This is no realist assault on mysticism: rather it is a search for new and better abstractions, new general ways of belonging which are more real and more generous than the old ones.

Playing through these themes is a deft use of the imagery of exile, a series of reversals and counterpoints. Monica, who stays at home, stays, for the most part, in her room in Drumcondra, is in internal exile above all because she is childless. Eoin who wanders all over the place and is in external exile is yet able to imagine himself at home in Germany because his children will be born there. Sterility and fertility are images which play off each other in the plays, lifting them out of what might be a parochial particularity and into common and recognizable human experiences.

In counterpoints like these, and in the imagery of trains (Monica's trains are confining: she watches *Brief Encounter* on the television, tensed up in case her dead husband will find her at it; Eoin's trains speak of dispersal), *In High Germany* gains much by being presented with *The Holy Ground* rather than on its own, as it was during the Dublin Theatre Festival. *The Holy Ground* gains less. Paradoxically, because its canvas is bigger and its relationship to events like the so-called Pro-Life referendum more public, it seems slight. It touches on more things that we want to know more about, that seem to be passed over too quickly because they cannot be dealt with within the narrow form. Pat Leavy's very solid performance gives body to the piece, but in a way that makes you want to see it more fully developed.

In High Germany, on the other hand, is deepened by all the counterpoints and contrasts, and helped considerably by a new set from Robert Ballagh which contains it beautifully while also giving more room for Stephen Brennan's increasingly confident and well-modulated performance. It becomes a more substantial and ultimately more moving piece, a fine piece of writing that also becomes a fine piece of theatre. It finishes tonight and is worth catching.

Prayers of Sherkin, by Sebastian Barry

Peacock Theatre
The Irish Times, 24 Nov 1990

Sebastian Barry's dazzling new play at the Peacock, *Prayers of Sherkin*, brings back into play in our theatre something that seemed happily dead: poetic drama. The very words 'poetic drama' have all the electrifying effect of 'rigor mortis' or 'current budget deficit'. They conjure up the forced earnestness of the verse play revival of the 1950s, of stuff that was unspeakable in every sense. In any word-association test they go with 'worthy but dull'.

Yet something real has been happening in Irish writing in the last few years, a hunger for the theatre on the part of poets, a re-invention of the theatre as the place where poetry happens. Seamus Heaney, Brendan Kennelly, Tom Paulin, Dermot Bolger, Aidan Mathews, Sebastian Barry himself with *Boss Grady's Boys*, have moved into the theatres. *Prayers of Sherkin* represents a very special fruit of this increasingly vigorous sapling.

It is a luminously beautiful work, enfolding and enrapturing, still and calm on the surface, teeming, like the glassy sea that is one of its favourite images, with life in its depths. It is 'poetic' drama in the obvious sense that it depends utterly on the lyricism of its language and in the potentially negative sense that it has little outward conflict. It has a loveliness that could so easily have been fey: all of the people in the play are intensely wonderful and utterly decent. Human evil is but a distant gloom beyond the horizon.

But it is not 'poetic' drama in the sense of the word that sends shivers of boredom down the spine. It has a crystalline clarity in its language, a well-driven narrative, a clear and deeply compassionate interest in character. It works through the

richness of humanity that it creates as much as through the
richness of language. And it is not for a moment boring.

It is striking that two of the best plays of the younger
generation of playwrights now finding a voice on the Irish stage
both began as poems and yet are deeply immersed in Irish
politics and society. Dermot Bolger's *The Lament for Arthur Cleary*
started life as an epic poem and became a richly dramatic play.
Barry's *Prayers of Sherkin* takes off from the title poem in his last
collection *Fanny Hawke Goes to the Mainland Forever*. The poem's
title sums up the action of the play: the departure from Sherkin
Island off Baltimore, County Cork, of a young woman, the last of
a failed community of millenarians from Manchester who had
come to Sherkin to wait for the New Jerusalem. Some of the
images are the same:

> Small smooth shells on the great strands
> come with her on her fingers as nails.
> She smells the lobster the boatmen found
> in the ghostly seas when she herself was
> asleep …

What is remarkable, though, is the extent to which the poetic
germ flowers into something infinitely bigger and incomparably
sharper. The translation of the poem into the theatre doesn't
make the theatre more obscure and wordy, it makes the poem
public, political, tough. Sebastian Barry has emerged as an
important playwright because he has found ways of matching the
private impulse of his work with a public impulse which plays
need if they are to be communicable to an audience.

In *Prayers of Sherkin* he has found a structure like a prism that
is itself completely clear but that lets a many-layered light pass
through and become visible in all its complexity. Or to use a
wonderful image from the play itself, it is like the delicate wind
vanes made of shells that fishermen used to tell them when they
had a favourable wind. It is itself a delicate object, but it contains
and makes meaningful strong and useful forces.

What this simple story of Fanny Hawke's departure from her
island, from her loving father, from her two aunts and her
baffled, dreaming brother, contains within its delicacies is a

moving and convincing meditation on Protestantism and Catholicism in Ireland. Fanny leaves in order to marry a Catholic, albeit an idiosyncratic one, a lithographer from Cork. Her departure is also an insertion of her hopes and visions, the Utopian dreams of her family, into the mainstream of Irish history and Irish culture, into Catholic Ireland.

The search of Matt Purdy, the Manchester artisan who led his small band of followers to Sherkin to await the New Jerusalem, is 'to find an Ireland where we could abide'. Since it is a search on which we are all engaged, Fanny Hawke's marriage of vision with survival becomes a wedding at which we are all guests. Slowly and with exquisite tact, her story develops into a political metaphor of great breadth and generosity.

The form of the play is as important to the metaphor as its content. It is a formal embodiment of the sort of Protestantism that the Hawkes live by, that strange mixture of vision and restraint. It shuns the temptations of strong emotional outbursts, of physical extravagances. And at the same time it is lyrical and visionary, reaching its turning point in dramatic terms with the intervention of an angel – Matt Purdy – on a visit from the kingdom of the dead to give Fanny his blessing for her departure. Most importantly, the play offers physical equivalences for its verbal sallies, even though they are not always made the most of in Caroline FitzGerald's production.

The play is full of detailed physical activity: the rowing of boats to and from the mainland, the making of candles, the measuring out of cloth in a shop, the collection and cooking of food. It has physical images, such as the making of the Easter Candle for the nuns of Baltimore by Fanny's father John, which match in their power the richness of the language. But they are not always used to their full effect. Bronwen Casson's set is beautiful in some of its details but not very successful at opening up the stage. The consequent impression of flatness is not ameliorated by the refusal to make more of the physical images and activities, to get the same sense of poetry into the movement as there is in the language.

The enormous strength of the production, on the other hand, is in its sure touch with the performances, the way it not only

allows for a whole series of really fine pieces of acting, but also
forms those pieces into a coherent whole. It is a compliment to
the actors that while you always feel you are watching very good
work, you are aware of them together and not separately. There
is a fundamental understanding that understatement and restraint
are where the dramas of the play lies, that the emotion is
infinitely more moving for being suggested and only half-spoken
rather than shouted out.

Wonderful Tennessee, by Brian Friel

Abbey Theatre
The Irish Times, 10 July 1993

In the introduction to the Methuen edition of Euripides's *The
Bacchae*, J. Michael Walton describes the Dionysus of the play as
'the Dionysus of the faith-healer and the trance-dancer'. Given
that Brian Friel's greatest play is *Faith Healer* and that his most
successful, *Dancing at Lughnasa*, has a trance-dance at its core, it is
hardly surprising that he should have approached *The Bacchae* at
some stage. What is surprising is that, in his new play, *Wonderful
Tennessee* at the Abbey, he should have done so in a way that does
so little justice either to his own great achievements or to
Euripides's.

As with most Friel plays, *Wonderful Tennessee* pulls together
strands from his earlier work. Since *The Enemy Within* was
produced in 1962, Friel has been struggling in his plays with the
idea of faith, with the pull between the chaos of life and the
intimations of the inexpressible that surround it. *Wonderful
Tennessee* continues that struggle. It also draws on the isolated
island where an act of violence occurs of *The Gentle Island*, the
rumours of dark paganism and the desire to move beyond
language of *Dancing at Lughnasa*, the barely-speaking character of
Translations (with George, the accordion-player, taking the role of
Sarah in *Translations*), and the celebration (Terry's birthday) that
becomes a kind of wake of so many Friel plays.

This kind of obsessive return to the same themes and images
is an essential part of Friel's greatness, and it does not in itself
suggest that there is anything stale about *Wonderful Tennessee*. Nor

is there anything in itself worrying about Friel's borrowings from classical literature and imagery. He has borrowed before, often to brilliant effect. The great final scene of *Translations*, for instance, is an amalgam of the end of *Juno and the Paycock* and Virgil's *Aeneid*, with an allusive pun on the goddess Juno tying these disparate sources together.

In previous plays, though, these borrowings have been re-imagined and transformed, taken full possession of and are made to arise from an entirely new dramatic situation. The problem with *Wonderful Tennessee* is that none of this seems to happen. Friel's borrowings, even where they are borrowings from himself, remain second-hand. Almost from the moment that the three married couples of the play arrive on Ballybeg pier and begin to talk of the imminent arrival of Carlin the ferryman to take them to Oileán Draíochta, it doesn't take a classical scholar to recognize that the image being worked is that of Charon the ferryman who takes the dead across the Styx into the Underworld and, if they are fortunate, to the Isles of the Blessed. The play, you realize, might have been called *A Day Out in the Styx*. This is fine.

The allusions, however, begin to pile in like rugby forwards into a ruck, leaving the poor story of the six people on a Donegal pier crushed and gasping beneath the weight. There's Dionysus and *The Bacchae*, providing incidents in the play which have no more genuine source in the actual dramatic situation. There's the story of Demeter and Persephone. There's *The Canterbury Tales* – pilgrims obliged to tell stories to shorten the road. And then there's a rake of religious references, from holy wells and the turas on Inish Keel Island to Protestant hymns, Catholic miracles and the life-belt stand that doubles as a Celtic cross.

There is, however, no dramatic yeast to make all these heavy ingredients rise, and they remain indigestible. Little effort is made to establish the characters in their own right, and what we learn of them is not especially interesting. That Terry and Angela have had an illicit affair, that George is dying, that Berna is suffering from chronic mental illness – these are the sorts of dramatic commonplaces that should be in the stage directions, not the body of the play. And as an image of human yearning for the

Other, the misty Oileán Draoíchta and a few dancing dolphins (a classical symbol of salvation, don't you know?) comes dangerously close to the banal.

In truth, the use of all of the source images is relentlessly reductive. The fearful dismemberment of Pentheus in *The Bacchae* becomes the tearing-off of the sleeve of Terry's shirt, more You-Rip-a-Dese than Euripides. The madness of the women of Thebes becomes Berna's nervous breakdown. The return of Demeter to the Earth and Dionysus's re-birth become Frank's bunch of flowers and Terry's determination to 'rise again' after financial death. The Nietzschean struggle of the Apollonian and the Dionysiac, the great play of the sacred and the profane, becomes an alternation of pop songs and hymns.

In all cases, less is not more. Instead of the ordinary becoming imbued with the mythic, the mythic is reduced to a very ordinary dullness. Big forces are shut up in a very small and static play like a tiger in a cat basket. The production tends to exacerbate rather than limit these problems, emphasizing the cramped nature of the setting, and throwing away the opportunity for a different dimension offered by the songs by trying to fit them within a naturalistic framework.

Actors of the stature of Donal McCann, John Kavanagh, Ingrid Craigie and Marion O'Dwyer are always worth seeing but the play, forcing lines like: 'You'd never guess – my wife teaches Classics' on them in its attempt to provide a justification for the allusions, has them up against it all the time.

The final irony of *Wonderful Tennessee* is that the joyous throwing off of political responsibility which Friel accomplished in *Dancing at Lughnasa* may also account for the weakness of his new play. Removing his characters from society, placing them at the end of a pier, between sea and land, is the ultimate attempt to throw off the shackles of Irish complication. But without the weight of a wider world pressing on his characters' lives, they come to seem, for all the heavy-handed attempt to attach a mythic meaning to them, insignificant and curiously weightless.

For good or ill, it seems, Friel cannot escape the messy social world of modern Ireland and remain the playwright of stature that he has proved himself to be. It is hard to blame him for trying, and we should respect his right to fail. That he does fail is, amidst all the hype, a salutary reminder of the precarious and unpredictable business of theatre to which he has given himself with such courage for 30 years.

Brothers of the Brush, by Jimmy Murphy

Peacock Theatre
The Irish Times, 16 October 1993

Perhaps because of all the solvents they inhale, house painters have an important place in Irish writing. Jimmy Murphy's play *Brothers of the Brush* at the Peacock, widely seen as the most successful new play of the Dublin Theatre Festival, has respectable antecedents, and seems quite conscious of them. One of the most influential Irish novels, though seldom seen as 'Irish', Robert Noonan's *The Ragged Trousered Philanthropists*, credited, with some exaggeration, with Labour's victory in the 1945 general election in Britain, is centred on a group of house painters. More recently, the literary and dramatic output of the Behan family, including Brendan and Dominic, bears the brush-marks of their family trade. Brendan wrote an anthem for house painters that could well be a motto for Jimmy Murphy's play:

> In the cold hard wintertime they have us on a cross
> Stuck up like Christ between two thieves, the foreman and the boss.

In tone and, up to a point, in content, *Brothers of the Brush* takes up where Noonan and Behan left off. Its setting could be that of the start of Noonan's novel – 12 o'clock in a big house being refurbished by a gang of workmen. Its language is the demotic speech of working men. Its observations of the minutiae of the trade – jobs underpriced because of competition, leading to shoddy work and an undermining of the pride of the workers in their craftsmanship – could be straight out of Noonan. The mood of rough tragedy, of careless cruelty, is reminiscent of Behan. And the use of housepainting to illustrate the inequities of capitalism is in the tradition of both.

Yet, this sense of being on familiar ground, is, as the play unfolds, deceptive. Bit by bit, as Murphy's story proceeds, it becomes clear that we are in the presence not of an inheritor of the world of Noonan and Behan but of an elegy for that world; it is the darker, bleaker side of *The Ragged Trousered Philanthropists*, the sense of workers made mean and cruel, rather than noble and heroic, by their condition that is followed here. It takes up from the gloomy night-thoughts of that novel's hero Owen, rather, than from his daytime arguments for the socialist future, from his musing that 'under the present system, it was impossible for anyone to succeed in life without injuring other people and treating them and making use of them as one would not like to be treated and made use of oneself'.

Brothers of the Brush is precisely about that situation in which people, in order to survive and succeed, misuse others. And unlike in classic socialist rhetoric, it locates that impulse among the workers themselves as well as between them and the bosses. The result is a deceptively subtle and sophisticated piece of work, at once continuous with a traditional strain in Irish writing and, in the same breath, marking a breach with it.

At one level, Murphy's painters are like Behan's, crucified between the boss and the foreman. Johnny Murphy's Martin, owner of the firm, is a typically shifty small businessman, cutting corners, exploiting his workers, paying bribes, operating the black economy. But the foreman part of the equation is where Jimmy Murphy's hard-edged view of the workers comes into play. The basic device of the play is that, at one or other stage of the action, each of the three workers believes himself to be the foreman of the upcoming job in a factory. The workers are therefore decidedly impure, shifting in their class allegiances, constantly hovering between the horrors of the dole and the prospects of a bit of money and status.

It is this which marks the play as an elegy for the world it seems at first to celebrate. It is also this that makes it a successful piece of theatre. For the play's form, which is conventional, simple, cloth-cap realism, is subverted just as much as its apparent political simplicities are. By exploring the break up of old class identities, Murphy not only allows himself to create interesting and complex characters where stereotypes might have been expected, he also creates a theatrical world where identity is not nearly as fixed as the outward form of social realism would imply.

What is happening as the action proceeds is that the basement of an old house is being patched up. The cracks, literally, are being painted over. And this provides an accurate metaphor for the story itself, a story in which the characters find themselves more or less improvising an identity that is, in reality, falling. The identity of the tradesman and trade unionist, skilled worker and uncompromising champion of the dignity of Labour, which is articulated by Liam Carney's Heno, has been eroded by unemployment. The argumentative, proud, bolshie culture of Noonan and Behan is a rickety house that no amount of gloss will hold together. The skills, the bargaining power, the sense of solidarity, are memories. What remains is the war of all against all.

The prospect of being foreman is used by Murphy to create a highly theatrical sense of changing roles. As each of the three workers sense the chance of success, the place of each in the gradations of status and power changes. Within a simple storyline and an unadventurous form, we get a gripping zero-sum game in which each person's gain represents a loss for the others. This makes for a larger dimension than is physically present on stage, a dimension in which what is at stake is not the job prospects of three individuals, but the survival of a class and culture. What might have been a whinge about hard times of three workers becomes a lament for the death of the working class.

Murphy is relentlessly unsentimental. At times the atmosphere of his play is closer to an existential nightmare like Sartre's *Huis Clos* than to social realism – three men in a room using all their resources to destroy each other. The bitterest irony is that Heno's articulation of the language of solidarity, of principle, and of pride is, in the end, just another weapon of manipulation in the Hobbesian struggle. And Murphy carries this through considerable skill, constantly shifting the audience's sympathies from one character to another, so that we too take part in this game of gains and losses. By never allowing us to know which side we are on, Murphy gives us a real sense of a world in which there are no longer two clear sides at all, only a fractured and unstable system of alliances and betrayals.

David Byrne's clear, eloquent production allows the play its humour and its playfulness but keeps a tight hold of this ultimately bleak theme. In a softer production, this might have seemed a very slight piece of work, but here it is shaped and controlled in such a way that its seriousness is allowed to emerge with great clarity and force. The result is a piece that is both an entertainment and a sharp anatomizing of the forces that are shaping Irish society. That theatre can do both of these things even without the involvement of a great established writer is a salutary and hopeful lesson to emerge from a festival.

I Know My Own Heart, by Emma Donoghue

Andrews Lane Theatre
The Irish Times, 13 November 1993

In Myles na Gopaleen's novel *The Poor Mouth*, the Gaelic League speaker at the Feis in Corcadorca harangues his audience about the proper use of the Irish language. Not only, he thunders, must Gaels speak Gaelic, but they must speak about nothing but Gaelic in Gaelic. This linguistic hall of mirrors, in which the only proper subject of language is speech itself, was no mere parody. From the Revival of the 1890s until recently, the principal subject of Irish writing has been 'Ireland'. The story in a novel, the metaphor in a poem, the action on a stage have been understood to be held together in some way by an unspoken character: Ireland itself. From Daniel Corkery to the *Field Day Anthology*, there have been coherent and concerted efforts to exclude from the canon of Irish writing anything which does not follow this rule.

Thus, to give just one illustrative example, George Bernard Shaw's *John Bull's Other Island* is an Irish play because it deals with the matter of Ireland. But *Pygmalion*, because its setting and characters are English, isn't. Never mind that what it deals with — class, language and sexuality — are things which are as central to the experience of Irish people as they are to anyone else. Irish writers can only write about Ireland. On this definition, of course, Roderic O'Conor's paintings of Breton seascapes would not be Irish paintings, but somehow the absurdity has never occurred to us.

One of the great things that has been happening in Irish writing in recent years is that the writers have blown this nonsense apart. It is not that writers have turned away from the language, the experience and the history of Ireland, it is that they have at the same time felt free to ignore them. In plays like Frank McGuinness's *Innocence* or Sebastian Barry's *White Woman Street*, aspects of Irishness (Catholicism, exile) may still play about the action like flickering shadows on a wall, but the wall itself is built of different stuff – Italian painting and the Wild West.

Emma Donoghue's fascinating play at the Andrews Lane Theatre, *I Know My Own Heart* (subtitled *A Lesbian Regency Romance*) takes this process further than it has gone before. Based on the diaries of Anne Lister, a Yorkshire heiress who embarked in the 1820s on a homosexual odyssey that defied almost every convention imaginable, it has just one passing reference to Ireland.

If the play were a mere shrugging-off of inherited Irishness, it would probably merit a mere shrug of the shoulders. But what makes it fascinating is that its implicit rejection of one imagined community – 'Ireland' – is accompanied by a search for another. The very act of the play itself, its decision to put on stage an obscure Englishwoman 150 years dead, is an effort, not to awake from the nightmare of history, but to invent an alternative history in which a young Irishwoman can place herself. Stepping outside of one set of allegiances, it assumes another. Gender and sexuality replace nationality as the forces that constitute the play's characters.

It's interesting to see the play in the context of Emma Donoghue's short story *Going Back*, published in the recent *Ireland in Exile* collection. In the story, the lesbian protagonist, Cyn, asks: 'What's the age of consent for being Irish? [...] I mean, I don't seem to remember ever being consulted [...] All that cultural baggage foisted upon us without a by-your-leave. And what happens if you try and refuse it or leave it behind?

Everybody freaks out as if you've dumped a baby in a carrier bag at the airport'. Drawing up a list of 'Reasons for Not Living in Our Dear Native Isle', Cyn finds that the only entry on the positive side is 'crisps'.

The play, in a sense, is a self-conscious shrugging off of all that cultural baggage of Irishness. Even its subversions are subversions of a particular aura of England. The Regency setting, the drawing room conspiracies, the obsessions with social gradation, the sexual tremors beneath the drawing room floor, are all reminiscent of Jane Austen, and one specific name-check makes the intentions explicit. Anne's fumblings on the chaise longue with her inamorata Marianne, her seductions on healthy countryside walks, her social visits with dishonourable intentions, all reclaim pride against prejudice.

It is hard to expect that such a defiant withdrawal from both Ireland and sexual stereotypes would be accompanied by a fully resolved sense of what is to be put in their place. It isn't. Emma Donoghue's writing shows an awareness that the story she has chosen is one of rebellion against only one of many imprisoning stereotypes. Anne Lister refuses to be an object of male desire, but she is nonetheless an obvious beneficiary of the class system.

Nor, indeed, are the sexual stereotypes completely left behind, for even in the lesbian relationship between Anne and Marianne, there are still strong elements of stereotypical maleness and femininity, with the only real difference being that the 'gentleman' is a woman. Katy Hayes's production, while it is well organized and fully committed, seems a little weighed down by these contradictions and inhibited about being as playful and funny as much of the dialogue suggests it should be.

The writing is too sharp, too polished and self-conscious, for the writer not to be aware of these ironies, but they are never resolved. The play remains too close to its source to be able to really comment on the experiences it records. Emotionally, this creates a contradiction between what we are seeing and what Anne is telling us. The text tells us that we are to sympathize with Anne's lonely struggle for selfhood, yet from what we see – three love affairs in which she seems to enjoy herself enormously – she doesn't seem to be doing all that badly. To be fully achieved as a piece of theatre, the play needs to reconstruct and re-imagine the story it has to tell.

Nevertheless, it is unmistakably the work of a real writer with a gift for dialogue, a hard-edged wit and an admirable determination to make her own world. It takes guts, especially in the theatre, to abandon all the shared codes and meanings which come from sticking to the subject of Ireland. And it takes delicacy and suppleness to sustain a story which has no linear plot because it is about trials and explorations, advances and retreats. When you get guts, delicacy and suppleness in the same writer, then you might well have something besides crisps to put on the positive side of life in our dear native isle.

At the Black Pig's Dyke, by Vincent Woods

Gate Theatre
The Irish Times, 23 February 1994

In his fine book, *Irish Folk Drama*, Alan Gailey mentions an Ulster mumming company who, when playing in Catholic houses, enacted the defeat of Saint George by Saint Patrick, and in Protestant homes the defeat of King James by King William. Mumming slid in under the door of tribal animosity, a visceral bamboozler of opposites.

During the Troubles in Fermanagh in the 1910s and 1920s, mumming stopped. In times when people retreat into their fixed identities, its hidden faces and archetypal personalities have no place. When peace returned, the mumming plays were reinvented. Peter Flanagan, one of the old Fermanagh mummers, explained to Henry Glassie, whose *All Silver and No Brass* is still the most profound book on Irish theatre yet written, that mumming was reinvented 'to bring unity among them, and to show the opposite number that there was no harm in them. […] It broke down a lot of barriers. It changed public opinion altogether. If the mummin' had spread – if people had become more mixed – it really wouldn't have developed as it has at the present time. I really think that'.

Part of the reason for the astonishing force of Vincent Woods's play *At the Black Pig's Dyke* in Maeliosa Stafford's triumphant production for Druid is that it goes right to the heart of mumming's power and its tragedy. It takes a situation in which a form of theatre expressed the hopes of a community for peace but was driven out by war and makes it a powerful statement of the role and limits of theatre itself.

At the Black Pig's Dyke is a superbly eloquent and heartbreaking statement about tribal war in the Border counties. But it is also, in theatrical terms, one of the most radical gestures which the Irish theatre has managed in the 1990s, radical in the original sense of going back to roots. Modern Irish theatre was invented as an attempt to reconcile Protestant and Catholic cultures. Lady Gregory, Yeats and Synge attempted to bring a Protestant, cosmopolitan sensibility to bear on what they saw as an ancient, Gaelic tradition surviving around them. And, to a large extent, they succeeded.

What they failed to do, though, was to break out of a perception that the folk traditions they wanted to tap into were purely Gaelic and that they were entirely non-theatrical. The great irony of their achievement is that it completely ignored the theatrical tradition which was actually present in the folk culture – that of mumming. Mumming is not Gaelic but it is traditional. It is not Catholic but it does belong to the ordinary rural people. It screws up, in other words, all the categories by which modern Irish theatre invented itself. The one theatrical genius who actually tapped into its potential – George FitzMaurice – was banished from the Abbey and left to languish in obscurity.

This is one of the reasons why *At the Black Pig's Dyke* is such an important achievement for the Irish theatre. It doesn't just represent a remarkable piece of Irish theatrical invention, it reinvents the categories of Irish theatre. It reaches back beyond the Creation, grasps hold of the elements and puts them together in new combinations. But it also faces the fact that this joyous re-creation comes too late, it accommodates the brute facts of life. Set around and against the mumming is the story of Lizzie Flynn (Stella McCusker) and Jack Boles (Brendan Laird), Catholic and Protestant, wife and husband, trying to annihilate the categories into which they are born and ending up being annihilated by them.

Lizzie, fleeing to Fermanagh with Jack, is pursued by Frank Beirne (Seán Lawlor), whose desire for her is inextricable from his political conviction that people should not be allowed to escape the fate of their 'own kind'. He is the avenging angel of the tribe, the hammer of traitors, the asserter of fixed, inescapable identities. And as in life, he holds the field.

Maeliosa Stafford's direction has the courage and the skill to make the play's profound ambition manifest. The production works by creating a space that is permeable, a playing area into which different times and places can come, parallelling the fundamental condition of mumming: that people are not afraid to answer the knock on their doors, to allow masked men into their homes. And it gradually makes that openness more and more sinister, creating the sense that a space into which mummers may come is also a space which has no protection from whatever evil might wish to enter.

As performance, the play is thrilling. As a story it is an eloquent statement of what has happened to the Irish tribes, of anger and despair. As an exploration of theatre, though, it is wonderfully hopeful. Even in enacting the defeat of theatre, of Peter Flanagan's intention to 'bring unity among them', it reasserts the power and dignity of the imagination.

The Last Apache Reunion, by Bernard Farrell

Abbey Theatre
The Irish Times, 22 March 1994

At the end of the 1970s, there was what looked like a new generation of playwrights emerging in Irish theatre. The Abbey, under the artistic direction of Joe Dowling and the script editorship of Seán McCarthy, began to implement a coherent policy of developing new writers. With considerable courage and persistence, the theatre took the risk of giving first productions, often of very imperfect plays, to unknown writers.

By the early 1980s, that policy seemed to have paid off. Irish theatre had a new group of playwrights – the most prominent being Bernard Farrell, Graham Reid, Neil Donnelly and Frank

McGuinness – who seemed capable, not just of supplying the Peacock, but of filling the Abbey itself.

Most of this work was socially realistic, and much of it could have been on television. There were plays about the violence in Northern Ireland, about the IRA and wayward gardai, about strikes and psychotherapy. The work often lacked poetry and theatrical adventure, but there was no reason to believe that, so long as Irish society kept producing 'issues', this supply of solid, realistic contemporary work would dry up.

Yet it did. While Frank McGuinness went on to develop a highly individual and poetic style, suggesting that the relative naturalism of his first Peacock play *The Factory Girls* was somewhat against the natural grain of his work, the other three playwrights failed to live up to expectations. Reid's work gravitated more and more towards television. Donnelly's petered out. Most disappointingly of all, the menace, madness and theatrical inventiveness of Bernard Farrell's brilliant debut, *I Do Not Like Thee, Doctor Fell*, deteriorated into the shallow sitcom of plays like *All in Favour Said No!* and *All the Way Back*.

Last year, 14 years after *Dr Fell*, Bernard Farrell re-emerged as a real force with *The Last Apache Reunion* at the Abbey, now revived in an essentially unchanged production by Ben Barnes at the Tivoli in Dublin, revolving around the excellent performances of Frank McCusker, Don Wycherley and Jane Brennan. It is acutely observed, deeply funny and, just as importantly, honest and courageous in its dissection of male fears and inadequacies. It is so good that it immediately poses the question of what happened over those 14 years, of whether Bernard Farrell merely failed, or whether, in fact, Irish theatre failed him.

The play is not, on the surface, all that remarkable. It deals with what is almost a stock situation – the reunion of a gang of school buddies, the overgrown boys who used to call themselves 'The Apaches'. It does not have or pretend to have the metaphorical sweep of the Irish play it most resembles, Tom Murphy's *Conversations on a Homecoming*. And its 'secret', the legacy of bullying, is hardly surprising.

Beneath the surface, though, is a relentless probing of the fissures in Irish manhood. The very predictability of the scenario is turned, with real theatrical suppleness, into a kind of grim ritual in which The Apaches are doomed like uneasy ghosts to haunt the site of their cruelties and humiliations 15 years before.

In many ways, we are back with *Dr Fell*. There is the same exposure of the tyranny of the group, and its potential for destruction of the individual. There is the same satire on therapies, with the group therapy of the earlier play replaced with a kind of informal regression therapy, as the lads gradually shed their grown-up years and return to the state of late adolescence which, mentally, they have never left. Above all, there is the same dark and dangerous comedy in which characters are poised on the knife-edge between hilarious absurdity and hysterical breakdown.

What these similarities bring home is the sense in which Farrell is essentially a serious writer, one whose true comedy lies not in the mere tittle-tattle of social observation, but at the borders of human identity. He is concerned not with the foibles of society, but with the very basis of society itself: the way in which groups form, cohere and perpetuate themselves. Here, the characters' return to the past is a mark, not of nostalgia, but of how fragile their subsequent selves are, how insecure and vulnerable they feel without the reinforcement of the group to which they once belonged. Having so little sense of self, they must seek it in collective memories, even if those memories are, as it emerges, not happy ones.

The laughter is nervous laughter, the comedy a comedy of terrors. Farrell lays bare the fear at the heart of middle-class life, the fear that in spite of believing in individualism, you might be nothing without the group. His characters, having no sense of society, have to cling on to whatever vestige of it they can find in their past lives, even if they are only the grubby cruelties of The Apaches.

Beneath the knockabout, sometimes crude humour, there is a fiercely bleak view of lives in which the essential connection to other lives has never been made and which have therefore never really become adult. Like all true comedy, this drama is grounded in a moral vision.

It may be the case that *The Last Apache Reunion* is a mere return to form of a writer who has recaptured his original inspiration.

But it is hard not to conclude that the relentless demand for entertainment and for commercial success in the mainstream theatre did not play some role in blunting the cutting edge of his vision and diverting him into the shallows. Now that he has found his true voice again, it is important that he should be allowed to use it to the full, even, and perhaps especially, when he is saying uncomfortable things.

Asylum! Asylum!, by Donal O'Kelly

Peacock Theatre
The Irish Times, 9 August 1994

Placing Donal O'Kelly's new play *Asylum! Asylum!* in the Peacock alongside Shaw's *The Doctor's Dilemma* at the Abbey is a good piece of programming. The argumentative theatre of Shaw may be a problematic tradition, but it is good to know that it is not a dead one.

With *Hughie on the Wires*, about El Salvador and the international media, which played at the City Centre earlier this year and now with *Asylum! Asylum!*, O'Kelly has shown himself to be an unashamed follower of the Shavian ideal of theatre as a vehicle for political and social argument. Like Shaw, too, he understands that the argument must be entertaining if it is to be listened to, and his plays are lively and funny.

Argumentative theatre is still, nonetheless, problematic, and *Asylum! Asylum!* raises many of the problems. It is very obviously a play with a purpose: to expose the odiousness and cruelty of Irish and EU attitudes towards asylum-seekers from developing countries. This it does to real effect, fulfilling in the process one of theatre's most honourable functions: to make the audience think about something it may not have thought about before. This is no mean achievement, nor is it one which is irrelevant to the question of whether the play is 'good' or not.

The fact is that *Asylum! Asylum!* not only deals bravely and passionately with an important public issue, it also challenges, in a way that a national theatre should do, some basic aspects of our self-perception as a people. Our view of ourselves as a morally pure part of the Third World, as belonging to the oppressed rather than the oppressors, is blown away in O'Kelly's stark images of a Ugandan refugee, Joseph Omara (very powerfully played by Dave Fishley), being roughed up by Irish immigration officials. For that alone, it demands to be seen.

There are, nonetheless, other questions which need to be asked of a piece of theatre, questions of form. There is a perception that a play which has a direct and urgent political content must adopt the most immediate and direct of forms. Television has played its part in this perception, but so too has the Abbey itself, which has tended to equate 'issues' with naturalism in a fairly crude Ibsenist calculation.

Yet there is no good reason why this should be so. For one thing, many of the most powerful political plays of recent years in Ireland – think of *The Lament for Arthur Cleary* or *Observe the Sons of Ulster Marching Towards the Somme* – have been non-naturalistic. For another, Donal O'Kelly specifically is a writer whose greatest strengths are in the linguistic playfulness and surreal inventiveness that made *Bat the Father, Rabbit the Son* such a joy. That play was no less political for its adoption of an inventive form – on the contrary, its politics were all the more powerfully expressed because the language created its own utterly convincing world.

Asylum! Asylum! is most effective, too, when it is most strange. It is the oddities – Joseph's memories of torture and of his father's obsession with Churchill's descriptions of the Ugandan railway, the parallel memories of Leo and Mary, Joseph's interrogator and solicitor respectively, of their father in childhood, their father's memories of his courtship of their mother – that make the piece compelling and human. When it follows the logic of these moments, John Crowley's production achieves a real theatrical intensity.

In these moments, the play is not merely about the treatment of a refugee, it is itself an evocation of the nightmare of torture, of the strangeness of a strange land, of the way the world looks from the outside. By making familiar things strange, these passages of the drama don't just do what all art tries to do, but they also get to the core of the estrangement that Joseph is made to feel. The aesthetics and the politics reinforce each other.

The problem, though, is that all of this is hedged around by naturalistic conventions that simply can't work. You can't impose naturalistic conventions of cause and effect and then expect an audience not to demand that they be carried through consistently.

So we ask questions that undermine the power of the play: would an immigration officer really bring in his sister to act as an asylum-seeker's solicitor? Would she really kiss him during their first consultation? Is it likely that all the characters would end up in her father's back garden? In the theatre, once you start to explain anything, you have to explain everything, and it would have been much better if the play had been cast in a form that didn't offer explanations at all.

True Lines, by John Crowley et al.

City Arts Centre
The Irish Times, 18 October 1994

At least two things can be said with confidence about Irish theatre after the Festival. One is that the old hierarchy of centre and periphery, of 'mainstream' and 'fringe' has collapsed. The other is that naturalism is no longer the staple diet of our plays.

Both points were made with joyous force by Bickerstaffe's splendid *True Lines* at the City Arts Centre. The play shares little with the comfortable familiarities of traditional Irish theatre. It is not a literary creation, but a collective enterprise, devised by the director John Crowley and written with the excellent cast, Cathy Belton, Tom Murphy, Gwynne McElveen and Stuart Townsend. It is not from Dublin, but from Kilkenny. And it defies the classical unities with haughty disdain, with the action occurring simultaneously in Australia, Arizona, Berlin and Ethiopia.

There are, though, other things it is not either – not 'experimental', not self-indulgent, not precious. This is a tough, lucid, rigorously disciplined piece of theatre. Its clarity comes from an understanding that naturalism and realism are not the same thing, and that a play can have the texture of reality without pretending to be a slice of life. *True Lines* is in many ways a remarkable piece of social realism. For it is the best expression yet in our culture of the world of the new generation of Irish emigrants of the 1980s, a world without a centre, a world in which cultures and people are like colliding atoms, continually crashing into and bouncing off each other.

If there is a presiding influence at work, it is not from the Irish tradition at all but from the Canadian director Robert Lepage. But it is an influence worn lightly and Crowley's hypnotic succession of verbal and physical images has the tang of genuine originality.

The piece is constructed on a simple but beautifully-worked set of counterpoints between the intimate and the universal, between the body and the world. Images of bodily dysfunction – epilepsy, asthma, abortion, bodies falling from buildings – set off images of being adrift in an unbounded world where random encounters and casual partings have taken the place of certainty. Tying them together is the image of the Aboriginal songlines, the networks, at once physical and cultural, that traced unseen paths through a hostile continent. It acts as an image of the yearning of these young Irish people for something that will give them a connection, make them feel at home in the world.

Through it all runs a cry – Emmett's 'I just want to be continuous' – that should echo in the skulls of those who talk blandly on the 'global generation' of young Irish people. If the cry itself is despairing, though, it is uttered in a voice so full of wit, courage and imaginative compassion, that it is a tonic to hear it.

The Mai, by Marina Carr

Peacock Theatre
The Irish Times, 18 October 1994

The other new voice that will stay in the head long after the carnival has left town is Marina Carr's. For a while now, hers has been an insistent but unsure presence at the edge of Irish theatre, but with *The Mai* at the Peacock, she emerges in full voice at the centre. Here, the brighter elements of her earlier plays – the anarchic humour, the edgy language, the courage to play dangerous games – are combined with a critical new element: that mysterious but unmistakable sense of shape that separates an interesting playwright from an accomplished one.

Ostensibly, *The Mai* has more in common with the traditions of Irish theatre than *True Lines* has, but the appearances are deceptive. The trappings of the well-made play – a set suggestive of a real house, fixed props, unified action – are no more than a rough grounding for the piece. In fact, the play has little interest in plot or in describing events. It works by evoking an atmosphere rather than by enacting a story.

The atmosphere it evokes in Brian Brady's well-modulated production is doom-laden but not gloomy, compounded of myth and memory, of fierce longing and bitter elegy. Mai, played by Olwen Fouéré, who manages the difficult task of embodying an evanescent presence with her usual grace, is a woman whose foundations are undermined by her love for her faithless husband. But Carr expands this all too commonplace story into dimensions of myth and archetype, giving the play a generational sweep by balancing Mai with her ancient grandmother (Joan O'Hara) on the one side and her daughter Millie (Derbhle Crotty) on the other.

The effect of this is not very far from *True Lines*. *The Mai* builds slowly into a sense of a single female world of loss and desire, a world in which places and times are not held apart but form a continuous universe. Carr gives us five generations, so intertwined that it is hard to remember which is which. She evokes places as diverse as North Africa, New York, Paris, an island off the West coast, and a Midlands lakeshore. The Ireland she imagines is a porous place, its people seeping out, stray bits of the world streaming in.

It takes real and justified confidence for a writer to invoke such an unstable world, and Carr shows herself here to have her ear always well tuned to the pitch of the piece. Nothing of the zaniness of her imagination is lost, but the anarchy this time is purposeful – creative collisions rather than messy disorder.

The play is as deft as it is daft, with its head screwed on as well as screwed up. Again, the key is an understanding that realism and surrealism are no longer opposites for Irish theatre, that our reality is so strange that only strange images can encompass it. With minds like Carr's and Crowley's clicking into gear, there is every reason to believe that a new generation in Irish theatre will have the measure of the new world in which we live.

Chamber Music, by Hugh Leonard

Abbey Theatre
The Irish Times, 13 November 1994

The theory, put forward by Hugh Leonard in his columns, by Bernard Farrell in his programme note for Leonard's *Chamber Music* at the Abbey, and, more obliquely in one of the two playlets that make up the evening, goes like this: writers like Leonard and Farrell are undervalued by Irish critics and directors because they are funny. Sad, humourless theorists, led astray by the search for subtexts, miss the point and are too uptight to let rip and have a laugh. They drag in extraneous matters, especially politics.

It is an interesting theory, not least because it has, as Leonard's prize eejit Chas Mangan in *Senna for Sonny*, the first half of the double bill, would put it, a soupspoon of truth. The truth is that not only do critics tend to undervalue humour, but funny playwrights tend to resist criticism. Analysing humour is a mug's game – like tearing the wings off butterflies to see how they fly.

Yet, go to see *Chamber Music*, and what do you get? A farce about the nouveaux riches settling in after the Irish Civil War, and a monologue about the pain behind comedy. So, who's dragging in what?

Then pick an Irish farce, any Irish farce. Admittedly, there are not many to choose from. Ireland does not have the same tradition of boulevard farce that France and England do, for the simple reason that we did not develop a new urban middle class in the same way that other countries did. But Irish playwrights, among them Leonard, Friel and Murphy, have used farce as a form. Friel's *The Communication Cord* is a farce about linguistics and politics. Murphy's *Too Late for Logic* is a farce about a philosopher preparing a lecture on Schopenhauer. And Leonard's own farces – *The Patrick Pearse Motel* and *Kill* are attacks on nationalism and political corruption.

The point, though, is not just that Irish playwrights use farce as a vehicle for dealing with serious public issues. It is that in many of these plays the farcical elements are not very funny while the political elements are a scream. The best jokes in *The Patrick Pearse Motel*, for instance, are not the standard farce gags, but the wonderfully bad taste of the political mockery – like the motel restaurant called The Famine Room.

The same goes for *Senna for Sonny*. The bits taken from Feydeau – truly awful lavatory humour about chamber pots and laxatives – are about as funny as the Dow Jones index. But the bits taken from Leonard's own rage about Irish Civil War politics are brilliant and hilarious. The dialogue between die-hard Chas Mangan (John Olohan) and Free Stater General O'Horan (Des Cave) – fond reminiscences of torture and murder – is gloriously grotesque, in the best traditions of Denis Johnston's *The Old Lady Says No!* or of Myles na Gopaleen at his most splenetic.

Whereas the Feydeauesque elements are merely tasteless, the political stuff is in wonderfully bad taste. Bad taste – the artful inversion of decency – is funny; tastelessness – the artless reversion to infantile indecency – isn't.

It is a real pity that the political satire is overwhelmed by the toilet humour to such an embarrassing extent, particularly since Patrick Mason's production shows so much skill and intelligence in its efforts to push the form to its limits and create a human Punch and Judy show on stage. Freed from the shackles of dreary farce, an Irish *Ubu Roi* just might have emerged, trailing some real vulgarity to commit sacrilege in the Abbey. As it is, we just get a stifled guffaw at the back of the church.

Hidden Charges, by Arthur Riordan

Project Theatre
The Irish Times, 25 October 1994

When Irish theatre is discussed, a discreet silence is maintained about much of its history. The story that is told is a succession of masterpieces from Synge to Friel. What is forgotten is that huge tracts of the theatrical landscape are planted not with great and enduring oaks but with quick-growing and carelessly felled pines. The Abbey stage, for instance, was occupied for much longer by the plays of George Shiels and John McCann than by their contemporaries Samuel Beckett and Brendan Behan.

Watching Arthur Riordan's first play, *Hidden Charges*, presented by Rough Magic at the Project and soon to go on tour to Kilkenny, Cork, Galway and Limerick, I couldn't help thinking of John McCann. John McCann's plays of the 1950s were the staple diet of the National Theatre. Their ingredients were constant – lower-middle class Dublin families, stock comic characters, awkward families, topical allusions, plots revolving around marriage and money.

Hidden Charges has all of these elements. Its plot, concerning the tension between a young upwardly mobile Dublin couple and her country aunt is straight out of the 1950s. It has topical allusions – divorce, abortion, a thinly disguised version of the Anne Lovett case. Its central question – will Mark (Darragh Kelly) and Carol (Anne Byrne) move in together, or will Carol's country and western auntie Kitty (Bernie Downes) disrupt their relationship? – is a 1990s version of McCann's first hit, *Twenty Years A-Wooing*, in which our hero Henry's progress towards the altar is thwarted by his family.

The comparison is not made as a put-down. As a piece of writing, *Hidden Charges* is infinitely better than most of the tradition from which it comes. Arthur Riordan shows a real mastery of stagecraft, albeit the stagecraft of the 1950s well-made play. He has a terrific sense of pace, which is exploited to the full in Lynne Parker's sharp, snazzy production. Three of his four characters (the exception being Kitty's friend Bill, who plays an increasingly important part in the plot without ever being properly established) are pinned down like specimens in a display case, even though the idea that a left-wing newspaper columnist like Mark would be vain, opinionated and liable to drink more than the odd pint, is patently unrealistic. And the dialogue, for most of the play, buzzes with wit and verbal exuberance. At least half of the play is funny, a very much higher proportion than most so-called comedies.

So what's the problem? The problem is that you can't write 1950s kitchen comedies (or in this case sitting-room comedies) about 1990s Ireland. The Ireland of the 1950s was, in its own way, as complex and as tense as today's society. But it was much better at hiding its complexities and its tensions. In cultural forms, the illusion of a nice, cosy petit bourgeois world still had real clout, and for the most part Irish theatre was devoted to its maintenance. It took plays of extraordinary courage and ferocity – Tom Murphy's *A Whistle in the Dark* and John B. Keane's *Sive* in particular – to unsettle it.

By now, though, it is well and truly unsettled, and the theatrical methods of the 1950s no longer suffice for the creation of even a vaguely workable version of the place. Social comedy like *Hidden Charges*, however light it may seem, actually requires a whole set of agreements with an audience about how certain characters are to be seen. This is all the more obviously the case since Riordan's play tries to engage directly with the bitter battles between liberalism and conservatism in Ireland in the last decade.

Hidden Charges depends, for instance, on the idea that a middle-class Dublin journalist like Mark would have a mortal dread of 'culchies'. Around this notion the play tries to build a tension between Mark's liberal agenda and Kitty's supposed conservatism.

But that premise itself is so weak – an import from the world of John McCann – that the structure of argument built on it collapses in on itself. By the middle of the second half of the play, the action is caught uncomfortably between bedroom farce and Shavian dispute, unable to do justice to either. We have been led, by a most pleasant route, into a dramatic cul de sac.

It would be nice to think that things didn't have to be like this, that with a little polishing, a play of this nature would come off.

The prospect of a writer who could produce old-fashioned, well-made comedies from the material of 1990s Ireland would have theatre managers all over the country driven wild with anticipation. But the fact is that *Hidden Charges* is the product of a writer with all the necessary talents and it still doesn't work. Our reality is just too perverse and too elusive to fit into the discarded moulds of 40 years ago.

Danti-Dan, by Gina Moxley
Project Theatre
The Irish Times, 28 March 1995

Irish theatre has never been very good at dramatizing the world of children. When you think of how successful some Irish playwrights have been at writing prose about childhood and adolescence – think of Brendan Behan's *Borstal Boy* or Hugh Leonard's *Home Before Night* – and when you remember how dominant the theme of childhood was in the Irish writing of the 1940s and 1950s, this is quite remarkable.

It is not even that there has been any reluctance to explore the difficult and sometimes dangerous terrain between childhood and adulthood. Irish plays, especially since the Sixties, have often featured the man-child, the adult self projected back into childhood years. Hugh Leonard in *Da* gives us an older self watching an imagined younger self. Brian Friel in *Dancing at Lughnasa* deploys a narrator who is allowed to switch between his presence on stage as a middle-aged man and his memories of himself as a kid among his aunts decades before. Tom Murphy, in *A Crucial Week in the Life of a Grocer's Assistant*, gives us something more disturbing and pointed: adults who are still children, trapped in a time and place that will not allow them to grow up.

The originality of Gina Moxley's first play *Danti-Dan*, currently presented at the Project by Rough Magic, is that in it we approach the wild borderlands of adolescence almost entirely from the point of view of the child. The oldest of the characters is 18, the youngest 13. The adult world is somewhere out on the margins of the story, unseen and unheard. And because there are no adults, there is no nostalgia, no warm glow of remembrance.

Danti-Dan is a fierce and raw play, whose humour and control mediate but do not mitigate its bleakness. Only Paul Mercier's plays *Wasters* and *Spacers* offer any parallels in Irish theatre to *Danti-Dan*'s exploration of an adolescent group taken entirely on its own terms. But whereas Mercier's concerns are primarily social and political, Moxley's are much more nakedly sexual. *Danti-Dan* steps, courageously and with admirable integrity, into the minefield of adolescent female sexuality.

It is hard, in the wake of the X case appeal judgement, to think of any area that could be more difficult to traverse safely. To walk a line between two explosive lies – one that pretends that young girls are innocent of sexual desires and feelings and another that pretends that they are in control of their sexuality and thus players in the sexual market – and still retain some theatrical poise is a fair achievement. For the most part, Gina Moxley pulls it off.

It is the tension of walking that line that makes the play more than just an admirable apprentice piece. In form and structure, it is little more than an extended sketch. We meet the five characters in a small town in Cork – Cactus (Sophie Flannery), a 13-year old hormonal tidal wave; her 14-year old friend Dolly (Eileen Walsh), Dolly's 16-year old sister (Dawn Bradfield) and her 18-year old boyfriend (Donal Beecher); and Danti-Dan (Alan King), who is 14 but has a mental age of 8, early on. The action plays itself out quite predictably towards its inevitable conclusion. If there was nothing else going on, *Danti-Dan* would be a display of promise rather than achievement.

But what gives this rather flat dramatic structure a real grip on its audience is the remarkable skill and unflinching determination with which Moxley pursues an uncompromising vision of the relationship between sex and power. Beneath the dull surface, there is a turbulent interplay of countercurrents and reversals. Moxley gives us two male and two female characters who mirror each other, with Dolly as the innocent enmeshed in their power games. If the play doesn't move forward with any great conviction, it circles round itself, one role bouncing off another, with the hypnotic fascination of a deep and dangerous whirlpool.

Thus what looks like it might be a story out of Frank O'Connor ends up being more like something out of Jean Genet. Each gender has its victims and its victimizer. Cruelty and desire become the exclusive property of neither sex. To the familiar drama of a dominant male exploiting a sexually vulnerable female, Moxley counterposes the unfamiliar and uncomfortable story of Cactus's sexual exploitation of the even more vulnerable Danti-Dan.

This creates the effect that most art strives for, making the familiar strange and therefore powerful. An old story of cruelty and power gets retold with a freshness that demands a hearing.

It is not, in spite of being laced with humour, a pleasant tale, but Moxley refuses to cop out of the task of telling it clearly. And Lynne Parker's production lives up to this integrity. It manages to do justice to the ultimate bleakness of the piece without itself being bleak, and above all to give a fine young cast the confidence to take emotional risks. And it also manages to suggest that if Gina Moxley can add a subtler sense of theatrical form to her skill with language and her courage in deploying it, she will become a formidable playwright.

A Little Like Paradise, by Niall Williams

Peacock Theatre
The Irish Times, 4 April 1995

Death, in Niall Williams's new play at the Peacock, *A Little Like Paradise*, is not so much the ruffian on the stair, as the familiar guest, already well settled in the biggest armchair.

Like Eugene O'Neill's *The Iceman Cometh*, the play is set mostly in a bar, in this case Jay Feeney's bar-cum-grocery in the remote village of Caherconn. And as in O'Neill, William's barroom is an anteroom of death's dominion. Jay Feeney is also the local undertaker. Of his two customers at the start of the play, one – the small farmer Mick Maguire (John Olohan) – is about to die, and the other, Cissie Reidy, has just lost her beloved husband. As we meet the other characters, we discover that two of them are widowed and a third, the local priest, is dying of cancer.

The play is nothing like as grim as all of this might suggest, but there is no doubt that its tone is downbeat and wistful. Caherconn, the fictional village where Williams's first play, *The Murphy Initiative*, was also set, is a dying place, a remote corner of rural Ireland from which the life is inexorably draining. The sea is eroding the coastline. Emigration is eroding the social fabric.

But if *The Murphy Initiative* was a funny play driven by desperation, *A Little Like Paradise* is a play of desperation driven by humour. Things are desperate but not serious.

The hardest trick to pull off in theatre, indeed in any art form, is that of making the physical and the metaphysical, the mundane and the eternal, chime. It is the trick of creating an ordinary, credible situation and imbuing it with the resonance of the great abstract forces of life and death, heaven and hell, making the story work all the time on both levels.

O'Neill does it in *The Iceman Cometh*. Tom Murphy does it in most of his plays. Dermot Bolger does it in *The Lament for Arthur Cleary*. Niall Williams is not yet a dramatist of that quality, but in *A Little Like Paradise* he comes close enough to make for an ambitious and often moving piece of theatre.

We are certainly invited to view the play on both levels. People are dying, but so too is the place. Caherconn has been abandoned by Brussels and Dublin, but also by God. The characters yearn for Structural Funds and National Lottery grants but also for a more awesome answer to their prayers, for some indication that there is still someone up there watching. Jay Feeney's bar counter serves also as a bier and as a kind of shrine.

Mick Maguire 'dies' and is resurrected, bringing back visions of the afterlife. The hosts of children he claims to have seen floating above the bar are spirits of the dead but also an image of the village's yearning for young life to replace the dying.

It takes tremendous confidence with the form of theatre to make this kind of allegorical drama work, and Williams doesn't always manage it. At times the two layers of reality he plays with come together like one photograph superimposed on another, making for an image that is confused and out of key. But when the images do match, the picture stands out with remarkable depth and force.

Where the play is at its weakest is in the relationship between Senator Marty McInerney (Vinnie McCabe), the local politician who has made promises he cannot deliver, and Kay Breen (Fedelma Cullen), the former matron who has campaigned with him for a local hospital. The two should have married decades ago, and now that both are widowed Marty's hopes of reversing history and standing up to the inexorable ravages of time by persuading Kay to marry him is the play's metaphor for the broader yearning of the village to defy its doom.

But the play allows too little space for their relationship to become genuinely persuasive, and given how much weight it bears in the whole metaphorical structure, this is a serious failing. There are strengths, however, to counterbalance this weakness, and Brian Brady's astute production finds the balance between bleakness and hope that is the most important of them.

A Little Like Paradise is flooded with a tender sympathy for its characters, and this depth of compassion gives real force to their plight. Vinnie McCabe brings a touch of Lear to Marty's disillusion with the political world and raging loneliness. Des Nealon rises to the grief and loss of a priest who can no longer answer for the deaths that God permits, including his own. And Brendan Conroy's Feeney is a splendid comic creation, a likeable huckster casting a cold eye on death and life, measuring corpses and measuring out whiskies with equal resignation.

It all adds up to a play of real accomplishment. Niall Williams is finding a style that allows him to express an urgent social critique without becoming didactic and to explore a broader spiritual yearning without becoming mystical or obscurantist. He is finding, in other words, the level of concrete metaphor, the combination of physical reality and resonant image, at which theatre begins to be powerful. He is getting to the place where reality is both re-enacted and transformed. *A Little Like Paradise* may not be the final destination, but it is a transit camp at which it is well worth stopping.

Hard to Believe, by Conall Morrison

Andrews Lane Theatre
The Irish Times, 18 April 1995

Goodness, in the theatre, is seldom any good. The idea of a piece of theatre commissioned by a group such as Cultures of Ireland, which seeks to 'encourage mutual understanding between the island's divided people' is admirable but also off-putting.

Decency, respect and enlightenment may be wonderful qualities in life but theatre, which thrives on conflict, darkness and mutual incomprehension, is not very hospitable to niceness. So the heart sinks a little at the thought of Conall Morrison's *Hard to Believe*, presented by Bickerstaffe and Cultures of Ireland and playing at Andrews Lane Theatre in Dublin until the end of this week. As it happens, though, such apprehensions merely add surprise to the array of emotional disturbances released by this ferocious piece.

Hard to Believe is a one-actor show performed by Seán Kearns, thus, in my case at least, adding to a dread of one-actor shows the initial fear of being subjected to a modern morality tale.

Within a minute, though, both prejudices are blown away by the edgy, manic and dangerous presence of Kearns's John Foster. As a creation, Foster is certainly distilled from the ether of the Northern Ireland conflict. He is a British Army psychological warfare operative, and the offspring of a mixed marriage in which, as we discover, his father's Protestant origins have been obliterated. Put like that, the character sounds contrived, a cipher from some pre-ordained schema. But this is not a simple lesson about the origins of the Troubles, and John Foster is not a vehicle for a theatrical sermon.

The relationship of the play to politics is, in fact, as real and as obscure as that in the nineteenth century Irish Gothic novels of which *Hard to Believe* is so reminiscent. Morrison explores the dangerous borderlines between the real and the invented; placing himself in that 'frontier between two adjacent realms' in which the critic Neil Cornwell locates the Gothic imagination. This is why his play seems closer to the world of Charles Maturin and Sheridan Le Fanu than it does to, say, anything by Graham Reid or Marie Jones. Like the Gothic writers, he takes the literal co-existence of two worlds – a Catholic one and a Protestant one – and re-shapes it as the co-existence of the natural and the supernatural, the real and the unreal. Like them, too, he pursues the meaning of horror until he finds its source.

We enter the borderland between the real and unreal through Foster's gleeful, funny and harshly sardonic account of his favourite operations. These are real episodes from the history of the Troubles: the undercover army agents who posed as laundrymen, the spreading of the rumour that static electricity in women's knickers could set off explosives (designed to stop women from carrying bombs in their underwear), the Kincora scandal, the planting of media stories about the lovable army dog Rats and so on. These stories are culled from newspapers, and Foster's description of his job clearly owes a good deal to the claims and revelations of the army black propagandist Colin Wallace.

But this layer of realism – the realism of the unreal – is overlaid all the time with Foster's memories, fantasies, and madness. Kearns, in a performance of extraordinary virtuosity, makes Foster not just demented but truly demonic, a creature from a Gothic horror movie but with all the dangerous immediacy of a big man on a little stage. He seems both oppressively present and yet weirdly empty, a man who forces his existence on us but cannot himself keep a hold on it.

He has gone so far into the world of the invention and manipulation of reality that he keeps veering off into their personalities in his search for a meaningful self. Past and present are shuffled and reshuffled like a deck of marked cards in his increasingly unhinged apologia, so that we move back and forth over four generations.

He dresses and strips, dresses and strips, becoming now his Catholic mother, now his fundamentalist Protestant grandfather, now his brother, now his great-grandmother. History spins like a top, its patterns blurring in the dizzy speed of his frantic transformations. The language of religion – the Bible, saints and scapulars, astral travel – takes over from the language of black propaganda, until, imaginatively at least, it is hard to tell the difference between one and the other.

This is made most explicit in the dominant image of the play, that of the all-seeing eye. As a child, Foster is told that God is watching everything he does. As an adult, no longer believing in God, he places his trust in the human equivalent, the army spy in the watchtower who might or might not be able to hear and see everything that happens behind every closed door. In a society obsessed with different religious versions of the unreal, Morrison seems to suggest, reality itself becomes impossible to grasp. Because so much has been buried and denied, there is no longer any way to tell truth from lies.

This is a grim conclusion to a sometimes grotesquely brilliant play. *Hard to Believe*, in fact, feels much more like an expiation than a reconciliation. It lets out a pent-up anger rather than trying to assuage it. It travels a long way from realism in order to get close to the bone. It is not at all nice, but it is a relentlessly honest and utterly compelling enactment of the failures of past generations that the present one has to overcome.

Red Roses and Petrol, by Joe O'Connor

Project Arts Centre
The Irish Times, 16 May 1995

Joe O'Connor's first play *Red Roses and Petrol*, presented by Pigsback at the Project Arts Centre in Dublin, looks, at first glance, like a drama about the Irish family. It has all the familiar conventions: the father's funeral as an excuse to gather the scattered children and set in motion a train of remembrances and arguments; the bitter after-effects of childhood rivalry for parental affection; the stoic mother and wayward father; the gradual revelation of family secrets. In other words, it contains everything that seems to have made up every play about the Irish family since the 1940s.

At a second glance, though, the play is not so much about the Irish family as it is about the *image* of the Irish family. What gives the play its particular force and originality is its extraordinary self-consciousness about itself as both a counterpoint to, and a part of, a received Irish literary and theatrical tradition. For all that it looks like a 1990s replay of 1950s domestic drama, with a snort of cocaine replacing a cup of tea.

Red Roses and Petrol is in fact a relentlessly post-modern piece, knowing and playful, always moving between reality and pastiche, between direct speech and quotation marks. The one problem with Jim Culleton's production is that it doesn't always seem to be as aware of this as it should be.

The literary self-consciousness is obvious. Mammy and Daddy (Anne Kent on stage and John Kavanagh on video) are, as we are constantly reminded, inseparable from literary and dramatic archetypes. She used to be an actress, and played Mary Boyle in *Juno and the Paycock*, so her children call her Juno. He is a university librarian and would-be poet.

The first edition of Douglas Hyde's *Love Songs of Connaught* and the love poem he may or may not have written for her bear a heavy weight in the dramatic action. Their son Johnny (named, presumably, after Juno's son Johnny) remembers as a pivotal moment in his fraught relationship with his father the time he was caught trying to steal an edition of Yeats's *Collected Poems*. And through most of the action, the dead father's books – Yeats, Synge, Auden, O'Casey, Hyde – are being sorted.

Just in case there was any danger of the audience missing the point, the play is punctuated by a series of dramatic in-jokes and burlesques of theatrical versions of the family. *Juno and the Paycock* is there, of course. But so too are *Philadelphia, Here I Come!*, *Mother of all the Behans*, and *Three Sisters*. There is even, for readers of Joe O'Connor's fiction, a reminder that Johnny is a version of O'Connor's anti-hero, Eddie Virago.

Previous literary and theatrical images of Mother, Father, Daughter and Son haunt the stage at every turn. The effect is comic and mock-heroic, and the savage side of O'Connor's humour – wit as a weapon of mutually assured destruction – is given full rein. But it is also, at times, chilling and bleak, making all the characters seem like pale images of themselves. The video of the dead father that brings his ghostly presence into the room is only slightly more spectral than the eerie light of other plays on the still-living characters.

This constant need for double-takes makes the play much more challenging to produce than it might seem. It has to both look like and mock the Irish family drama. It calls for a straight narrative and a crooked smile at the same time. And Jim Culleton's solid and skilful production doesn't really manage the difficult job of simultaneously entering into and subverting a dramatic form.

In the tricky balance between playing the lines and playing with the lines, the production falls much too heavily on the side of the former. Fiona Leech and Fiona Whelan's set hedges its bets, giving us a straight sitting room with an angled back wall, that ends up being in effect a minor variant on the dutiful reproduction of domestic detail. Likewise Jim Culleton's direction ends up being too well made: it has all the traditional virtues of convincing character detail from Kathy Downes, Deirdre O'Kane, Barry Barnes and Paul Hickey, good pacing and well-worked entrances and exits.

But it reproduces the form of the conventional family drama so well as to be trapped within it. Careful but dull naturalistic action all but crowds out the desire to play with theatrical form that seems inherent in Joe O'Connor's script. The non-naturalistic elements – the in-jokes, the powerfully edgy presence of John Kavanagh's odd, discontinuous interventions from the television screen, the brief flashbacks to the mother and father's courtship in the late 1950s – sit uneasily with the conventions of domestic drama in the rest of the action. A freer, more imaginative and less literal use of space would probably do more justice to the play's sophistication.

Within those limitations, though, there are real strengths, especially in Anne Kent's quiet and fierce portrayal of the mother, Moya. She maintains for a long time the potent ambiguity of a woman who seems to see and hear nothing but who actually knows much more than she wants to. And she takes us on a dramatic journey from her comfortably familiar exterior to her dark and complex interior. In doing so, she embodies perfectly the play's unillusioned tenderness towards family life, its reluctant but inevitable embrace of the realities beyond the image.

Sick, Dying, Dead, Buried, Out, by Barabbas Theatre Company

Project Arts Centre
The Irish Times, 15 August 1995

'Are these ageless sons of absurdity, are they human at all?', asks Thomas Mann of clowns in *The Confessions of Felix Krull.* 'Are they, I repeat, human beings, men that could conceivably find a place in everyday life? In my opinion, it is pure sentimentality to say that they are "human too", with the sensibilities of human beings and perhaps even with wives and children. I honour them and defend them against ordinary bad taste when I say no, they are not, they are exceptions, side-splitting, world-renouncing monks of unreason, cavorting hybrids, part human and part insane art'.

What Mann put his finger on in this passage is the uncomfortable truth that lies behind all the clichés about the tears of the clown. Clowning exists for our pleasure, but the clown is also a kind of monk, a devotee of a harsh and unblinking god. The great clown always gives the appearance of being only half-human, of existing in rigorous isolation from the rest of society, cut off from the comforting associations that make humanity what it is.

It is not for nothing that the archetypal clown personality is that of the tramp, the homeless wanderer without money or family, stuck in the spotlight with an eternal sidekick. Not for nothing, either, that Beckett, in his search for a theatrical image of human isolation in the world took his first heroes – Didi and Gogo in *Waiting for Godot* – straight from the tradition of clowning.

In spite of Beckett, though, there is very little in the nature of an Irish clown tradition. Ireland had a strong vaudeville culture, but its laughter was generated by comedians rather than clowns. Jimmy O'Dea, Maureen Potter, Cecil Sheridan, and the other great vaudevillians relied almost entirely on wordplay and characterization, not on the physical, bodily presence of the clown. There is no Irish equivalent of Bert Lahr or Chico Marx or Max Wall, much less of the venerable European tradition of *commedia dell'arte*.

Why this should be so is a matter of speculation, but I would hazard a guess that an important factor is that the idea of an Irish clown was too close to the tainted tradition of the stage Irishman. Especially in the early years of this century, when playwrights like Yeats and George FitzMaurice were experimenting with a kind of theatre that might well have been hospitable to clowns, the stage Irishman was the great taboo. Because it was politicized and turned to nefarious social purposes, the native clowning impulse locked up in the stage Irishman was effectively inaccessible.

Barabbas, the first coherent attempt at an Irish clown theatre, is thus an expedition into unknown territory, so much so that the progress of the company in little over two years is simply astonishing. With their most recent work, *Sick, Dying, Dead, Buried, Out*, which finished a successful run at the Project in Dublin on Saturday night and is likely to tour, they have definitively established themselves as a serious force. They have ended once and for all an era of stray experiments in mime and physical theatre that has straggled on in Irish theatre for 15 years, and brought an utterly convincing sense of purpose to an idea that seemed to be going nowhere fast.

The clowning of Mikel Murfi and Raymond Keane, under the direction of Veronica Coburn (the show is written and devised by all three in collaboration) is not that of mere tomfoolery, but of monks of unreason at their devotions. The laughter they evoke is that of cavorting hybrids, rooted not in levity of spirit but in the unsettling ferocity of true clowning. They seem to have the kind of demented dedication to their art which alone can give the clown the slightly inhuman air of loneliness and isolation.

Murfi and Keane play out a life-and-death struggle of two brothers, whose performances as clowns are intercut with their alternating loves and hates as people. Clowning is set explicitly on the edge of everyday darkness, the clown shown as a kind of half-human substitute for human relationships. The travelling act in which Ultan and Pádraig becomes the clowns Ultie and Paurie is very funny, but we are never allowed to forget the intimate struggles that lie beneath its surface.

What is most impressive about Murfi and Keane is the way they combine athleticism and delicacy. Their wordless, though far from noiseless, comedy depends on an ability to move between a rigorous physical drama, drawing as much on tag wrestling as on dance, and a finely observed, subtly evoked playing-out of scenes from ordinary life. Add to the skills employed in these contrasting styles a brilliantly inventive use of props, a confident deployment of magic tricks, and a very clever excursion into puppetry, and it becomes obvious that Barabbas is drawing on a formidable range of theatrical strengths.

Even within that impressive range, of course, there are limits to what two actors can do, and there are times when the interplay becomes repetitive to the point of tedium. With time, Barabbas will almost certainly have to expand and to open itself to a wider set of theatrical connections. But it is obvious from *Sick, Dying, Dead, Buried, Out* that the company has the potential for the kind of development that could make it as powerful a force in Irish theatre as Théâtre de Complicité has become in Britain. Seeing how far Barabbas has come in two years, there is no obvious limit to the seriously inspired madness they could yet unleash.

April Bright, by Dermot Bolger

Peacock Theatre
The Irish Times, 29 August 1995

Irish theatre, from the late 1950s to the late 1980s, was driven by the intensely dramatic conflict between tradition and modernity. In the plays of Tom Murphy, Brian Friel, John B. Keane and Hugh Leonard, the whole idea of what is dramatic is bound up with a clash of generations that is also a collision of worlds. A young generation, shaped by ideas of individuality and sexual independence, struggles with an old generation still living with nineteenthcentury values and attitudes. The conflict between these two worlds is intense, often violent, usually tragic. We got not just great plays but great dramas.

There is no dramatic conflict between tradition and modernity in Ireland any more. Daniel Corkery's holy trinity of traditional Irishness – land, nationality and religion – has been dethroned. Insofar as it still exists, traditional Ireland is alienated, angular and embattled, as strange, with its moving statues and paranoid visions, as any avant-garde has ever been. Its image in the theatre is no longer John B. Keane's proud, confident, dangerous Bull McCabe but Sebastian Barry's odd, sad, comic, encircled Boss Grady's boys, waiting for death.

Dermot Bolger's new play at the Peacock, *April Bright*, marks very strongly both this change in Irish society and what it means for Irish theatre. It is a play about generations, imbued with both the contrasts and the continuities of family life now and then. An unmarried couple (played by Denis Conway and Sian Quill), expecting a child after two miscarriages, is moving into a terraced house in Dublin. The arrival of a mysterious visitor (Fedelma Cullen) calls up the ghosts of previous occupants and the haunting spectre of a pre-Noel Brown Ireland, wracked with TB and fear.

What is immediately striking about the play, though, is that this co-existence of generations is a source, not of conflict but of sympathy. As the play unfolds, we soon realize that past and present are there, not to wage war, but to fulfil each other. The ghosts of the visitor's past inhabit the place, not to scare away the newcomers but to give a meaning and a content to the empty spaces and threatening silences of the bare house. The new arrivals, for their part, are there to fulfil the frustrated destiny of the place, to provide the happy ending that was denied to the story of the Bright family.

Sympathy, of course, is the opposite of conflict and in the absence of conflict there is none of the drama that we became used to in what now looks like a golden age of Irish playwriting. But in this, *April Bright* is not especially unusual. Not only is the work of most of the younger Irish playwrights generally undramatic in this sense but so are the later plays of Tom Murphy, Brian Friel and Hugh Leonard. The social roots of conflict in the Irish theatre have, for the time being at least, all but withered.

Theatre, though, can do something else as well as enacting conflict through drama. It can also, as the plays of Yeats do, evoke a world through language and ritual, call things up to 'the eye of the mind'. And, as it happens, Dermot Bolger's plays have never been as far from those of Yeats as their angry social content might suggest. Bolger has always used social realism as a way in to spiritual quest. Plays of his like *The Lament for Arthur Cleary* and *One Last White Horse* are deeply involved with ideas of death and the afterlife. Others, like *In High Germany* and *The Holy Ground* imbue the idea of home with an almost metaphysical resonance.

April Bright, in fact, brings these two quests together, connecting grave invocations of death with a deep longing for home. And at its best, in David Byrne's serene and supple production, it has the evocative power of a religious ritual or a stark fairytale in which the birth of a princess is attended by malign and benign witches, each vying to curse or bless the newborn child.

This is not to say that the absence of drama is not a problem. The interweaving of the two families does at times become schematic and abstract. There are times, indeed, when the play seems to cry out for the two families to stop circling round each other's lives and to enter more boldly into each other's presence, breaking free from the residual remnants of realism and pushing further into a poetic territory where past and present not merely brush against each other but enter into sustained dialogue. That never really happens.

But if such dramatic yearnings are never satisfied, narrative and structural ones are. The world of the past is brilliantly evoked in Bolger's writing and superbly enacted by Dawn Bradfield and Eithne Woodcock as April and Rosie, the Bright children whose imagined future will never be unfolded. And especially as the play moves towards its lyrical ending, death itself, is recast, not as an immutable fact, but as a story. The idea takes hold that the meaning of a story depends on where you choose to end it and that by choosing as an end-point not the conclusion of one generation's life in the house but the beginning of another's, you can turn a death into a birth. That kind of transformation, achieved with great emotional control and a powerful sense of dignity and sympathy, reminds us that so long as it can manage to turn one thing into another, theatre doesn't always have to be dramatic.

The Steward of Christendom, by Sebastian Barry

Gate Theatre
The Irish Times, 9 May 1995

In Sebastian Barry's marvellous play *The Steward of Christendom*, which has just moved on from the Gate in Dublin to Brighton, Luxembourg and Liverpool, the central public image is that of the surrender of Dublin Castle to Michael Collins in 1922. Thomas Dunne, the play's central character, is the chief superintendent of the Dublin Metropolitan Police, and the surrender marks the end, not just of his public role, but of his meaning in history. When we meet him, ten years later in the County Home in Baltinglass, he is flitting in and out of lucidity, a man who cannot make sense of things because he himself does not make sense. The world in which he had a meaning was lost in that moment of surrender.

Barry's brilliant series of plays, of which this is the fifth, are in a sense all about surrender. His people are the footnotes, the oddities, the quirks of history. The tide of time sweeps them beyond familiar ground, and their part is but to surrender to its implacable swell. The miracle of each of the plays is that as each piece of human flotsam floats by we see its head still above water, kept buoyant in an invisible web of words and tenderness. These poor, meaningless people come to mean everything to us.

The miracle in this case happens through one of the great performances of modern times in Irish theatre – Donal McCann's Thomas Dunne. We have seen acting of this unutterable greatness only twice in the last 20 years – Siobhán McKenna's Mommo in *Bailegangaire* and McCann's own Frank Hardy in *Faith Healer*. Like those other performances, this one is sublime in the sense that Edmund Burke had in mind when he wrote that 'whatever is analogous to terror is sublime'. The terror and the stark beauty come from the same source: the cutting away of everything superfluous so that, in the face of approaching death, the bare bones of humanity, pure and unadorned, stand clear.

In this unadorned humanity, McCann, like King Lear, on whom Thomas Dunne, who has lost a kingdom and is now dependent on his three daughters, is partly modelled, presents an 'unaccommodated man […] no more but such a poor bare forked animal as thou art'. Talking to himself, at the beginning of the play, he pictures himself as an animal 'like a dog that won't work without using his teeth, like a dog under sentence'. But at the end of the play, travelling back in memory, he is no longer a dog, but a boy beside a dog, coming home, at last, to his father. In the movement of the language, a human figure comes to stand beside an animal one. In the movement of his great performance, McCann achieves the same transformation, conjuring, from a poor forked animal, an unaccommodated man.

McCann has always been one of the great voices in the theatre, but here he brings an astonishing physical presence to bear as well. The play, in many ways, draws its power from a tension between language and the body, between the stately syntax of Thomas Dunne's speech and the tormenting and humiliation of his body. The language is noble and biblical, the action ignoble and biblical, Thomas Dunne, stripped and tied and beaten like Christ. Often, the writing itself achieves a stunningly simple balance of the spiritual and the physical, the momentous and the everyday: 'The midwife came over immediately and placed her bundle in my arms. It was like holding a three-pound bag of loose corn'.

McCann's genius is to express both the delicacy and the immediacy to their utmost and at the same time. In the course of the play, its political metaphor – a man who has kept order being himself disordered in mind and body – is brought to life in the contrast between speech and action. He speaks the words with magnificent control and dignity. At the same time he turns his body into a despised object. The mountain of flesh that once stood between the queen and her enemies now crumbles and dissolves before our eyes.

As the play goes on, McCann manages to create the impression of a man who is further and further removed from the bag of bones that encases him. The relish with which he eats in the first half of the play becomes a complete lack of interest in food. The urgent concern at the beginning of the play about how he should be dressed becomes a physical indifference so total that he seems not even to feel the blows that rain upon him.

And we come, through the sheer weight of humanity in McCann's performance, to feel this growing indifference as a gradual liberation, a release from the brute reality of the body into the imaginary realms of memory and love. Barry's beautiful metaphor, the repeated phrase 'just as the need for candlelight fails', perfectly poised between death and life, is played out in McCann's performance of guttering candle and rising sun.

Everything else in the production, inevitably, merely plays its part in making space for McCann's extraordinary act of grace. As smaller lights become invisible in proximity to great sources of illumination, so the seven other actors in Max Stafford-Clarke's production are often hard to see, and only Tina Kellegher as Thomas Dunne's Cordelia, Annie, lingers in the mind. Such a fate for an actor might be, in an ordinary play, a disappointment. In this play, and in this extraordinary company, it is a privilege.

The Ginger Ale Boy , by Enda Walsh

Project Theatre
The Irish Times, 12 September 1995

Myles na Gopaleen, in the darkest yet most brilliant of his *Irish Times* columns, employed the disturbing power of ventriloquism to expose the skin-deep culture of modern Ireland. An artists' trade union, seeking work for the horde of unemployed ventriloquists on its books, hits on the idea of hiring them out to theatregoers as escorts for opening nights. The ventriloquists will save the ignorant arriviste of the new middle class from embarrassment by carrying on both sides of the foyer conversation sufficiently loudly for the wise and witty comments on the play to be overheard. The scheme, however, goes wrong when unscrupulous ventriloquists embark on a campaign of blackmail, threatening to utter not merely social solecisms but downright insults unless they are given large amounts of cash. Soon, the foyers of Dublin are ringing with curses and jeers and the veneer of civilization crumbles.

Myles's savage fantasy played on the element of fear that the art of ventriloquism inevitably arouses. The ventriloquist's dummy, though usually employed for children's entertainment, has always had an unmistakable air of menace. Like some kind of humanoid automaton, it occupies a disturbingly uncertain space – a machine with a human voice, a moving statue, a cruelly wooden parody of human gestures. It is a mockery of human individuality, and the dialogue between the dummy and the ventriloquist is a parody of conversation. A man talking to himself with his hand up the back of a gangly doll may be funny, but he is also inevitably an image of madness.

This ambiguity was exploited most memorably, of course, in the film *Magic*. Enda Walsh's play *The Ginger Ale Boy*, presented by the Corcadorcha company at the Belltable in Limerick from tonight after a short run at the Project in Dublin last week, is, so far as I know, the first Irish play to do so, even though the Myles fantasy would have made a wonderful black farce. And it goes straight for the heart of the matter – the bleak gulf between the outward show of fun and the innate intimations of cruelty, isolation and madness in the act of ventriloquism.

It combines, in fact, two familiar themes – that of the sinister undertow of the talking dummy and that of the mother, denied fulfilment in her own life using her son as a vehicle for her dreams. Bobby (Eanna Breathnach) is 28 and still living with his mother, his silent father and his dummy, Barney (Bríd Ní Chionaola). Mother (Fiona Peck) places on his fragile shoulders the burden of making up for the bitter disappointment of her marriage and her move from England to Cork. From the grim paradox that she is trying to make their lives better by having Bobby tell jokes, while knowing that they themselves are 'the joke on everyone's lips', Walsh fashions his sorrowful mystery.

So familiar are these themes, though, that we know exactly from the start how they will be played out. And this is the weakness in a play that manages, in spite of it, to be intermittently compelling and consistently imaginative. There are some variations on the themes. The dummy is less an alter ego for the disturbed Bobby than an indicator of his lack of a stable ego at all. The mother is not an Irish Mammy, but an Englishwoman disgusted by the Ireland in which she has ended up. But they are not sufficient to give the piece the one element that any drama in whatever form must have – a sense of change.

The play has, in other words, one of Aristotle's elements of tragedy – pity – but not the other – fear. Bobby and Mother are genuinely pitiful, and Breathnach and Peek perform so well that they manage to make characters with almost no freedom and no choice much more than mere ciphers of urban despair. Breathnach conveys utterly the anguish and confusion of a man with the ambitions of an adult but the emotional equipment of a frightened child. Peek gives to his torment a context, both in personal history and in social environment, creating with passionate conviction the dilemma of a woman caught between her own sense of destiny and the realities of poverty and deprivation.

What the play doesn't do, though, is to exploit the nightmarish quality of the ventriloquist's dummy, or the dramatic possibilities of Bobby's act. Ní Chionaola's creation of Barney the dummy is so complete, so accurate in gesture and voice, that you expect a much more coherent and purposeful use of the opportunities she creates for a real voyage into the terrifying depths of the broken mind. That doesn't happen, and as a consequence the play sacrifices both the drama of fear itself and the simple narrative drive for an audience wondering what is going to happen next. Because the basic elements of the story remain exactly the same all the way through, the piece loses its ability to surprise long before the end.

To some extent Pat Kiernan's production makes up for this loss with its vigour, invention, and clever use of space. It fills the gap with any material to hand – songs, video, dances, even a mini-drama on an ice-cream van, all performed by a four-strong chorus. Before you can say 'a gottle of geer', there seems always to be another trick to throw in. But these are, perhaps inevitably, hit-and-miss weapons, and the musical numbers in particular struggle to justify themselves. The most memorable images are the simplest ones: Bobby interviewing himself on make-believe TV while Mother scrubs the toilet-bowl, Bobby kicking his way out of a cupboard, Bobby's Love Interest (Sorcha Carroll) describing a blind date with him while the dummy enacts it. In images like those we glimpse a writer and a company with the skills to match a laudably boundless ambition.

Monkey, by Michael West

Peacock Theatre
The Irish Times, 7 November 1995

The writer C.S. Lewis once had to mark school exam papers which asked a question about Chauntecleer and Pertelote, a cock and a hen in Chaucer's *Nun's Priest's Tale*. The answers were written by 'boys whose form-master was apparently a breeder of poultry. Everything that Chaucer had said in describing Chauntecleer and Pertelote was treated by them solely as evidence about the precise breed of these two birds [...]. They proved beyond doubt that Chauntecleer was very different from our modernized specialized strains and much closer to the old English 'barn door fowl'. But I couldn't help feeling that they had missed something'.

Equally, faced with criticism of Michael West's short wordless play *Monkey*, which ran at the Peacock last week based on the assumption that it is essentially about monkeys, one can't help feeling that something has been missed. Nobody really believes that Mickey Mouse cartoons are about mice. Nobody imagines that Aesop's fable of the hare and the tortoise is a study of motion in mammals and reptiles. So why, in the theatre, faced with three actors behaving like monkeys, should we assume that what is at issue is the behaviour of our fellow primates?

It helps, in a sense, that *Monkey* grows very obviously out of a familiar visual image, that of the three monkeys See No Evil, Hear No Evil and Speak No Evil. By starting from such a well-known point, *Monkey* puts itself forward as a variation on a theme rather than a radical new departure. One monkey is deaf, another dumb, the third blind, the disabilities signalled simply by the placing of cloths around the ears, eyes and mouth.

This is not, of course, unlike Beckett's games with dislocated bodies in which a mouth or a torso, or a pair of eyes become disassociated from the rest of the human frame. There is the same surreal feeling of the senses at war with each other. The three monkeys are bombarded alternately with harsh sound and blinding light, so that what affects Deaf and Dumb will not affect Blind, and what affects Dumb and Blind will not affect Deaf. The complex of sense that makes up human consciousness is thus sundered. Split from each other the parts begin to collide and struggle, until in the end each has acquired the other's disability.

This links the piece, via Beckett, to the Yeats of *The Cat and the Moon*, who is in turn using images from Schopenhauer, and, less obviously, to Tom Murphy's last play, *Too Late for Logic*. There is also, in *Monkey*, the same feeling of a mathematical process that you often get in Beckett, of a careful series of operations being performed in sequence until every variant has been tried and found wanting. To some degree, this gives *Monkey* the sense of a trial piece, of a series of exercises within a set and predictable pattern.

What saves it from being dull, though, is a very Beckettian sense of humour and a very unBeckettian freedom of movement. West's clever direction incorporates elements of farce and slapstick which provide welcome relief from the bleakness of the theme. His work has always shown a strong interest in physical comedy, the hysterical chaos of things falling apart, and to a degree what happens here is that the actors become objects, thrown around in the same haphazard way that props are used in a farce.

But more importantly, *Monkey* depends on the kind of physical expressiveness and precision that used to be alien to the Irish theatre. The assurance with which the actors move and shape themselves and the fluidity with which West uses both pace and space are impressive reminders of just how far Irish theatre has come from stilted naturalism.

This kind of work is never going to be complete in itself – especially at this stage in the twentieth century game, when everything that there is to say about the absurdity of the human condition has been said already. It has to feed back into a process of development for a writer. But in Michael West's case there is more than enough evidence of intelligence, boldness and assurance to make the process as well as the end result well worth watching.

A Night in November, by Marie Jones

Andrews Lane Theatre
The Irish Times, 5 December 1995

Marie Jones's *A Night in November* is probably the most successful Irish play of the last 18 months. Since it opened in West Belfast in August, 1994, it has toured almost continually in the North, the Republic and Britain, winning awards and praise. After its second run at Andrews Lane Theatre in Dublin (where it has been receiving standing ovations) finishes on Saturday night, it is off to New York. It has just been published by New Island Books.

And it is easy to see why all of this is so. It has a very skilful script, full of acute observation, wicked humour and compelling verbal energy. The production by Pam Brighton for Dubbeljoint is as tight as a drum, with the kind of variety of pace and rich use of the stage that ought to be impossible in a simple, one-actor show. It has a performance of extraordinary virtuosity by Dan Gordon, full of charm and grace and passionate conviction. And, unfortunately, it tells a Catholic audience exactly what it wants to hear: that Northern Protestants are just like us, except that they're too tight-arsed to admit it.

Behind all its charm, *A Night in November* depends on a very simple opposition. On the one side, there is our hero Kenneth Norman McAllister. He is not just a Northern Protestant but, explicitly, a representative Northern Protestant. He and his family are, he tells us 'the perfect Prods, we come in kits, we are standard regulation, we come from the one design […], our dimensions never vary, and that's the way we want it'. And that

standard-issue Ulster Prod, is, the play tells us, a pathetic
creature: a sly bigot, a control freak afraid to step on the grass, a
sexless automaton trapped in a loveless marriage.

On the other side, there are Catholics. Catholics have untidy
houses, great sex lives, teems of children, happy-go-lucky
attitudes. Protestants have on their bookshelves unread uniform
volumes of the world's classics bound in burgundy leather.
Catholics have 'books of all shapes and sizes, books that looked
read, had dog ears, piles and piles of them'. Protestant football
fans scream sectarian abuse at 'Fenians'; Catholic football fans
want to have Paul McGrath's babies. And the play is the story of
how Kenneth goes from being a perfect Prod to being part of
Jack's Army, a delirious, liberated real Irish man in tricoloured
shorts.

If this story sounds familiar, that's because it is. It is every
Noble Savage story ever written. It is *The Last of the Mohicans*. It is
Mutiny on the Bounty, with Kenneth starting out as Captain Bligh
and ending up as Fletcher Christian, garlanded by Tahitian
maidens with Dublin accents. It is Matthew Arnold's stereotype
of rational Saxons and imaginative Celts. It is the Irish Revival,
with dissatisfied Protestants inventing a Catholic Other to fill in
the gaps in their own desires. And it is all of this in an
astonishingly crude, apparently unselfconscious form, without
the slightest leavening of irony or complexity.

Even more surprising, coming from a writer with a passion
for exploring the lives of ordinary women, is the fact that this
crude opposition is also played out in terms of gender. Kenneth's
liberation is not just out of dour Protestantism and into the good
company of Irish Catholics, it is also out of the company of his
'stupid empty-headed bitch' of a wife and into a state of grace
defined by the fact that 'I was one of the lads and the lads all
looked out for each other'. His great act of rebellion involves
taking all of the money he can lay his hands on, slipping out of
the house in secret, and leaving his wife and children behind. The
play's sexual politics, in other words, are about as profound as its
ethnic politics are.

However misguided it may be in the North to attack
sectarianism by playing to such blatantly sectarian stereotypes, it

is even more so in the South. For an audience that might share Kenneth's Northern Protestant identity, the play could be challenging and uncomfortable, even if not always for the best of reasons.

But for a Southern audience, it is merely ingratiating. It heaps on the flattery with an unctuousness that would make Uriah Heep sick. It tells us that we are a great bloody crowd altogether, a 'wild, untameable' bunch who 'look after their own'. And it tells us that the only thing that stops the perfect Prods from joining our 'parade of the best there is in human nature' is their own stupidity. Why wouldn't we be on our feet cheering and clapping?

The answer to that question should be not just that self-deluding stereotypes make for bad politics, but that flattering the audience is a betrayal of theatre. I have never seen a play that required a Dublin audience to put less on the line, to expose so few of its own assumptions and prejudices to the risks that engagement with a piece of theatre ought to entail. In contrast to the play it most resembles on the surface – Dermot Bolger's one-man play about Irish soccer fans, *In High Germany* – it buys into every soft-focus cliché ever invented about what it means to be Irish. And in doing so it sells short the great theatrical skills that go into its making.

The great irony of all of this is that the flattery is really the old bigotry reversed. *A Night in November* replays bigoted images of Irish Catholic vices – shiftlessness, unpredictability, wildness – as virtues. And in that sense, the play can be excused any taint of bias. It is equally insulting to both sides, the only difference being that it insults the identity of Protestants and the intelligence of Catholics.

The Beauty Queen of Leenane, by Martin McDonagh

Town Hall Theatre, Galway
The Irish Times, 6 February 1996

As well as being one of the most auspicious debuts by an Irish playwright in the past 25 years, Martin McDonagh's *The Beauty*

Queen of Leenane, which opened last week at the new Town Hall
Theatre in Galway, is also the most intriguing Anglo-Irish fusion
since Jack Charlton first pulled on a green tracksuit.

In it, Harold Pinter and Joe Orton blend seamlessly with Tom
Murphy and John B. Keane to create a vibrantly original mixture
of absurd comedy and cruel melodrama. McDonagh's London-
Irish background allows him to hold in perfect tension an
extraordinary range of elements from both sides of the Irish Sea.

As in Pinter, everyday banality acquires sinister undertones. As
in Orton, mundane speech is bent into outrageous shapes
without ever losing its demotic feel. But there is also a dark
comedy of yearning and despair reminiscent of Murphy, and a
situation – a 40-year-old spinster trapped with a monstrous old
woman in a remote house in the West – that echoes his great
play *Bailegangaire*.

There is a wildly melodramatic plot of which the early John B.
Keane might have been proud. And all of this is held together
with an utterly 1990s sensibility, in which knowing and playful
pastiche becomes indistinguishable from serious and sober
intent.

The mixture of elements makes sense because the country in
which McDonagh's play is set is pre-modern and post-modern at
the same time. The 1950s is laid over the 1990s, giving the play's
apparent realism the ghostly, dizzying feel of a superimposed
photograph. All the elements that make up the picture are real,
but their combined effect is one that questions the very idea of
reality.

One of the superimposed pictures is a black-and-white still
from an Abbey play of the 1950s: west of Ireland virgins and
London building sites, tyrannical mothers and returned Yanks. In
it, Marie Mullen's Maureen lives with her terrible mother (Anna
Manahan) in a house up a Connemara hill. A meeting with Pato,
a local man back on holiday from the building sites (Brian F.
O'Byrne) holds out the promise of happiness that you know
from the start will be destroyed by the mother.

But the other picture is a lurid Polaroid of a post-modern
landscape, a disintegrating place somewhere between London
and Boston, saturated in Irish rain and Australian soaps, a place

in which it is hard to remember anyone's name, in which news of murders floats in through the television screen, in which the blurring of personal identities makes the line between the real and the unreal dangerously thin. And behind these garish colours, there are shadows in which madness and violence lurk, waiting to emerge.

Looking at both pictures at the same time, you experience a series of double takes. You are drawn into the comfortable, melodramatic rush of the plot, knowing all the time that it is taking you to places you don't want to go, wondering why conversations keep throwing up images of violence and death, wondering why Maureen's party dress looks as if it could be for a funeral as well as a hooley. You find yourself in two minds most of the time.

And as the real and the unreal become for Maureen increasingly hard to tell apart, the whole idea of theatrical realism becomes itself the biggest double take of all. The conventions of domestic drama are at once followed and parodied. The kitchen sink is present and prominent, but only to provide a pungent running gag. The domestic details – Kimberley biscuits, lumpy Complan – that are meant to provide a 'realistic' backdrop to the action are instead pushed relentlessly into the foreground by McDonagh's brilliant dialogue. And the domestic appliances that dominate Francis O'Connor's subtle set become gradually less cosy and more sinister, as objects like the cooker, the cooking oil and the poker become portents of violence and cruelty.

All of this is accomplished with an assurance astonishing in a first play. There is just one scene, dictated by the need to tell the audience the contents of a crucial letter from Pato to Maureen, where the stylistic integrity of the piece is broken. But what is really important is that McDonagh is more than just a very clever theatrical stylist. His tricks and turns have a purpose. They are bridges over a deep pit of sympathy and sorrow, illuminated by a tragic vision of stunted and frustrated lives, that make any comparison with Quentin Tarantino, prompted by outward similarities of violence and language, merely superficial.

And in Garry Hynes's superb production, perfectly pitched between the comic and the grotesque, it is Marie Mullen who embodies that vision. In one of her finest performances, Mullen combines a minute sense of detail in her movements and expressions with the ability to suggest all the time that those details don't ever add up to a stable whole. Her Maureen is now girlish, now old, now vulnerable, now cruel, now warm, now cold – a bundle of tentative possibilities in search of a personality. With the disciplined, assured work of Manahan, O'Byrne and Tom Murphy as Pato's brother Ray around her, she forms the broken heart of the play's clever games of form and meaning.

In his stunning final scene, McDonagh brings together the trivial and the tragic, an ascent into the heights of loopiness and a descent into the depths of despair. The effect is hysterical in both senses – wildly funny in its incongruity, crushingly bleak in its madness – and deeply unsettling. And as it starts to sink in, you realize that a new force has hit Irish theatre.

The Gay Detective, by Gerard Stembridge

Project Arts Centre
The Irish Times, 20 February 1996

If Gerard Stembridge's new play at the Project, *The Gay Detective*, were really, as it almost is, a film of a Raymond Chandler novel, it would be hard to cast Philip Marlowe. The usual suspects – Robert Mitchum, say, or Humphrey Bogart – wouldn't do.

For, even though *The Gay Detective* is a self-conscious journey down Chandler's mean streets, his hero has none of the hard-bitten, down-at-heel ambiguity of a Philip Marlowe. He is that oddest of things, an innocent man, almost entirely good, played by Peter Hanly as such. And the play itself is just as odd – a pastiche that is actually more serious than the original, a clever exercise in style that is also an excursion into good and evil.

Like Tom Murphy in *The Blue Macushla*, Stembridge uses the film noir of the 1930s and 1940s as a metaphor for social and political corruption in modern Ireland. *The Gay Detective* is a simpler play than Murphy's, the language less highly wrought, the allegory less ambitious. It doesn't have the same complexity of texture. But at its core is a sense of moral darkness no less profound. And the relative simplicity of the play has the advantage of making that vision entirely clear.

The play, in other words, is simple but not naive. It takes a well-tried form – a standard detective thriller – and makes use of its main advantage for a writer. The great thing about detective stories is that they provide a form in which an audience can be led through a cross-section of a society. Stembridge uses the investigation of a crime – the murder of a TD in a gay sauna in Dublin – as the excuse for sending his Garda detective sergeant, Pat, on a journey through a looking-glass Ireland.

What makes this journey work as a play, though, is the fact that it is not just a social odyssey but also a sexual one. Woven through it is the detective's search for sex and love, as he goes from casual encounters to real commitment. As well as a political metaphor, the play offers a moral one, as Pat struggles to distinguish the sexual roles he plays in his undercover investigation from the realities of his relationship with his lover Ginger (Eddie Tighe).

What makes the play original is the way it puts these sexual and political, private and public, themes together. *The Gay Detective* is far from being the first Irish play to deal sympathetically with homosexual characters. But it is, I think, the first to take those characters entirely for granted. What might be called gay issues – decriminalization, queer-bashing, staying in the closet, homophobia – run through the play, but as facts of life, not as issues.

The play is emphatically not about male homosexuality, in that it treats the state of being gay as in itself perfectly normal and morally neutral. The hero and his lover are gay. So are the villains. What the play does is simply to use gay subculture as a mirror for Irish society. Seeing it reversed in that mirror, you pay more attention to the writing on the wall.

It is important in achieving this that, when it comes to sex, the play is explicit but not literal. Sexual encounters are played out on stage, but never in such a way that they become naturalistic. And this is as important to the play's content as it is to its style. It makes you aware all the time that these sexual encounters are not just private actions, but also social performances. What the gay context does is to show us that sex is hedged around with rules and dangers that derive from the world outside. That what matters, in other words, is not whether sex is gay or straight, but whether it is human or inhuman.

To keep hold of this idea, the play needs to unfold with great discipline, and here the advantage of the writer also being the director is immense. As Pat's quest takes him deeper and deeper into a corrupt underworld of political and personal abuse, the tone of the play has to change very slowly from light to darkness, and yet retain its formal coherence. Stembridge paces the change with great skill. More importantly, he keeps control of the degree to which the characters are stylized (most have animal names, emphasizing their unreality), and the degree to which the style gives way to serious substance.

Not only does Peter Hanly's earnest, fresh-faced Pat gradually take on an obsessive air, but the characters around him are almost entirely transformed. Almost everyone starts out as a comic caricature: Pat's Garda boss Bear (the superb Tom Hickey) as a harmless Inspector Plod, his lover Ginger as a fairy queen, Ginger's neighbour Puppy (Shelly McGlynn) as a scatty fag-hag. But all of them become over time more real – the boss a cynical bigot, the lover a dying man, the neighbour a lost woman. The effect is like that of characters slowly emerging out of a movie world into something very like a real one.

And the writing works the same way, moving from a dry, brittle wit that makes the first half hilarious to a brusque and brutal realism that makes the second increasingly uncomfortable. It is a transition that some may find hard to take. But it comes from a determination to use a command of style and humour for a serious moral purpose, a refusal of easy options that makes *The Gay Detective* not just a clever play but also a genuinely brave one.

Portia Coughlan, by Marina Carr

Peacock Theatre
The Irish Times, 2 April 1996

The landscape of Marina Carr's plays is both literally and metaphorically watery. Her Midlands ground is soft underfoot, boggy and unstable, bounded by lakes and rivers. And the language of her characters flows with the same lazy meander, words oozing into each other until the distinctions between them are blurred, and all the hard, clear consonants are drowned.

At the start of her new play at the Peacock, *Portia Coughlan*, a factory owner (Seán Rocks) slips home in the morning to see his wife, the eponymous Portia, already working her way through a bottle of brandy. He says: 'Tin a' clache i'tha mornin' an ya'are ah ud arready'. Normal speech is so slurred that it becomes impossible to tell drunk from sober. The words, like the landscape, are flat and slow, and they suck you down into treacherous depths.

And both landscape and speech belong to the wider set of metaphors that hold the play together, images in which clear distinctions keep breaking down. Portia and her twin brother Gabriel are still locked together, as they were in the womb, even though he drowned himself in the river 15 years before, on their joint fifteenth birthday.

And in that awful psychic entanglement, the borders between the living and the dead, between male and female, between the born and the unborn, between the past and the present, dissolve in the river's interminable flow. The dead boy and the living woman are the same person, a single personality that has been sundered and that can only be made whole again by Portia's death.

It is terribly unsteady ground for a piece of theatre to stand on. If the basic oppositions by which we understand the world cannot be taken for granted, then clearly the simple rules of cause and effect that drive most plays cannot be maintained. It takes great courage to go out on stage without them, and even greater skill to make it work. With great direction, and acting of extraordinary coherence, it does. The play becomes a dark and difficult passage over ground that constantly seems about to give way, but one that does reach some commanding heights.

As in her last play, *The Mai*, Carr is concerned with the notion of family lines, and stretches the story over four generations. And that story is unremittingly bleak. Though Portia Coughlan draws most openly on Shakespeare's *The Merchant of Venice* (Portia's name, the fact that she comes from Belmont, her choice between suitors), its tragedy is much more Greek than Shakespearean.

This is the world of Aeschylus and Sophocles in which a course of action is set in motion in the distant past and works its way unrelentingly through the present. Portia has never really entered the world at all, but remains trapped in the womb of the past, 'where there's no brathin', no thinkin', no seein', on'y darcheness an' heart drums …'.

Just in case the audience might have any illusions of escape, Carr places the action in the middle of the play, cutting off all hope. What we watch thereafter is a kind of psychic autopsy, a cold delving into the soft tissues of Portia's mind to discover and pluck out the cause of death: the knotty, incestuous society of a rural Ireland that has seldom been painted in such dark colours.

To act the part of someone who knows from the start that she is doomed and helpless is a ferocious challenge for Derbhle Crotty as Portia, and in meeting it she shows again why she is such a superb resource for playwrights of daring. Here she combines ferocity with vulnerability, lightning intelligence with dark self-destructiveness, to give off the angry, hopeless energy off a bee trapped in a bottle.

That energy is essential, for if Portia once settles into any single emotional mode, the play would sink under its own weight. Crotty is able to remake the mood from moment to moment, to flow like the Belmont River that marks the limit of Portia's life, and to carry the play along with her.

This achievement is consistent with everything else in Garry Hynes's brilliant production. Knowing that there is no clear line of cause and effect to thread through the play, Hynes holds instead to the language. Instead of reacting against the indistinct, blurry quality of the speech, she works with it to fashion a style in which there are few full stops. Using the freedom of Kandis Cook's minimalist design, and very few props, she draws the play away from its roots in naturalism and towards a vivid poetry of movement in which places and actions melt into each other.

In this style, neither the difficulty of the speech nor the bleakness of the story is in any way mitigated or softened. On the other hand, going all the way with what is inherent in the play produces performances that are not just individually admirable but also full of collective integrity. It is rare to see a play cast with such depth (Tom Hickey, Des Keogh, Stella McCusker, Pauline Flanagan and Marion O'Dwyer proving the adage that there are no minor roles, only minor actors), even rarer to see all the actors so closely attuned to each other and to the play.

The result is never easy and always grim. But it has, like the boggy landscape on which it is set, a harsh, heavy beauty all its own.

True Lines and Double Helix, by John Crowley et al.

Peacock Theatre
The Irish Times, 18 June 1996

For most of this century Irish theatre has been obsessed with a sense of place, and one of the most pertinent questions you could ask about any Irish play was what part of the country it came from. It made sense to talk of Synge's Mayo and Yeats's Sligo, of O'Casey's Dublin and Leonard's Dalkey, of Keane's North Kerry, Murphy's Tuam and Friel's Donegal. Almost everything on the stage – language, character, action – seemed to have not just a setting but a location. Surrounding it was not just a fictional context, but a local habitation with a name. And surrounding that vividly imagined place was a bigger place called Ireland.

This sense of place hasn't evaporated overnight, and it remains obvious in, for instance, the relationship between Billy Roche's plays and the town of Wexford, or between Marina Carr's work and the Midlands. But even in these cases, there is also a feeling that the individual places have become free-floating and disconnected from any larger whole. They have become porous and diffuse, bitterly aware that their apparent stability is maintained only at the cost of the continual export of instabilities.

In two devised plays for Kilkenny's Bickerstaffe Theatre, *True Lines* and *Double Helix*, John Crowley and his actors have taken this process much further, and defined Irishness not as a sense of place but as a sense of placelessness. In both pieces the main characters are Irish. In neither does any of the action happen in Ireland. *True Lines* was set in four continents – in Berlin, in Arizona, in Australia, and in Ethiopia. *Double Helix*, now at the Peacock in a co-production between Bickerstaffe and the Abbey, takes place in Paris, Montreal, Rome, Turin, New York, Rio, and Manaus.

Here, dislocation is so extreme that there is no real sense of location left at all. Ireland is no longer, for these young travellers, even a stable point of reference from which to measure the distances they have traversed. Their only fixed centre lies in the play of motion and emotion, in the confused but still powerful bonds of love that tie them to the people they have left behind.

These are not exiles pining for a native place, but people who exist, as actors, photographers and students, within an abstract, highly mediated universe. One of the most powerful aspect of the piece, indeed, is the glittering stream of projected images – maps, paintings, photographs – that flows over and around the characters, placing them, if anywhere, in the teeming flush of signs that is the contemporary world. They are inhabitants of a global village where place has ceased to be a physical reality and has become instead a set of visual stimuli, emotional connections and professional networks. Even when set adrift in foreign cities, they see familiar faces. In the world of the play, coincidence is not even worth remarking on, because it is a world in which random encounters are the norm.

If this were all that is going on in *Double Helix*, it would be more interesting as a symptom of the times than an exploration of them. But, as with *True Lines*, the drama comes from the fact that for all their homelessness, the characters have to acknowledge one inescapable home – the body.

They carry within them, written into the very genes that make them what they are, connections to history and geography, to their ancestors and their contemporaries. Andrew (Martin Murphy) carries the genes for Huntingdon's disease. Jennifer (Gertrude Montgomery) carries inside her Andrew's child, who may also carry the fatal genes. Seán (Stephen Kennedy) has inherited from his parents both diabetes and an obsession with the Beatles *White Album*. Julie (Derdriu Ring) suffers the most inescapably bodily fate of all – death.

Through a simple but beautifully worked set of counterpoints between the intimate and the universal, between the body and the world, the piece asks what the meaning of heredity can be. The only tie to the past, to a sense of place, is what is in the blood: the genetic codes that link one generation to another. And the play follows, in the end quite literally, these blood lines across the continents.

Double Helix explores rather than answers these questions, and indeed it is at its best when it is most content to enjoy connections rather than to explain them. The more literal moments – the explanations of basic genetics, the rather undigested chunks of *Hamlet* – are the ones with the least energy. Conversely, some of the most unlikely visual and verbal conjunctions of private and public space – between a map of the Amazon and a blood transfusion, between Andrew's image of the monster he will become as a result of his disease and the Turin Shroud, between the image that haunts the photographer Jo (Olwen Fouéré) of a map of New York tattooed onto a man's body – have all the startling clarity of a metaphysical conceit in a John Donne poem. When the play strikes out most boldly for the poetic logic that may be the only kind of logic available in the culture of the 1990s, it can be exhilarating.

Strawberries in December, by Antoine Ó Flatharta

Peacock Theatre
The Irish Times, 17 September 1996

Theatre and youth culture seem, these days, to be increasingly at odds. Theatre needs time and concentration. Though it can be tricked out with all sorts of spectacle, it depends inescapably on very bare necessities – space, time, human presence. It is no good at grabbing the attention quickly. An audience is usually required to put up with a period of uncertainty during which not merely the characters and the situation but the very conventions of the piece, have to be learned. It is, in an age of instant replay, unrepeatable: you get it first time or not at all. In an MTV world of instant excitement and immediate boredom, of short attention spans and rapid eye movements, it can seem like a doomed anachronism.

The admirable thing about the National Youth Theatre's production of Antoine Ó Flatharta's specially-commissioned *Strawberries in December*, which ended its run at the Peacock on Saturday night, is that it never pretended otherwise. It would have been very easy for NYT, in its first production since 1989, to put on a nice Shakespeare or a modern classic, pretend that all was right with the future of theatre and accept a ritual pat on the head from its elders.

But NYT doesn't need to be patronized. The number of youth theatres has grown phenomenally, from three in 1986 to more than 50 now. The youth theatre movement has fed indirectly into the work of Gerard Stembridge and Paul Mercier. Brian Brady, who directed *Strawberries in December*, is himself a product of youth theatre. Both as an end in itself and as a long-term resource for Irish theatre as a whole, the movement has no need to justify itself.

It deserves great credit, therefore, for not taking the soft option of pretending that theatre has a natural and stable place in the hearts and minds of young people now. Instead, it had the courage to produce a piece as angular and hyperactive as contemporary culture itself. If the result was very far from being a well-made play, it was something much more honest and adventurous.

Strawberries in December could be seen in one sense as a play that asked fundamental questions about its own existence. Instead of making blithe assumptions, it implicitly asked whether 'youth theatre' is not in itself a contradiction in terms: is it possible to be at one and the same time true to the cultural experiences of young people now and to operate within the conventions of theatrical form? It matters much less that the answers it suggested were equivocal than that they were asked in the first place.

Antoine Ó Flatharta's work has always been concerned with the tension between a hankering after stability on the one hand and the placeless and amorphous feel of the contemporary technological village on the other. Television and film, karaoke and computers, saturate his landscapes, unsettling identities and undermining language itself. *Strawberries in December*, though set in a supermarket, was also dominated by disembodied technologies – irradiated fruit, mobile phones, tapes, late-night radio confessionals, coded electronic security devices. On Feargal Doyle's excellent set, the supermarket shelves were deliberately reminiscent of a bank of television monitors. In the story played out around it, the real and unreal were virtually indistinguishable. The young woman market-testing margarine was hardly more grounded in reality than the young man obsessed with messages from aliens.

The piece went further than Ó Flatharta has gone before, though, bringing a sense of disconnection right into the heart of the play itself. The nod in the direction of plot and character, a thin storyline about a young woman returning from Spain to manage her dead father's supermarket, was more like a barely perceptible tic. The play was at its weakest, indeed, when it tried to keep up the pretence of a conventional storyline, suggesting motives for the actions of characters who hardly existed as such.

For the most part, the laws of cause and effect were discarded in favour of a jerky jumble of appearances in which neither time nor place could hold good, and no fewer than 26 characters moved in and out of view. The play worked off the idea of layers of reality – the ghosts of the past, the confusions of the present, the desires of the future – coexisting. The effect was as enervating, but also sometimes as mesmerizing, as a 90-minute, non-stop session of channel-hopping with the remote control, snatched sounds and fragmented visions succeeding each other in an almost random order.

It is hardly surprising that this did not produce a theatrical classic. But it is hardly very important either. With Brian Brady's disciplined direction and Ó Flatharta's ability to create powerfully expressive moments, a sense of theatrical form did emerge from the relentless flow of barely connected images. Brady imposed a visual coherence, culminating in a striking tableau of candlelit faces stacked on the shelves, and managed to move 26 actors into and out of a small space without ever succumbing to chaos.

And Ó Flatharta allowed a simple yearning for wholeness to emerge unsentimentally from all the excess of images. What more should be asked from a National Youth Theatre than evidence that the theatrical desire to give a shape to formless existences remains alive?

In a Little World of Our Own, by Gary Mitchell

Peacock Theatre
The Irish Times, 18 February 1997

Tragedies tend to be written at very specific times and in very particular places. To write one, you need to be able to draw on a society that is caught between two worlds. You need the chance to imagine people who are so divided within themselves between one world and the other that whatever they do will be wrong.

In the late 1950s and the 1960s, the Republic was such a place at such a time, and its theatre produced some remarkable tragedies. Gary Mitchell's *In a Little World of Our Own* at the Peacock suggests that contemporary Northern Ireland may offer the same possibilities.

Tragedy, oddly enough, seldom emerges from utterly bleak circumstances. If there is no change and no hope – as in Northern Ireland for most of the last 30 years – you can get plays that are grim, sad and violent. But you can't get the tragic tension, the idea that there are credible grounds for hope that will, in the course of the action, be blighted. In that sense, Gary Mitchell's play, though it is dark and sombre, is a tentative sign that something has changed. The dashing of hopes that it enacts implies at least that there was in the first place some possibility of hopes being fulfilled.

This is, in other words, very much a play of the Peace Process, of a time when people have been stretched between hope and despair, between longing and revulsion. Like the current return to violence, its action is all the more terrible because an alternative is just about imaginable. The opening exchanges of the play create a specific political context: tension within the UDA about whether to follow a path towards peace and politics or whether to accept, as the hardman brother Ray (Stuart Graham) does, that 'the world is a violent place'.

The play is set in the Protestant Rathcoole estate in North Belfast, and, declaring its tragic intentions, follows the classical unities – a single action (the destruction of three brothers), played out in a single place (the garish sitting room of their house), over a single day. As in a Greek tragedy, all of the violent events – beating, rape, murder – take place off stage. And one character, Walter (superbly played by Lalor Roddy), acts as both Chorus (filling in offstage details, prompting the action, laying out the alternatives) and Messenger, bringing word to and from the paramilitary leadership.

The play never leaves this political context, and at one level it is almost an allegory of paramilitarism, in which the family stands for the tribe. The action is driven by forces that are felt in the public world as well as the private – the resort to irrational violence that comes into play when the survival of the family is threatened, the scapegoating of a 'Taig' for the family's own sins.

The strength of the writing, though, is that this political division is reflected within the family, not through abstract argument, but through a struggle over who is to look after the mentally disabled brother Richard (the excellent Marc O'Shea). Is he to go to a new house with Gordon (Seán Kearns)and his God-fearing wife-to-be (Andrea Irvine) thus becoming part of a new, respectable future in which the past is left behind? Or is he to stay with Ray, who, in spite of his violent outlook, treats him with tenderness and respect?

Mitchell shows great skill in turning what might have been a rather mechanical opposition into a complex interaction: the 'bad' Ray is also intelligent and loving; the 'good' Gordon is priggish and weak. As in a Tom Murphy play, there is a sense that the two together might make one decent human being. But, split as they are, dreams of decency are doomed to slip away, slowly at first, and then in an avalanche of disaster. By the end, everything – Ray's power, Richard's innocence, Gordon's hopes for a normal life – is in ruins.

Conall Morrison's production is terrific: very well cast, perfectly paced, always on edge but never hysterical or bathetic.

The only misjudgement is the decision to go for a naturalistic set, well designed by Kathy Strachan, in which the fussy furniture sits oddly with the classical form and the Old Testament resonances that echo through the play as the family's fate comes to resemble a distorted echo of Abraham and Isaac. A starker, less literal, setting would have been riskier – and there are plenty of risks associated with a play like this anyway – but it might also have taken away the nagging feeling that the characters are not quite big enough to operate on a truly tragic scale.

This is, nonetheless, an utterly compelling piece of theatre and, for all the bleakness of the action, an oddly hopeful one. If it is true that terrible events can only really be seen when they are over, then the relentlessness of Gary Mitchell's gaze and the quality of his vision suggest that his play may in its own way mark a beginning of the end.

Catalpa, by Donal O'Kelly

Gate Theatre
The Irish Times, 25 March 1997

Considering how much popular interest there is in Irish history, it is remarkable there are so few history plays in our theatre. In most European countries, and especially in England, there is a substantial body of drama in which the past is recapitulated, recovered and redefined.

Here – perhaps because history still has a present tense – there isn't. What we have are not history plays but plays about history: how it is made and why. In its title and content, Brian Friel's *Making History*, a play not about Hugh O'Neill but about the construction of a historical narrative around him, is emblematic.

Recently, two brilliant plays have gone even further, and reversed the usual relationship between theatre and history. Instead of taking a historical event and then dramatizing it, they have taken a theatrical event and given it a historical reference. In Tom Mac Intyre's *Good Evening, Mr Collins* and in Sebastian Barry's *The Steward of Christendom*, the border between the past and the present has ceased to exist. The chronological logic of history has been replaced by the radical openness of theatre in which all that matters is, as Tom Murphy puts it in *The Gigli Concert*, that 'you and I are alive in time at the same time'.

Donal O'Kelly's magnificent *Catalpa*, originally produced by Red Kettle in 1995 and now at the Gate in Dublin, belongs in the same company. It makes use of a historical event, the extraordinary jailbreak of the 1870s in which an American whaling boat snatched six Irish Fenian prisoners from Western Australia and brought them all the way to New York, but it is not about that event. The story is refracted through a double prism of cinema and theatre, so the white light of historical truth is broken up into a fabulous rainbow whose colours are fact and imagination, triumph and failure, sex and politics, the public and the personal.

From the very start of the play, we are unsure what century we are in. Giles Cadle's set – a big, bare and decrepit Georgian room – suggests a nineteenth century slum. But when Donal O'Kelly enters, he is wearing 1990s cycling gear. Nothing in the room suggests our world, yet he is clearly of it, for as he begins to speak, his talk is of Hollywood moguls and Tom Cruise. He has failed to sell his epic movie script on the voyage of the *Catalpa*, so he is going to tell us the picture.

The feel is a bit like *Kiss of the Spider Woman* played by one actor. There is the same mixture of movie fantasy and political intrigue, but instead of being alternative worlds, they have melted into each other. And this isn't just as aspect of the writing: it is embodied in O'Kelly's extraordinary performance.

It is not just that he plays the entire cast and, literally, crew – though he is possessed by more spirits than Linda Blair in *The Exorcist*: he is, among other things, a seagull, a little rich girl, a bored clerk pining for the sea, a dying old woman, a cynical whaling agent, an Oirish port commissioner, the Fenian John Devoy, a bluff Dublin conspirator, a Scottish first mate, a drowning Indian, a whale, a pregnant French maid, a British colonial governor and an awkward Australian.

What is really remarkable, though, is not this feat of multiple impersonation, but the deeper idea that allows it to happen. For what Donal O'Kelly manages to do is to abolish the distinction between showing and telling. The device of telling a movie allows him to be both actor and narrator, so that we forget to ask whether he is recounting a story or playing it out. And this ability is at the heart of the play's reflection on history. History tells a story; theatre enacts it before us. By doing both at the same time, he makes the difference between one form and the other, and thus between the past and the present, shrink to nothing.

The result is a brilliant unravelling of the heroic epic and a subtle questioning of all kinds of official history. The story of the *Catalpa* doesn't fit into Hollywood's view of the world. But the stories of many of those who sailed on the *Catalpa* don't fit into a comfortable nationalist history either. The big story, the daring rescue, ends in a ticker-tape parade down Fifth Avenue. It is public history. But the other, private histories that are interwoven with it have no such triumphant ending. The captain, George Anthony, doesn't get the money that was his main reason for undertaking the voyage. The Pawnee Indian in the crew ends up on the bottom of the sea. The West Indian ends up selling relics of the *Catalpa* cut into shamrock shapes. The pregnant French maid is, like Ariadne, abandoned and betrayed.

And that reminder of the story of Theseus's voyage to slay the Minotaur is appropriate to the feel of the play. *Catalpa* is, above all, a homage not to the facts that make up history but to the imagination. And when the imagination is brought to bear on great events, the result is myth.

Donal O'Kelly has made a narrative that has the rough, magical qualities of the Greek mythic tales: directness, vigour, spellbinding narrative, cruel humour and a sense of the human failures that so often underlie heroic deeds. And though it runs only until Saturday night, *Catalpa* deserves to linger in the imagination for a long time.

Mrs Sweeney, by Paula Meehan

Project Arts Centre
The Irish Times, 20 May 1997

One of my favourite cartoons is from *Dublin Opinion* in the 1930s. In it, two formidable, Dublin, working-class matrons are squaring up to each other with evil intent. One of them is fixing her narrowed eyes on the other and saying: 'Looka here, Mrs Murphy, we'll have none of your Abbey Theatre realism in this here tenement'. It is an acute comment on the difficulty that so often faces anyone trying to dramatize urban, working-class life: where does the realism end and the reality begin?

Paula Meehan's first play for adults, *Mrs Sweeney*, produced by Rough Magic at the Project in Dublin, could almost have been called *Juno and the Pigeon*. It is, at one level, an updating of Sean O'Casey's early plays. The old Georgian tenements have given way to a place not a million miles from Fatima Mansions but there is the same sense of working-class people living simultaneously at the end of their tether and in each other's ears.

The tough, hard-bitten mother has, like Juno, to cope with a useless husband and his talkative crony, though her daughter's disaster is not pregnancy but death from AIDS. The Covey-like know-all, well played by Anto Nolan, still likes the sound of his own voice but the theories he expounds are gathered not from Jenerski's thesis on the origins of the proletariat but from New Age books and obscure television programmes.

At another level, though, Paula Meehan reaches back much further than O'Casey for her inspiration. As her title suggests, the play is also a feminist take on the Irish legend of the mad birdman, *Sweeney Among the Branches*, a story that has attracted the interest of, among others, T.S. Eliot, Seamus Heaney and Flann O'Brien.

Again, as with O'Casey, the myth is brought both up to date and down to earth. This Sweeney is a middle-aged Dubliner so traumatised by the slaughter of his beloved racing pigeons that he begins to imagine that he is one. In taking on the myth, Meehan turns, as she put it in an early poem, to the figures of women 'Hollow of cheek with poverty! And the whippings of history!'

Within this rich weave of resonance and allusion, the problem is to find the room for realism. For on this highly decorated platter, the play also tries to serve up an old-fashioned slice of life. While playing with aspects of literary and theatrical tradition, it also tries to simply draw attention to present-day social realities. The world we are asked to envisage is that of a marginalized Ireland, where crime, drugs, domestic violence and AIDS prey on the lives of three women (played by Ger Ryan, Neili Conroy and Gina Moxley). The play is, in other words, trying to be both a knowing exercise in style and an honest revelation of an often hidden reality.

The surprising thing is not that it doesn't work but that it comes so close. The flaws are obvious enough. It is too long and slow. It has too little development. Too much of what the characters have to say lies uncomfortably between dialogue and declamation. Some of it is more like a bad parody of O'Casey than an improvisation on his themes. (Does any working-class Dublinman, outside the Abbey stage, talk about himself in the third person, as the drunken husband does here – 'Nobody says a word to Jimmy O'Reilly'?) And, though she makes brilliant use of the spaces opened up by Barbara Bradshaw's excellent set, director Kathy McArdle sometimes allows the actors to talk into empty spaces rather than to each other, exacerbating the disembodied feel of some of the language.

But with all these difficulties, there are also extraordinary moments of theatre. Somewhat paradoxically for a play written by a very fine poet, *Mrs Sweeney* is at its best when the focus is on the action, not the words. And what is striking is that the further the action moves away from realism, the more convincing it gets. In the second half of the play, when the mechanics of setting up a realistic plot are left behind and the writer's gift for a hard-edged, angry absurdity is given full rein, there are some startling and gripping scenes.

As Sweeney becomes all bird, and as strange objects – a Starry Plough flag, a hideous Virgin Mary lamp, the weird carnivalesque costumes that the women don for a Hallowe'en party – take centre stage, the play acquires not just a darkly anachronistic sense of humour but a vivid theatrical life.

Ger Ryan as Lil Sweeney and Mick Nolan as the birdman of Maria Goretti Mansions begin to occupy the stage with a new conviction. The blacker the humour, the starker the imagery, the better the performances and the more enthralling the theatre.

What this suggests is that it is the wild myth of the Sweeney story and not the apparent social realism of O'Casey that is best able to get to the heart of lives on the edge of Irish society today. The challenge is not so much to show the way we live now but to shape it through the imagination into images that will burn themselves into the brain. When she has the courage to pursue such images, Paula Meehan proves that she certainly has the imagination to forge them.

The Leenane Trilogy, by Martin McDonagh

Druid Theatre Company
The Irish Times, 24 June 1997

At a key point near the end of Martin McDonagh's great Gothic soap opera, *The Leenane Trilogy*, one of the characters looks guiltily at another and says: 'We shouldn't laugh'. It is a simple line, but, for the audience, a devastating one. We have, at that point, spent nearly six hours laughing ourselves sick at some of the blackest, bleakest stories that have ever been told in the Irish theatre. We have laughed at the Famine, at murders and suicides, at children drowning in slurry pits and old men choking on vomit. And the question that McDonagh asks us is: when does the laughing stop and the thinking begin? For at its core, the trilogy is a comedy about the need to take some things seriously.

It is often said, with a great deal of truth, that the characteristic mode of Irish theatre is tragicomedy. And in that sense, McDonagh, for all the complexity of his background and influences, is clearly an Irish playwright. The difference, though is that whereas in the classic Irish repertoire, comedy and tragedy tend to alternate in the same play, here they become indistinguishable. These plays are so brilliantly entertaining that we are still laughing halfway down the street. But because we know we shouldn't laugh, they are also deeply disturbing.

The disturbance comes from the sense of being in a world where the kind of responses implied by words like comedy and tragedy just don't work anymore. It is not accidental that the Ireland of these plays is one in which all authority has collapsed. The family, from *The Beauty Queen of Leenane* onwards, is a site for psychological and even biological warfare. The law, in the shape of Garda Tom Hanlon (Brian F. O'Byrne) in *A Skull in*

Connemara, is a joke, and everyone is literally getting away with murder. The Church, embodied by David Ganly's Father Welsh in *The Lonesome West*, is a lost, despairing young alcoholic, whose flock console him with the thought that at least he is not a paedophile. The Catholic Church's great point, says Maeliosa Stafford's Coleman Connor in the same play, is the ability to supply good vol-au-vents at funerals.

This is a world where the difference between the real and the unreal is increasingly hard to grasp. On the one hand, there is a sense of isolated people clinging to a remote and inhospitable landscape. But on the other, this isolation is also suspended in the airwaves. From the start, through television and emigration, bits of other places – Australia, America, England, Trinidad – float into consciousness. And the plays themselves are plugged into the television screen – with its continual references to Australian domestic dramas, American detective series and, in *The Lonesome West*, to *The Odd Couple*. The trilogy is a giant soap opera, but one that makes *Twin Peaks* look like *The Riordans*.

At one level, then, the trilogy maps a very real and immediate Ireland. However grotesque the exaggerations, they inflate a recognizable truth so that it can be seen more clearly. But at another level, the world that is imagined in this way is also a version of one of the great mythic landscapes – the world before morality. It is the ancient Greece of *The Oresteia* – a cycle of death and revenge before the invention of justice. It is, perhaps more to the point, the Wild West of John Ford's westerns or Cormac McCarthy's novels, a raw frontier beyond civilization.

McDonagh's brilliance, though, lies in the way he drains the heroics out of the myth. He suggests that what happens when order collapses is not just the big, epic horrors, but a hysterical riot of incongruities. What makes his characters so like old, mad children is that everyone has forgotten what adults are supposed to learn – the difference between what matters and what doesn't.

Much of the best of his comedy comes from the contrast between the savage intensity that the characters invest in unimportant objects – Kimberley biscuits, Tayto crisps, plastic figurines of saints – and the carelessness with which they treat each other's lives. The appalling hilarity of this contrast reaches its logical conclusion in *The Lonesome West* when Coleman, about to be knifed by his brother Valene, realizes that the best way of defending himself is to point his shotgun, not at Valene, but at the latter's beloved new gas cooker. In this demented pre-moral world, things matter much more than lives.

If Martin McDonagh had not existed, Garry Hynes would have had to invent him, for all of this is uncannily in line with what she and Druid have been about over the last 21 years. For one thing the trilogy is the culmination of a long demythologization of the West that she and the company have conducted through such great productions as *The Playboy of the Western World*, M.J. Molloy's *The Wood of the Whispering* and Tom Murphy's *Bailegangaire* and *Conversations on a Homecoming*. At a profound level, McDonagh's plays represent a final reversal of Romanticism. To the Romantics, the West was proof of the Utopian belief that life was better and purer before the imposition of modern society. Here, the West, without a functioning society, proves the opposite.

The plays fit in with Garry Hynes's work at Druid in another way, too. The company's veterans – Marie Mullen, Maeliosa Stafford, Mick Lally – have often been at their very best when exploding naturalism from within, starting with the apparently familiar and making it very strange.

This is precisely the way McDonagh's writing operates. It takes the conventions of kitchen sink drama and exaggerates them into a kind of dirty naturalism. As Hynes has done so often, it takes the elements of literary Western speech and writes them out with the kind of fluorescent pens that Maryjohnny Rafferty in *A Skull in Connemara* uses for doing bingo. For these people not only talk – they talk about talk, discussing curses, insinuations, aspersions, insults, and coinages: 'There's no such word as un-bare'. They have a theatrical self-consciousness that has been the hallmark of so much of Druid's work.

This confluence of Druid's history with McDonagh's intentions makes for a magnificently seamless production in which play and players are inseparable. There are great technical achievements – the simplicity which designer Francis O'Connor distils from a very complex use of space, the odd grandeur of

Ben Ormerod's lighting, the flawless pacing and relentless physicality of Hynes's direction.

But this is above all a triumph in the direction of actors. The sheer facility of McDonagh's writing for the stage is such that it would be difficult to imagine an entirely bad production. But an entirely good one is a ferocious challenge for it requires an ability to maintain a highly distinctive tone over three plays.

McDonagh's style is not quite like anything else on earth. The characters are cartoon creatures who really die when someone fires a shotgun at their heads. They are sitcom people in desperate situations and horrific comedies. They are puppets who continue to move around long after the strings of logical control have been cut. To inhabit them, the actors have to both believe in them utterly and yet maintain the kind of cool distance they would bring to a farce or a knockabout silent movie.

They do it – collectively and almost perfectly. Brian F. O'Byrne's achievement in creating three different characters with the same accent and the same age who are yet utterly different is the most remarkable. But there are brilliant performances, too, from Anna Manahan, Marie Mullen and Maeliosa Stafford, and all the acting is extraordinarily intelligent.

The result is undoubtedly one of the great events of the contemporary Irish theatre. It would be greater if Martin McDonagh had managed to find, in his exploration of a world that has imploded, some basis for the new morality he seems to be seeking, some ground for reconciliation. But given that he has not yet found it, there is something deeply admirable in the way he refuses to concoct it merely for the sake of completeness. The openness of his ending suggests that he is still on a journey and the exhilaration of this strange stretch of the road suggests that anyone who travels it will want to go all the way with him.

The Cripple of Inishmaan, by Martin McDonagh

Public Theatre, New York
New York Daily News, 8 April 1998

With *The Beauty Queen of Leenane* due to transfer to Broadway later this month, the young Anglo-Irish playwright Martin McDonagh has already made his name in New York.

In that production, though, he will be among friends: the director and cast are all Irish. For *The Cripple of Inishmaan* at the Public, on the other hand, director Jerry Zaks and much of the cast are American. The production therefore poses a question: Can McDonagh's work survive outside its native element?

The answer here is a qualified 'yes'.

Comparing the two plays is a bit deceptive. Th*e Cripple of Inishmaan* has the same West of Ireland setting and the same very black comedy as *The Beauty Queen of Leenane*. But it is less realistic, more mythic.

The central character, Billy, played by the convincingly fragile Ruaidhri Conroy, is a disabled orphan on one of the rocky Aran Islands in 1934. He lives with his crazy aunts, is besotted with the wild, violent Helen, and dreams of escape. When the American film maker Robert Flaherty comes to the islands to make the famous *Man of Aran*, he escapes to Hollywood for a screen test.

Oddly enough, there is no great problem in having American actors play some of these isolated, remote people.

For one thing, the play is in part a send-up of the American Romanticism of *Man of Aran*, so the tinge of American in some of the accents is actually rather apt. For another, McDonagh's language is in any case a playful pastiche of stage Oirish. To worry about authenticity is to miss the point.

In fact, two of the best performances of the evening are those of Elizabeth Franz and Roberta Maxwell as the aunts. Both they and Aisling O'Neill as Helen get exactly the right balance of exaggeration and credibility.

The other strengths of Zaks's production are its deft storytelling and good, old-fashioned comic timing. Zaks paints in broad strokes on the open canvas of Tony Walton's impressive set. Especially in the first half, when the tone is mostly light, the play is very, very funny. McDonagh's talent for taking banal dialogue and giving it a subtly demented twist is given free rein.

As the play moves on and the mood gets darker, though, the weaknesses show through. There is not enough of the tiny, precise detail that grounds a yarn in reality. When Billy's journey is no longer a trip to Hollywood and becomes a voyage into love, death and shame, the production is not able to travel all the way with him.

There is enough enjoyment to suggest, nevertheless, that McDonagh is much more than a one-hit wonder.

The Weir, by Conor McPherson

Walter Kerr Theatre, New York
New York Daily News, 2 April 1999

About 50 years ago, a journalist asked an old woman in the West of Ireland if she believed in fairies. 'I do not, sir,' she replied, 'but they're there'.

Conor McPherson's *The Weir*, which opened last night after arriving from London's West End loaded with awards, is about that kind of uncertainty.

The characters don't really believe in fairies or ghosts or the afterlife. But they can't shake off the feeling that there's something there.

Critics like to use the word 'haunting' to describe plays whose images linger in the mind long after the stage lights go out. *The Weir* certainly deserves that description.

But it is haunting in a more literal sense. The play is a series of ghost stories that shade gradually from mere spookiness to awful, heart-rending grief.

The Weir is set in a small bar in a lonely corner of Ireland. Soon, in summer, the place will be jammed with tourists. But for now, it is still in hibernation, and the quiet, melancholy owner, played by Brendan Coyle, depends on a few local bachelors for customers.

There's Jack, a pompous scarecrow in his fifties who lives with memories of what might have been. And there's the almost silent Jim, still, in his forties, living with his ancient mother.

Into this weary world, the flashy businessman Finbar brings Valerie, an attractive city woman who has come to live in this dull backwater. To impress her, the men tell scary stories of fairies and Ouija boards. She seems unusually alert to these tales of the supernatural.

Then she tells a story of her own, an ordinary, terrible account of the death of her little daughter. Somehow, their lurid yarns have given her the confidence to speak. Somehow, too, these awkward men find the dignity to listen and respond.

On one level, all of this is utterly simple. There is no high drama, no complex plot. They meet, they talk, they leave. But this careful understatement allows a larger subject to emerge. For *The Weir* is really a play about death, and the need for a language in which to speak about it.

The ghost stories, McPherson implies, are the way people used to explain the feeling that a departed loved one is somehow still present. If this larger subject is to come through, it has to emerge from the calm unfolding of a mundane evening.

Director Ian Rickson and his fine cast hold their nerve through the long moments when nothing seems to be happening. The pay-off is a profound sense of dignity.

The hardest role is that of Valerie, who has to move quite suddenly from passive observer to passionate participant. Michelle Fairley handles it with emotional grace.

But the most extraordinary performance is that of Jim Norton as Jack. A ridiculously talkative figure at the start, he gradually acquires an ability to listen, first to Valerie and then to himself. Norton plots this inner journey with an uncanny sense of direction.

Together, these actors tell McPherson's strangely uplifting tale. They tell us that, even though the ghosts may be gone, the 'something' that remains is the haunting memory of those we have lost.

Lovers at Versailles, by Bernard Farrell

Abbey Theatre
The Irish Times, 8 March 2002

Long, long ago, there was a time when the Abbey stage was filled with plays about ineffectual shopkeepers, spinster daughters who pass up their one chance of marriage because their mammies won't let them, and contrived happy endings in which the spurned beau reappears to offer a second chance. The drama was of the kind where, in moments of crisis, someone always puts the kettle on. The jokes were generated by the repetition at strategic intervals of the fixed number of predictable quirks that came ready-assembled with each character.

How long ago was all that exactly? Well, to be precise, Wednesday night, when Bernard Farrell's *Lovers at Versailles* opened at the Abbey. It is an extremely strange event, like one of those living museums where unemployed actors pretend to be Vikings or Ancient Celts. Welcome to Blythe World, where audiences can experience what it was like to go to the theatre in the days when Ernest Blythe reigned supreme and the harmless domestic comedies of George Shiels, Louis D'Alton and John McCann kept bad thoughts at bay.

It is all the stranger because Farrell's reputation rests on two admirable qualities: his accuracy as a chronicler of middle-class mores and his ability to unleash a dark anarchy within the apparently banal confines of mundane lives.

From his first Abbey play, *I Do Not Like Thee, Doctor Fell*, in 1979, to his last one, *Kevin's Bed*, in 1998, he has often combined these qualities into a potent cocktail. It is deeply puzzling, therefore, that our finest observer of urban middle-class life should produce a play in 2002 that, except for its last 10 minutes, could have been written in 1952.

Social comedy demands credibility, and the basic problem with *Lovers at Versailles* is that we are given no reason to believe in its central character, Anna. The play is set in 'the present in suburban Dublin'. Anna ages in its course from late 20s to late 30s, suggesting that the early scenes to which we continually return take place sometime around 1992. Yet we have to believe that an intelligent, competent woman in her late 20s at that time is so hopelessly dominated by her harridan of a mother that she leaves her much-loved husband-to-be literally standing at the altar.

Even if Farrell gave us some reason to believe this - and he doesn't – we then have to ask why we should care about a character who is a mere cipher for someone else's hang-ups. In the course of a rather long evening, we actually learn very little either about Anna or about her parents, her snooty sister Isobel, or her boyfriend David.

Each character has a single, unchanging quality. Anna is a mouse. Isobel is a stuck-up, selfish bitch. Mammy is a dried-up, selfish bitch. Daddy is a nice, harmless old codger. David is a nice, harmless young codger. Isobel's husband Tony is unimaginably stupid. And the comedy, such as it is, is sealed up in these packages. Mammy is forever giving withering looks. Daddy is always forgetting David's name. Tony is a bottomless well of numbing stupidity.

All of this has obvious consequences. One is that Mark Lambert's cast is operating well within its comfort zone. Any competent actor can do this sort of stuff while half the brain is still working out the last clue to a crossword puzzle. Only a genius, on the other hand, could make it remotely exciting. And while Tina Kellegher as Anna, Barbara Brennan as the mother and Vincent McCabe as the father are all actors who have a spark of genius within them, none of them finds a reason to go beyond competence here.

The other consequence is that a play as inert as this one can only be resolved by a plot contrivance that makes the old deus ex machina of the Greeks seem subtle. The descending goddess in this case is Jeananne Crowley, and such is the dullness of what has gone before that the outrageous sentimentality of the device she delivers is inordinately thrilling.

Ariel, by Marina Carr

Abbey Theatre
The Irish Times, 4 October 2002

After the first few minutes of Marina Carr's new play *Ariel*, we know we are in a crumbling world. The very title comes from the feverish vision of the Biblical prophet Isaiah, foreseeing the destruction of a city. On stage, at the sixteenth birthday party of the eponymous daughter of a rising Midlands politician, the three pillars of the old Ireland – Church, State and Family – are in an advanced state of decay.

The politician, Mark Lambert's Fermoy Fitzgerald, is a strange beast, driven by dark compulsions and fanatic visions of destiny. His brother Boniface (Barry McGovern) is a monk whose sole remaining duty is the care of his decrepit and demented colleagues. And the wider Fitzgerald family is a cauldron of simmering resentments.

In all of this, Carr is laying out the ground that the best Irish dramatists of the younger generation must now occupy. The society that gave form and meaning to the work of their older contemporaries is in disarray. Playwrights such as Carr and Sebastian Barry, whose recent work, *Hinterland*, bears many resemblances to *Ariel*, have to start almost from scratch. They have to find a way to make their own private myths fuse with the public world they now inhabit.

This is a journey into unmapped territory, and when you have no map and no clear sense of a destination, you tend to wander. It may well be that Ariel is the kind of play we will have to get used to: a meander into an unknown landscape where we see some breathtaking views and stumble into some treacherous bogs.

The grand house that the Fitzgeralds have built with the fortune they have made in the cement and gravel business is, we are told, fronted with Greek columns. So is Carr's play. Given her recurrent concern with family dynasties riven by violence, death and inescapable destiny, it was perhaps inevitable that she should seek her public myth in the Greek tragedies.

Ariel is clearly a version of the story of Iphigenia, sacrificed by her father Agamemnon to appease the gods and gain a fair wind for the voyage to Troy. The Fitzgeralds are a 21st-century Irish House of Atreus, with Fermoy as Agamemnon, Ingrid Craigie's precise, contained Frances as his disaffected wife Clytemnestra and Elske Rahill's Ariel as Iphigenia. There are elements of Electra and Orestes in the Fitzgeralds' other children, Stephen (Dylan Tighe) and Elaine (Eileen Walsh).

This in itself is an enormously ambitious undertaking, but *Ariel* is also trying to be an Irish version of Tony Kushner's *Angels in America*. Carr, too, is trying to fuse an immediate vision of political crisis with a large sweep of religious and Biblical images. She tries this, moreover, over a span of 10 years, with the first act set in the present and the other two in 10 years time. This is quite simply too much for one play, even for a dramatist of Carr's bold and relentless imagination. Euripides and Aeschylus - no mean playwrights - felt it necessary to unpack the myth in a series of plays. Kushner split *Angels in America* into two very long epics. By squeezing it all into one evening of conventional length, Carr risks the kind of literal overkill that comes when bodies pile up in a rapid succession of catastrophes.

Nor does she manage to get to the core of the Greek plays: a sense of necessity. In the Greek world, the killing of Iphigenia is as necessary as its terrible consequences are inevitable. Here, Fermoy's sacrifice of his daughter is driven, not by the logic of the story, but by a rhetoric drawn from psychotic visions. We never get a convincing reason why it has to happen.

These are serious problems, all the more so because the play does not pretend to work on the level of social realism. Fermoy is not remotely convincing as a contemporary Irish politician, and his religious ravings in an extended television interview don't sound like the kind of stuff that could make him the next Taoiseach.

What is most remarkable, however, is that with all of these gaping flaws, Ariel is still curiously compelling. This is partly because of the sheer, gutsy integrity with which director Conall Morrison and his cast engage with Carr's quest. Lambert and

Craigie in particular don't just push the boat but steer unflinchingly into the uncharted waters.

It is also, though, because of Carr's own courage. It takes vision and generosity to accept the task of trying to find public myths for a society that no longer knows what anything means. If Ariel doesn't find them, there is nevertheless an excitement in the search.

Irish Revivals

Famine, by Tom Murphy

Seapoint Ballroom, Galway
Sunday Tribune, 12 February 1984

It is one of the commonplaces of modern writing about the theatre that it is no longer possible to write tragedy, that tragedy as a form has been superseded by contemporary sensibilities. One of the few contemporary plays which challenge this assumption is Tom Murphy's *Famine*. There is a sense of an individual overwhelmed by inescapable forces in *Famine* which brings classical Greek tragedy to mind. The central figure, John Connor, is a residual tribal elder, a village leader whose people were once kings, a ragged Agamemnon. 'What's right in a country when the land goes sour?' asks his wife as Connor insists that he will always do what's right. Running through the play is an almost supernatural sense of blight, of an evil that is too immense to be comprehended. And Murphy's writing has much of the Greek tragedy about it, with individual moments of passion counterpointed by choruses of the general populace.

But the analogy goes only so far. For the real protagonist of *Famine* is not an individual locked in a losing battle against the gods, but a society in a struggle to the death against history. And for this, forms other than tragedy are needed and adopted. These are the forms of epic theatre and of opera. Epic theatre developed at a time when the central question of *Famine* was being asked in a different context, and with different resonances, on the European mainland. As the black night of Nazism descended on Europe, the question that Murphy's John Connor must ask himself was asked by Brecht and others: what can survive of humanity when the world is overtaken by disaster and barbarism? *Famine* is an epic in the sense that John Connor is not intended as an individual 'character'. He is specifically a last representative of the Gaelic civilization that is to be destroyed once and for all by the Famine. With him will go the idealism, generosity and nobility of his culture, to be replaced by the hard, calculating practicalities of survival which hunger teaches. For the play to work Connor's actions must be understood, not by their psychological motivation, but as the embodiment of historical processes.

The strength of Garry Hynes's production of *Famine* for her Druid company is that it operates on this basis. Because of its affinity with Greek tragedy, with epic theatre and with opera, *Famine* has been a difficult play for Irish directors, actors and audiences – it does not deal in 'characters', the common currency of the Irish theatre. Garry Hynes goes for expression rather than character and, for the most part, succeeds.

Her method is largely operatic – full of choruses and counterpoints, huge set pieces and individual arias. There is an operatic flourish in the entrances and exits. From the opening scene where a tableau of mourners keens and chants in the 'cottage' at the back of the playing area, counterpointed by the rough chatter of a group of men on the ditch outside, the tone is established. The men on the ditch form a chorus against which the more minute tragedy of the Connor family is measured.

The style grows naturally from Murphy's language, which is usually speech reaching towards song and is here an actor in its own right. It is rich and poetic, but also at times harsh and brittle in the manner of biblical prophecies, and the disintegration of language in the play, the inability of the characters to form sentences or to finish them is the clearest expression of the loss of meaning in the society.

It is impossible to speak this language as if it were 'natural', impossible to present these actions as if they were imitations of surface reality, and Druid's production seldom attempts to do so. It seeks instead a complex pattern of images and rhythms, and achieves some startling crescendos. Performances like those of Mick Lally, Mary Ryan, Marie Mullen, and Tomás Ó Flaithearta have a clarity and intelligence about them which is extraordinarily effective.

There are times also when the delicate and complex balance of the play falls apart, when the actors lapse into naturalism or the images just fail to make it. The failure on the opening night seemed to be more one of energy than of intention, and the unfamiliarity with the space of the Seapoint Ballroom didn't help a production which needs absolute concentration and confidence. But the failures are rare and the strengths out of the ordinary.

The ultimate test of *Famine* in production is whether the performances allow for a sufficient distance from the action so that the audience can see that it is not events in the nineteenth century which are in question, but the effect of those events on the twentieth century, on the way we live now. Druid's production does that to a great degree and to that degree it is a success.

The Sanctuary Lamp, by Tom Murphy

Abbey Theatre
Sunday Tribune, 3 November 1985

Tom Murphy's play *The Sanctuary Lamp*, now revived at the Abbey, is an anti-Christian play. But it is not a mere rejection of religion. Instead it uses a religious setting, Christian imagery and the Christian concern for prayer, forgiveness and redemption and places them in a world long since abandoned by God.

The clergy, the confessional and the pulpit are here, but the vision that is proclaimed from the pulpit, the vision that is at the heart of all of Murphy's theatre, is the blasphemous dream of a dishevelled showman, a vision of Jesus calling to his side, not the sheep but the goats: 'All those rakish, dissolute, fornicating goats, taken in adultery, and what-have-you'.

The setting of *The Sanctuary Lamp*, here Bronwen Casson's abstract and atmospheric arrangement of church pillars, pulpit, pew and confessional, brings together two people in search of forgiveness and redemption.

The circus strongman Harry (played by Peadar Lamb) comes to the church in search of help and healing. He is joined by Maudie (Bairbre Ní Chaoimh), an innocent young girl seeking to be forgiven for her sins. It is entirely in keeping with Murphy's theatre that Harry should find that healing, not at the hands of the priest (Des Perry) who gives him a job as clerk of the church, but from the man who proclaims the play's vision from the pulpit, Francisco.

The priest represents an illusion of salvation through an act of redemption located in the past – the sacrifice of Christ. Francisco, on the other hand, is the nightmare of Harry's own past, the man he is both seeking and fleeing from.

Francisco has stolen Harry's wife Olga, and it is he who reminds Harry of the torment of his own experience: 'There was no one there but myself to kiss away the tears of that poor, unhappy, lost unfaithful wife'. It is only by embracing that past reality without illusion that Harry can find the healing he seeks.

What makes *The Sanctuary Lamp* such an extraordinary play is that this complex excursion into the roots of religion is dealt with theatrically through a story that borrows from both melodrama and from fairy tales. Looked at simply, *The Sanctuary Lamp* is the story of a strongman, one of the strongest in the world, who loses his strength because he refuses to face reality, finds salvation and regains his strength. It is a parable as simple as any in the New Testament.

The Bible itself is undoubtedly the major influence on the language and the action of the play. The dialogue is full of ironic, steely, biblical echoes. The sacred symbols are humanized, translated into the world of fallen man, so that the Holy Family, present in a statue at the back of the church, becomes also Francisco the blasphemous juggler, Olga the unhappy, unfaithful wife and Sam the performing dwarf.

It is this simple quality of the parable, the accessible symbolic story, which is missing from Ray Yeates's production at the Abbey.

The most important theatrical moment of the play concerns Harry's regaining of his physical strength. He has tested himself by trying, and failing, to lift the pulpit in the church. But when Francisco, railing from that pulpit, confronts him finally with the reality of his relationship to Olga, Harry rushes at the pulpit and lifts it with a mighty effort. His strength has returned.

It is a moment of theatrical magic, making clear and concrete the fact that a point of transformation has been reached in the play. But in this production it is a moment that is mistimed and largely lost. The simple story that makes the play accessible is submerged.

Without that sense of being a parable, *The Sanctuary Lamp* remains powerful, but lacks the kind of immediacy it needs. The moment when Harry lifts the pulpit is as important in the play as the moment when Gigli sings in *The Gigli Concert*.

Both moments represent a leap into new possibilities, testifying that once the shackles of illusion have been broken, some sort of new life is open to Murphy's characters. After it, Francisco and Harry go on to formulate their own religions, to picture the world for themselves, to face up to possibilities.

Ray Yeates's production has fine moments in the performances of Garrett Keogh (as Francisco), Peadar Lamb and Bairbre Ní Chaoimh. Peadar Lamb captures Harry's mixture of open yearning and defensive, wounded perplexity. Bairbre Ní Chaoimh's Maud manages to inject a great emotional range into a childlike performance. And Garrett Keogh performs Francisco's speeches from the pulpit with an utterly convincing mixture of passion and irony.

But Murphy's careful orchestration of sound, the interplay of voices that is the only real point of human contact in his work, demands a minutely balanced relationship between the actors. That relationship seems to be missing here.

The production does however have the mark of a great deal of care and commitment and the play is still one which demands to be seen. In a country which is steeped in Catholic imagery and in which Catholicism is still the language of most people's yearning for a better life, *The Sanctuary Lamp* is a rare and courageous voyage into the heart of those images and that language.

It isolates and gives voice to those yearnings which religion is supposed to satisfy. If in the end of the play there is no sanctuary, no refuge, from reality, not even in madness, there is at least the quest and an image of new possibilities.

A Whistle in the Dark, by Tom Murphy

Abbey Theatre
Sunday Tribune, 12 October 1986

Tom Murphy's *A Whistle in the Dark*, revived at the Abbey in a superb production by Garry Hynes, is a first full-length play rich enough for all its apparent simplicity to contain the seeds of 25 years of theatrical achievement.

A play with a classically direct plot and clean lines of action, it yet embodies many of Murphy's continuing concerns: the impossibility of flight, the destructiveness of illusion, the centrality of the outsider.

To a certain extent Garry Hynes uses the benefit of hindsight, emphasizing the elements which subsequently emerged most strongly in Murphy's work, and in doing so brings out the full power and moral complexity of the play.

Most of Murphy's plays are set in some space which the characters have established as an attempt at a sanctuary, a destination in the flight from themselves and their world.

In *A Whistle in the Dark* the Carneys have come to Coventry from Mayo. Though Michael, the eldest of the brothers, does not recognize this, they are exiles and outsiders.

They are caught between two illusions: the vainglorious king-of-the-rubbish-heap rantings of Dada, who comes to join them, a belief that so long as they can assert themselves through violence then they have the right to be proud, and the integrationist efforts of Michael, who believes that by keeping their heads down they will be accepted and prosper.

Garry Hynes uses hindsight to bring out a third force in the play, and to make it central. Here, the character of Harry, in a wonderful performance from Seán McGinley, is placed at the core of the play, as the most vicious and despairing of the brothers and the one who therefore speaks the most truth.

The production, while strong on a sense of detail, also moves away from a straightforward naturalism, making much of the musical elements in the play, and using design and lighting to make the setting non-specific and to give the action a stark but slightly distanced quality

By doing this it emphasizes the ritualistic inevitability of the action. The performances are tough, clear and above all beautifully in tune with each other, making for a seamlessly savage piece of theatre whose power is not only undiminished by the years but actually enhanced by our heightened sense of violence in the recent past.

Nightshade, by Stewart Parker

Project Arts Centre
Sunday Tribune, 8 February 1987

Stewart Parker's play *Nightshade*, revived by Rough Magic at the Project after its first Dublin performances in 1980, is one of the deftest, richest and most engaging Irish plays of the Eighties. It is also very much a Protestant play, wrapped up in the Puritan struggle between the soul and the body, and desperately seeking a way out of the blind alley of Puritanism. It is in one sense a paradigm of Northern Protestantism, with all its sense of loss, its revulsion at the things of the body and its contradictory yearning for bliss, blessing and release. Yet all of this is contained within a play that is superbly theatrical, very immediate and often playful.

The central vehicle for the struggle between soul and body is the figure of Quinn, who is both a mortician and a magician, engaged at once in the most inescapable of physical realities, death, and in the world of illusions and insubstantial trickery. As the play goes on, however, we realize that these are not opposites, that Quinn's occupation as a mortician is just as much a matter of making things disappear as is his hobby of magic. One of his assistants, Kane, explains: 'We're invisible men to the public,' and the mortuary business is seen as being primarily about waving a magic wand over the unpleasant realities of death and making them go away.

Nightshade is itself like a magician's show, with rabbits and images popping out of hats, people and props disappearing up sleeves. This is a good production of a terrific play.

I Do Not Like Thee, Doctor Fell, by Bernard Farrell

Olympia Theatre
Sunday Tribune, 6 September 1987

The number of amateur and professional productions it has been given must make Bernard Farrell's *I Do Not Like Thee, Doctor Fell* the most popular Irish play of the last decade. From the sturdy revival now at the Olympia, it is easy to see why the play has survived so well since its first production at the Peacock in 1979.

Not only is it very well made and often very funny, it is also one in the eye for the Yanks, telling the story of how a smug, glib American gets her comeuppance at the hands of a dark, devious Irishman. Beneath its façade of social criticism, *Doctor Fell* essentially belongs to one of the most popular genres of theatre and then cinema, the revenge story, and there is nothing we Irish like better than seeing the underdog get his own back on the upstarts.

It used to be, of course, that the upstarts which we got our own back on were the English. Irish folklore is full of tales of the way the seemingly stupid Irishman uses his apparent dimness as a disguise to outsmart the English. What is interesting about *Doctor Fell* is that it is now the Americans, and not the English who get their comeuppance.

The immense popularity of the play suggests that, in the Republic at least, we now think of the Americans as the masters who need to be outfoxed. In this, *Doctor Fell* is very much a play which reflects the increased Irish dependence on American capital and American culture since the Sixties.

The hero of the play, Joe Fell, excellently captured here by David Herlihy, is almost a stock character. He appears to be shy, withdrawn and stupid. The first words of the play are his awkward stammer 'Ex ... excuse me'. He is apologetic, lost, worthy of pity but hardly of serious respect. We soon realize, however, that he has treacherous depths, that he knows more than he says, that he may be way ahead of the game. His façade of stupidity is a ruse, the weapon of the underdog with which his opponents are made to drop their guards.

Joe's opponent Suzy Bernstein is American, slick and energetic, the coordinator of the group therapy session into which Joe has apparently wandered. She represents everything American: brash confidence, pop-psychological jargon, the 24-hour clock, the glib assumption that problems can be solved by the power of positive thinking. Suzy is the 'Me Generation' personified.

The play is not so much an attack on group therapy itself as on the culture which created it, the culture of relentless self-improvement which has no time for real misery and unhappiness. It is that which Joe Fell is set against.

Two of the other participants of the session, Peter and Maureen, represent the awkwardly developing Ireland into which this American culture has been transplanted. Peter is Sixties Man, a builder of bungalows. His success has brought him only misery, the terrible insecurity of feeling that Maureen is deceiving him behind his back with his business partner and any other man she can lay her hands on. In the course of wreaking his revenge on Suzy, Joe also demolishes the hope of an easy fix for Peter and Maureen.

The delight of the play is in its subtlety, its refusal to point big fingers at what is happening, preferring to allow hints to hang in the air long after they have been let slip. Barry Cassin's production takes this somewhat too far in an opening half which is muted almost to the point of insignificance, but the pace becomes considerably less monotonous as the play moves into the second half.

At the heart of the production is David Herlihy's Joe, which is less energetically evil than Garrett Keogh's original performance in the role, but which becomes more and more menacing while retaining outwardly the appearance of a benign simpleton. His lumbering bulk and slow impassivity also contrast nicely with Billie Morton's neat briskness as Suzy.

Hatchet, by Heno Magee

Olympia Theatre
Sunday Tribune, 1 May 1988

Though the writer and performer of one are involved as actors in
the other, it would be hard to imagine two more sharply
contrasting views of Dublin than those presented by Seán
Lawlor's *The Watchman* at the Peacock and Heno Magee's *Hatchet*
at the Olympia.

Perhaps because it changed so quickly and so traumatically in
the Sixties, Dublin has been peculiarly susceptible to nostalgic
sentimentalization of its poverty, squalor and violence, the rare
oul' times that were all too common. Though in a far from
objectionable way, *The Watchman* is sufficiently distant from that
past to be somewhat dewy-eyed about it. *Hatchet* is too close for
such comforts.

The contrasts often express themselves in terms of ideas of
escape from the city centre. In *Hatchet*, emigration to England is
an ideal, the object of Bridie's fierce desire; in *The Watchman*,
emigration to England is a nightmare which can be awakened
from only by return to dear dirty Dublin. In *Hatchet*, the new
housing estates of Cabra and Crumlin are places where people
can breathe; in *The Watchman*, anything beyond Ballybough is the
country. As the need to escape is replaced with the desire to
return to the past, so the alternatives to overcrowded claustrophobia become less and less attractive.

Hatchet was first produced by the Abbey in 1972, before the
current wave of Dublin nostalgia had begun to roll. It remains a
remarkably powerful and eloquent testament to the feel of
entrapment which the pressure-cooker atmosphere of slum
conditions produced. It is also many other things, among them a
play about the dichotomies of emigration and a play about the
convolutions and contradictions of the extended family. There is
a tendency to talk about working-class socially realistic writers
like Heno Magee as raw and instinctive, but now that the shock
of its violence has been muted by the passage of time it is
possible to see *Hatchet* as a very self-conscious, sophisticated play.

Peter Sheridan's production at the Olympia has its share of violence and tension, but it also allows the other elements of the play to emerge. With an open, geometric, almost abstract set by Frank Hallinan-Flood, it gets away from strict naturalism and in the process draws attention to just how unusual Hatchet's family is. Like John B. Keane's *Sive* whose impact in rural Ireland is matched for Dublin, *Hatchet* presents an extended family under pressure from the competing ideal of the nuclear family.

Hatchet's wife Bridie is determined to build a nuclear family of the orthodox kind, and is determined not to have children until she is able to do so. But she is living with Hatchet, Hatchet's mother and a 'touched' male relative Ha-Ha. What impels Hatchet towards tragedy is not so much the gang violence of the slums as his inability to make up his mind between these two ideas of the family, an inability which leaves him paralysed in the face of danger.

The sophistication of Magee's writing shows in the way in which, without straining the conventions of domestic drama, he gives us concrete images of this family in chaos. Nobody sticks to their allotted roles. Hatchet's mother (a very strong performance from Eileen Colgan) refuses to be the virginal Irish Mammy and remains sexually available. Hatchet himself refuses to behave like a son and acts towards his mother more like a combination of censorious father and jealous lover, ticking her off about her immodest behaviour, her lewd dress, her suspect morals. Bridie refuses to be the good wife, resisting sex and children.

And to complete this image of a family that doesn't know how to play out its expected roles, the only child on stage, the one who uses baby talk and sucks sweets, is a middle-aged man, Ha-Ha. In the midst of all this confusion about the family, Hatchet is supposed to declare his loyalty to the family honour by avenging an insult in tribal warfare against the Mulallys. It's small wonder that he has problems coping with the situation.

David Herlihy's Hatchet captures both his physical strength and his emotional impotence. Herlihy begins with the swagger of a shape-thrower, his physical confidence is sapped as his emotional uncertainty increases. Herlihy suggests the turmoil subtly, with the eyes and the face, giving a complex impression of a man who is neither naturally vicious nor strong enough to impose himself on events.

The strength of performance continues down the line, with Eileen Colgan and Dave Carey (as Ha-Ha) particularly effective, though Aisling Tóibín's Bridie is too often given to hysteria. Overall, this is a very capable production of a play which continues to grow in stature.

Summer, by Hugh Leonard
Abbey Theatre
Sunday Tribune, 10 July 1988

In the public mind, Hugh Leonard is probably marked down unambiguously as a comic writer, a one-liner man guaranteed to be good for a laugh. Yet the truth is something else entirely – Leonard's humour is nearly always laced with despair, and a strong streak of melancholia runs through his work. In Leonard's plays, humour struggles with desperation, disgust with resignation.

Nowhere in his work do the desperation and disgust win out as honestly and as unflinchingly as they do in his very fine 1974 play *Summer*, now revived at the Abbey. There are jokes in *Summer*, but more often than not they are conscious attempts on the part of the characters to gloss over the pain that is just below the surface.

The roots of *Summer*'s melancholia are made very clear. The three couples who meet on a hillside overlooking Dublin, first in 1968 and then in 1974, are all, with varying degrees of success, riding the rising tide of new money in the Irish economy.

Not only are they nouveaux riches themselves, they also make their money out of supplying the nouveaux riches, Richard selling them antique books for their walls ('This isn't reading, this is owning'), Stormy building their houses, Jess travelling in wallpaper. As Stormy puts it near the start of the play, 'there's a few quid in the country now'. No one before or since has taken the pulse of that new money with such relentless accuracy as Leonard does in *Summer*. The despair comes from the fact that by the time the second half of the play opens, these people have got where they were going. Stormy is now building corporation houses, Richard's business is slipping, and Jess is on the skids. The have no ties with the past, and no future to look forward to. All that awaits them is death. And in the course of the play they come to realize this.

Leonard spatters the play with images of death. Within a few minutes of the start, Richard is linking his business success with death: 'People die, their libraries are sold off'. Stormy has an attack of indigestion that looks for a few moments like a fatal heart attack. He composes in his mind the ad that his company will put on the back of *The Irish Times* 'as a mark of respect to our late managing director'. Later, Jess convinces himself that he is dying.

In a vain attempt to make time stand still, Richard and Stormy's wife Jan engage in a furtive affair. But as a way of warding off death, it is doomed in advance by Leonard's imagery. The writing links sex with death: Richard's description of Jan makes her sound already dead – 'Thin as a lath and cold as January'. Stormy starts thinking about female flesh and ends up thinking about the graveyard: 'The modern girdle has more bones in it than Deansgrange cemetery'. All of this gives *Summer* a tone and texture which, for all the familiar trappings of middle-class life, are closer to Beckett than to Feydeau.

Summer has worn very well in the 12 years since its first production. Leonard has made some changes which, in particular, sharpen up the portrayals of the two members of a younger generation on stage – Richard's son Michael, and Stormy's daughter Lou, but, if anything, the play expresses the mood of the times even better now than it did in 1974. It remains a difficult play to direct, needing both a feeling of real intimacy with the characters on the part of the audience and at the same time a sense of undercurrent, of things going on behind the action that we are not entirely in touch with. Eamon Morrissey's production gives us all of the surface waves but not enough of the ripples and undertow.

Apart from a set which is rather too monumental to allow for much intimacy, it is not so much a matter of what is on stage as of what is not. The performances – Clive Geraghty's Stormy, Catherine Byrne as Richard's wife Trina, Barbara Brennan's Jan, Des Cave's Jess – are good, and the direction is tight and smooth, moving well from the duologue to monologue to general chatter.

But there is seldom much of that unspoken current between actors which makes the stage come alive. The tension when Jess's devoutly Catholic wife Myra discovers Richard and Jan's affair should be intolerable. Instead, it is merely interesting. Instead of terror and despair, there are anxiety and disappointment. *Summer* is made to look a good play but not as good as it deserves.

A Crucial Week in the Life of a Grocer's Assistant, by Tom Murphy

Abbey Theatre
Sunday Tribune, 4 September 1988

John Joe Moran is five years older. When Tom Murphy's *A Crucial Week in the Life of a Grocer's Assistant* was first produced at the Abbey in 1969, John Joe, its central character, pulled between the compulsion to leave small-town Ireland and the desire to stay, was a twenty-nine-year-old boy still struggling to emerge into adulthood. Now in Garry Hynes's splendid revival of the play, John Joe is thirty-four, and the subtle change is a devastating comment on the failures of the last twenty years to resolve the dilemma of emigration.

It is as if nothing has happened except that we have all got older and more desperate. Instead of calling to John Joe in his dreams: 'Quick, before you're thirty,' his girlfriend Mona now calls: 'Quick, before you're forty'. The effect is to make the play at once funnier and more darkly acerbic.

The times have conspired to make *A Crucial Week* again a crucial play. It was written in 1962 and is set in 1958 and its mood is very much that of those years, plumbing as it does the frustrations that led to the opening up of the country in the Sixties. When the play was finally produced in 1969, it must have had the feel of history, so fundamentally had the mood changed.

Now *A Crucial Week* matches our mood again as the whole question of what freedom we have to go or to stay becomes again a central one. It is in communicating this urgency that Garry Hynes's production is so powerfully effective. The play is intensely funny, and there are times when you want to shriek with laughter, but the laughter is of a special kind – it is the laughter of recognition. *A Crucial Week* is still funny because we can still recognize its people, and the fact that we can still recognize them is a mark of how desperate we are. That's the complex emotional equation which adds up to superb writing and a production of rare confidence and mastery.

The key success of Garry Hynes's direction is in handling the degree of stylization involved in the play. Many of the details of the play belong to 1958 – the clothes, the bikes, the size of the wage packets, the nature of the business conducted in the shop in which John Joe works – and it could be undertaken as an exercise in social history. But Hynes understands that fact that the details have changed matters little, because the play is not essentially about psychological and naturalistic detail.

The characters are brilliantly drawn, but as so often in Murphy's work, they are encapsulated by the sounds they make, by the waves they make in the world. The other characters are not so much individuals but representatives of the social forces around John Joe, of the church, the state, the town, most especially of the Irish Mother.

By getting the degree of stylization involved in this right, Garry Hynes allows for a succession of wonderfully accurate cameos, each of which fulfils its function perfectly but, with admirable discipline, is not allowed to spill over its proper bounds in an attempt at misplaced depth.

What Hynes does is to blur the boundaries between the dream sequences and the other scenes – by for instance declining to light the dream sequences differently – narrowing the difference between the dream caricatures and the 'real' characters, giving a shuddering nightmarish quality to the whole thing, even at its funniest. The excellent design work of Monica Frawley and Roger Frith enhances the effect.

A very strong cast responds brilliantly to this clarity of purpose. Stanley Townsend's Mr Brown, Martin Dempsey's Father Daly and John Cowley as John Joe's father are the most hysterically funny, but the quality extends through the whole cast. Most of the complexity, quite rightly, is left to the central relationship of the play – between John Joe and his mother, and the performances of Seán McGinley and Joan O'Hara.

McGinley is typically understated – but uses the awareness of John Joe's older age to inject a sense of terror at the passing of time, making us aware of just how much the play is concerned with the approach of death. O'Hara's performance has a genuinely tragic quality, capturing both the mother's clinging, manipulative oppressiveness and her real heroism. Together they give the play its heart. It all makes for a piece of theatre that is funny, savage, absorbing and angry.

Talbot's Box, by Thomas Kilroy

Garter Lane Theatre, Waterford
Sunday Tribune, 11 September 1988

The last few years in the Irish theatre, when only a relatively small number of significant new plays has been produced, has been, above all, a period of revivals, a time of taking stock. The theatre in Ireland has begun to form something like a contemporary repertoire for itself, to winnow the accumulated stores of the last quarter century. Plays which in some cases had received no more than one professional production in Ireland, have had their soundness tested – Keane and Leonard at the Abbey, Murphy at the Abbey and Druid, Parker and Kilroy by Rough Magic. The results have been, on the whole, very encouraging, to a point where the remarkable explosion of new playwriting talent that emerged from the late Fifties to the mid-Sixties begins to look like a second Renaissance.

Red Kettle's production of Thomas Kilroy's play *Talbot's Box*, first performed at the Peacock in 1977, is a genuine and heartening addition to the process. For their first venture into the contemporary Irish repertoire (apart from the work of their artistic director, the playwright Jim Nolan), the young Waterford company would have been hard put to find a more difficult challenge, but it is one with which they cope impressively. Kilroy's play is complex, expressionistic, full of play-acting, its central character consciously inaccessible and inexplicable. They come to grips with it well enough not only to do justice to its complexity and integrity, but also to bring out its humour, playfulness and inalienable theatricality.

Talbot's Box is one of those plays where the form and the content are inextricable. Kilroy has long been concerned with the imagination of the performer, with the way in which the actor transforms the world before our eyes. Much of what Kilroy has to say, about our images of ourselves, about the way different worlds are superimposed on each other, about the ambivalence of life and death, can only be said physically, in the way in which actors, while we watch, become one thing and then another. In *Talbot's Box*, as in other Kilroy plays, even the most fixed and obvious of human relationships – father, son, brother – become confused and threaten to melt into each other. Matt Talbot's struggle is to stop himself becoming, through drink, his father or his brother, and this struggle is embodied before our eyes as the boundaries of character slip and slide. It is this business of embodiment which makes Kilroy, in spite of his considerable stature as a novelist and critic and the cinematic elements in some of his plays, so inescapably a playwright.

Jim Nolan's production appreciates this theatricality. It jettisons Kilroy's original idea of having the action played out in a box which is opened at the start and closed at the end, but maintains the spirit and the style which Kilroy is after. In a play which opens with its hero on a hospital trolley in a morgue and then brings him back to life, which makes a great display of the actors turning into Talbot's family, foremen, employers, Countess Markievicz, doctors and stand-up comics, and which uses its sets and props with abandon, there is no room for literal and heavy-handed characterization, and Red Kettle avoid it deftly.

What Kilroy is after is the sense in which Matt Talbot's pain and loneliness and yearning cannot be appropriated to any cause, even that of the playwright, and the consequent untrustworthiness of historical, religious and fictional images of the man. To get this across, Talbot himself has to remain enigmatic, and it is a real difficulty for an actor to have to express the power of a personality which cannot be explained or redefined or 'motivated'. In this context, Aidan Walsh's Matt Talbot is for the most part very effective, his rough passion and physical presence leaving room for the darkness of Talbot's soul.

The rest of the cast is equally good, Frieda Ryan, Jenni Ledwell, Conor Tallon and Brian Doherty all strong and forceful without losing the looseness and lightness that the play demands. They are helped by Jim Nolan's direction which, though it has its swampy moments and occasionally struggles with the acoustics of the otherwise excellent Garter Lane space, is also fluid and marked with some fine and appropriate comic touches. The display of Talbot's chains in an impromptu fashion show or the businessman's horse smoking and studying the racing form are the kind of touches which both add to the theatricality and keep within the spirit of Kilroy's playfulness.

Big Maggie, by John B. Keane
Abbey Theatre
The Irish Times, 26 November 1988

Almost all of the major contemporary Irish playwrights have given us their version of Mother Ireland. There are the mothers in Brian Friel's *The Loves of Cass McGuire* and Hugh Leonard's *Da* and Mommo in Tom Murphy's *Bailegangaire*. Most directly of all there is John B. Keane's Big Maggie, the most literal Mother Ireland since Yeats first put Cathleen Ní Houlihan on the stage. Maggie is both a particular and well-defined individual and a metaphor of Ireland after Independence.

Like the country as a whole, she wins her freedom, in her case through the death of her husband. 'Tis only now,' she says at the graveside, 'I know what freedom means'. But, like the new Irish state, she wants to use that freedom to keep her children under control, and in particular to rein in their dangerous sexual urges. And in doing so she pays the price that the country paid for its economic harshness and sexual repression – the emigration of her children, the gradual descent into proud isolation.

This element of metaphor, of allegory even, in *Big Maggie*, means that it can't be treated as a simple naturalistic melodrama. Maggie has to be two things at once – a character and a symbol – and a successful production of the play has to mix naturalism and symbolism in a difficult chemistry. Ben Barnes's production at the Abbey and particularly Brenda Fricker's tough central performance manage to achieve this remarkably well, Barnes's mixture of production styles held together by the clarity and continuity of Fricker's acting.

Big Maggie is a play with serious faults. Much of it is overly schematic and most of the parts are little more than cameos. Some of the dialogue is too compressed and consequently incredible. The ending is formally unsatisfactory and Keane's new closing monologue, written for this production, though it helps considerably, still leaves some confusions.

But for all of this it remains a remarkable play containing an extraordinary dramatization of the sexual tensions within a family and of the relationship between economics and sexuality. Money and sex are inextricably linked in Maggie's motivations. On the one hand she wants to control her children's sexuality so that she can keep them under her thumb economically, working for her in the shop and the farm she has been left by her husband. But on another, deeper level she is punishing them for her own sexual frustration, visiting on their heads the knowledge, and fear of the body's power which she has acquired in a misbegotten marriage.

Maggie's world is genuinely tragic: she acts to protect her children from what has happened to her, but she does not understand that their world might be different. She is caught in the middle between two different worlds and no matter what her motivations, her actions cannot produce good results. In tragedy, there is a disjunction between cause and effect, and this is what happens to Maggie.

Keane's new ending to the play offers Maggie at least the tragic blessing of self-awareness. It is a powerful monologue in which Maggie analyses her sexual self, her relationship to her

own body and to men and the way in which the Church has
moulded that relationship.

But it is confusing because, along with its bitter clarity in
analysing the past, there is a vision of the future which seems to
bring back illusions. Maggie vows to take advantage herself of the
new sexual freedom of the Sixties and the problem is that we just
can't imagine her doing this. We have seen her emasculation of
both Teddy and Byrne, her would-be lovers, as well as of her
own sons; and those images of sexual hatred far outweigh any
aspirations to sexual fulfilment which come at the end. This
leaves the end of the play hanging by a very thin thread.

The central scenes, though, are very effective in this
production. Ben Barnes takes the risk of moving from the virtual
expressionism of the opening graveyard scene, all blacks and
greys with a defiantly unrealistic set, to the detailed domestic
drama of the middle scenes set in Maggie's shop and on to the
final monologue which again discards naturalistic conventions
and addresses itself straight to the audience.

It is the kind of mix that can very easily become a mess, but
there are three things which make it work. The first is the
conscious artificiality of Barnes's blocking which keeps a strong
pictorial element even in the most domestic of scenes. The
second is Frank Conway's fine set which successfully mixes
realistic detail and symbolic statement, and the third and most
important is the careful equilibrium of Brenda Fricker's
performance.

The sparks in Fricker's Maggie come from the cold beat of
flint on flint rather than the vulgar display of fireworks. Like
Niall Tóibín in Barnes's production of *The Field*, she underplays
what might otherwise be an ogre, emphasizing the rationality and
self-protectiveness of the character's actions. Fricker refuses to
sway with the play's alternating emotional winds, but remains as a
rock over which all of the storms break. By remaining rooted and
outwardly undemonstrative, she not only gives us a credible
Maggie, she also gives the production's changing styles a constant
core.

By refusing to over-act, Fricker also refuses to do our thinking
or our feeling for us. *Big Maggie* is full of dark corners – the

relationship of father to daughter, the sexual usurpation of daughter by mother – that are worthy at times of Strindberg, and it is important that the production resists the temptation to fill them in. Fricker's very impassiveness makes us face the nightmares ourselves.

The Gentle Island, by Brian Friel

Peacock Theatre
The Irish Times, 17 December 1988

There is something not only logical but almost inevitable about Frank McGuinness choosing Brian Friel's 1971 play *The Gentle Island* for his first full-length professional production as a director. It is not just that Friel and McGuinness come from the same part of the world and speak the same language. It is also that they are the same kind of playwright.

Both are excavators rather than explorers, staking out their own ground and digging deep for its truths. Both are concerned with the tribe, its boundaries and its logic. And in *The Gentle Island*, of all Friel plays, the logic is sexual as well as social and political, making it the closest of all his plays to a work like McGuiness's *Observe the Sons of Ulster Marching Towards the Somme*. Like McGuinness's Protestants in that play, Friel's islanders are physically cut off and that isolation is embodied in the image of homosexuality.

If anyone could restore *The Gentle Island* to the contemporary Irish theatrical canon, it is McGuinness. In a wonderfully acted and beautifully paced production at the Peacock, he has done so, making for perhaps the most impressive piece of theatrical restoration since Garry Hynes rediscovered M.J. Molloy's *The Wood of the Whispering* some years ago. *The Gentle Island* has never figured as an important Friel play and it reads badly, its seemingly naturalistic frame coming across as too rickety for the burden of symbolism which it must bear. But McGuinness plays down the naturalism and allows the symbols to emerge lightly and easily. *The Gentle Island* still does not appear as a great play, but it does stake its claim as a rich, absorbing and very brave one.

One of the things that the production makes you realize is the extraordinary continuity of Friel's work. That breathtaking efflorescence of his writing in the late Seventies which produced *Aristocrats*, *Faith Healer* and *Translations* seems to have come almost from nowhere. *The Gentle Island*, though, is the missing link, belonging perhaps to his early work, but with haunting echoes of *Faith Healer* (the old man Manus describing his return to the island to face his enemies is unmistakably reminiscent of Frank Hardy's encounter with his fate); *Translations* (Peter and Shane, the urbanites who arrive on the island foreshadow the English soldiers Yolland and Lancey arriving in Baile Beag); and even of his most recent play, *Making History* (the mocking references to the Flight of the Earls, the notion that 'every story has seven faces').

Like so much of Friel's work, *The Gentle Island* is highly Chekhovian, but it is also unexpectedly Wildean in its taste for paradoxes, for turning expectations on their heads. The symbols tend to work like Wildean epigrams, reversing the conventional direction of a cliché.

Manus's dead wife, Rosie Dubh, may be a Dark Rosaleen, an image of lost romantic Ireland; yet the 'ocean green' is not her salvation but, when she drowns herself in it, her death. The sea throws up dead bodies, not live saviours; clocks and binoculars from torpedoed freighters, not wine from the royal Pope. And the paradoxes continue – homosexuality is normal, humdrum, heterosexuality strange and problematic. The strangers are innocent and unsophisticated, the supposedly innocent islanders convoluted and enmeshed in conventional lies.

The Gentle Island is a brave play, not just because it is unflinching in its laying bare of the viciousness and unhappiness of a rural idyll, but also in its willingness to break the rules of the well-made play in the search for some kind of truth. In a play which has depopulation as its background, Friel makes us feel that depopulation, rather than be told about it. He brings on a succession of tantalizingly interesting characters at the start of the play and then makes them disappear, leaving us, like the Sweeney family left alone on the island, deprived of company, stuck with whatever's left.

Friel also prepares for the total break with naturalism which was to come in *Faith Healer* by giving us a play which is nothing but a tissue of stories, a set of conflicting narratives, in which we are told everything and shown nothing. Daringly, we are given no evidence of anything; the crucial events of the past and the present that fuel the play may or may not be as we are told they are, since none of them happens before our eyes. It is a hugely risky strategy but one which Friel carries through here with enormous skill.

It is in understanding and embodying this that McGuinness's production is so good. A lesser director would have seen the play's incompleteness as a failure and done everything possible to fill in the gaps, to round out the characters, and explain the mysteries. McGuinness, helped considerably by Wendy Shea's stark but subtle set, goes for restraint, precision and formality. Very good performances from a disciplined and intelligent cast leave central characters like John Cowley's Manus and Gerard McSorley's Philly, his elder son, dark and enigmatic, but with the darkness of infinite possibility rather than the emptiness of a blank.

All of this makes for a sombre, ritualistic piece of theatre, often witty and brilliantly written – there is a scene in which Manus writes a letter to a young woman for his youngest son Joe which ranks with anything that Friel has done – but always intense and unsettling. It is an *Island* rescued from the theatrical tide that threatened to engulf it – craggy, daunting and inhospitable, but with a savage power that is always compelling.

Waiting for Godot, by Samuel Beckett

Lyric Theatre, Belfast
The Irish Times, 25 February 1989

Is Godot worth waiting for? Samuel Beckett's play has been performed by practically every major Irish theatre company in the past decade. In the past two years it has had productions from Druid in Galway and from the Gate in Dublin and it is currently running in a new production at the Lyric in Belfast, until March 4th. It has recently had a much-hyped production in

New York and is probably, like the Mass and McDonald's hamburgers, one of the few things that is now the same the world over, or like the old British Empire, something on which the sun never sets. It has become so much a part of contemporary western culture, its title has become so much a part of contemporary language, that it is difficult to even ask the most basic question which needs to be asked about any play: is it any good or not?

Waiting for Godot raises in its own way the question which George Bernard Shaw asked in relation to his *The Devil's Disciple* – to what extent can a play which reflects current avant-garde ideas outlast the popularization and vulgarization of those ideas? *Godot* is not, of course, a play of ideas in the Shavian sense, but even more profoundly than a Shaw play it does reflect the philosophical currents of its time, the fashionable absurdities of the 40s and 50s.

When the play was new, there were those – Sean O'Casey among them – who thought it proper to discuss and attack the play's ideas. Now, the play has such unchallenged classic status and we are so used to its ideas that no one bothers to even mention them. Critical reaction has been replaced by the sort of hunt-the-symbol games that are a sure indication that a work is no longer seen as dangerous, radical or challenging.

Arguably, *Godot* is a play that everyone should see once and that no one would really want to see twice. You could see *Hamlet* every night for a week and if the productions were different, the experience you would have in the theatre would be equally different. But the precision, the control and the minimalism of *Godot* mean that, essentially, the play does not change, or rather it changes only in peripheral details, in tiny nuances. If it changes more than this – if, for instance, it is set in a concentration camp or played entirely by women or by actors dressed in tutus and pig masks – then it may be all sorts of things but it is no longer *Godot*.

And yet, *Godot* does survive and the main reason that it does so, ironically, has very little to do with the philosophical currents in which it swims. The thing which initially attracted so much attention to it – its absurdist vision – seems relatively unimportant now. The thing which hardly seemed to exist at all when the play was new – its overwhelming theatricality – is now everything. *Godot* survives as a superb piece of theatre, as a play on and a play about the idea of theatricality.

This conclusion is prompted by watching a production which gets the play's philosophy right, which catches the absurdity and the humour that arise from it, which is careful and clear about the play's statements, and which yet fails to work, precisely because it makes too many mistakes with the theatrical mechanism of the play. If *Godot* was primarily a philosophical piece then it wouldn't matter so much that Tim Webb's production at the Lyric in Belfast misjudges its theatrical temper.

For there is, after all, so much that the production does right. It has a really intelligent and effective set by Laura Pritchard which, with its subtle suggestions of a road to nowhere, has a perfect mixture of symbol and reality. It has two beautifully contrasted performances from Ian McElhinney and Mark Drewry as Vladimir and Estragon, with the fact that one is Irish and the other English adding a properly understated element of personality to the performances without descending into a misplaced attempt at naturalistic characterization. It uses suggestion of time and place without becoming literal and reductionist.

But there are also fatal misjudgements which are all to do with the theatricality of the play. *Waiting for Godot* is essentially a joke on the whole theatrical experience, an extended invitation to the audience to get up and leave. Nothing is going to happen, the play keeps telling us, it's going to get more boring, the second half is going to be the same as the first. Why do you insist on hanging around in a futile expectation? Like Didi and Gogo, our decision to stay is the triumph of hope over experience.

Tim Webb's production fails to make use of this essential nature of the play and it suffers accordingly. The great running joke of the play is the way that the actors are self-conscious of themselves as actors on a stage trying to keep going, all the time half-nodding in the direction of the audience, sharing the audience's panic, boredom, frustration. The actors all the time threaten to break the invisible barrier between themselves and the audience, to do an Alan Devlin and announce that they can't do it anymore, that they're going for a pint. The joke is that they never actually do so.

Now the one way to ruin this joke completely is to have the actors break the barrier, have them come down into the auditorium among the audience, in the way that the recent New York production reportedly does. And this is exactly what Tim Webb has his actors do. It is a judgement that is of a piece with the general lack of feel for the way the play works as a piece of theatre, rather than as a set of ideas about man and the universe that the production manifests.

Thus, the Pozzo and Lucky episodes of the play are woefully ineffectual. Pozzo and Lucky may have importance as symbols of oppressor and oppressed – and Webb tries to clarify this significance – but first and foremost they are there as a theatrical device. Their arrival holds out some, quite illusory, hope that something of significance is about to happen, that we are about to get away from Didi and Gogo and their inconsequential banter. Pozzo is himself a theatrical joke – florid, hammy, pretentious. For this to work, he and Lucky need to look and sound different, to attract attention, to promise something interesting. Here, Lucky and Pozzo are slow, grey and dull.

In its desire to explicate and clarify what has been said in the play, to point it up with inventive stage business, the production misses the way it is being said, which is infinitely more important. As a result, the whole rhythm of the language is lost and *Godot* becomes, not less, but more difficult to sit through.

The Death and Resurrection of Mr Roche, by Thomas Kilroy

Abbey Theatre
The Irish Times, 3 June 1989

The anthropologist Margaret Mead said something to the effect that the problem civilizations face is that of defining the male identity. Certainly, in Thomas Kilroy's play *The Death and Resurrection of Mr Roche*, putting your finger on Ireland is about putting your finger on the Irish male.

Because it was, in its first incarnation in 1968, the first Irish play to have an overt homosexual at its core (the gay men in Brendan Behan's *The Hostage*, for instance, are appallingly insulting caricatures), it is easy to misread *Mr Roche* as a play about homosexuality. In fact, as Frank McGuinness has pointed out, it is concerned with heterosexuality – 'one of the hardest and most uncompromising statements on heterosexuality in the Irish theatre'. Just as you only become aware of silence when a noise stops, Mr Roche's homosexuality is there to make the 'normal' maleness of the other characters visible. And with this light shone on it, we can see it as troubled, insecure, full of mistrust, terror and sheer downright misogyny.

What makes the play so fascinating, though, is that it both uses this probing of sexual identity to sound the state of the nation and does so in a way which also lays bare the fundamentals of theatre as a public ritual, as a kind of secular religion. *Mr Roche* remains in a sense a shocking play, not in the fact that it has a homosexual character sympathetically treated or that is uses bad language about dirty filthy things, but for what it does with rituals and symbols of the One, Holy, Catholic and Apostolic church. Many people in Ireland found Godard's film *Hail Mary* shocking because it portrayed the Blessed Virgin as a modern young Frenchwoman. If those outraged only knew it, *Mr Roche* goes much further in giving us Jesus as a genteel, middle-aged Dun Laoghaire homosexual.

The state-of-the-nation aspect is straightforward enough. As a whippersnapper in 1959, Kilroy was writing about the need for Irish theatre to engage the social currents of its time. 'A theatre which creates something permanent absorbs some of the conflicting topical social issues around it and gives a public interpretation of current values'.

Mr Roche, at one important level, is very much a public interpretation of current values, the values of the 1960s and the rising tide of the new Ireland. One of the main characters, Myles, a flashy car salesman, embodies these values to a tee and tries to assert that 'it's now that counts'. The central character Kelly is himself a classic example of upward social mobility, caught in the no-man's-land between rural nostalgia and a sordid city.

Throughout the play, Kilroy is dramatizing the gap between the fantasies of infinite desire and the realities of male frigidity and self-loathing.

The use of religious images, though, is more complex. Kilroy's protagonists in a number of his plays are inclined to see this world as hell, or at best as limbo. In *Mr Roche*, this world is a place populated by the play's imagery. Roche is both Christ suffering crucifixion, burial and resurrection and the buried Christ who descends into limbo (the mundane limbo of Kelly's basement flat) in order to release the souls of those who have been awaiting salvation. And he is also none of these things, for like so many of Kilroy's heroes, Roche is a richly empty figure. He is what he is perceived to be by others. He is dead because they think he has died; he is risen because they thought he was dead and were wrong.

For all its apparently gritty naturalism – the stout bottles and the soup, the obscene language and the almost real smell of stale socks which rises off the situation – it should be clear, then, that *Mr Roche* is working on far too many levels to be a naturalistic play. Mr Roche is probably the most Joycean figure in the Irish theatre. Just as Joyce could make a Dubliner Homeric, Kilroy can make a Dubliner Christ-like – in a spirit of irony, but not of parody. In other hands, such parallels would be mocking and mock-heroic. In Kilroy's visionary, apocalyptic style, they are a testament to humanity's power to transform itself.

To get the full power of that transformation requires a particularly supple sense of theatricality. Ben Barnes, in his production, understands that you can't play *Mr Roche* as a naturalistic drama of psychology and motivation. Working on Frank Conway's raked and jutting set which emphasizes shape and space over physical detail, Barnes underplays the emotional swings of the piece. Eamon Morrissey's Kelly, in particular, looks for an even, curiously uninvolved sense of a man drained of the capacity to feel anything deeply. This pays dividends in the comic tempo of the piece, but at a cost to the drama of desperation and salvation which is unfolding.

What we don't get at any stage is a real sense of just how low Kelly has fallen during this dark night of the soul. Morrissey's very comic energy, his slightly madcap air, gives the impression of a man who will keep going no matter what. What we need though, is something different – the sense of a man who has come to a full stop. Christ's resurrection wouldn't have had much effect on the Apostles if they'd been no more than comically disconcerted by the Crucifixion. Kelly, here, seems more disconcerted than devastated and the impact of Mr Roche's return from the dead is somewhat diminished as a result.

At the very beginning of the third act, for instance, Kelly is entirely alone and abandoned by both God and man, desperately praying for forgiveness and cursing his friends who have left him. It should be a moment of utter nakedness, of emotional truth. Instead, it is played here as basically funny, played for the comic contrast between Kelly's prayers and his cursing. This is fine in itself, making for a good, funny moment. But the price is paid soon afterwards when Roche's return is lessened in its impact. We should get the sense that the real resurrection is Kelly's, but because we have not seen Kelly buried, we do not see him rise. The evenness of the performance works against its realization of the full power of the role. The wonder of the last part of the play, the irony on which it turns, is the fact that Kelly (not Roche) is alive at all. To feel that wonder we have to feel that at some stage he had died.

This is a criticism, not a condemnation, however, for in other respects this production is extremely effective – lucid, well acted, beautifully paced. It continues and brings further one of the most positive enterprises of the Abbey's recent work, the sifting and testing of the major Irish plays of the 1950s and 1970s, the establishment of a contemporary Irish theatrical repertoire. That repertoire has been emerging with remarkable power and eloquence. There is more than enough pleasure, terror and courage about *Mr Roche* to guarantee its place in those ranks.

Aristocrats, by Brian Friel

Gate Theatre
The Irish Times, 10 February 1990

It can be said of many playwrights that their work is more political than it looks, that there are implications for the big, public world that don't at first seem to be there. With Brian Friel, the opposite is often true: his work is frequently less political than it seems.

The Freedom of the City may seem to be 'about' Bloody Sunday, but it is much more about the impossibility of writing about Bloody Sunday. *Translations* may seem to be 'about' the colonization of Ireland, but it is much more about the dodgy relationship between words and events. And *Aristocrats*, revived in an often splendid production at the Gate Theatre in Dublin, seems to be about the decline of a social class – the Big House Catholics – but that apparent theme is largely irrelevant to the heart of the play, to its desire to set the dynamics of memory dancing to the still, sad music of humanity.

The mistake in approaching *Aristocrats* is to see the Big House as a theme rather than a form, a subject rather than a genre. The play is set in a Big House because it is a Big House play in the sense that Chekhov's plays are. Its characters are Big House Catholics because Friel does not write about Protestants. But it is no more a play about Big Houses than *Philadelphia, Here I Come!*, which is set mostly in a kitchen, is a play about kitchens. *Philadelphia* is an extension and a subversion of the kitchen comedy; *Aristocrats* is an extension and a subversion of the Big House play.

There is almost nothing that is important to the people in *Aristocrats* that is specific to their class or station in life. The central relationship of the play, that between the dying father and the long-dead mother, is an exact replay of the relationship between Gar O'Donnell's more plebeian parents in *Philadelphia*. The refusal or inability of the dandy Uncle George to speak is repeated in the figure of the peasant girl Sarah in *Translations*. In its essentials and many of its details, *Aristocrats* is not tied to class, except in an ironic, mock-heroic way.

So why then does Friel need the Big House form at all? The reason, I think, has to do with the play's central concern: the relationship between a family and the passage of time, between family and history. Only rich or once-rich families have histories, a sense, however spurious, of themselves as being an entity that has remained constant over time. Friel needs this sense of history in order to show its collapse. *Aristocrats* is a play about memory, its failure and its force, and memory is something that becomes important when real, historical continuity has collapsed.

The history that matters in the play is not the comic version of the inheritance of the years that Casimir, the failed successor to the family's heritage, holds onto, nor is it the academic study of the role of the Catholic Big House that the American Tom Hoffnung is engaged in. It is the history of the ten years before the play was first performed, the bitter backwash from the Civil Rights Movement's collapse into terror.

Two members of the family – Eamon, the local boy who married into it, and Judith, who has been left literally trying to hold the house together – rode the civil rights wave and have been beached on desolate shores, he in London, she among her father's soiled sheets. History has been warped, bent out of shape, and with that warping, memory, the mechanism of our personal histories, becomes misshapen, untrustworthy, treacherous.

In that warping of memory, the play becomes – if such comparisons are needed at all with Friel – much more like Beckett than Chekhov. *Aristocrats* is full of disembodied voices, sounds that are already replays from the past. Father's voice is heard through the baby alarm, his words rambling reruns of his past self, imagining himself to be in another time, another place. Casimir tapes his sister Claire playing Chopin, then replays it the next day, so that we forget which music is being played now and which is from the day before. A taped message from the missing member of the family, a nun in Africa, is played for the comic effect of her failure to move out of the past, but turns out to have a dramatic effect in the present. Past and present melt into each other and invent each other, the past a fiction invented by the present, the present a lie determined by the past.

And the collapse of memory means the collapse of the family, because the modern family is held together only by memory. The family – Casimir in Hamburg, Eamon and Alice in London, Judith's baby in an orphanage somewhere, Claire a refugee in Chopin's cadences, which is the place where she really lives – exists only when it is remembered. Unless that memory can be brought back into some contact with reality, then the family will no longer exist at all. And without the family, without some acceptable version of it in their heads, its members will cease to exist too.

What we observe as we watch the play is a number of people teetering on the edge of nothingness. It is the achievement of Friel's skill and compassion that we care about his people enough to want them not to be annihilated, to shrink from the depths to which they sink by the middle of the third act.

Because it is about capturing such slippery things as memory and pain, and not about big, tangible things like politics and social classes, *Aristocrats* is a particularly delicate mechanism. It needs a director's sympathy as much as his understanding, and, it needs the actors' compassion as much as their rigour. Music is played almost all the way through the action, and the play is itself like a piece of music. At the Gate there is a delicacy of touch, an ear for the sound of human yearning, that are just what the play needs.

Joe Dowling's direction attends to the mood and the rhythms of the piece with grace and tact. Where there are interventions, like having Eamon move to physically attack Judith towards the end of the play, they rise out of the situation rather than being imposed on it. The depth of the playing by the entire cast is such that anything fussy or flashy would be out of place. Their playing is detailed, restrained, often richly ironic.

The actors evoke the air of absurdity that hangs over their characters without allowing that consciousness to become superiority, to lose either the exuberance of much of the humour, or the respect that sorrow must be given. Seán McGinley in particular is stunning, the dry wit and the understated viciousness of previous performances of his coming together perfectly to create something new and powerful.

This tact and perfection, though, would lack something without the oddness, the jagged extravagance of Tom Hickey's central performance as Casimir. Hickey has done something extraordinary in his acting, which is to bring the wildness of gesture and utterance which he developed in his work with Tom Mac Intyre and Patrick Mason into mainstream, conventional parts. Here, he is both completely a character in a well-made play and a set of gestures and sounds.

The effect is strange, startling, and at times bizarre. At first, the hyped-up edginess threatens to break the perfectly controlled rhythms of the piece, to shatter the unity of the mood. The performance, though compulsively watchable, seems to be in the wrong place. Then, gradually, the energies converge. The stillness and restraint of everybody else meets the strangeness of Hickey's presence and the effect is of an energy being accommodated, of Casimir's oddness both drawing sustenance from and giving point to the lives of the others. It is a risky, uncomfortable and ultimately brilliant piece of acting, like the crazy deliberate flaw that gives life and meaning to the beautiful patterns of a patchwork quilt.

Faith Healer, Brian Friel

Abbey Theatre
The Irish Times, 2 December 1990

He holds his left arm stiffly across his solar plexus like a man in pain or a man bracing himself for a kick in the stomach. Yet his face is mobile, mocking, alive and superior, parodic theatricality. The face is the face of a cynical, arrogant performer, the body is the body of a wracked, anguished man. Already, although there is just Donal McCann alone on the stage, there is drama, a clash of contradictions, a war within.

And then you are shocked by how big he looks on that all but empty stage. It is partly the effect of the way the set recedes from the eye in painterly perspective, but when you see other actors against the same set, you realize that it is mostly him, that he has this extraordinary ability to fill a stage in a way that nobody can explain. You could call it presence, except that presence usually means a quality of the personality, and this is something physical, something you can actually see before your eyes. He looks larger than life-size.

The play – Brian Friel's *Faith Healer* at the Abbey – is a play of words, four monologues interlocking and, crucially, contradicting each other. It is storytelling, but the storytelling of a fractured, troubled world where the story refuses to be just once upon a time and refuses to end happily ever after. The words bring the narrative forward, but they also bring it backwards, ensnare it, make it ricochet off the walls.

They are utterly untrustworthy, these words that tell the story of the Fantastic Francis Hardy, Faith Healer, of his wife Grace and his manager Teddy, of miracles and a stillborn baby and a wedding and a death. Yet they are all we have and so we cling on to them. And in order for us to be able to do that we need an actor who can make them real for us, almost a physical presence. Donal McCann, magician that he is, can do that.

When, in the second part of the play Grace (Judy Geeson) talks about the way Frank has with words, 'releasing them from his mouth', you know what she is talking about because you have seen him do it, seen him hold a word captive behind his lips, stop everything in its tracks, and then release it like a bullet is released by a slowly squeezed trigger, delicately but explosively. Donal McCann has a way of stopping, holding up his hand with his palm open as if feeling the weight of the word he is about to say, scrutinizing the as yet unsaid word, mouthing it silently and then letting it go, saying it out, already distanced from him before he says it aloud, already tested in the mind and found wanting.

In the gap of a few seconds that has been opened up while he is doing this, your own mind is supplying the word he is waiting to speak, running through possibilities, sometimes hitting the right ones, sometimes not. The drama starts to happen, not on the stage so much as in the mind of the audience. You are creating your own shadowy language, your own alternative set of words, words that can be wrong, words that don't match whatever it is may have happened to these people. You don't learn about the untrustworthiness of words, you experience it.

In one of Flann O'Brien's books there is the mad theory that the onset of night is caused, not by natural phenomena, but by the opening of a box full of noxious darkness which seeps out into the air and turns it black.

It is the best analogy I can think of for Donal McCann's great and terrible performance as Frank Hardy, one of the few great pieces of acting that any of us is likely to see in our lifetimes. McCann walks on stage and opens a box of darkness which seeps slowly into the air, into the theatre, into your bones. Nothing happens. There are no writhings of angst, no physical violence. But McCann radiates a cold energy, the energy of death. Like the corpse of a man who has died from an overdose of radiation, he is no longer sentient, no longer able to feel anything but the urge to finality, yet he is dangerous, abuzz with deadly beams, untouchable. Those who are exposed to him will either be healed like cancer patients or destroyed as Grace has been.

At first the performance seems jauntier, more playful than it was ten years ago, when McCann and director Joe Dowling first brought the play to the Abbey stage. It is more actorly now, full of wry rakishness. You wonder if he has lost it, if he just doesn't want to take the lid off that box of blackness anymore. Then the play-acting becomes colder, more terrifying, more the work of a man who creates and destroys others at will as an actor does with his characters, as Frank Hardy does with his 'patients'. He does a touch of Micheál MacLiammóir and it is coldly funny. Then he does Grace's mad mother talking to him in a restaurant and it chills the blood. The play-acting puts him even further outside of people, more in command of others. And it heightens his terrible irony: that he is not in command of himself.

Going back to this play after ten years you experience something of Frank Hardy's own dilemma. What haunts him is that he has a power but cannot turn it on at will. The fear you have going back to the play is that the magic will not return just because everyone wants it to.

Dowling's original production of the play, and McCann's performance in it, are a touchstone of excellence in modern Irish theatre, and asking miracles to happen in the same place twice is tempting fate. But there is no need for the fear. This production is different, but it is no less wonderful.

The play is indisputably a great one, and the production is equal to it. It seems more expansive, more elaborated than it was before and there are times when Frank Hallinan-Flood's set seems to be much too much. But it comes into its own along with Trevor Dawson's superb lighting in the closing monologue, the receding lines creating the sense of a vanishing point, of a point at which Frank Hardy will be no more.

The use of the English actors Judy Geeson and Ron Cook as Grace and Teddy adds richness to the play's themes of exile and homecoming, of English romanticism and Irish darkness. The highest praise that can be given to both of them is to say that they are not out of place beside McCann's towering performance. Cook is a superb Teddy, rat-like but dignified, a wounded barrow-boy. Geeson is distraught in a perfectly controlled way, harrowing but not hysterical, stroking the heartstrings rather than plucking them. She shows amazing skills with accent, creating a voice that is Northern Ireland with English overlays or vice versa, leaving open the question of whether she or Frank is telling the truth about her origins. At times, the energy of the performance drops too much, but this will probably change as the pitch becomes clearer. If this production were merely an exhibition of acting, it would be wonderful. That it is also a riveting and ultimately devastating probing of faith, hope and charity makes it simply unmissable.

Sharon's Grave, by John B. Keane

Gate Theatre
The Irish Times, 8 August 1995

When the Abbey rejected John B. Keane's wild psychodrama *Sharon's Grave* in 1959, the reported reasoning of its managing director Ernest Blythe was that the play was 'too grotesque for words'. Blythe was right in his reasoning, if wrong in his decision. The play is indeed too grotesque for words alone. Its mad concoction of Irish myth and *grand guignol* – imagine Hitchcock's *Psycho* written by the early Yeats – could not be encompassed within the literary word-bound traditions of the Irish stage. It has taken all of 35 years for a credible production of the play to emerge in the shape of Ben Barnes's uneven, but boldly imaginative, re-invention of the text at the Gate. Not surprisingly, the most important elements of that reinvention are visual.

Sharon's Grave is a naive play in the sense of that term more often used in visual art. It is all flat surfaces and garish colours, entirely innocent of perspective and subtlety. But it also has the vivid boldness and the sense of the eternal that, say, the Tory island painters can bring to a canvas. There is no characterization worth talking about. The moral universe in which the action unfolds is positively Manichaean: the struggle at its heart has been accurately described by Keane himself as 'a conflict between a physically abnormal sex-crazed delinquent and a young upright lad whose heart is pure [...], an extension of the everlasting clash between the diabolical and the angelical'.

The almost-mediaeval association of physical disability with moral evil is the dark, ignorant side of the play's naivety. It is the most formidable problem for a contemporary production, but one that is largely overcome by Ben Barnes and by Mark O'Regan who, in a superbly compelling performance, plays the aforementioned sex-crazed delinquent, Dinzee Conlee.

The strength and the weakness of Barnes's production both lie in his decision to treat the play entirely on the mythic level, as a clash of angels and devils. On Frank Conway's great set, a stark and minimal space that is yet extraordinarily rich in colours and possibilities, brilliantly lit by Tina MacHugh, Dinzee and his antithesis, the pure-hearted Peadar (Stephen Hogan), play out an almost ritual struggle for control of Trassie (Catherine Byrne) and her land.

By heightening this mythic dimension to the exclusion of all else, setting the play effectively in a pagan Ireland that is much closer to Africa than Europe, Barnes largely overcomes the problem of Dinzee. He imagines Dinzee and his brother Jack (the excellent Pat Kinevane) who carries him around on his shoulders, as a version of the Blind Man and the Fool from Yeats's *The Cat and the Moon* and *On Baile's Strand*, borrowed in turn by Yeats from Schopenhauer as an image of mind and body.

Since the image is also at the heart of Beckett's *Endgame*, this gives the production access to the store of Beckettian imagery with surprisingly little strain.

O'Regan and Kinevane seize this opportunity triumphantly and make themselves into a two-back beast with all the horrifying fascination of a mythic monster. They stalk the stage like a minotaur the wrong way round: Dinzee a human head full of bitter sorrows and dark desires, Jack a bull's body ready to charge blindly at the word of command.

The problem, though, is that as Ben Barnes himself showed in his Abbey productions of *Sive*, *The Field* and *Big Maggie*, these early Keane plays, however much they draw on mythic types, are also fuelled by the playwright's sense of social change. The ambivalence of the plays, the contradictory impulses that make them so infinitely better than his later work, is that they at once draw on a traditional folkloric world and celebrate the death of that world. *Sharon's Grave* is no exception – it is fascinating for its mythic grotesqueries, but it also depends on a social project. The triumph of Peadar over Dinzee is also the triumph of a modernizing Ireland over its dark past.

By making the play entirely mythic, and indeed by deliberately disrupting any tendency to identify the action with a real rural Ireland of the 1920s (when the play is set) or the 1950s (when it is written), Ben Barnes makes those elements that are not mythic look at best displaced, at worst ludicrous.

The realistic characters – Trassie and Peadar – struggle to maintain any real presence on the stage. The scene in which keening women gather for the wake of Trassie's father is stylized out of existence and loses virtually all its force.

The medicine man Pats Bo Bwee, who has one foot in social reality and another in myth, is, in John Olohan's incarnation of him as some kind of eastern shaman, cut off from any relationship with an imaginable Irish reality, and becomes faintly ridiculous. Only Brian O'Byrne as the simple Neelus, dreaming of the mythic Sharon and her dramatic death, manages with any conviction to seem part both of a folkloric world and of a real one.

The problem is at its worst in the wildly misjudged, tacked-on ending, in which the formalized conclusion of the play in a blessing of Trassie and Peadar as symbols of a new, emergent Ireland, is undercut by a fey sub-Riverdance tableau of Sharon and Neelus in the underworld that misses the obvious point that the mythic is powerful precisely because it is unseen.

Such failures, though, arise from a sense of adventure and a brave willingness to come to grips with one of the strangest and most tormented explorations of sex, land and imagination in the post-war repertoire of Irish theatre. If it risks the ridiculous, the production also achieves the sublime, and it is very much worth seeing both for its moments of visceral force and for its reminder of just what a pagan place Ireland was until very recently.

The Field, by John B. Keane

Abbey Theatre
The Irish Times, 21 May 1996

Certain theatrical characters become like exiled acquaintances, encountered on the occasional visit home. They are recognizably the same but altered by the intervening years and by life in a strange country.

John B. Keane's Bull McCabe, the protagonist of *The Field*, now in its umpteenth incarnation in Ben Barnes's production at the Gaiety, has been on the go for a little over 30 years. Every few years we have an intense evening in his company. Each time, he does and says exactly what he did the time before. But, even as he does so, we can see that he has lived, in the intervening years, an unsteady life. The Bull is now, if not quite a reformed character, then certainly a much altered and much more sympathetic one.

I didn't see Ray McAnally's original Bull but from all the descriptions of it in print, it seems to have been a terrifying creation, full of rage, menace and dark power. Beginning with Ben Barnes's first production of the play in the Abbey in 1987, this elemental force has become gradually more explicable. In that production, Niall Tóibín began the process of making the Bull almost a tragic figure, caught between the values with which he grew up and the new ethic of a changing, industrializing Ireland. Then, in Jim Sheridan's film version, Richard Harris gave psychological and political meanings to the Bull's violence, locating him both as a failed father and as a vestige of atavistic nationalism.

Now in Ben Barnes's second visit to the play, the Bull, embodied in a compelling and consistently intelligent performance by Pat Laffan, has been entirely humanized. He is no longer an obscure force rising up from the depths of post-Famine Ireland but an infinitely weary Atlas trying to hold a dead world on his shoulders. His violence – the brutal murder of an interloper who tries to buy a field the Bull believes to be his by right – is now an act of desperation and defeat, proof, more of impotence than of power.

There are very good reasons for this shift of emphasis; one of them external to Keane's text, the other an integral part of it. The first is that the Ireland in which the play now finds its audience is a world away from the one in which it was written, and not just because murder is no longer an almost unbelievable act of sacrilege against the order of things but a mundane occurrence. When Keane wrote the play, the Bull's world was still present all around him, still dangerous and frightening.

Now it is definitively gone. It is an ancient temple that we visit, not as people who might become a sacrifice on its altar but as curious archaeologists, able to contemplate in some comfort the peculiarities of a distant civilization. Since we're not afraid of the big, bad Bull, we need to replace fear with understanding.

The other reason is that for all its continuing force, *The Field* has weaknesses. Midway through the second half, after the climactic moment of the murder, it loses some of its grip. All that is left is what doesn't happen – nobody spills the beans, the Bull gets away with it, justice is not done. As a reflection of reality, this is brave and truthful but as a piece of drama, it is less than satisfying.

The strength of this production is that it solves both of these problems in the same way: by making the Bull much more remorseful, and much more obviously haunted, than he has been before. Pat Laffan has the physical presence to ensure that the

Bull is no less domineering. But, from the start, he plays the large scale of the Bull's physique against the small scale of his emotional and psychological horizons. His rage for control is in inverse proportion to the amount of his world that he actually controls.

In all the universe there are just three things on which he can exercise his power – a field, his doltish son Tadhg (Pat Kinevane) and the miserably sycophantic Bríd O'Donnell (Mark O'Regan). And none of them is worth it. The field is just a bit of ground.

Kinevane and O'Regan, for their part, manage, quite brilliantly, not just to play their own parts but to become reflections of the Bull's doom. As the agents and objects of his attempts to control the world around him, they are so obviously inadequate that everything he does seems, from the start, to be assured of ultimate failure.

With that knowledge, the murder, instead of being the climax of the play, becomes much more openly pointless. Barnes plays up the essentially accidental nature of the killing, so that, instead of being triumphant, the Bull's later acquisition of the field is merely the meaningless playing out to the end of a game that has gone hopelessly wrong. Grief and horror, not glee, are etched into Laffan's face in the last scenes, giving them a poignancy and a dramatic complexity that they have not had before.

Such revelations of psychological complexity, in a play that once seemed more like a folk tale of clashing elemental forces, more than justify the decision to give an old war horse another run. In a society that has changed as much as ours has over the last 30 years, even the most familiar parts of the culture have, it seems, the capacity to catch the light at ever-different angles.

The Loves of Cass McGuire, by Brian Friel

Town Hall Theatre, Galway
The Irish Times, 16 July 1996

When, in the third act of Brian Friel's *The Loves of Cass McGuire*, one of the residents in an old folk's home asks who General Custer was, another, an Englishman, replies: 'Wasn't he one of the leaders of your Easter Rebellion?' Written at a time when the

Republic was wallowing in the celebration of the 50th anniversary of the Easter Rising, the play is, among many other things, an astringent antidote to the historical self-congratulation of the time. Its Ireland is a place where history – both personal and collective – is a series of insistent inventions. Watching it 30 years later, on the night that the Orangemen swaggered down the Garvaghy Road, the play's startling freshness and unblunted accuracy was cause for both pleasure and despair.

That it is still so vigorous has a great deal to do with the courage and truthfulness of Friel's vision at the time. In the story of Cass, a raucous 70 year-old returned Yank, he laid bare the sense of displacement so often at the heart of Irish reality. To an official view of Ireland as a nation on the march, passing down a simple continuity from one generation to the next, he opposed a bleak dissection of a place caught between meaningless memories and banal desires, unable to tell its own story because the beginning, the middle and the end keep slipping out of sequence.

At the start of the play, a senile old woman is rambling through a remote landscape of disjointed memories. Beside her, her grandson is reading out snatches of an American *True Detective* magazine. One generation is unable to hear anything but its own confused recollection. The other is unable to talk in anything but a borrowed voice. That scathing little vignette sets a tone of disillusionment that gives the play, especially in Garry Hynes's stark and hard-edged production for Druid at the Town Hall Theatre in Galway, the feel of a piece written much more recently than 1966.

The play is not a great work, but it is manifestly the work of a great writer. Brian Friel has described it as 'a concerto in which Cass McGuire is the soloist'. The analogy is as accurate as it is problematic: the idea of a soloist and a supporting orchestra sits uncomfortably with twentieth century ensemble styles of acting. Cass is a great part for Marie Mullen, and one of the most vividly written characters in modern Irish theatre. The other parts – Cass's brother Harry (Mick Lally), his wife and son (Marion O'Dwyer and Eric Lacey), and her fellow inmates in the old people's home – are brilliantly accurate but rather small and static cameos.

To this limitation is added what is not so much a weakness as a complication. The play betrays an underlying uncertainty about whether or not its overwhelming sense of homelessness is caused by emigration. On one level, Cass's psychic displacement is linked all the time to the physical displacement of 52 years in New York, and the power of Marie Mullen's deeply moving performance lies in its embodiment of *émigré* experience. Her Cass seems to belong almost to a different species than the specimens of Irish humanity around her. Her movements are jagged and sprawling, while theirs are neat and halting. Her voice, full of decibels and damnations, has an acoustic entirely different to their soft murmurings.

And these differences add a terrible poignancy to the ruins of an old Irish self that stick like bare bones to the thick second skin of her American persona: the Irish country pronunciations that lurk behind her New York bawl; the way she sings *Oft in the Stilly Night* in a raucous Yankee caterwaul in the second act but with a quieter, truer voice in the third.

On another level, though, Friel seems to suggest that homelessness and displacement are parts of the human condition, that we are all exiles from our own imagined selves anyway. Those who have stayed at home ultimately fall victim to the same confusion of fantasy and reality, the same feeling of dizzy weightlessness, as Cass does. Trilbe, Cass's fellow resident at the old folks' home, is terminally homesick even though she has never been out of Ireland.

Garry Hynes's production tackles these difficulties by imagining the play less as a concerto and more as a ghost sonata, tilting it away from a specific social reality and towards an unsettling surrealism. Rob Howell's superb setting of doors and skies, reminiscent of one of those uncanny Magritte paintings of hollow people and fluffy clouds, strips away most of the few naturalistic elements in Friel's stage directions. Against it, all the human figures except Cass become strangely disembodied, making a virtue of the lack of detail in the way they are written.

Rosalind Knight and John Rogan, in superb performances as Trilbe and her sidekick Ingram, achieve an insidiously sinister quality that gives the play an unexpectedly Gothic feel, as if they were undead spirits calling Cass to join them. And in this context, the borders between the real and unreal become so blurred that it becomes possible to believe that even Cass's American history is all in her head. Without losing robustness and humour, the play gains in poetry, becoming evocative, haunting, and ultimately mesmerising. So much so that, in spite of its absence from the repertoire for so long, it seems sure of a place long after the likes of Cass have faded from memory.

Da, by Hugh Leonard

Abbey Theatre
The Irish Times, 12 July 2002

Fathers generally had a rough time in twentieth-century Irish male literature. Synge's Christy Mahon kills his Da – twice. Joyce's Stephen Dedalus ponders the idea that paternity is a legal fiction. Brian Friel's Gar O'Donnell doubts whether he has any real connection with his father at all. Tom Murphy's Dada in *A Whistle in the Dark* is a living nightmare. Dark paternal shadows fall over the characters in much of John McGahern's fiction.

In this respect, Hugh Leonard's 1973 play *Da*, for all its obviously autobiographical elements, is also a variation on an Irish archetype. It hovers between intimate memories of real events and a bigger, mythic story.

On one side, there are specific reminders that this is a kind of theatrical memoir. The shape of the play is similar to Leonard's classic memoir, *Home Before Night*.

The central character, Charlie, is the adopted son of a Dalkey gardener and his wife. He is the same age as Leonard himself. And even if the audience knows none of this, it learns quite early on that Charlie is a playwright. This, clearly, is the author's own story.

On the other hand, the mythic element is strong. Leonard's first international success was the Joyce adaptation, *Stephen D*, and both the form and the content of *Da* remind us of this fact. Charlie, like Stephen, is pulled between alternative fathers, in his case the amiable, infuriatingly passive Da and the dry, intellectual Drumm, whose protégé he becomes.

What all of this means is that *Da* is a much tougher piece to stage than its reputation as a well-worn Irish comic classic might imply. The element of autobiography pulls it towards a kind of photographic realism but the mythic impulse demands a bigger brush and more sweeping strokes.

The comedy, moreover, is mostly of the subtle kind, the sort that is completely embedded in the action. Some of the funniest lines are not funny lines. Drumm's deadpan responses, simple phrases such as 'Yes, I would' depend on minute movements of expression for their comic effect. They are, in cinematic terms, close-ups. Yet the broad thrust of the action is seen in wide shots. The form, moving with great skill from past to present and back again, deliberately prevents the tight focus of realism.

These challenges can be met, of course, and in Patrick Mason's new production, the first at the Abbey since Joe Dowling's in 1983, there are two consummate examples of how it is done. One is Anita Reeves's luminous portrayal of Da's wife, Maggie. The character is at one level an archetypal Irish mammy but the archetype is filled out with intimate and illuminating detail. Reeves fuses these two elements into one bustling, ferocious force, a portrayal so energetic and fast on its feet that it never freezes into mere cliché.

The other great success is John Kavanagh's Drumm. The character has his own play, *A Life*, and Kavanagh brings to it here the experience of playing that role two years ago. The result is that Kavanagh's Drumm is far richer and more complex than we have a right to expect from a character whose onstage presence is largely confined to three short episodes. Drumm, the dry old stick, is filled with life, so that his sardonic, embittered personality becomes an intelligent man's response to the world as he finds it. One delightful effect is that Drumm becomes by far the funniest presence on stage.

Otherwise, though, these rich possibilities remain unfulfilled. Stephen Brennan's Da is a fine feat of acting. But because the character is for the most part so much older than the actor, it is impossible not to be aware of it all the time precisely as a feat. Every old man's movement is questioned by Brennan's young voice. The effect, in a play whose structure depends so much on the passage of time, is continually disconcerting.

Elsewhere, the balance between the real and the mythic is never quite struck. Ronan Leahy's Oliver is almost entirely cartoonish. Seán Campion and Alan Leech, as Charlie and his younger self, on the other hand, are too one-dimensionally realistic. Neither seem to quite fit into Paul McCauley's beautifully dreamlike set, nor to feel at home in a play that is, essentially, a ghost story.

Sive, by John B. Keane

Town Hall Theatre, Galway
The Irish Times, 12 September 2002

For much of the last 50 years, Ireland has been conducting an argument between tradition and modernity. The row is over now. Looking back, we can see how crude these terms are, how inadequate such a simple opposition has always been. Irish culture has always had the ability to be more than one thing at any one time.

John B. Keane's extraordinary 1959 play, *Sive*, is a case in point. We can see it as an almost mediaeval work, whose story of the sale of a poor young girl to a rich old man could be set, with few changes, in almost any part of the world at any time in the last 700 years. Or we can see it as a sharp, realistic response to the exhaustion of the Ireland of de Valera and the birth of the Ireland of Lemass.

And now, thanks to Garry Hynes's fierce yet poetic production for Druid, we can see it as both. As the first posthumous staging of Keane's greatest play, this one has the feeling of a retrospective view that can take in the entire landscape he travelled.

Roughly speaking, *Sive*'s history has had two chapters. In its early days, when it welled up from the very roots of rural Ireland with an unstoppable force, it was seen as a folk drama – powerful but primitive. Then, in 1985, Ben Barnes's superb production at the Abbey humanized it into a realistic social drama, with the central character, Mena Glavin, becoming less a wicked witch and more a tragic heroine.

Hynes has now added a third chapter, which is a synthesis of the other two. The core of *Sive*, she suggests, is that it unfolds in a world that has layers of reality. There is a social and economic reality: Mena desperately trying to escape from poverty, to establish a modern nuclear family, to be part of the new Ireland that is struggling to be born. And there is a spiritual reality: a world of curses and blessings, of pure goodness and pure evil, of paganism fused with Christianity.

The trick, of course, is to make these two realities cohere on the stage. Hynes, her terrific design team and her outstanding cast achieve this by following a rather neglected aspect of Keane's achievement: his language.

Keane's language is realistic, in the sense that it uses a recognizable version of the Hiberno-English of north Co Kerry. But in the mouth of the magnificent Derbhle Crotty as Mena, and the wonderfully mad Eamon Morrissey as greedy matchmaker Thomasheen Seán Rua, we remember that Keane must also have been reading Shakespeare and Synge.

All the actors use thick rural accents, so that Keane's language becomes as viscous as clotted cream. And the rich strangeness of what we hear is matched by what we see. Francis O'Connor's long, hollow rectangular set is like an old Abbey box set that has scorched in a fire. Its dirty grey tones are lit by Davy Cunningham in glimmers and afterglows that place us in the perpetual gloom of a world before electricity.

These inspired designs have the effect of pushing every streak of colour that enters the frame to the limits of visual intensity. When Ruth Bradley's sparkling Sive enters in the last act, decked out for the sacrifice in a garish red dress, the effect is genuinely shocking. Her abandoned red high-heeled shoes, sitting towards the front of the stage, have all the power of the strange portents that presage doom in a Greek tragedy.

What Hynes is doing here is placing Keane in an Irish Gothic tradition that hovers between the real and the fantastic. She reinforces this shift through brilliant use of the minor characters. Liam Scuab, often a too-good-to-be-true drip, is played by Barry Ward as a kind of village Christ. The men of the roads, Pats Bocock and Carthalawn, become, in Frank O'Sullivan and Peter Halpin's trance-like performances, ghostly emanations from an otherworldly realm. Noel O'Donovan plays the rich old farmer, Seán Dóta, as a sinister compound of childish idiocy and monstrous lust.

Yet all of this poetic stylization is applied with enough restraint to allow for the more recognizable social and psychological realities to be given their due. Crotty's performance as Mena, Gary Lydon's as her husband, Mike, and Anna Manahan's as his mother, Nana, are all beautifully attuned to the human truths of people trying to achieve decent goals in an indecent world.

Held in a masterful balance, these forces create a sumptuous drama that could not tackle harder or drive on more relentlessly if it had been written by Roy rather than the late, great John B.

Frank Pig Says Hello, by Patrick McCabe

Liberty Hall, Dublin
The Irish Times, 1 November 2002

'When I was a young lad twenty or thirty or forty years ago I lived in a small town where they were all after me on account of what I done on Mrs Nugent'. It is now all of 10 years since, with those opening words of *The Butcher Boy*, Patrick McCabe launched Francie Brady on the world.

In that time, he has become, almost literally, a legend. The pity and terror of Francie's slow transformation from innocent child to psychopath are so convincingly drawn that he seems more real than the literal truth. We are less likely to see the book as a reflection of actual events than to interpret a terrible outbreak of violent madness in rural or small-town Ireland through the book.

Culturally, the impact of the novel remains enormous. Neil Jordan's film of *The Butcher Boy* is arguably the finest Irish movie of the 1990s. In literature a whole school of Irish rural Gothic has emerged under McCabe's influence.

One of the questions around the revival of *Frank Pig Says Hello*, McCabe's dramatic version of the novel is, therefore, the extent to which all of this will blunt the edge of what was, when it first appeared, a startling show. It is a mark of how well fashioned it was in the first place that the answer is very little.

Frank Pig is not, in the usual sense, an adaptation. Not only is it McCabe's own work, but it emerged more or less contemporaneously with the novel in 1992. The story is broadly the same, but its shape and focus are inevitably different.

For a start, the great technical achievement of the novel – the insidious intimacy of the narrative voice – is missing. The story becomes more external, a set of things that happen rather than a succession of words in a man's head.

The irresistible charm of Francie, his heartbreaking amiability, is largely lost. On screen, in Jordan's film, this could be recaptured by having Francie played by a child. On stage, this is a practical impossibility.

Frank Pig is not, then, as brilliant a play as *The Butcher Boy* is a novel. But the great virtue of Joe O'Byrne's supremely confident staging is that it wastes no time crying over spilt milk. It does not try to capture qualities that are beyond the grasp of theatre but rather sets about the task of reconstructing the story in theatrical terms.

The key to this is an almost complete disavowal of realism. There are just two actors. David Gorry plays the younger, active Francie, here called Piglet. Denis Conway is the older Frank, who is not so much a recollecting narrator as the mind in which the whole story is re-enacted.

Thus we get, not an adaptation, but a translation. The language of fiction becomes the language of theatre. The internal verbal world of the narrator becomes the external physical world of the stage.

In O'Byrne's own design, this is an invented space, half-real and half-abstract. One of the great advantages of this revival is that the new Liberty Hall space, with its open, uncluttered stage, is perfect for this style of fluid staging.

None of this would mean very much, though, were it not embodied by the performers. David Gorry's re-creation of his original role as Piglet is no less remarkable than it seemed a decade ago. Gorry goes back for inspiration beyond the naturalism of the modern Irish stage to the world of silent movies. He uses a language of movement and gesture that draws on the terrifying strangeness of Buster Keaton and the apparent innocence of Stan Laurel. And he achieves the same kind of visual eloquence, at once distant and engrossing.

Denis Conway is very different, but scarcely less impressive. Filling in a large array of other characters, he has to be slower and more subtle. But his assurance allows him to create the structure which Gorry can illuminate with his pyrotechnics. Their telepathic relationship lends the whole thing an air of absolute conviction.

This certainty that these people are completely in command of what they are doing is rare enough in the theatre, and it forms a powerful shield against the rush of passing time. Anyone who saw the show a decade ago should welcome it back. For anyone who didn't, it's time to say hello.

The Development of the Critic

Julia Furay

Theatre companies in Ireland have continually worked to define a modern canon; this means, of course, that contemporary classics get habitually reproduced and rethought. Frequent productions of classics lend importance to the issue of re-reviewing. The following segment reprints the reviews of four plays that Fintan O'Toole saw numerous times: *Happy Days*, *The Hostage*, *Philadelphia, Here I Come!*, and *Translations*.

The first review of *Happy Days* was one of the first pieces of criticism that O'Toole published, so his development as a critic is particularly noticeable here. He has certainly developed an O'Toole form and style since he began: while he was always inclined to analyse rather than describe, his ability to weave these elements together has visibly improved.

Look at his *Translations* reviews together, for instance: by 1996, a clearer and snappier style had emerged since he wrote his first review of the play thirteen years earlier. His sentences have more personality ('Hands up anyone who has seen the play and didn't think of the Provos whenever the invisible Donnelly Twins were mentioned?') and a greater acuity of perception in explaining exactly why the production doesn't work. Most noticeably, the 1996 *Translations* review features the structural coherence which is a hallmark of the O'Toole style.

Nowadays, theatrical description, contextualization, even discussion of the play's core – all of these are used not unto themselves, but as points of argument within a larger thesis. All of the elements of his writing must act in coherence with this argument.

And as his knowledge of the theatre grew, so did his repertoire of references and comparisons to outside influences or comparative works. His analyses have therefore gained depth: while he explores meaning in his first *Happy Days* review, his analysis expands to a reflection on Absurdism and Protestantism two reviews later.

But from the beginning, O'Toole has been alert to the contemporary resonances in classic plays. He forces a play to continually justify itself: *The Hostage, Philadelphia, Here I Come!* and *Translations* all seem to him problematic plays for contemporary audiences, and with each review here, he tries to define why.

Happy Days, by Samuel Beckett

Players Theatre
In Dublin, 27 June 1980

'So that I may say at all times, even when you do not answer and perhaps hear nothing, something of this is being heard, I am not merely talking to myself, that is in the wilderness, a thing I could never bear to do'. In *Happy Days* we hear a rare snatch of Beckett's own voice, the voice of a writer so painfully aware of the gulf between himself and his audience that he must ask whether there is any relationship at all between words and action, the artist and the world. Winnie, confined up to her waist and later her neck in sand, is incapable of meaningful action and must fill the silence with words. Willie, who is free to move, can speak only in single words or short phrases from newspaper advertisements. There can be nothing between these extremes.

Stressing the sterility of mere words, Beckett makes fun of abstract intellectualism. There is a comic reduction of the search for truth in Winnie's attempt to discover what is 'fully guaranteed, genuine, pure' on the handle of her toothbrush, and a mockery of the play's own attempt at meaning in 'What's the idea? ... What's it meant to mean?' The realization of Beckett's ideas on stage needs a production sensitive to this humour and to the compassion in the portrayal of a middle-aged housewife confined in an empty relationship to her husband. Brendan Ellis and the Cogitandum Company at Players' Theatre unite all these strands in an outstanding production. Claire Mullan as Winnie combines cruel discipline with creativity in a remarkable performance. Ellis is not always faithful to Beckett's stage directions, but after the dullness of Beckett's own direction of *Endgame* at the Peacock, that may not always be a bad thing.

Peacock Theatre
Sunday Tribune, 25 May 1986

Marie Kean has a particular ability with Beckett. Her acting always has an angular edge to it. She can produce the emotions without being totally caught up in them. This is a good basis on which to approach the playing of Winnie in *Happy Days* (at the Peacock). Winnie, stuck first up to her waist and then up to her neck in sand, is not completely a character in the realistic sense, but then neither is she a mere symbol of some metaphysical dilemma. The play calls for something halfway between domestic drama and cosmic comedy. We need to be able to see Winnie as a particular person with particular emotions and at the same time as a representative and significant specimen of humanity. Marie Kean's style of acting allows her to do this.

Happy Days is about the human propensity to make do, to concentrate on what is available and ignore the terrible limitations that surround our actions. It deals with the way in which things become significant in their absence. The fact that Winnie can hardly move makes every move she makes seem terribly meaningful, even when it is completely banal and pointless. The fact that her husband Willie (very well played by O Z. Whitehead) hardly ever talks to her makes every noise he makes seem important even when he is only reading out useless headlines from an old newspaper. *Happy Days* is not about absurdity but about our relentless search for meaning.

The movement of the play is towards a narrowing of the focus. In the first half, we can watch Winnie's frantic attempts at making herself busy as she uses the things around her to create the impression of activity. In the second half, deprived of these things, every twitch and detail of expression become important. Marie Kean does this superbly. She changes her tone from the frantic breeziness of the first half to a harsher, more hollow note of pain and desperation. She makes the way each phrase is said cut the ground from under its ostensible meaning, opening up the gap between word and meaning which is at the core of the play.

There were, on the opening night at least, too many moments when the essential flow of the speech was stopped by uncertainties. These will presumably be ironed out in later performances. When they are, this will be a very fine *Happy Days*.

Andrews Lane Theatre
The Irish Times, 30 June 1990

Absurdism did not begin with Beckett or Camus, but with the extreme scepticism of the philosophers of the seventeenth and eighteenth centuries. Protestantism begins with the notion that it is up to each individual to find God for himself, to validate the world by his or her own inquiries. Implicit in that notion is an absurd time, a time before that validation has been found when everything is meaningless and without purpose.

In Descartes, in Locke and in Berkeley we have that process of extreme doubt, that gap between the question and the answer which we would later learn to call absurd. We don't think of it as absurd because, of course, those philosophers always found the answer they knew they wanted, always ended up with a God who gave meaning to everything. The only real difference between Berkeley and Beckett is that the former finds the answer he is looking for and the latter knows there is no answer. Absurdism is a godless Protestantism.

All of this lurks somewhere behind Beckett's play *Happy Days,* currently playing in a fine production at the Andrews Lane Studio in Dublin. It was one Protestant Irishman, out on the margins of Protestant Europe, George Berkeley, who wondered whether a flower that bloomed unseen in the desert could be said to exist at all. It was another Protestant Irishman, out at the margins of a dying Protestant class, Samuel Beckett, who put this idea on the stage in the form of a woman buried in the sand of the desert who wonders whether she can be said to exist at all if she is not seen and heard. It was Berkeley who said 'esse est percipi': to be is to be perceived. It was Beckett who gave us people on the stage who only exist because we are looking at them, who made the perceiving audience the central character of his plays.

This is not just philosophical rambling. If there really is a connection between Berkeley and Beckett, if the Beckett of *Happy Days* can be said to be using an Irish Protestant tradition as much as a French Absurdist one, then this has a bearing on how we might see the play.

There are two ways of being wrong about Beckett. One is to be too literal, to see his plays as being 'about' external events like the French Resistance or the threat of a nuclear holocaust. The other is to be too allegorical, to see the plays as being about things that can only be expressed with capital letters: Man, God, the Human Condition. Beckett is both and neither of these things: he is a philosophical realist, a writer trying to deal with general things in particular ways. If you can say that there is a specifically Irish Protestant dimension to *Happy Days*, then you can see the part of humanity through which it explores the human condition.

Winnie, stuck first up to her waist, then up to her neck, in sand, remembers or imagines her past life. The world she conjures could well be an Anglo-Irish one. It is a world of bishops and balls, of tool sheds and boats on the lake, of steep wooden stairs and old nursemaids. Her constant refrain of 'the old style' makes it easy to imagine her as an Anglo-Irish matron lamenting the decline of the Big House. Certainly, for an Irish audience, it is that specific world that is evoked.

And this sense of the decline of an old order and its culture is reinforced by the play's literary references. In one sense, the whole play is a parody of the decline of English and Anglo-Irish romanticism. Winnie in her mundane torment is a down at heel version of Shelley's heroic Prometheus. He is chained to a rock, his liver torn by eagles. She is 'stuck up to her diddies in the bleeding ground'. He laments: 'no change, no pause, no hope'; she echoes the lament while rummaging for her toothbrush: 'no change – no pain – hardly any – great things that – nothing like it'. The heroic style is reduced to absurdity. And the mock-heroic impulse comes closer to the Irish Protestant bone when Winnie takes up the chorus from Yeats's Cuchulain plays: 'I call to the eye of the mind ... One loses one's classics', Winnie remarks, and the sense is of being at the tail end of a dying culture.

If you take away the sand dunes and the blazing light, *Happy Days* could easily be a domestic play set in a decrepit Big House. It is certainly the most domestic of Beckett's big plays, following as it does the trivia of the daily routine – the alarm clock, the toothbrush, the tonic, the lipstick, the morning paper – and using, to an extent that is rare in Beckett, a marital relationship.

What all of this amounts to is that the play is one which, without being too specific or literal, can bear a little grounding in a recognizable reality. In Brendan Ellis's production it gets the right amount of that grounding. Teresa Mitchell's Winnie is nicely ordinary and recognizably Irish, not quite a filled-out conventional character but close enough to avoid abstraction.

If there is a criticism it is that this is sometimes achieved, particularly in the first act, at the expense of the humour and self-conscious theatricality of the piece. The joke, as in most of Beckett's plays, is on the audience: 'What does it mean? he says – What's it meant to mean? – and so on – lot more stuff like that- usual drivel …' It is the situation of theatre itself that is being sent up and from which much of the humour derives. And too little is made of that here. The loss is greater because the production is exceptionally slow, and tends to ignore whatever opportunities for a bit of diversion there are in the text.

The Hostage, by Brendan Behan
Abbey Theatre
In Dublin, 8 January 1982

In the minds of most people involved with the business of theatre, there is some kind of general distinction between art and entertainment by which most productions can be categorized. The possibility that this distinction might be a false one is seldom considered, and certainly not at Christmas time when what the punters want is Entertainment. This kind of categorization is fine when it comes to a show like *The Pirates of Penzance* but it hardly does justice to an ambivalent play like *The Hostage*.

Because it is structurally such a mess, it is easy to regard *The Hostage* simply as an excuse for a bit of a romp and Behan himself encouraged this by talking about how 'the music hall is the thing to aim at for to amuse people and any time they get bored divert them with a song or a dance'. In one way *The Hostage* is just a great variety show, with some very funny songs, lots of bad language and a few good gags. In this respect Joe Lynch is well cast as Pat the brothel-keeper, bringing a nice touch of the music-hall MC to the proceedings, and Tom Hickey does a hilarious impersonation of Beaker from the Muppet Show in the role of the idiotic Volunteer.

But, on another level, that Volunteer is a man with a gun, and since the play was written, in 1958, we have learned once and for all that men with guns are not very funny. The great strength of Behan as a writer was the fact that he had experienced personally and painfully the disintegration of militaristic nationalism as a moral force in this country. Beneath the layers of vaudeville, there is a core of political meaning in *The Hostage* that is both relevant and contentious today. Behan's IRA officer who 'might take a bottle of orange and me after the high caul cap in a Gaelic measurement at an Irish ceilidhe, but not at any other time' is not entirely a joke.

This being the season of good will, however, Tomás MacAnna has directed as if political violence had ceased to exist in Ireland in 1958 and we can all look back at history and have a good laugh. His IRA men are pretty harmless and the spectral figure of Monsewer is played by Ray McAnally as a lovable eccentric rather than as the raving madman he is. An incidental, but highly objectionable result of the director's refusal to look at the play with any degree of hindsight is the uncritical acceptance of Behan's stereotypical limp-wristed homosexuals Rio Rita and Princess Grace. Instead of being played down, these insulting caricatures are milked for cheap laughs.

As with so many recent Abbey productions, this version of *The Hostage* seems to have been staged because it fits the bill for a Christmas show rather than because anyone had any real idea what to do with it.

Jesuit Hall, Galway
Sunday Tribune, 1 November 1987

Because it came to international attention through London it is easy to forget that Brendan Behan's play *The Hostage*, which has opened in a Druid production at the Jesuit Hall, Galway, has a very specific Irish background. Its Irish-language predecessor *An Giall* was written early in 1958, just after the collapse of the IRA's ill-conceived and disastrous Border Campaign of 1957.

The IRA had come close to farce and even within the Republican movement a lacerating process of self-criticism was underway. *The Hostage*'s criticism of militant nationalism and its depiction of the IRA have much to do with these circumstances. It is this which makes the play so difficult to perform now that the IRA has been reborn as something very far from farce. Jim Sheridan's production looks for a way of distancing the play from its origins while preserving its spirit and its vision.

The text used for this production is practically an adaptation, since it blends elements of the Joan Littlewood-inspired *The Hostage* with Behan's original *An Giall*, adding elements of its own. The action is moved forward to 1960, presumably to distance it from the atmosphere of the 1957 campaign.

Some of the more farcical characters, Miss Gilchrist and Mulleady, are dropped altogether; the songs from the Littlewood production are used with a great deal of freedom, some dropped, others placed differently in the action; and, most importantly, the hostage of the title, the young English soldier Leslie Williams, here a Geordie rather than a Cockney, emphasizing his distance from the establishment in his own country, dies not in a chaotic police raid, but in the more haphazard and meaningless manner of *An Giall*, suffocating in a fridge where he has been hidden. All of these decisions are good ones.

The cumulative effect, however, is still somewhat odd. What Sheridan has done is to make the realistic more believable. The relationship between Leslie and Teresa, the skivvy, is more touching and genuine, and Eanna MacLiam and Rachael Dowling consequently do very well, capturing the innocence and loneliness of the characters without neglecting their essential toughness. Similarly, John Murphy's Pat is less of the music-hall master of ceremonies and more of a coherent character in keeping with Teresa's accusation, imported from *An Giall*, that 'It's not the Six Counties that's bothering you. You are trying to get back two things you can't get back, your lost youth and your lost leg'.

And yet all of this relative realism has to sit with the farcical elements that remain. The IRA officer who wears a beret, trench coat and *fáinne* and drinks only a *buidéal oráiste* at the *céilí* is a very funny caricature of the self-righteous ultra-conservative patriot of the Fifties, and is played well by Dave Carey as such. But the IRA just isn't funny anymore, and this cartoon character is from a different world to the rest of the production. By heightening the realism elsewhere, Sheridan also heightens the problematic nature of the depiction of the IRA.

The first half of the play suffers most from this ill-fitting mixture, the confusion of tone leading to uncertainty and flatness. But the production is rescued in the second half by some superbly inventive stage business, by a growing use of stylization and the symbolic and by the genuineness of the relationships which are established.

The real test of a production of *The Hostage* is whether it is possible to end the play convincingly with Leslie's resurrection from the dead as he emerges singing: 'The bells of hell go ting-a-ling for you but not for me'. In order for this to work there has to have been the sense on the stage of another world, a world of images and symbols in which such things can be made to happen. Sheridan's production, as it advances, creates this world through the songs. Terry Neason sings magnificently, in her role as Meg, dramatizing songs like 'The Laughing Boy' and 'Who Fears to Speak of Easter Week?' to a degree where her voice becomes an alternative presence on the stage, literally out of this world.

Allied to this is the use of light and space, of Andy Phillips's supple and atmospheric lighting and Brian Vahey's excellent set. The set creates a picture-frame at the back of the stage, and Sheridan uses this space more and more as an area of stylized action, framing expressionistic tableaux within it and making it a sort of magical space from which the resurrected Leslie can convincingly emerge. Here, stagecraft and ideas work together to sometimes stunning effect.

For all that it is not entirely satisfactory, therefore, Sheridan's production passes its most crucial test and remains memorable for it.

Abbey Theatre
The Irish Times, 19 March 1996

We talk of 'putting on a play' as if a piece of theatre was an off-the-peg outfit, sitting in the wardrobe of repertoire, waiting to be dusted down and worn. But the metaphor is misleading, and never more so than in the case of Brendan Behan's *The Hostage*.

What we have is not a play text but merely the record of a production, an indication in print of what happened when Joan Littlewood staged a play in the Theatre Royal, Stratford East, in October 1958. Kenneth Tynan noted at the time that 'no one can be sure how much of the dialogue is pure Behan and how much is gifted embroidery'. By now, not just the embroidery but all the seams of the piece need to be restitched. Otherwise, it just won't wear.

The fascination of the play lies in the very choice that Behan made when he allowed his little Gaelic melodrama, *An Giall* (no more than an extended one-act sketch), to be transformed into *The Hostage*. To put it another way, the most profound critique of the IRA in the play, the real break that Behan makes, lies not in the content of the play but in its form.

The plot – Republicans kidnap young English soldier and glimpse the futility and inhumanity of their own assumptions in the cruelty of killing him – was written in the 1930s, by Frank O'Connor. Behan adds nothing in the way of emotional or moral insight to O'Connor's *Guests of the Nation*. What is original and important is the way in which that plot is placed in an entirely different cultural context.

Guests of the Nation and *An Giall* may raise questions about the political and moral assumptions behind militant Irish nationalism, but they leave its cultural assumptions untouched. Both remain firmly within the Irish literary movement; the attempt to create a separate and distinctive cultural space. But *The Hostage*, as re-invented by Littlewood and Behan, destroys the cultural assumptions as well.

It depends on the idea that the popular vulgarities of vaudeville are as much at home in Dublin as they are in London. It suggests that the British soldier's Old Kent Road is not much different from the Old IRA Man's Russell Street. It shows that Ireland is not a pure place in any sense of the word, that it is sexually heterogeneous and culturally promiscuous.

And, above all, it makes a choice for the here-and-now instead of for tradition and posterity. Where *An Giall* is trying to place itself within a literary tradition, to win a place in a national cultural canon, *The Hostage* is, above all, *live* theatre, reckless of past and future, concerned only with what can happen between actors and an audience at any given point in time. That choice is where the play's real politics lie. By choosing the here-and-now, the contingent, the living, over the long view, the dead generations, and the abstract future, it challenges most profoundly the Republican belief that the present can be sacrificed on the altar of history.

In doing this, it presents a director with a stark choice – either reinvent it and make it truly a live event, or don't do it at all. Brian Brady, who directs the Abbey production, seems fully aware of this choice. But he also seems too timid to really make it. His production starts, and continues for a while, as if it were going to be bold and radical. But it lacks the courage of its convictions.

One sign of the timidity is that the action is moved forward, but only to 1962, as if the director wishes to acknowledge the need to shift the play out of its original context but is afraid to do so in a way that would make any real difference. Likewise, contemporary references – white ribbons, peace talks – are interpolated, but in a way that is so marginal that the effect is almost invisible. And Brendan Conroy's IRA officer is still a comic and absurd figure, as if a 1996 Dublin audience knew no more about such things than a 1958 London audience might have done.

There are good things in the production. It is mostly well cast, and it has in Donal Donnelly and Barbara Brennan two performers who, if they have no opportunity for great art here, at least display great craft. Robert Price as the English soldier and Janet Moran as the country girl who falls for him both have the sophistication it takes to play naive characters well. Tony Flynn manages, amazingly, to lift the male prostitute Rio Rita out of the dated clichés in which he is written. And even if the songs – in many ways the glory of the piece – are truncated and butchered, David Hayes's musical arrangements subtly reinvent the tunes.

But there are also bad things, not the least of them that there is a gaucheness about the approach to the play's exuberant vaudeville, a vague but unmistakable embarrassment about the vulgar, unsubtle directness that is what it's all about. The contingent humanity of the piece is still 'put on' and, like any borrowed garment, it comes apart at the seams.

Philadelphia, Here I Come!, by Brian Friel

Abbey Theatre
In Dublin, 28 May 1982

Philadelphia, Here I Come! was not only Brian Friel's first international success, it is also a seminal work for much of his subsequent dramatic writing. Friel's plays, particularly his two most recent works, *Faith Healer* and *Translations*, are concerned chiefly with the question of identity – personal, national and political. Friel has always used a sense of place as a metaphor for the relationship of the individual to his world, a metaphor in which physical dislocation comes to represent a state of personal homelessness. The problem for Gar in *Philadelphia* is that moving from one place to another, from his native Ballybeg to the United States, will do nothing to alter the fact that he has no place in the world.

Friel expresses this sense of spiritual dislocation in a simple and forceful dramatic device by dividing the character of Gar into public and private personae, played by different actors. The consequences of this device crop up again and again in Friel's plays. The dissolution of individual identities in *Faith Healer* and the fissure of consciousness brought about by the invasion of an alien language in *Translations* are the deepest expressions of concerns which surface in *Philadelphia*.

The best piece of dramatic writing in the play is echoed directly in *Faith Healer*. In a last desperate effort to establish some communion with his father, Gar speaks to him of his memory of a single day when they were happy together, an idyllic image which has sustained him for many years in silence. But his father has no such memory, and the last semblance of relationship, a relationship which might allow Gar to define himself, is shattered.

A revival of *Philadelphia* at this time might be expected to look at the play in the light of Friel's later work and to seek to clarify the elements in it which are of abiding value in the context of Friel's relentless formal experimentation. It is interesting to note, however, that the most effective elements in this production are the performances of two old stagers of the Abbey tradition, Ray McAnally and Marie Kean, who are individually excellent in their naturalistic roles. The main element of formal innovation which Friel introduced in the play – the anti-naturalistic division of the character of Gar – is handled less successfully, however.

The production does nothing to clarify the relationship between Gar's private and public personae. Stephen Brennan and Gerard McSorley never seem to connect, a failure which has its most serious consequences in the scene where Gar is visited for the last time by his old cronies.

In spite of its lack of depth, however, there is much to enjoy in Joe Dowling's production. It is stylish, well paced and maintains a good balance between humour and desperation. For admirers of Friel the opportunity to see one of his most important plays is very worthwhile.

Gaiety Theatre
Sunday Tribune, 20 April 1986

A lot has changed since 1963, when Brian Friel's *Philadelphia, Here I Come!* was written. When the play was first produced, towns like Ballybeg and all-purpose shops like S.B. O'Donnell's were ten a penny. For an Irish audience then, there would have been an immediate recognition of the stultification, the sexual frustration, and the sheer dullness of a place like Ballybeg.

Now, the dullness of small-town Ireland may not have changed, but it takes different forms. Things like air-conditioning and hamburgers and colour TV are no longer credible as an attractive alternative to the life of Ballybeg. Immersed as we are in all of those things, the old stabilities of Ballybeg, with its innocence and its simplicities, are more exotic than the bright lights of Philadelphia. The bitterness of Friel's portrayal of Ballybeg can become nostalgia.

This, to a certain extent, is what happens in Joe Dowling's superbly capable and well-acted production of the play at the Gaiety. Without deliberately going for softness and sentiment, it is dominated by both. It is not that the director has any dewy-eyed vision of the play, just that he has done nothing to counteract the nostalgia-inducing effects of the passage of time.

Just as, for instance, Pat O'Connor's film of *The Ballroom of Romance*, a vicious, depressing vision of the Ireland of the Fifties, invoked in its audiences, not bitterness, but a wave of the warm reminiscence for the supposed innocence of the times, nostalgia creeps into *Philadelphia* without invitation, because nothing has been done to stop it.

So what's the problem with nostalgia? In the case of *Philadelphia*, it's quite a big problem. The play focuses on the dilemma of Gar O'Donnell, a young man of 25, torn between the attractions of emigration to America and the ties of his own hometown.

In order to fully understand that dilemma, it is important that a careful tension is maintained between Gar's alternatives. The pull of flight has to be strong, and the impossibility of staying in Ballybeg has to be clear. Nostalgia for the life of Ballybeg, life before McDonalds, *The Late Late Show* and *The Sunday World*, disturbs that balance, and robs the play of some of its urgency.

The feel of the production is epitomized in Rosaleen Linehan's performance as Madge, housekeeper to Gar and his widowed father, and the one living person in the play for whom Gar feels an uncompromised love. The performance is in itself a miracle of comic timing, understatement and attention to physical detail, summing up the sheer quality of the acting in the production.

But at the same time it is soft-centred, making Madge a saintly and charming woman impervious to disappointments and betrayals. She embodies the old Ireland of homeliness, resignation and imperturbability so attractively that it is hard for us to see why that old Ireland was no longer sufficient for young men like Gar. She is a wisecracker on Walton's Mountain. It is hard to understand that she is part of the stultification which Gar must escape.

From the start, there is this touch of softness. The first thing we hear is the sound of Dinjoe on the radio, a sound which evokes, not a sense of claustrophobia, but of innocence and warm reminiscence.

S.B. O'Donnell himself, Gar's begrudging, uncommunicative father, is, in Seamus Forde's strong performance, rather more venerable than cantankerous, never as mean-minded as he could be. In some of the smaller roles, however, there is a counter-current to this softness, with Ray McBride's edgy despair as one of Gar's ageing bunch of 'lads' and the enormously impressive cameo from John Cowley as Master Boyle, capturing the pathetic dignity of a man locked in a world that is too small for his aspirations. Here there is the hard edge of a hellish existence, the awfulness that Gar cannot abide.

The great strength of this production, however, is in the interplay between Gar Public and Gar Private, the inner and outer sides of the hero, played respectively by Lorcan Cranitch and Garrett Keogh. The two actors are physically alike, but their performances are beautifully contrasted, Cranitch still and passionate, Keogh ironic, unstable and vulnerably ostentatious.

Dealing with this relationship, the production is full of wit and invention, finding ways of commenting on the action with touches like having Gar mime an exaggeratedly Americanized song using his hurley as a guitar.

The playing of the two sides of Gar clarifies and brings to the fore the most interesting and effective device of the play. What happens around Gar is that reality, the world he is living in, is already becoming a memory, so that he is consciously trying to create moments which will sustain him as his last memories of the people he is close to, rather than deal with them in the present.

And that reality itself comes to depend on a memory – the crucial question for him is whether or not his father can remember an idealized incident from many years into the past.

This playing with time, so that the present becomes the past and the past shapes the present, is the most characteristic concern of *Philadelphia* in relation to Friel's later work, and Joe Dowling, who has directed much of that later work, draws it out with a sure hand.

It is interesting that what wears best in the play is what was, in 1963, its 'experimental' side, the splitting of the main character into two parts, while the play's affinities with the small-town naturalism which dominated Irish theatre until the end of the Fifties are what make it problematic now. What the Gaiety production plays to those strengths, it is very fine indeed.

Abbey Theatre
The Irish Times, 28 February 1995

As they say in all the best exam papers, compare and contrast:

> (a) I'm going to Philadelphia, to work in an hotel. And you know why I'm going, Screwballs, don't you? Because I'm 25, and you treat me as if I were five – I can't order even a dozen loaves without getting your permission.

> (b) My mother died yesterday. Well, not my mother as such. She didn't raise me or anything. [...] I was adopted. Apparently she asked that I be told of her death and given these. A photograph and a shoe. That's all. I don't know what her name was. What she died of or where she died. It doesn't matter now. What was slightly less negotiable was my ex-boyfriend turning up at the departures lounge for his final farewell. I know he means well, but so did Charles Manson.

These are passages of dialogue from two Irish plays. Both speakers are Irish people in their early twenties. Both are on their way out of Ireland and intending to work abroad. Both have strained relations with their parents. But there the similarities end. The first, Gar O'Donnell from Brian Friel's classic *Philadelphia, Here I Come!* lives in a world so intimate and closed that leaving his native Ballybeg for America is like leaving Earth for Mars. The second, Siabhra from Bickerstaffe's *True Lines*, one of the most important Irish plays of last year, lives in a world where departure and disjunction are taken for granted, whether you go or stay.

The 30 years that separate *True Lines* from *Philadelphia* could be a century. Neither play is 'about' emigration, but each is unimaginable without emigration. The persistence of emigration should create a real sense of continuity between Gar O'Donnell's generation and Siabhra's, but it doesn't. To look at Patrick Mason's production of *Philadelphia* at the Abbey after seeing a play like *True Lines* is to realize just how foreign and distant the world of Gar O'Donnell has become. The Ballybeg of 1964 has become much more foreign than Philadelphia.

The contrast is not just between soiled shop-coasts and cool Raybans. It is, more profoundly, between one mental universe and another. Critical words like 'memory' and 'home' have changed their meaning. The whole dramatic premise of *Philadelphia* – that Gar's departure from Ireland is a huge turning-point in his life – is unimaginable in *True Lines*, which is set in Kansas, Australia, Berlin and Ethiopia, and whose characters never had anything fixed and stable to depart from.

What makes *Philadelphia* a brilliant play, lifting it way beyond the kitchen tragedy it might have been, is the way it dramatizes Ireland and America, not just as two places, but as two states of mind. Ireland is a place haunted by memory, America, a place haunted by forgetfulness. Gar and his father are tormented by inescapable memories which may be mere inventions. But Gar's American aunt, Lizzie, superbly played in this production by Stella McCusker, is unable to remember even where she has been a few hours ago. Ireland is unbearable stasis and claustrophobia, America terrible anonymity and impermanence.

But this polarity is impossible now. In *True Lines* the young émigrés already live in a world of anonymity and impermanence. They travel not to escape an Ireland that is too numbingly continuous, but in the hope that they might find some kind of absent continuity on their journeys.

The problem that all of these huge changes of mind pose for a serious production of *Philadelphia* now is how to avoid nostalgia. A contemporary audience approaches the play as a reflection not of a bitter present but of a half-remembered past. It is too close, and too often revived, to be exotic, but too distant to be contemporary. It has the same problems as O'Casey's Dublin trilogy had in the 1950s, and runs the same risks of being blunted by an over-familiarity that allows neither for freshness nor for radical reappraisal.

Patrick Mason seems aware of the problem, and his production goes at least some distance towards solving it. *Philadelphia* is rich enough to allow characters previously on the sidelines to move centre stage. Oddly enough, in a play that is so much about the condition of the Irish male, it is the women – especially McCusker's Lizzy and Rosaleen Linehan's Madge – who now seem much the most interesting characters. A whole other play about the lives of women, present in deep layers beneath the surface of the main action, suggests itself in the undertow of Linehan's profoundly truthful performance, which seems even more deeply rooted than it did when she first created it for Joe Dowling's production of the play.

The immediacy of these performances, however, serves to highlight the weary and even dreary nature of much of the rest. Mason's staging suggests that he thought about Gar Private as a kind of Gar Future, a version of Gar returning to Ballybeg to replay the eve of his departure in his mind. This is an intriguing idea, and, if carried through, it might give Philadelphia a new resonance by making it a memory play. But Darragh Kelly's performance is too lightweight and glib to give it substance, and it remains merely a notion. And without some coherent new approach, the play is bathed in the light of other days, a light much softer and dimmer than the light in which this great theatrical creation deserves to be seen.

Translations, by Brian Friel

Abbey Theatre
In Dublin, 25 March 1983

What could the Abbey have done with *Translations*? On the one hand a production by the National Theatre of a play that has been hailed as a national classic raises certain expectations about the definitive stature of that production; on the other hand the Abbey's current position is such that it clearly has not a sufficient range of actors to be able to mount a definitive production of a play that demands extraordinary strength in every part. Furthermore a director approaching *Translations* now must on the one hand have due regard for its depth and seriousness as a play while on the other hand taking into account the fact that Brian Friel followed it with *The Communication Cord*, a play which showed a great deal of scepticism about the undue deference afforded to *Translations*. These contradictions and uncertainties bedevil Joe Dowling's new production, making it bewilderingly uneven and inconclusive.

The strategy which Joe Dowling seems to have adopted is to orchestrate the play towards a series of major setpieces, hoping that their impact will carry through some of the more dubious performances and also allow for a mixture of tones which might overcome the problem of excessive reverence. This is not a solution, but as a strategy it does have the advantage of allowing for some moments of really great theatre to coexist alongside the inadequacies.

The problem is really summed up in Eamon Morrissey's performance as Doalty. Perhaps as an effort to lighten the overall tone, he plays Doalty almost exactly as he played Tony Lumpkin in *She Stoops to Conquer* a year ago – as a lovable, idiotic bumpkin. It is a serious piece of miscasting. Central to the play is a perception of Doalty, in his ignorance of the Classics, his lack of interest in the mythological dreaming of Jimmy Jack, as the possessor of an alternative knowledge – the wisdom of the soil. This perception is entirely absent in this production.

Of the actors in fact only Clive Geraghty, Dearbhla Molloy and Éamon Kelly present their characters with conviction. But these are superb performances, particularly Éamon Kelly's as Hugh. In Hugh's great closing speeches, the despairing oratory practiced throughout by Kelly is twisted and wracked into an almost ceremonial keening in which the grandeur of his beloved myths and the agony of the present intermingle. The play's themes of history and language, permanence and change are sharpened to a clear crystal in the voice and movements of a great actor. It is an exhilarating and terrifying moment, a moment which vindicates both Friel's play and ultimately Joe Dowling's production as well.

Gaiety Theatre
Sunday Tribune, 24 April 1988

Joe Dowling's new production of Brian Friel's *Translations* at the Gaiety takes its cue not so much from his previous and not particularly successful production of the play at the Abbey as from something completely different: his last collaboration with Donal McCann, in O'Casey's *Juno and the Paycock* at the Gate. I had never thought of the old hedge-schoolmaster Hugh and his sidekick Jimmy Jack as a sort of Captain Boyle and Joxer Daly before, but here, with their fantasizing about the ancient world and their final drunken entrance, they take on some of that colouring. Not, I hasten to add, the colouring of the traditional O'Casey buffoons, but of the downbeat, desperate Boyle and Joxer of Dowling's production. The effect is largely salutary, making for a warier, less romantic and more wry version of the play.

The initial burst of piety which exploded on *Translations* after its first production in 1980 was such that Friel felt obliged to write the deflating farce *The Communication Cord* as a counterbalance. This new production of *Translations* is very much post-*Communication Cord*, more sceptical of the pieties, more hesitant about picking sides among the play's competing forces. This sometimes makes for a lack of drive in the production, but it has compensating strengths and is certainly pursuing the right lines.

Dowling helps us to see what a complex and in some ways properly evasive play *Translations* is. Set in 1833 as the British

military are carrying out an Ordnance Survey around the fictional
Irish-speaking townland of Ballybeg in County Donegal, a
process which involves the translation of the familiar local place
names from Irish to English, the play is about the loss of a
language but also about the whole business of historical change.
Dealing as it does with pleasant, well-educated, peaceful people
being undermined by ignorant and ultimately violent aliens, it is
open to dangerous simplicities. Here, those simplicities are
warded off.

There are three things which contribute to this process. In the
first place there is Frank Conway's set, which is stripped bare of
most of the comfortable rustic images that are meant to adorn it:
hay, milking stalls, lobster pots, cartwheels; and is instead grey,
cold and somewhat suggestive of a prison yard, making it much
less of a bucolic utopia.

In the second place, Dowling has found in Conor Mullen the
first completely satisfactory Lieutenant Yolland I have seen.
Yolland is an important figure in the play, a young idealistic
English soldier who falls in love with both Ballybeg and Máire,
the girl who is meant to marry Manus, the schoolmaster's son.
Mullen's performance brings out the fact that the vision of
Ballybeg as a utopian community is given to a naive sentimental
outsider (In the *Communication Cord*, after all, the equivalent to
Yolland is a mad German tourist) and is therefore not to be
trusted.

And thirdly, of course, there is Donal McCann and Patrick
Laffan, playing very effectively together as Hugh and Jimmy Jack.
Laffan's Jimmy Jack is less of a romanticized tramp and more of
a lost fantasist, less charming and more robustly pathetic.
McCann's Hugh is decidedly unheroic, bullying, conceited,
cynical and full of self-contempt. His cries of, 'A bowl of tea,
strong tea, black', are roared at his son Manus with a violent
contempt. His dismissal of Máire's desire to learn English is
imperiously sneering. McCann's Hugh is an intelligent and
perceptive man with a gift of coherent expression, but he is not
an attractive person, and the interpretation strengthens and
deepens the play. The performance has its eccentricities and
uncertainties, not least the fact that you are sometimes convinced

that you are listening to Ben Kiely on *Sunday Miscellany*, but it is essentially very good.

It has its price, though. McCann's relative youth in the part means that his sons also have to be younger, and while Mark O'Regan's Manus is fine in itself, the fact that he is so young takes away much of the poignancy of the ageing Manus, trapped in the shadow of his domineering father, delaying his marriage to Máire until it is too late. Darragh Kelly is slight and insubstantial in the role of Hugh's other son, Owen, who works for the army as an interpreter and ends up being torn in the great divide. Róisín Sheerin's Sarah lacks the symbolic power which the part of the mute learning to speak should have. Otherwise, though, this intelligent, often witty production is exceptionally well cast and has fine performances from Peter Gowen as Doalty, Orla Charlton as Máire and Ruth McCabe as Bridget.

Abbey Theatre
The Irish Times, 13 August 1996

To a play already brimful of ironies, the current Abbey production of Brian Friel's *Translations* adds new ones of its own. There is already the layer of *double entendre* implicit in a story about the loss of the Irish language being acted out in English: English serves in the text both as itself and as a surrogate for Irish, so that the play's governing idea – the irreparable loss that a society incurs when it shifts from one language to another – is continually undercut by the fact that, in terms of what the audience actually hears, there is no difference between one language and the other. And there are the most specific ironies – the subtle presence of America in this confrontation of Ireland and England, for instance – that Friel continually points up.

But there is, at the Abbey, a further paradox, arising from the circumstances of the production rather than the nature of the play. This play about the cultural imperialism practised by England on Ireland is presented on the stage of the Irish National Theatre by a British director, designer and leading actor.

There is, I hasten to say, nothing at all objectionable about this – the close relationship between the theatre cultures of Britain and Ireland is for the most part mutually beneficial, and the director in this case, Robin Lefevre, has a brilliant record of work with Irish writers and actors. The problem, though, is that the production refuses to acknowledge its own reality, and tries instead to ignore the heavy British presence in a play that is, in another sense, an attack on that very presence.

This attempt is doomed to failure for one very obvious reason. Directors and designers declare their presence indirectly and implicitly. But actors declare themselves openly with every word and gesture. In this case the actor in question, Kenneth Haigh, not only has a very considerable stage presence, but also occupies the central role in the play, that of the hedge schoolmaster Hugh. And it is patently obvious at every turn of hand and phrase that he is not, and cannot convincingly pretend to be, a pre-Famine Donegal man.

This open incongruity ought to be an opportunity rather than a problem. *Translations* is not a play that necessarily requires the suspension of disbelief on the part of the audience. Indeed there are very good reasons for asking the audience not to enter into the play by pretending that we have been transported by means of the realistic illusion back into the 1830s.

One reason is that, if it is indeed taken literally, *Translations* is wide open to the charge of distorting history. Things didn't happen as they seem to happen in the play, and at a time when the destructive power of myths about history has never been more obvious, it is dangerous to create the illusion that what we are seeing is 'real'.

And besides, the play itself actually invites the audience to engage in an almost Brechtian double take. It issues that invitation both through the conceit of having Irish spoken as English and through very deliberate analogies with the present. Hands up anyone who has seen the play and didn't think of the Provos whenever the invisible Donnelly Twins were mentioned?

Because of these elements in the very nature of the play itself, it was open to Robin Lefevre to use the presence of Kenneth Haigh as Hugh in a deliberate and self-conscious way, disrupting the easy assumptions that the play can seem to reinforce. At the very least the result would be challenging. It was also open to Julian McGowan as designer to push away the temptation to indulge in a kind of touristic voyage into the past, and to give us something more than a virtual reality Irish barn, however beautifully realized. I recently watched on video a production of the play at the Stadttheater in Mainz, in which the designer Klaus Baumeister created a big, stark expressionistic space whose epic qualities both echoed the play's references to the classical world and established quite clearly that its action was unfolding in the here-and-now of theatre and not in some pretend past.

Neither of these openings is exploited. Instead, we are offered the play as a kind of intellectual costume drama. Kenneth Haigh tries to convince us that he really is a drunken schoolmaster in Donegal in 1833 by doing his best with the appropriate mannerisms and accent. The result is something very strange indeed, reminiscent at times of W.C. Fields playing Mr Pickwick and at others of what Jigs from the old Jigs and Maggie cartoon might look and sound like if he could get up off the page and tread the boards. The keynotes of the character, pathos and a mock-heroic grandeur, are never sounded. Since Hugh is the human flesh on the play's intellectual bones, the embodiment of its dying world, this failure is in spite of all the good things on offer in the production, decisive. The pace and rigour of Lefevre's stagecraft, the splendid sense of comic timing that makes the most of Friel's wicked humour, the fine ensemble playing and the strong performances of Ali White as Máire, Lloyd Hutchison as Owen and Gary Lydon as Manus all make for an acceptable enough production. But since this is at least the fifth major professional production of the play in the Republic in 15 years, the time for accepting the merely acceptable is surely long gone.

General Irish Theatre Commentaries

Redmond O'Hanlon

For O'Toole, theatre is above all else defined by its public, therefore political nature. It continually engages with the issue of community, of threats to community and with the possibility of making new, vibrant, even festive, communities. We can sense his enormous relish for this aspect of theatre in his fulsome review of Andy Hinds's *Siege of Derry Pageant*.

In his early years as a critic O'Toole may have been somewhat ideological in his reviews but his openness to new forms of theatre, new styles of acting was impressive. The work of companies like Footsbarn, Theatre Unlimited, Els Comediants and Barabbas really excited him, broadened his theatrical education and exploded his inherited notions of what theatre can be.

Towards the end of the 80s O'Toole began to see a seismic shift in Irish drama: for him, the primary agon from the 60s to the late 80s was the conflict between traditional and modern Ireland. But then this collapsed and Irish playwrights had to deal with 'a series of more or less isolated, more or less angular Irelands'. The result was the discarding of conflict as a basic principle of drama and, with it, plot, action and narrative. Out of this came a theatre of transformation, of linguistic evocation in which things are called up rather than merely enacted. His review of Barry's *Prayers of Sherkin* perhaps best encapsulates his new openness to a poetic theatre and its capacity to articulate post-modern Ireland.

It may surprise many people that O'Toole has little time for agitprop and, since the late 80s, for an old-style naturalism which he saw as incapable of dealing with the fragmented, often surreal reality of contemporary urban Ireland. For him, this was excitingly explored by companies like Passion Machine and Wet Paint who created large new audiences for theatre without patronizing them or lowering their own commitment to theatrical innovation.

Another feature of O'Toole's criticism is his sensitivity to convention, despite his tenacious holding on to a firm content/form distinction which was radically unsettled years ago by Beckett's early critical work on Joyce. He argues repeatedly for coherence in theatrical conventions and playing styles and is always sensitive to disjunctions between a given directing style and the conventions implied by the written text; his review of Jimmy Murphy's *A Picture of Paradise* epitomizes this.

O'Toole has been for some time uneasy about the future of theatre in the MTV generation and critical of naive attempts to confront the issue (such as John McArdle's *Something's in the Way* (*Irish Times*, 12 November 1996). He does wonder how the youth of today with its tiny attention span, its hunger for buzz and brief sensation, can ever be open to the depths of experience that theatre can provide. But he doesn't counsel despair: his review of *Pop* (*Irish Times*, 14 March 1995) reveals great enthusiasm for director Caimin Collins's risky, exuberant attempt to give some shape to the incoherence of life in the post-modern cultural supermarket and to realize some of Marinetti's aesthetic aspirations towards an electromagnetic theatre of the future which would combine myriad sensations, explosive energies and modern technology.

The canon of Irish theatre has for some time now been a focus of O'Toole's concern. He consistently argues for the absolute necessity of reassessing Irish classics in terms of playing styles and contemporary resonance. In my own view, O'Toole himself has made no mean contribution to the construction of a revised, more inclusive, Irish canon, something he berates Field Day for narrowing so shamelessly in terms of a rigid political agenda.

On the macrocosmic level, O'Toole has been a trenchant critic of the anomalies and randomness of theatre funding in Ireland. He has always argued for the importance of financial and institutional support in the development of theatrical creativity, pointing to the key role played here by the Project in the 70s and Joe Dowling's Peacock in the 80s. He often berated those who funded ground-breaking companies like Rough Magic and Passion Machine so inadequately and so sporadically. His experience of theatre in New York did nothing to shift his conviction that subsidy and public institutional support are essential to excellence and creativity in theatre.

The Myth of Our Renaissance

Sunday Tribune, 9 November 1986

Ask any readers of the theatre columns of the English quality papers and they will tell you that there is at the moment an extraordinary flowering of playwriting in Ireland, a renaissance which again puts Irish theatre on the international map. Led by the highly respected Michael Billington, the English critics have been taking notice and coming to conclusions.

With the usual Irish tendency to believe in the worth of our own work only when it has been validated in England, there is a growing sense in the Irish theatre that this is indeed true, that we are in the midst of a great new upsurge. There are ironies and dangers in this belief, as well as a grain of truth.

It is important to bear in mind that over the last year there has been an unusually large number of Irish productions in Britain, concentrating years of work into what looks like, at least to British eyes, a sudden explosion. English and Scottish audiences have seen, in the recent past, Frank McGuinness's *Observe the Sons of Ulster Marching Towards the Somme*, which is likely to be a contender in the major London theatre awards this year, Tom Murphy's magnificent *Bailegangaire*, Tom Kilroy's *Double Cross*, Tom Mac Intyre's *The Great Hunger*, Theatre Unlimited's *The Murder of Gonzago*, Anne Devlin's *Ourselves Alone*, and Barry McGovern's Beckett show *I'll Go On*.

For Irish audiences, these have been highlights of three years of difficult and often sparse theatre times. For British critics, they have found their way to their shores within a much shorter period.

If the impression is somewhat unbalanced, however, the list remains extraordinarily impressive. There can be no doubt but that there is playwriting of a kind and of a quality going on in Ireland at the moment that makes Irish theatre important internationally.

We have to remember, however, that this playwriting is taking place in spite of, and not because of, the institutions of the Irish theatre. There has not, for a very long time, been so little in the way of a commitment to new writers by Irish theatres.

In the Seventies and early Eighties, the emerging playwrights had some sense of an institution around which they could work. The Project under the Sheridans and for a while afterwards did provide a space and a context for new work. When it went into decline, the Peacock began a vigorous policy of promoting new work under Script Editor Seán McCarthy and Joe Dowling.

Some half-formed, unsatisfactory but nevertheless interesting and novel work was seen. There was a place for new playwrights to learn and to see their work on the stage. Out of the policy emerged Graham Reid, Neil Donnelly, Aodhan Madden, Bernard Farrell and Frank McGuinness.

Not only has the Peacock in the recent period been bereft of new playwrights; but its original triumvirate of Reid, Farrell and Donnelly has been developing an, at best, ambivalent relationship with the theatre. The screen has been reaping the rewards of the Peacock's work: Graham Reid is now essentially a television writer, and for the BBC at that; Farrell is about to embark on writing *Glenroe* for RTE; and Donnelly is currently writing a film script.

Only Frank McGuinness has emerged unequivocally as a major new force in Irish playwriting, and it is at least doubtful whether, if he had not already established a reputation with *The Sons of Ulster*, his current play *Innocence* would have found a theatre prepared to take the risk with what is a difficult and often consciously ugly work. If that generation of Irish playwrights has not gone on to fully develop the promise of its early years, then the previous generation, which dominated the Irish stage from the early Sixties onwards, is also in an ambivalent position.

Hugh Leonard is now more committed to the screen than to the stage and has declared his intention not to write any more plays. Brian Friel, after a stunning burst of plays in the late Seventies and early Eighties, has been silent for five years and may well have exhausted a whole seam of his work.

John B. Keane seems to have been unable to make the transition to writing plays for a more complex society and is now making his mark much more strongly in prose fiction with *The Bodhrán Makers*. Only Tom Murphy, having reached an amazing climax to nearly 25 years of his work in *The Gigli Concert* has managed to go on and push himself up against new boundaries in *Bailegangaire*.

If the Peacock has failed so far to regenerate itself as a centre for new Irish playwriting, the other major subsidized theatres, the Gate and Druid, have not really tried to fill the vacuum. *Innocence* apart, the Gate has produced only one new Irish play, Hugh Leonard's *The Mask of Moriarty*, which was not in itself either a commercial risk or a testing of theatrical boundaries.

Druid has always been cautious about new work and faces a very major challenge in finding new Irish plays after the conclusion of its relationship with Tom Murphy.

It is an astonishing fact, therefore, that the major centre of new Irish work has been an unsubsidized venue concentrating on the work of one writer. Paul Mercier's three plays for Passion Machine, *Drowning*, *Wasters*, together with his new work *Spacers*, represent a major achievement.

But it is an achievement that has been made possible only by two unusual factors: Mercier's ability to stage his own shows as director, and the courage of John Sutton at the SFX who has been prepared to look beyond immediate profit.

But had Mercier not been able to physically put the plays on the stage himself, an ability which hardly any other Irish playwright shares, there is a strong chance that the work would not have been presented for the audience which he wants to reach.

The point is that the institutional context of playwriting matters just as much as the creative inspiration, and without the former, it is going to be difficult to sustain the latter.

It is right to recognize the superb achievements of Irish playwrights in the last few years, and also to recognize that their success in Britain has been gained purely on their own terms. But it is just as important to recognize that without a vibrant theatre to sustain it, that achievement could be ephemeral.

Banking on miracles

The Irish Times, 24 September 1988

[...] Each Festival is therefore an attempt to calculate the incalculable, to work out the mathematics of money, seats, venues, transport, ticket prices, dates, in such a way that the equation adds up to some kind of collective excitement. What will work in one year will be insignificant in another. In 1979, a new Tom Mac Intyre play was virtually jeered off the stage of the Edmund Burke Theatre. By 1983, Mac Intyre's *The Great Hunger* had found an audience. In 1962, Séamus Byrne's *Little City* was the most daring thing in the Festival. This year, Druid's plans to bring their production of it to the Festival were abandoned – the play seemed hopelessly stolid. And what goes for home-based production is doubly true for the imported companies. It is not enough that they be good; they have to be good in a way that meets the needs of the audience at a particular time.

In facing this awesome and perplexing task, the Eighties have been, for the Festival, the best of times and the worst of times. On the one hand there have been bigger audiences, more and better venues, more commercial sponsorship, more new plays, more exotic foreign companies. But on the other hand, this greater scale of operation has come together with continuing insecurity [...].

At the root of the problem lies the fact that the Festival was never established with clear aims, rational structures and guaranteed funding. [...] It is, indeed, doubtful whether the Festival could have survived at all, or at least survived with any stature, had its first decade not coincided with the extraordinary resurgence in Irish playwriting in the late Fifties and early Sixties. The Festival, for all its meagre resources and shaky structure, happened at a time when the four playwrights who still dominate the Irish theatre – Brian Friel, Tom Murphy, Thomas Kilroy and Hugh Leonard – were emerging. It was able to present the plays with which Hugh Leonard (*Stephen D* in 1962), Brian Friel (*Philadelphia, Here I Come!* in 1964) and Thomas Kilroy (*The Death and Resurrection of Mr Roche* in 1968) gained international prominence, as well as Tom Murphy's theatrical rebirth with

Famine in 1968. During the Sixties, the Festival was also able to present early plays by John B. Keane, Eugene McCabe, Patrick Galvin and Conor Cruise-O'Brien. Not only were there new plays, but new playwrights of stature, making virtually every Festival of the period a journey into the unknown. The Festival did not have to import the exotic and the novel – Ireland was becoming a different country and its new playwrights were able to show the audience, amid the familiar landscape, things they had not seen before.

But this ready supply of novelty also served to disguise the Festival's underlying unsteadiness. Since so much was new and unforeseen, there was little point in planning from year to year. Since the theatre of its own accord was producing so much of real interest, there was little need to work out the relationship between the Festival and the Dublin theatres. Since the emphasis of the Festival was so much on home-grown work, there was little need to work out a way of dealing with the international touring circuit. From the mid-Sixties to the mid-Seventies, the Festival was practically guaranteed that it would have each year a new play by Hugh Leonard and another by either Tom Murphy or Brian Friel. With such certainties, why think ahead?

Those days of certainty have gone. It is five years since the Festival premiered a new Murphy; 11 years since a new Kilroy was unveiled during the Festival. Brian Friel's openings are all now in Derry and tend not to arrive in Dublin until the Festival is out of the way – his new play, *Making History*, will not play Dublin until November. And even Hugh Leonard, at one time virtually the Festival's resident playwright, hasn't had a new full-length play in the Festival since *Kill* in 1982. And only Frank McGuinness has replaced them. His contribution to recent Festivals has been quite amazing in its quality and quantity, and he is again one of the mainstays of the 1988 event, but even he cannot single-handedly guarantee a supply of significant new work to the Festival.

With the collapse of such certainties, some of the underlying problems have become clearer. The most acute one remains that of the relationship between the Festival and the major theatres. Dublin is not, and is not likely ever to be, in the position of

Edinburgh, able to combine selectivity with a free-for-all, choosing an official programme and at the same time throwing open the doors to any company which wants to set itself up in the unofficial 'fringe'. Dublin is simply too small to have a fringe.

The Dublin Theatre Festival must either select its programme and present it to the public as its considered choice of what is best in Irish and international theatre, or else it must simply announce a free-for-all and stick the label 'Festival' on whatever happens. At the moment it does a bit of both. If a company is small and powerless, it has to get the Festival's imprimatur in order to be included in the programme. If it is large and powerful, it simply tells the Festival what it is doing and gets on with it, whether the Festival likes it or not.

The Festival is, in effect, the prisoner of the large theatres. As it happens, this year the large theatres are doing precisely what the Festival would want them to do. The Abbey is staging three new plays, by Jean Binnie, Frank McGuinness and Aodhan Madden. The Gate, exemplifying the spirit of the Festival, is matching an Irish playwright, McGuinness, with a European classic, *Peer Gynt*. And the Gaiety is co-producing with the Festival a new play based on the writings of Christopher Nolan. But equally, the Abbey might have decided, as it did last year, not to do anything special for the Festival. The Gate might have decided, as it did last year, not to make itself available for the Festival at all. And if they had done so, the Abbey and the Gate would have been included in the programme anyway, their shows sold to the public as considered choices of the Festival's programme director.

The Abbey, in particular, has always had a somewhat ambivalent attitude to the Festival, taking the benefits in publicity and extra ticket sales but being prepared to go its own way. […] Under Tomás MacAnna, the Abbey's participation in the Festival was more wholehearted, but in recent years the Abbey has again shown itself to be happy enough with a second-hand Tom Stoppard or an old Hugh Leonard at Festival time. There is no guarantee that this year's change of heart will be permanent.

The problem for the Festival in this regard is that it has no real sanction against the major theatres. It does not put money into their Festival-time shows, and therefore is in no position to ensure that they come up with a suitable production. The one sanction that it does have – the power to decide not to include shows which it doesn't wish to stand over in the Festival programme – it has been reluctant to use. Arguably, in this the Festival has underestimated its own strength for inclusion in its programme is of real economic benefit to the theatres. It is also arguable that a decision to exclude shows which it doesn't want, while it might result in a smaller Festival, would also make for a more coherent one, as well as showing more honesty towards the theatregoing public which tends to assume that every show in the Festival has been specifically chosen by the programme director.

The other underlying problem has to do with the Festival's international content, which since 1981 has become steadily more important. The visiting companies are far more than the icing sugar on the cake. There is no doubt, for instance, that the visits in 1981 and 1982 of the Brazilian Macunaima company and the Wroclaw Contemporary Theatre from Poland had an important effect in opening up both Irish audiences and the Irish theatre profession to the physical and visual dimensions of theatre itself. Not just the acceptance of Tom Mac Intyre's work from 1983 onwards, but the greater physical assurance of Irish theatre in general owes a great deal to those visits. And the Polish connection continued to bear fruit, not only in the subsequent visit of Contemporary Theatre's director, Kazimierz Braun, to work with Irish actors, but in the move to Ireland of a member of the company, Maciek Reszczynksi. He became the driving force behind Theatre Unlimited and his new show *Penelope* features in this Festival as a home-grown production.

This engagement with world theatre, however, is considerably stunted by the uncertainty which has been so much a feature of the Festival's finances. Visits by the major international companies take years rather than months of planning. The Royal Shakespeare Company and the Australian Circus Oz, for instance, are in the 1988 programme because of work done three years ago by Michael Scott. The inability to commit money in advance has often meant that the Festival has missed the most important companies. The most highly acclaimed production of recent years, Peter Brook's *Mahabharata*, didn't come to Dublin. Michael Scott wanted it; Peter Brook wanted to come and was prepard to drop the asking price to a minimum. But the Festival couldn't commit the money far enough ahead, and the production was lost.

This problem has now, to an extent, been tackled. The Arts Council has agreed to give the Festival a three-year commitment on financing, making real long-term planning possible for the first time.

Ultimately, though, the only way in which the Festival can become the master of its own destiny is for it to take a much more active, interventionist approach to the theatre. At the moment, it acts as an independent producer for almost all of the foreign shows which it imports, mounting the production and taking the commercial risks. Ironically, it doesn't do the same for the Irish shows. Only two of the home-produced shows in the 1988 Festival, Christopher Nolan's *Torchlight and Laser Beams* and Antoine Ó Flatharta's *City Mission*, are Festival productions. Until the Festival is in a position to commission plays, mount its own shows and take its own risks, it will always be hoping for the best. For the most part, over the years, its luck has held. But banking on annual miracles is a risky business.

Revivals touched by the mood of the Eighties

The Irish Times, 31 December 1988

If it can be credited with such a thing as a collective purpose, then the Irish theatre seemed to be engaged in two things in 1988. One was the establishment of a contemporary repertoire, the continued sifting of the achievements of Irish playwrights in the Sixties, Seventies and even the early Eighties in the attempt to sort the wheat from the chaff. The other was the discovery of the extraordinary fact that there are playwrights from Dublin.

Not since the Sixties has the generation of Irish playwrights which emerged in that decade been so dominant – between them John B. Keane, Hugh Leonard, Tom Murphy, Brian Friel and Thomas Kilroy accounted for 10 major productions and only one of those (Friel's *Making History*) was a new play. And never before has the year's new writing been so dominated by the work of young Dubliners. Aidan Mathews, Paul Mercier, Brendan Gleeson, Sebastian Barry, Donal O'Kelly and Joe O'Byrne made it a year in which, were it not for the amazing ubiquity of Frank McGuinness, virtually all of the significant new plays would have come from Dubliners under 35.

The conjunction of the these two facts is both good news and bad news. The ransacking of the store of recent Irish drama can be seen as complacency and lack of imagination as much as it can be held up as a process of re-evaluation. This is particularly so when it continues to be the case that it is, on the whole, the less well established and less subsidized companies who are doing the new plays and the big companies who are tending to go for the revivals.

The Gate did no new Irish play and neither did Druid. The main Abbey stage gave us only the off-colour *Colours*. It was left to Passion Machine, the Dublin Theatre Festival, the Peacock, Rough Magic, Theatre Unlimited and Co-Motion to risk new and untried plays and playwrights.

There is certainly, then, a case to be made for seeing the Irish theatre as a dying beast living on its own past and showing signs of life only at the extremities. But there are two things which make me think otherwise about the spate of revivals. One is that the range and diversity of the companies involved in them argues that not all of them can be merely marking time, that there is something else going on. From the Gate, the Gaiety and the Abbey to Red Kettle and Druid, there is a process of re-evaluation.

The other thing is that it seems to me that there are good objective reasons why we should be looking again at plays like *Big Maggie* and *The Scatterin'* and *A Crucial Week in the Life of a Grocer's Assistant* and *Hatchet*, reasons which are not to do with safety but with discomfort – with the awkward feeling that in some sense at least we have returned to the dilemmas of the time in which those plays were written.

In a lot of ways it would be much better for us if we could find *Big Maggie*, for instance, as quaint as we find Frank Carney's *The Righteous are Bold* which, in spite of having the same director,

Ben Barnes, came across in revival as rightly forgotten. But we can't. Those four plays I've just mentioned are all about going and staying – the pain of going and the seeming impossibility of staying – and we find ourselves again, 20 years one, faced with that same old story.

The harshness of Mother Ireland in Keane's Maggie or Murphy's Mother is something which her children again have to live with. Or the social schizophrenia of Dublin which can be seen emerging in *Hatchet* and *The Scatterin'* is now everywhere around those of us who live in the city. These plays seem like immediate mirrors of ourselves in a way that even five years ago they wouldn't have.

This sense of parallel concerns between the playwrights of the Sixties and ourselves at the fag end of the Eighties is confirmed by looking at the new work of the young writers. In the Passion Machine plays – Mercier's *Home* and Brendan Gleeson's *Breaking Up* – and even, in a much less obvious way, in Aidan Mathews's *Exit Entrance*, the whole business of searching for a home or a homeland, for a place to settle in, is very much at the heart of the drama.

None of them is a play *about* emigration – and *Breaking Up* in particular is a hilarious corrective to keening about the lost Irish Diaspora – but all of them are very much shaped by the questions that arise *around* emigration – what is a home? How are we related to those around us? How do those relations survive constant flux and mobility?

With such questions in the air, the mood of Irish theatre is no longer one which allows much room for pure playfulness. The sort of visual and physical consciousness which was in the air a few years ago has been absorbed by the mainstream theatre but in a context which roots it quite firmly in some perception of social reality. With this mood of social perplexity it is probably not accidental, for instance, that 1988 seemed to be the year in which, with *Snow White*, the Mason-Mac Intyre-Hickey project at the Peacock ran into fundamental problems of purpose.

The successes of the Gate – and 1988 was undoubtedly the best year of Michael Colgan's tenure there – have similar resonances. On the one hand, the Gate's programme was almost entirely non-realistic, with only Joe Dowling's fine production of Friel's *Fathers and Sons* falling into the general category of nineteenth century naturalism. On the other hand, the theatre's explorations of poetic theatre (*Salomé*, *Peer Gynt* and *Twelfth Night*) all worked so well because, rather than going for timeless images, they were deeply touched by the mood of the Eighties.

Steven Berkoff's *Salomé* undoubtedly owed much of its mood of decline and decadence to Thatcher's Britain, Mason's *Peer Gynt* took its concreteness from both Irish idiom and Irish history and Dowling's *Twelfth Night* had very specific parallels with 1920s Hollywood and the darkness of the Eighties. Elements of the visual, the poetic and the imagistic were very strong in each of the productions, but rooted in a heavy underlay of politics. With crises crowding around us, we were not, in 1988, in the mood for playfulness alone.

Overturning a favourite theme

The Irish Times, 12 August 1989

Fathers have had a pretty bad press in Irish literature and the Irish theatre. Joyce in *Ulysses* has Stephen Dedalus decide that paternity is just a legal fiction and replace his Da with a different model. In *The Playboy of the Western World*, Old Mahon has his skull split not once but twice by his son Christy and ends the play decidedly under Christy's thumb. In O'Casey's *Juno and the Paycock*, a father is replaced by 'two mothers'. In Tom Murphy's *A Whistle in the Dark*, Dada is an ogre, a terrible mixture of whinge and bully who blights the lives of his sons. In Brian Friel's *Philadelphia, Here I Come!*, Old Screwballs is at the heart of his son's dilemma, ineffectual and unable to speak his love.

Even when we get a more tender and affectionate portrait of a father, in Hugh Leonard's *Da*, it is one which reinforces the idea of paternity as a legal fiction and which is also mixed with fear and resentment. 'When,' says Charlie of Da's kindness, 'did I ever get a chance to pay it back, to get out from under you, to be quit of you?' At last, in Donal O'Kelly's extraordinary theatrical odyssey, *Bat the Father, Rabbit the Son*, which finishes its run at the Peacock tonight, the tables are turned: here it is the father who occupies the moral and dramatic high ground and the son who is down below.

What is interesting about this whole theme of father and son (or rarely, as in O'Casey, father and daughter) is that it is intimately bound up with history and politics. In the period of the Irish Renaissance, with Joyce and Synge and O'Casey, the father is overthrown – as young reborn Ireland is overthrowing the old Empire. In the Sixties and Seventies, when Murphy, Friel and Leonard in their different ways return to the imagery of father and son, it is with the rueful awareness that nothing has been overthrown, that nothing, psychologically, has changed. Now the fathers are not vanquished but remain to haunt the sons who cannot shrug them off.

That this does have to do with contemporary history, and with the contemporary history of the Irish Republic at that, is attested by how utterly different is the way this theme is handled North of the Border. There, love for the father oozes out of the poems, whether the poet be Protestant or Catholic. […] These elemental gestures are possible in the Northern poets because the images of father and son have not become images of political change and political stultification. Their relative simplicity is just not possible in the South, where the terms 'father' and 'son' have come to bear a historical weight for writers.

One of the fascinating things about Donal O'Kelly's play and performance (the two are indistinguishable) is the way it consciously confronts this inherited set of images. O'Kelly very deliberately takes on the whole historical load that comes with fathers and sons in Irish writing. Bat the Father represents his time – the Citizen Army, working-class life in Dublin, a kind of authenticity of feeling. Rabbit the Son, who has made his fortune in the haulage business, is everything that his father is not: powerful, corrupt, rich, literally and figuratively adrift from his moorings. If father and son have unavoidably become images, then O'Kelly rejoices in the fact, using them to embody a whole set of political, social and historical changes, to sum up, indeed, the history of the modern Republic.

But O'Kelly does much more than take the tradition on its own terms. He turns it upside down and inside out. When Synge or Joyce or Friel or Murphy dealt with the theme, they did so in the awareness of being at a point of change, a time when a line was being drawn (between Imperial Ireland and the Irish Republic or between traditional Ireland and modern Ireland) with fathers on one side of it and sons on the other. O'Kelly is concerned not with the drawing of lines but with the blurring of distinctions. Here, history is not a turning point but a telescope, with the past and the future jumping in and out of each other. 'That's history for ya,' he says in the play, '[…] all gone grey.' Father and son occupy the same body, are part of the same performance. This is not about one generation set against another but about the split personality of modern Ireland, carrying its unresolved past around in its head.

The dominant images in O'Kelly's great rush of language are of things mixing and of things returning. His main metaphor is the sea, churning things up, sending them back, retaining the human deposits of decades. It is an imagery in which everything mingles – past and present, the beautiful and the ugly, all held together somewhere out in the bay, all waiting and waving about. There is something of the sense of contemporary Ireland which you find in a very different play, Tom Murphy's *Bailegangaire*, the sense of unfinished history, of a story that won't stop telling itself.

In keeping with this sense of things, O'Kelly overturns the distinction between the father and the son. It is Bat the Father who is childlike in his simplicity, his rhymes and jingles, his pranks and delinquencies; Rabbit the Son who acts the big man with his imperiousness and pomposity about his own achievements. Rather than a confrontation of different generations, O'Kelly gives an inspired enactment of an unholy mess, a mess in which the pieties of both generations are reduced to farce and absurdity.

Bat's only injury in the 1916 Rising was the wound he received in breaking the window to put his rifle through and his trip to Frongoch prison camp on a boat is equated with other abortive and ludicrous boat-trips: a frustrated honeymoon voyage to Garnish Island, a disastrous fishing trip to Howth and his mad journey up the Tolka as Rabbit seeks his lost moorings. Rabbit's pieties of profit and power and pulling yourself up by your bootstraps are more directly and more unmercifully reduced to ridicule.

In overturning and messing up one of the favourite themes of Irish literature and theatre, Donal O'Kelly subverts both literary and political traditions. This gives the piece an anarchic energy that makes it unique in Irish theatre.

Into the 90s: Setting the stage for an exciting, dizzying decade

The Irish Times, 8 January 1990

In the 1980s, arguably for the first time in its history, the Irish theatre set out to define itself, to establish a coherent sense of its own repertoire. It was, with few qualifications, a job well done.

Garry Hynes and Joe Dowling created new ways of presenting and performing Irish classics, principally the works of Synge and O'Casey. Yeats was rescued from the drawing-room by Jim Flannery. A half-forgotten writer like M.J. Molloy was rescued from obscurity by Druid and tested against the new times of modern Ireland. And those writers who emerged in the 1960s were also successfully re-assessed. The early works of Tom Murphy were produced with renewed power at the Abbey and at Druid. Ben Barnes's series of engagements with John B. Keane's early work at the Abbey stripped the plays down to their tough and explosive essentials. A whole series of different productions of Thomas Kilroy's plays by a range of companies revealed again their theatrical and intellectual eloquence.

All of this was necessary and immensely productive. It exorcized the ghost of the Revival by showing both that what has happened in the Irish theatre since the 1960s is at least as important as the Revival itself, and that the plays of the Revival period are not a sacred trust but a rich store of contemporary possibilities. Necessary and important though this was, however, it was also a way of living off accumulated fat. It added substance to a theatrical experience that might otherwise have seemed considerably thinner. Without the Revival and the 1960s, the 1980s would not have been what they were, an exciting time in

Irish theatre. Maintaining that excitement with new work will be the challenge of the 1990s.

It is not that the 1980s did not produce its own masterpieces, most obviously from Tom Murphy and Brian Friel, or that the work of defining the repertoire will not continue. But it is noticeable that Friel's and Murphy's great plays of the 1980s were themselves the culmination of a quarter of a century of work in the theatre. And, as I have argued before, the idea of a masterpiece itself is coming under severe strain in the Irish theatre. Masterpieces are plays which somehow manage to encapsulate the movement of an entire society, of a whole moment in history. But Irish society itself is becoming so fragmented, so slippery and indefinable, that that kind of achievement is becoming highly problematic. The 1990s are going to have to face this fragmentation without being defeated by it.

And one part of this process is going to have to be a facing up to our relationship to other countries and other national theatres. The tone of the 1980s was set by Brian Friel's statement early in the decade that Irish theatre was learning to talk to itself, to be *for* itself, rather than *for* London or New York. That determination fuelled the search for an Irish repertoire and had a great deal to do with the confidence that has been gained. But as the lives of Irish people are being more internationally determined, becoming more fluid in terms of their national boundaries, so also is the theatre going to have to use its new confidence to cope with that fluidity.

And here, particularly in relation to Irish theatre's links to Britain, some very, very strange things are happening. Common sense would tell you that the cosmopolitan, European work that is being done here would find an echo in Britain, while the socially realistic, specifically Irish work, wouldn't. But precisely the opposite seems to be the case.

People who are going to be crucial to the Irish theatre of the 1990s, Garry Hynes and Frank McGuinness in particular, have, in the last 18 months, been heavily involved with theatres in England, particularly the Royal Shakespeare Company. But the relationship seems to have been somewhat fraught in both cases.

Garry Hynes's links with the RSC seem to have ended for the moment. Frank McGuinness's recent English productions have met with a fair degree of bafflement, from critics at least. And what is particularly significant is that the play which McGuinness wrote for the RSC, *Mary and Lizzie*, is a stunning piece of work, probably his best play to date, doing exactly what needs to be done in using Ireland and Irish history but using them to get at the world as a whole, at the sweep of modern history, West and East.

Irish theatre needs to connect internationally, but the most obvious point of connection, England, seems unable to connect with us. And the irony is that new Irish work which is much more specifically Irish, much more rooted in the details of everyday Irish life, like the work of Billy Roche, is being successfully produced in London, not in Dublin. One way or another, Irish theatre is going to have to rethink its relationship to the rest of the world in the 1990s.

The other perplexing area for the 1990s arises from the failure of the last decade to produce the kind of progress in the prominence of women in the theatre that might have been expected. There are women – directors like Garry Hynes, Caroline FitzGerald and Lynne Parker, actors like Rosaleen Linehan, Olwen Fouéré and Catherine Byrne, designers like Monica Frawley and Wendy Shea – who are to the fore, but overall, the position of women is scarcely better than it was 40 years ago. Part of the problem is that feminist publishing has tended to encourage women to write in a confessional mode which is antithetical to good theatre. Part is the Irish belief in 'genius' as something which emerges naturally. Unless and until there is a coherent attempt to produce plays by women, playwrighting will remain largely male.

The good news is that the difficulties of the Nineties do not have to be faced unarmed. Not only have companies emerged – Passion Machine and Wet Paint in particular – which have the ability to create new audiences with new work, but those companies have an impressive toughness about them. In the place of the wide-eyed idealism which often marked the 'community' theatres of the past, they have been careful, coherent and highly efficient. They are in for the long haul. The struggle of a playwright like Paul Mercier to balance increasing theatrical adventurousness with a large audience should be one of the fascinations of the 1990s, one from which unpredictable things may come. If the work of theatre-in-education companies could be taken seriously by the Department of Education, one might also be confident about a steady expansion of the audience for theatre in the next decade. And not only are the new playwrights (Michael Harding, Aidan Mathews, Roddy Doyle, Anne Hartigan, as well as Barry and Bolger) writing across a whole variety of forms besides theatre, but the distinctions within the theatre itself between different roles are breaking down. Brendan Gleeson is an actor and a playwright, Paul Mercier and Jim Nolan (of the exciting Red Kettle Company in Waterford) are playwrights and directors, as are Frank McGuinness and Peter Sheridan. The distinction between the designer and the director is breaking down (Patrick Mason and Joe Vanek, Joe Dowling and Frank Conway).

Forms, including the distinction between high art and low art, are becoming fluid, the division of labour is falling apart. In this, the Irish theatre has already been anticipating the protean nature of 1990s culture, and seems in good shape to make something of it. If the structures which contain and give force to this fluidity can be strengthened, if, in particular, the Abbey can give itself a sound basis for the 1990s when it appoints a new Artistic Director this year, then the next decade could be an exciting, if also a somewhat dizzying, time for Irish theatre.

Right and wrong roles for theatre design

The Irish Times, 19 May 1990

Theatre design is all about space, but theatre space is not all about design. Space is the essential language of theatre: it is first and foremost about people being in the same place at the same time. The way that space is used, filled, shaped, is what determines the extent to which something can be said to be theatrical or not.

That use of space is so fundamental to theatre that it is largely independent of what a set designer does. Some of the best theatre I have ever seen had no sets at all; some of the worst had elaborate and detailed sets. It is in this sense that set design is a secondary activity in the theatre – it has to function in itself only insofar as it opens up and articulates spaces for the actors.

This is something that you could be forgiven for forgetting in recent Irish theatre. On the one hand, set design has improved immensely in the last few years. The old attitude to set design described by Eric Bentley when he directed at the Abbey in the 1950s – 'Scenery is a matter of repainting the standard box-set representing a kitchen' – is finally dead. Clumsily naturalistic sets which attempt to convince us that this isn't really a theatre at all are relatively rare now.

Directors and designers now tend to work much more coherently together, to the extent that Patrick Mason and Joe Vanek or Joe Dowling and Frank Conway are, in some productions, virtually co-directors, the design forming a crucial part of the interpretation of the play. You have only to look at either the Gate or the Abbey at the moment, at the radiant set designs by Bob Crowley and Joe Vanek respectively, to realize that set design has been both liberated and liberating in recent Irish theatre.

On the other hand, though, the new consciousness of design has been ambivalent in its effect. In an age when corporate image and sexy packaging are at least as important as the quality of the product itself, theatre has not always been immune to the bug. There is designer theatre as much as there are designer jeans, designer stubble and designer water. When you go to an opening night at the Gate and find the audience applauding the set as if it were the main event, then you wonder if the theatre wouldn't be better off without sets at all, if the design isn't providing a substitute for, rather than a support to, the communication between actors and audience that theatre is all about.

It is appropriate to talk about the Gate here, because Michael Colgan has been the single most important factor in stimulating the new awareness of theatrical design. In his determination to provide the customer with a sense of being cherished and doted on, he has ensured that no hint of tat or vulgarity will infect his productions. This has raised standards throughout Irish theatre, and has contributed hugely to the best things the Gate has done.

It has also, at its worst, created a kind of consumerist theatre in which, because the whole thing *looks* gorgeous, you can get away with having nothing much to say. Design can be used as a safety net, a level below which things will not fall, robbing theatre of the naked risks which are its air supply.

What is really new about the new wave

The Irish Times, 25 August 1990

The great thing about the new wave of Dublin writing, the surge of suburban explorations that encompasses work as diverse as that of Paul Mercier, Roddy Doyle, Brendan Gleeson, Dermot Bolger and Michael O'Loughlin in poetry, fiction and theatre, is that it has finally broken the hold of social realism in Ireland. This is not necessarily what might have been expected, and the reasons why it has happened are worth speculating about in the context of the revival of Mercier's fine play *Wasters* at the Andrews Lane Theatre this week.

When you think about this work, what is most obvious is that it reflects a new kind of life, a new kind of Ireland. This is crucial to any understanding of it, but it also has its limits. It tends to imply that the thrust of the work is essentially documentary, that it is gritty, that it is a realism that created *Kes* and *Cathy, Come Home*, and *Saturday Night, Sunday Morning*. But that implication is simply wrong.

Something funny happened to the whole notion of naturalism or slice-of-life realism or whatever we choose to call it, in its Irish version. It is normal to call the mainstream of Irish theatre, embodied in the Abbey, naturalistic and the term is the most useful one we have. It implies the absence of overt stylization, of breaks in the chain of cause and effect, of attempts to break the audience's suspension of disbelief by reminding them that they are, after all, sitting in a theatre watching other people make a show of themselves. And in this negative sense, the term is accurate as far as it goes. What can be missed in seeing things this way, though, is that Irish naturalism also reversed the usual process.

The difference is this: in Europe, naturalism grew out of the need to convince the audience of the reality of urban and industrial life, the new life of the nineteenth century. Zola's *Germinal* or Ibsen's *A Doll's House* need to be as 'realistic,' as 'natural' as possible because they need to convince their audiences that an industrial conflict or an urban household can be the site of the great human dilemmas. When Ibsen's plays are set outside of the town or city – *Brand, Peer Gynt, When We Dead Awaken* – they tend to be symbolic and poetic. Naturalism is for and about an urban audience.

In Ireland, on the other hand, naturalism grew out of the need to convince the audience of the reality of rural life. The followers of Ibsen in the Irish theatre – Edward Martyn in *The Heather Field*, James Joyce in *Exiles* – had little impact or influence. The only significant follower of Zola in Irish fiction, George Moore, had his impact here not with his novels of urban life, but with his little book of short stories on Irish rural life, *The Untilled Field*, which became the starting point for Frank O'Connor, Liam O'Flaherty and Seán Ó Faoláin.

Naturalism in Ireland was there to convince an urban Irish audience – the playgoers of the Abbey for the most part – that rural life was not just real but super-real, the essence of Irish life, the Real Ireland. If you were producing a play about the West of Ireland, it was essential that the Dublin actors convince themselves and others that they really were peasants, that you went to the Aran Islands to get real pampooties and real three-legged stools to dress the actors and the stage. Naturalism is for an urban audience but about a rural ideal. Far from being up-to-the-minute ultra-contemporary stuff, it is already nostalgic, already looking to the past.

So what? So, if you are a writer in a Dublin suburb in the 1980s and 1990s, you can't do what your nearest counterparts in urban Britain did in the late 1950s and early 1960s. You can't appropriate naturalism, a documentary style, rub-your-nose-in-the-dirt stuff, as a way of reflecting a new urban experience. In Ireland those styles, far from saying 'This is *now*' and 'This is *real*', say instead 'This is *Then*', 'This is *some other place*'. You have to do something else, and something else is what the new urban writers have done.

They have given us no descriptions of daily life in Finglas or Kilbarrack, or even in Rathgar (it should be remembered that a novel like Aidan Mathews's *Muesli at Midnight* is as much an image of the sensibility of its kind of middle-class suburb as Roddy Doyle's *The Commitments* is of its own place). They have not documented the movements of the 13 bus or the exchange value of butter vouchers. They have given us instead fantasies, dreams, hopes, games, road movies, action replays, waking nightmares, comic flights. They have given us more rock and roll than sex and drugs. Beneath the grit of the undeleted expletives, there is a sense that only a surreal style can reflect the surreal reality of modern Ireland.

Wasters, for instance, is set in a field, but it is an unspecific field. There is no attempt at realism in Anne Gately's set. You know that this is the world of a Dublin working-class suburb, but you also know that it could be a working-class suburb in Liverpool or in Ankara, anywhere where there are young people with nothing much to do and a metropolitan centre beckoning them as temporary, uncertain migrants. This kind of suburb is everywhere and nowhere. By being true to the nature of a new Irish reality, the play is true to the nature of a much more universal reality, a reality that may well become institutionalized after 1992.

The point is not that *Wasters* does not reflect a reality, but that the reality it reflects is a shifting, surreal, often fantastical one. Think of it in relation to, say Brian Friel's *Philadelphia, Here I Come!* – a play from a different era which deals with the same feelings of stagnation and the need to emigrate – and you understand that a fundamental shift has occurred. In *Philadelphia* emigration is a dramatic either/or choice. You go or you stay. You build a play around that moment of decision. But now, you go and you come back and you go again. You don't have moments of decision, merely moments at which it has become intolerable to be where you are, moments which will recur wherever you are. You can't build a play around the same sense of dramatic choice, for now there are no real choices, only impulses which can be followed or denied.

'Today,' John Berger writes in *A Seventh Man*, 'the temporary migrant worker suffers a kind of imprisonment in a prison without frontiers.' The people of *Wasters* exist in this temporary state and imprisonment is the play's central metaphor. And even that metaphor cannot be static: it has to be played with, fantasized about, made up as you go along.

This gives the play a frantic energy, a bitter humour and also a poignancy that comes through even more sharply in this present production than in the play's first manifestation in 1985. It may be the intimacy of the Andrews Lane compared to Passion Machine's usual venue of the SFX, but, while the play remains constantly entertaining and often very funny, the blackness comes through more clearly than before. As with Mercier's recent revival of *Studs*, everything is tougher and harder. There is a new urgency that makes these plays not just very good theatre, but also one of the few ways of understanding this place that we have.

Double Worlds
The Irish Times, 16 November 1991

Ten years ago, if you had looked at the overall direction of Irish theatre, you would have been sure of only one thing: that by 1991, Irish theatre would have moved very substantially away from the text, from the play as a highly wrought literary creation and towards the physical, the visual, the imagistic.

That was the pattern then, and to some extent it has been carried through into the mainstream. It is not, for instance, accidental that the most stunning moment in the most successful Irish play of recent years, Brian Friel's *Dancing at Lughnasa*, is a wild dance, a moment beyond words.

Nor is it accidental that the physical richness of Irish theatre has grown immeasurably in recent years, to the degree where even in the most stodgily verbal of productions, there is a far greater awareness of the action, of what is happening as well as what is being said, than there would have been a decade ago.

Yet the remarkable thing about all of this is that, far from fading away, the literary text has become much more literary. That most abused of notions, a poetic theatre, has, all by itself and without manifestos or deliberation, come back into play. The distinction between physical theatre on the one hand and literary theatre on the other has been blown apart. What we are getting is both at the same time.

All of this is a sign of a very profound change, a shift in the nature of Irish theatre which has not yet been grasped, never mind analysed. It seems to me that if the first phase of Irish theatre in this century was the Revival, and the second was the flowering of new writing that began at the end of the 1960s, then we are now moving into a third phase, with all the shifts of perspective and values which that implies.

To understand the nature of this shift, you first have to grasp the most important general characteristic of the Irish theatrical masterpieces of the last three decades – their essential doubleness. This idea of doubleness was itself a very profound shift from the uniform, singular world of Irish theatre of the classic period.

The plays which established and sustained the idea of an Irish dramatic movement are ones based on at least the idea of a uniform society. If you look at (to give just two of the more famous examples) *The Playboy of the Western World* or *The Plough and the Stars*, you see how essential to them it is that there is in each a close, bounded society sharing a common ground which is so absolutely assumed that it does not need to be referred to at all.

It is not that outsiders are not important to the plays – on the contrary, Christy Mahon or the British soldiers who occupy the stage at the end of *The Plough* are crucial – but that precisely in order for the outsiders to function like this it has to be utterly clear that they are outside this tight community. To have a functioning outside, you have to have a palpable inside. And the dramatic uses of this are huge: it allows you to assume that there is a metaphorical connection between this close community and a place called 'Ireland'. The idea of a single, an essential, Ireland lies behind the form and nature of these plays.

This fell apart in the late 1950s and early 1960s. We literally couldn't sustain the notion of a single Ireland, self-sufficient and bound in both its culture and its economy, and we had to acknowledge and allow in other things: industry, television, urban life, the modern world. All our singles became double. Instead of having one Ireland we got two, a constant clash between the traditional and the modern. This clash was inherently dramatic and out of the diverse approaches to it by what were then the new, young playwrights, we got extraordinary plays, extraordinary devices, and powerful theatrical experiences.

If there is a characteristic image of Irish theatre in the last three decades, it is the image of the split personality. The clash of the traditional and the modern was first powerfully articulated by John B. Keane in a relatively external way in plays like *Sive* and *The Field*. But as time went on this division became internalized, mixed itself into the psyche and the spirit of the people who inhabited our stages.

Brian Friel's Gar Private and Gar Public in *Philadelphia, Here I Come!*, Hugh Leonard's Charlie in *Da* who is played by two different actors, one now, the other then, Tom Murphy's succession of literal or spiritual brothers, two different people who between them make up one dramatic character, Thomas Kilroy's Brendan Bracken from *Double Cross* with his other self buried inside him or emerging as a haunting brother who waits at the lamp post outside his window. What began in society, and with the attempts of playwrights to dramatize the traumas of change in that society, ended up in the depths of the mind and soul, pushed way beyond realism into highly inventive and original drama.

The basic conflict between the old Ireland and the new led us into extraordinary and often exhilarating territories of theatre. But it is now at an end. We no longer have a new-fangled modern Ireland on the one hand and an old, coherent and conservative traditional Ireland on the other. We have a series of more or less isolated, more or less angular Irelands. Tradition is a dead duck, its adherents every bit as marginalized, as unsettled and as at odds with the mainstream as any seeker after novelties.

On the other hand, the modernizing impulse is in deep trouble. It hasn't delivered the goods. It hasn't done what it was supposed to do: stop emigration, create jobs, give us a new confidence in ourselves. The poles of the great division which has fuelled our theatre for 30 years are collapsing. By a curious irony we are moving back to the isolated, remote (culturally if not geographically) communities of the Revival. The difference is that these can no longer function as images of the whole country, only as images of themselves.

There isn't space to go into all the signs of this collapse, but two are obvious and very profound in their consequences. One is that many of the major plays of the very recent past move quite consciously out of a theatre of conflict. The basic conflict which fuelled the previous flowering isn't there any more.

If you look at four very different plays in other respects, Tom Murphy's *Too Late for Logic*, Brian Friel's *Dancing at Lughnasa*, Sebastian Barry's *Prayers of Sherkin* and John McGahern's *Power of Darkness*, you can see the discarding of conflict as the basic principle of drama. In each, conflict, and the things which pertain to it – suspense, the playing out of the unpredictable con- sequences of actions – are deliberately undercut either early on or in the course of the play.

In *Logic* we discover at the beginning that the play's protagonist is already dead, thus taking away the sense of an ending which was always so crucial to Murphy's work. In *Lughnasa* suspense is undercut with extraordinary daring by having the narrator reveal things to us before we see them enacted. In *Sherkin*, what will happen – Fanny Hawke's departure from the island – is clear from early on and the play works without a single point of external conflict. In *Darkness*, a narrative of suspense and action literally stops, refuses to go any further and collapses in on itself. Together these plays, and others from the recent past, suggest a shift in the most fundamental techniques of drama – plot, action, narrative, conflict.

Yet this is not without parallel in the theatre. Greek plays, for instance, are among the great classics of theatre, and yet they are predicated on the idea that everyone in the audience already knows the story. What they want to see are the images and structures – in the broadest sense, the poetry – which can be evoked from the stories. And this is the second sign of profound change in our theatre: we are moving from a theatre of linguistic evocation, one in which things are called up rather than simply acted out.

What is to be evoked in this new theatre is a particular, singular, isolated world (Murphy's urban underworld, Friel's house and family, Barry's island, McGahern's family into which no outside point of social or moral reference can enter), not the double worlds of the last three decades. That, too, is a reflection of where Ireland is now, just as much as the theatre of conflict reflected Ireland as it has been.

But the methods have to evolve even further beyond naturalism, because if you can't give an audience conflict, suspense and action, you have to give them something else: an all-embracing, hypnotic sense of atmosphere in which everything – words, images, movements – is deployed in the same direction. Language has to evoke a work as much as it has to describe one, and this is why our theatre is becoming more and more poetic in its impulses. This is not a move away from the reflection of Irish society, merely the reflection of a different kind of society.

The Field Day Anthology of Irish Writing
The Irish Times, 30 November 1991

[…] In an anthology which has not been afraid of making bold leaps in many other directions, the treatment of Irish theatre is relentlessly conservative. Taken as a whole, the sections on dramatic writing tend to confirm a stultifying myth: that Irish theatre has always been bound up with the paradoxes of Ireland and England and that a really Irish theatre didn't exist until Yeats and Lady Gregory set it up.

One of the most important jobs to be done in looking at the canon of theatre is to establish once and for all that theatre and theatres are not like love and marriage or horse and carriage. You can have one without the other, and it is the failure to grasp this which has always retarded the development of a more complex and interesting notion of what Irish theatre is. There were, for instance, folk plays in Ireland for hundreds of years, and at least some texts survive. Yet in an anthology which goes out of its way to acknowledge the tradition of popular ballads and songs in the countryside, the existence of popular plays in the countryside (so brilliantly analysed and put in context by Henry Glassie in recent years) continues to be ignored.

Even more surprising is that in areas where a great deal of more traditional scholarship is available, theatre still remains unacknowledged. There is in the anthology a substantial section on Latin writing in Ireland. It is recognized by most scholars that one of the finest existing Latin ecclesiastical plays of the medieval period is the Dublin *Visitatio*, performed by the clergy in Dublin churches to celebrate Easter. Yet it doesn't appear in the anthology.

The job of establishing this tradition of theatre in Dublin before there were theatres is all the more important since none of the morality or miracle plays which were performed in the city survive. One of the most important precursors of the Elizabethan flowering of theatre was John Bale, who staged his Protestant religious plays in Kilkenny. Even in a case like this, where there are available texts, the opportunity of placing theatre within the context of the evolution of Irish literature is passed up. It may be objected that Bale was English not Irish, but the same can be said of Spenser and Cromwell – who do get in.

The importance of these omissions may seem to be very minor, but it becomes clearer as you move nearer to the present time. What is acknowledged in the anthology is essentially the two established 'traditions' of Irish writing for the theatre, the great comic tradition, essentially geared to the London stage, stretching from Farquhar and Sheridan to Wilde and Shaw on the one hand, and the post-Revival Irish tradition on the other.

But there is a whole other side to Irish theatre, concerned not so much with a straight Irish-English axis, but with a Dublin-New York-Chicago-Liverpool-London-Paris axis, the milieu of the Victorian urban masses brought into being by the industrial revolution. This is the theatre of the melodramas and the music halls.

Boucicault, for instance, is represented by a few pages of *Arrah-na-Pogue*, which appear not in the section on drama, but in the 'Political Writings and Speeches' section, under the heading 'Fenianism'. What you miss by leaving out Boucicault is not only that aspect of Irish culture (urban popular culture) which has more connection to the industrial cities of Britain and America than it has to a notion of 'Ireland', but also a theatre which is confidently and brashly at home with modern technology. When you leave out this urban, modern strain of Irish theatre, you begin to seriously distort the nature of what the theatrical canon might be.

The logical but still outrageous consequence of this creation of a narrow canon is the exclusion from the anthology of Hugh Leonard. [...] As a result, if you look at the Contemporary Irish Drama section, you get the impression of a theatre inhabited only by gnarled farmers, people caught up in the northern Troubles, and people acting out in one way or another the conflict between Britishness and Irishness.

I'm relieved I was wrong

The Irish Times, 19 August 1997

[...] In the late 1980s, two things seemed to me obvious about the future of Irish theatre. One was that it would gradually move away from text-based plays to a much more physical, visual and direct style of performance. The other was that, if this didn't happen, theatre would lose its central place in Irish culture, becoming increasingly marginal as television and film fulfilled a changing society's need for drama.

Neither of these predictions was entirely foolish, but have proved, in essence, wrong. There is no doubt that Irish theatre now pays much more attention to what can be seen, rather than just heard, by its audience. Audiences are seldom asked now to sit through what are in essence animated radio plays. Younger actors are, in general, more visually literate, more at ease with physical display. Directors are no longer people who stop the actors from bumping into each other, and the primary job of designers is no longer to make the stage look as much like a sitting room as possible. The days when an Irish play was five people sitting around a table may not be entirely gone, but they are clearly numbered.

Yet Irish theatre is, for all that, still overwhelmingly literary in the simple sense that its great driving force is the production of new plays written, for the most part, by single authors sitting at home rather than theatrical collectives. Not merely has the death of the author in the Irish theatre been greatly exaggerated, but there is a new one born every month. A decade ago, the number of established professional Irish playwrights was tiny – Brian Friel, Tom Murphy, Hugh Leonard, John B. Keane, Bernard Farrell, Tom Mac Intyre, Frank McGuinness. Now, at least twice as many have a really substantial body of work.

Arguably, indeed, no decade in Irish theatre history has seen the emergence of as many really accomplished playwrights as the last one. If the work of Sebastian Barry, Marina Carr, Billy Roche, Martin McDonagh and Conor McPherson alone is considered, it is clear that this has been an amazing period for Irish theatre writing. But there are, besides, at least another dozen new writers who have produced significant plays and seem likely to go on doing so. This is not to say that the kind of plays being written is the same. On the contrary, the epic social drama of the 1960s onwards is no longer being written and the newer work is more odd, more angular, and more oblique. But it is also, if anything, more literary. Texts have become, in general, denser, more poetic, more highly wrought. As naturalism has waned there has been a return to highly charged, self-consciously stylized language.

Strangely, Irish theatre now has more in common with the early years of the twentieth century than with, say, the 1970s. If this has made it in one sense formally conservative, it has also given it an extraordinary sense of life.

And this upsurge of new writing relates to the second area in which my expectations of a decade ago have been confounded: theatre has not been shoved aside by television and film. This may be in part a negative phenomenon – the fact is, Irish films are still rather rare and one-off television plays are even rarer. But there is a more positive sense in which the attraction of a theatre for a new generation has proved much more resilient than I had expected.

Theatre audiences may be predominantly middle-aged, but that is hardly news to anyone. And the striking thing is that theatre is still a form that interests many outstanding young artists. The belated development of professional theatre schools has resulted not, as some feared, in a production-line for careerist clones, but in the emergence of an amazingly self-confident new generation of performers, at least some of whom are good enough to rise to whatever challenges innovative directors are willing to give them.

And what's important is that the new generation is not using theatre to hide from the problems of late twentieth century culture. In the work that, for instance, John Crowley has done with the Bickerstaffe company in Kilkenny, there is an obvious search for forms that will make sense of the broken narratives and discordant voices of an increasingly generalized world. Theatre is being used not as a playground for nostalgia but as a way of tracing contemporary experience. So long as this is happening, it will hold its place in Irish culture.

Modern Irish Dramatists

Hugh Leonard
Sunday Tribune, 26 June 1983

The 1960s swept the comely maidens off the village green and into the discos. The clash of the ash of de Valera's robust youths was replaced with the flash of the cash in Lemass's New Republic. For the first time in Ireland, upward social mobility was on offer. The fields of South County Dublin yielded a new crop of semi-detached estates. The middle class had arrived and Hugh Leonard was the man to articulate its fears and insecurities.

His own career has been emblematic of the Irish success story. Talent and hard work (in thirty years he has written 24 stage plays, 70 television plays and series, half a dozen films, countless episodes of *The Kennedys of Castlerosse*, a volume of autobiography and a newspaper column) have taken him from the poverty of Kalafat Lane in Dalkey, where he was raised as the adopted son of a gardener, to a brash modern house overlooking Dalkey island and a maroon Rolls Royce. The social mobility of which he is so emphatically a part himself has dominated his major works.

From the point of view of international success, the great advantage of writing about the *nouveaux riches* is that they are the same the world over. In Dublin and Tokyo, New York, Berlin and London they are all living the American Dream. Synge's peasants and O'Casey's slumber-dwellers have a certain exotic interest but what the audiences for commercial theatre will pay for are plays about themselves. The want to see their own foibles on stage anaesthetized with laughter.

Hugh Leonard doesn't write tragedies. Tragedies are about the problems of striving, but the middle class has already fulfilled its aspirations. It has got where it wanted to be. Instead, those who have made it have a gnawing fear of returning to the past, of slipping down the ladder, back to where they came from. Their particular neurosis is schizophrenia; they are at once products of their own past and terrified of it.

Leonard's most successful play *Da*, which won him the Tony Award in 1978 (along with twelve other major American awards) and has been running ever since in five continents, makes this schizophrenia physically explicit. Its central device is the splitting of the character of Charlie (who represents Leonard himself) into two – one actor for his past self, one for the present.

Returning home for the funeral of his father, Charlie is haunted by his own childhood and the figure of Da. He has tried but failed to slay the ghost of his origins with money: 'Since I was born. "Here's a sixpence for the chairoplanes, a shilling for the pictures, a new suit for the job. Here's a life." When did I ever get a chance to pay it back, to get out from under you, to be quit of you?'

In most of the major plays written since he returned to Ireland in 1970, the past is vividly present on the stage as an admonishment, defying his characters' efforts to shake it off. In *Time Was* (1976) the dreams and fantasies of childhood years slip into the present to assault two Killiney couples. In *A Life* (1979), the main characters are again split into two, with different actors playing their past and present selves. In *The Patrick Pearse Motel* (1971), Irish history, the collective past, plays a farcical role. The motel in question has rooms named after great patriots and a restaurant called The Famine Room.

The estate in Killiney where Leonard lived when he first returned to Dublin was known to the locals as Disneyland. Social mobility and the fear of the past bring with it a sense of unreality, of displacement. The *nouveaux riches* have no history. The discontinuity of rapid social change shatters the connections which normally act as anchors to the world.

In plays like *Summer* (1974) and *The Patrick Pearse Motel*, Leonard's characters try to substitute individual moments of excitement for coherent ties with reality. History is problematic for them, but sex, however fleetingly, offers a way of standing outside of time. Adultery is the new suburban pastime. Gráinne in *The Patrick Pearse Motel* says: 'I would love to have a man just once, just once before my throat gets wrinkles and people look at my brooch first and then my ring, and then me, and I swear, I swear, I will never ask for another thing as long as I live – just one short fleeting night of harmless innocent adultery'.

Leonard is a writer of enormous skill, but he has had exaggerated claims made for his plays. (*The New York Times*, for instance, hailed *Da* as 'in a class with the best of Sean O'Casey'). Great theatre, like O'Casey's, is about quests, about change and people who confront it. Leonard's people, inextricably bound as they are to middle-class neuroses, fear change above all. They reveal their fears but always in a way made palatable by laughter, a laughter that is not a threat but a cushion.

Ultimately his plays end in resignation, not resolution. The humour makes the insecurity, the emptiness, the schizophrenia, easier to live with. His characters don't confront the lunacy of their lives, they just stop worrying about it.

Tom Murphy

Sunday Tribune, 6 January 1985

Brian Friel has written of his fellow playwright Tom Murphy that 'he has explored the fate of Fallen Men, Eden's expatriates, pining for restoration, hung between the soot and the perfection'. The people of Murphy's plays are indeed fallen and the biblical imagery is appropriate to a writer who has used language with a religious intensity and with a fierce intimacy with the Bible, but Tom Murphy does not look to a lost Garden of Eden. The pining in his work is directed more to a future wholeness than to a past paradise. His vision is apocalyptic rather than elegiac.

Of all modern Irish writers Murphy is the most at odds with Christianity. He does not merely reject religion, consign it to the dustbin of history. He turns it on its head. He writes about the great Christian themes of sin, redemption and forgiveness, but he does so in a way that rejects the fundamental preconditions of Christianity. Whereas for the Christian redemption comes from accepting an act of salvation located in the past (the Crucifixion and Resurrection), the characters in Murphy's plays can only be redeemed when they accept the world without illusion, and then take a leap into a new, dark future.

The vision at the heart of Murphy's twenty five years of playwriting is the blasphemous vision of Francisco, the dishevelled circus juggler in *The Sanctuary Lamp*, proclaimed in the course of a mad night from the pulpit of a church: 'The day is coming: The Final Judgement: the not too distant future: Before that simple light of man: When Jesus, man, total man, will call to his side the goats: Come Ye Blessed! – Yea call to his side all those rakish, dissolute, suicidal, fornicating goats, taken in adultery, and what-have-you'. The irony of Jesus, not God but man, calling the goats to his side on the Day of Judgement instead of the sheep is an essential key to Murphy's turn of mind.

What makes Tom Murphy such an important playwright is the fact that this secular mysticism, this poetic vision, is combined with a social realism that goes further in reflecting post-Lemass Ireland than any other creative writer of the last two decades. These two strands of his work are inseparable, but his plays can be divided into two rough groups according to the emphasis on one or the other of them. One group, consisting of *On the Outside* (1959), *A Whistle in the Dark* (1961), *A Crucial Week in the Life of a Grocer's Assistant* (1962 and 1969), *The White House* (1972), *On the Outside* (1974) and *The Blue Macushla* (1980), has direct social and political reference to the changes in Ireland since the Sixties. The other, which includes *The Orphans* (1968), *The Morning After Optimism* (1971), *The Sanctuary Lamp* (1975) and *The Gigli Concert* (1983) is more 'poetic' and the references are more oblique. *Famine* (1966), a crucial Murphy play, stands between these two groups as his most specific statement of the relationship between socio-economic conditions and the spiritual and emotional poverty they create.

There is a staggering consistency and coherence in Murphy's work over a quarter of a century. His first three plays – *On the Outside* and *A Whistle in the Dark*, which are published in the Gallery batch, the latter for the first time this side of the Atlantic, and *A Crucial Week in the Life of a Grocer's Assistant* which Gallery has also published previously – in fact form a kind of loose trilogy.

On the Outside ends with its main protagonist obviously on his way to the emigration boat. *A Whistle in the Dark* shatters the illusion that it is possible merely to flee from the evils of the world, as the move for the Carney family from Mayo to Coventry merely intensifies their violent tribal ties and sharpens their struggle for existence in a brutish world. It remains an enormously powerful play and one which is seriously overdue a revival on the Irish stage. *A Crucial Week*, written in 1962 but not staged until 1969, enacts the process whereby a young man in a small town in Ireland rids himself of illusions about the world around him and finds the freedom to make the choice of staying here rather than emigrating.

The apocalyptic nature of Murphy's vision, however, is at its clearest in *The Sanctuary Lamp*, now issued by Gallery in a substantially revised version, and in *The Gigli Concert*, published for the first time. The apocalypse seeks to sweep away the world, but in order to do so needs an alternative world to which access can somehow be gained. In *The Sanctuary Lamp* an assault is made on that second world, represented by the symbolic presence of Christ in the sanctuary lamp itself. In *The Gigli Concert* the citadel is gained, the leap into darkness is actually attained on stage, making this Murphy's central achievement to date.

In both of these plays the characters are desperate, but in Murphy's scheme of things desperation is a necessary first step, a rejection of the world as it is without which the leap into something new is impossible. Because it is an utterly alien place, the world as it is must be despaired of before it can be transcended.

It is Tom Murphy's achievement, culminating in *The Gigli Concert*, to find an image and a language to express man's striving against an alien world, without ever resorting to escapism. That is in itself a unique achievement in the modern theatre, and an achievement that is fittingly celebrated in these beautiful Gallery Press editions. If *The Gigli Concert* was a major theatrical event of the last year, its publication now has to count as a major literary event.

Brian Friel

The Irish Times, 7 January 1989

[…] For Brian Friel, both as man and playwright, the past and all our images of it are slippery and untrustworthy.

And yet, for all his doubts about making sense of the past, for all his restlessness in relation to his own career, it is the very darkness of the past, the tricks of memory, that continue to shape his work. The fiction of one's own life becomes the more ordered fiction of the theatre. […] 'An autobiographical fact,' says Friel, 'can be pure fiction,' but he adds, with a typical touch, 'and no less true or reliable for that'. In his case, the autobiographical facts, if in themselves untrustworthy and insufficient, are nevertheless crucial, for more than most writers Friel has been obsessively concerned with his own patch of ground, his own place in the world. He has quoted Seamus Heaney with approval: 'There are only certain stretches of ground over which the writer's divining rod will come to life'. Those stretches of ground for Friel are nationalism and Catholicism, both with the particular tribal connotations which they have in the North.

He was born in Omagh, Co. Tyrone, where his father was principal of a three-teacher school and his mother a junior civil servant. At the age of 10, he moved to Derry with his family, and that city's nationalist politics were a fact of his life. His father, Patrick Friel, was a Nationalist Party member of Derry Corporation until its suspension in 1969, representing the South Ward which included the Bogside and the Creggan. He himself was a member of the Nationalist Party for a time. And particularly since the fateful year of 1968, everything he has written has been imbued, however obliquely or indirectly, with the events of the northern crisis.

The given facts of his Catholic religious inheritance are less obvious, but darker and perhaps more profoundly influential. After five years at Saint Columb's College in Derry, he went, at the age of 16, to Maynooth College to study for the priesthood. He left 2½ years later. What happened in the meantime is the most private aspect of a very private life. It was, he said in 1965, 'an awful experience, it nearly drove me cracked. It is one thing I want to forget. I never talk about it – the priesthood'.

In Friel's plays, however, absences and darknesses are always potent, and the same seems to be true of those years at Maynooth. He has spoken of his work as the search for a 'faith' and his description of that search makes it sound remarkably like a religious goal: 'The patient assembly of a superstructure which imposes a discipline and within which work can be performed in the light of an insight, a group of ideas, a carefully cultivated attitude'. He has also spoken of the theatre as a 'theoretical priesthood'. In his plays, the figures who most closely represent the artist are priests or priest-like: Saint Columba, Archbishop Lombard, and above all the faith healer Frank Hardy.

Nationalism and Catholicism shape Friel the playwright, then, but not in any simple sense. 'A priest or a politician – which?' Columba is asked in Friel's first full-length stage play *The Enemy Within*, and clearly both alternatives were real ones for Friel, with his Maynooth training and his nationalist politician father. His answer to the question has been neither and both. He became neither politician nor priest but has sought in his work to evoke both an alterative politics and an alternative priesthood.

The priest and the politician have stayed with him, and his work has the feeling of being created out of the need to flee from both, to find another way of dealing with politics and another way to perform the priestly function of blessing and healing. In this, Friel's story is remarkably like that of James Joyce, with the exception that Friel's exile has been internal and imaginative rather than physical.

Like Joyce, too, Friel worked out the beginnings of his artistic identity in relation to his father. Until his early 30s, in spite of being reasonably well established as a short story writer with a contract from the *New Yorker*, he was still in significant ways a reproduction of his father: an Irish Catholic schoolteacher living in Derry and involved in its nationalist politics.

It is hardly surprising that the play he wrote after breaking with that background, leaving his job as a teacher and becoming a full-time writer, is about fathers and sons. At the core of *Philadelphia, Here I Come!* is Gar O'Donnell's simultaneous

yearning for his father's love and fear of becoming like him. And
the theme has remained a central one in his work, lying at the
heart of *Crystal and Fox*, *The Gentle Island*, *Translations*, and his
adaptation of Turgenev's novel, *Fathers and Sons*.

Repeatedly, in Friel's work, the mother is dead, at best a
haunting presence, paring down the emotional complexities of
the family to the single question of fathers and their sons.
Sometimes, the son is split in two, divided between a garrulous,
relatively sophisticated figure who hungers for new experience
outside of the cocoon (Gar Private in *Philadelphia*, Owen in
Translations) and a taciturn, pained one who longs for his father's
recognition (Gar Public in *Philadelphia*, Manus in *Translations*).

Sometimes, as in *Translations* where Hugh and Manus, father
and son, are both teachers going for the same job, or in *The
Gentle Island*, where a father writes a love letter for his son, the
identification of father and son is uncomfortably close and must
be broken.

As he became, after *Philadelphia*'s commercial success in
Dublin, New York and London, a more established figure in the
theatre, that confidence has turned to a fierce protectiveness
towards his work, culminating in the foundation of his own
company, Field Day, in 1980. He ·has always been somewhat
distrustful of actors and particularly of directors, and entirely
hostile to the idea that scripts should be open to change in
rehearsals. Those who believe this, he has said, really 'belong in
showbiz. But there are so many of them, and they have such
strong support from directors and actors that those of us who
believe in the responsibility of the script are considered cranks
and difficult to work with. So be it'.

Between the premiere of *Philadelphia* in 1964 and that of *The
Gentle Island* in 1971, however, Friel's development stalled. Plays
like *The Loves of Cass McGuire*, *Lovers*, *Crystal and Fox* and *The
Mundy Scheme*, have fine things in them but none is the work of a
playwright of international standing. It was as if, having
dramatized his break with his own past in *Philadelphia*, he needed
to be able to rework that play's clash of father and son in a new
way, as a metaphor of a larger conflict. And that possibility came

with his gradual and complex assimilation of the Northern troubles after 1968.

During the Seventies, Friel the politician and Friel the priest found common ground in work that reflects both political concern and the desire to heal and to bless. Typically, it is through his need *not* to be a political spokesman or a tribal druid that these forces find their way into his best plays. *The Freedom of the City* (1973), because it reflects on the events of Bloody Sunday, is often seen as a stepping into the role of political spokesman on Friel's part. In fact, though, it is the opposite: a statement of the impossibility of finding a single point of view which will encompass the truth of those events.

The approach of Friel's three greatest plays – *Faith Healer*, *Aristocrats* and *Translations* – al premiered within an extraordinary period of 18 months between March 1979 and September 1980 – is much more oblique and imbued with mystery than any direct or simple response to the Troubles would imply. His 'sporadic diary' kept during the writing of *Aristocrats* in 1976 gives a sense of the darkness of what he is trying to capture, a sense far removed from the stance of a public man fashioning a manifesto:

> November 7. I think I've got a scent of the new play. Scarcely any idea of character, plot, movement, scene, but a definite whiff of the atmosphere the play will exude. Something stirring in the undergrowth. At the moment I don't want to stalk what may be stirring there. No. I will sit still and wait. It will move again. And then again. And each time its smell will become more distinct. And then finally when that atmosphere is confident and distinctive, I and the play will move towards one another and inhabit that atmosphere.

What Friel found in his plays after the Troubles is not a clear statement which he wished to make, not even the 'faith', the 'carefully cultivated attitude' which he yearned for in his 1972 BBC radio talk. It is a way of including the big issues – history, myth, language – in the small lives of his closed communities. He found the way of embodying the disjunction between private feeling and public form, which is the experience of the Northern Catholic, in theatrical images, just as he had done on a more simple and personal level in *Philadelphia* when he split the main character, Gar O'Donnell, into a public self and a private self. And, in these great plays of the late Seventies and early Eighties, the source of that division may be political, but its images are more often priestly.

Faith Healer, Translations and *Aristocrats* are all shaped by a sense of the sacramental. The sacraments and their ceremonies of birth, death and marriage, are where the public world and the private world, the political and the priestly, come together, and these plays are full of them. The failure of the public world and public ceremonies to accord with the truth of private lives is symbolized in the failure of the rituals of birth, death and marriage to keep their allotted place.

In *Aristocrats*, the planned wedding for which the characters have gathered becomes a funeral when the father dies. In *Translations*, the christening which Hugh attends in the first act becomes a wake in the third act, when the baby dies. In *Faith Healer*, the birth of Frank and Gracie's child is quickly followed by its funeral. Both *Faith Healer* and *Translations* are shaped as a movement from a ceremony of naming (baptism) to the acceptance of death (the last rites). Just as politics is always shifting and uncertain in Friel's plays, so too the priestly function refuses to work, as its rituals turn into each other, always changing for the worse. What remains is the deeply ambivalent, deeply unhappy, but deeply rooted sense of the Faith Healer, Frank Hardy, that sometimes, in his practice of 'a craft without an apprenticeship, a ministry without responsibility, a vocation without a ministry' he did in fact have the power to bless and heal.

Friel's latest play, *Making History*, currently on a tour of Ireland and Britain, shows him still deeply sceptical about the achievements of the writer in a crumbling and violent world, still asking himself the questions which his Frank Hardy asks:

> *Am I endowed with a unique and awesome gift?'*– my God, yes, I'm afraid so. And I suppose the other extreme was *Am I a con man?* – which, of course, was nonsense, I think. And between those absurd exaggerations the possibilities were legion. Was it all chance? – or skill? – or illusion? – or delusion? Precisely

what power did I possess? Could I summon it? When and how?

For Friel, there may be no answer, but for those who have watched his plays, the one suggested by Gracie in *Faith Healer* is good enough: 'I'm sure it was always an excellence, a perfection, that was the cause of his restlessness and the force of it'.

Samuel Beckett

The Irish Times, 25 December 1989

He grew into his age and his age grew into him. In the first sense, old age seemed peculiarly becoming to him, seemed his proper element, its characteristics of isolation and immobility according best with his general view of humanity's lot. Even in the work written while he was still in his early forties, it is often the voice of an old man that we hear. And as he grew older, his life caught up with his metaphors, and his work came, therefore, to seem more human, and, in a limited sense, more autobiographical.

In the second sense, his age – our age – came to see him more and more as a representative figure. As time went on, it was not Beckett's formal boldness or his apparent strangeness that seemed most essential. It was a fact that would have seemed wildly untrue when Beckett first came to world attention in the 1950s: the fact that Beckett was a realist.

He was a realist in two quite separate senses – in his reflection of disembodied isolation as the condition of more and more people in the ageing western world; and in his reflection of the lack of meaning which came to seem more and more the common condition of post-war society. What made him such a great writer was the way in which he brought together in single metaphors both of these dimensions: the utter intimacy of personal isolation and the absolute immensity of the human condition.

To see Beckett as a realist, you have only to look at the three facts of his life that are important. One is the fact that, as Eoin O'Brien's splendid *The Beckett Country* has shown, Beckett's work always remained haunted by the South Dublin landscape of his early years. What matters is not that this landscape is Irish or that

Beckett was, therefore, an Irish writer in any narrow sense of the term, but that this landscape is real. To a large extent Beckett's work is, therefore, an act of memory rather than of pure invention.

The other relevant biographical facts are Beckett's decision to return from Ireland to a France facing terrible war and his subsequent survival of the war on the one hand, and, on the other, his work with the sick, the maimed and the hurt – the casualties of the conflict – after the end of war. Beckett was, in a literal sense, a survivor, and it is this above all which shapes his greatest work. His post-war work emerges feeling itself for broken bones, stunned at its own survival, wondering, as survivors do, why some have been annihilated and others, for no apparent reason and with no apparent meaning, have been spared to go on. It poses the question of human survival as something at once meaningless and marvellous.

After the war, after Auschwitz, the intellectuals asked whether poetry could ever again be written (and then most of them went on to ignore the question). The only moral response to Auschwitz, they said, was silence. To babble on as if the full horror of what had happened could be comprehended, expressed and forgotten, was to devalue that horror. Beckett, with his acts of memory, took these questions seriously.

Where his pre-war work is clever, relatively expansive and more than a little pleased with itself, the work he began to publish after the war is fastidious, weighed, every word a struggle against silence, a point on a trajectory that always approaches, but never quite reaches, silence. He turned to theatre because, in the theatre, there are audible silences, pauses around which the words can be constructed, voices that can be heard to emerge out of the quietness.

He turned to the theatre, too, because it is an area in which cruelty and survival collide. At a basic level, theatre is about manipulation – the manipulation of actors and audiences by writers and directors. With *Waiting for Godot* and Vivian Mercier's famous description of it as the play in which 'nothing happens, twice,' the image of Beckett's plays was one of something that was barely theatrical at all.

But in fact, Beckett's plays are extraordinarily theatrical, are, indeed, largely about theatre itself. Not theatre as some kind of incestuous in-joke, but theatre as a metaphor and an example, as the very type of manipulation, of cruelty, of the domination of some individuals by others. Both the black humour and the lyrical blackness of his plays have to do with this metaphor.

The humour of *Godot*, for instance, is the humour of the actors' awareness that they are trapped in their roles, the way they keep threatening to give up and go home, keep threatening to do a deal with the audience and conspire against the writer and the director so that they can all just forget about it and call it a day. The joke of *Endgame* is the deliberate tormenting of the audience, as in Hamm's horrified question: 'We're not beginning to … to … mean something?' or Clov's turning of a telescope on the audience 'I see … a multitude – in transports of joy. That's what I call a magnifier'.

In Beckett's later plays, this identification of theatre and torment becomes more, not less, explicit. In *Catastrophe*, the Director tortures and humiliates an actor. Significantly, *Catastrophe* was coupled by Beckett with another play, *What Where*, in which a prisoner is beaten and interrogated.

But, in the end, the cruelty is not the point. The point is the survival. Just as he distilled language down to its essence, so he boiled all action on stage down to its tiniest essentials, making every movement a struggle against the gestural equivalent of silence, immobility. He tortured his actors, burying them up to their necks in sand, putting them in barrels and wheelchairs, blacking out everything but their mouths. But he did so, not in order to degrade, but in order to concentrate everything on the survival of voice and movement when all logic says that they should cease. Like any survivor from a disaster, he did not seek to give that survival great significance or to celebrate it. But he forced us to see it for what it was, and is.

Thomas Kilroy

The Irish Times, 10 May 1990

Just over 30 years ago, a young UCD student wrote an article for the Jesuit journal *Studies* reflecting on the poor state of the Irish theatre and demanding something better. It was the summer of 1959, and change was in the air. Eamon de Valera had just won the presidential election and retired to the Park, ending his era. Whitaker's Programme for Economic Expansion was getting under way under the leadership of Seán Lemass. Hesitantly, but apparently unstoppably, the country was on the move. But not so the Irish theatre.

Over at the Abbey, Ernest Blythe was still very much in charge and had just rejected, or was just about to reject, such plays as John B. Keane's *Sive*, Brendan Behan's *The Hostage*, and Tom Murphy's *A Whistle in the Dark*. The world was moving but the stage wasn't. Into this curious contradiction Thomas Kilroy sent his first piece of published work, that *Studies* essay, called 'Groundwork for an Irish Theatre'.

Irish theatre in the previous two decades, he wrote, 'has not been a creative theatre, not rooted in the society which supports it. During the last 20 years few Irish dramatists have been in any way exciting technically. More often, however, our dramatists today are guilty of a worse defect than mere lack of technical proficiency. They are inclined to shirk the painful, sometimes tragic problems of a modern Ireland which is undergoing considerable social and ideological stress'. He called for a new Irish theatre that would thrive on 'social readjustments and reassessments,' that would absorb 'some of the conflicting topical, social issues and give a public interpretation of current values'. Replying to Kilroy's implicit attack on the Abbey, one of its directors, Gabriel Fallon, mockingly urged the young man to 'become in the shortest possible space of time a startlingly good dramatist'. He was not to know then that Thomas Kilroy would become precisely that.

He did not do so in terms that precisely matched his own prescription. The playwright he became would never talk of 'mere lack of technical proficiency', for the technique with which to invent illusions, to create dreams, has been crucial to his achievement. Nor would he be drawn to 'topical, social issues', for he would come to believe that, in the theatre, 'escapism has its own tragic truth'. But he would most certainly strive to create a theatre that would refuse to shirk the pain of modern Ireland, that would give 'a public interpretation of current values'.

Part of the difficulty critics have with Kilroy is with the absence of what every Irish writer is supposed to have: a sense of place. Place is what gives a writer in Ireland a public identity, the feeling of belonging. When we think of the other playwrights, their home places come with them: Brian Friel's Donegal and Derry, Tom Murphy's Tuam, Frank McGuinness's borderlands, Tom Mac Intyre's drumlin country, Hugh Leonard's Dalkey, John B. Keane's Kerry. Even when the places have become imaginary landscapes, they are constant presences, and they give a public, communal dimension to even the most intensely private work.

With Kilroy, this is not so. He was born in Callan, County Kilkenny, in 1934, but apart from his novel *The Big Chapel* (which won the Guardian Fiction Prize in 1971) Kilkenny is not a presence in his writing. His plays are usually set in Dublin, but it is really a place on a stage where anything can happen, not a representation of a city.

Nor is this absence of a sense of place merely accidental. One senses in his work that an enormous effort has been made to keep clear of autobiography, an effort not to use childhood, growing up, personal history, the things that most Irish writers use all the time. His one play that can be said to have directly autobiographical elements, in that it uses the situation of a playwright in his room trying to write a play – *Tea and Sex and Shakespeare* – is his least successful.

The best way to understand Thomas Kilroy's work is to say that he comes from Catholic Ireland but forces himself to write as if he didn't, to lose that implacable knowledge so that he might stand above it, shape it beautifully, make it dance and fly.

And much of what he plays with is Catholicism itself. Two of his plays (there are only four since the first in 1968, with another *The Madam MacAdam Travelling Theatre*, due later this year at the

Royal Court in London; a new novel is also in progress) have explicit religious dimensions. His first, *The Death and Resurrection of Mr Roche* has, in the eponymous Mr Roche, Christ as a Dublin homosexual, replaying the Easter story in a seedy flat. *Talbot's Box*, now on tour in an excellent Red Kettle production, is about Matt Talbot and the notion of sainthood in the modern world. And in both cases, the religious vision is converted from implacable knowledge into something either nightmarish or utopian, into a sense of the world as double, not single.

Matt Talbot wonders if this world is not already hell: 'D'ya ever think father, there's any foundation in the notion we might be goin' through hell on earth? I do often think so!' Mr Roche sees around him 'all the dead and the living dead'. And yet both have apocalyptic visions of the world transformed into something heavenly: Talbot says that 'I do often see a light like the beginnin' of the world'; Roche sees the sun rising 'like the beginning of life again … Breaking up into light … Breaking up into life'.

The civil servant Kelly in *Mr Roche* is haunted by his brothers from the country whom he sometimes meets in Croke Park. Brendan Bracken in *Double Cross* sees, or imagines he sees, his brother standing under a lamp post outside his window: 'To be haunted by one's own brother dressed like a Soho pimp and with manners to boot. There are times, darling, when I truly fear that he may never go away from beneath the lamp post there'.

The people who have the power to forgive and bless in Kilroy's plays, therefore, are those who can truly forget the past. Mr Roche can bless his tormentors because 'I never remember anything, ever'. Matt Talbot can nullify history, sweeping away its opposing forces in a religious vision that unites all opposites: 'Blessed be the policeman 'n his stick/ For he bates the people outta our anger. / Blessed be the soldiers o' the king/ For the hungry wind takes away the smoke o' their guns'.

But that forgetfulness can equally lead to madness and self-destruction as it does for Brendan Bracken and William Joyce in *Double Cross*. In Kilroy's contradictory vision, things exist only when they are denied. Mr Roche's tormentors can reassure themselves of their sexual normality only by beating up a homosexual. Joyce and Bracken can assert their nationality only by the act of treason to it. And in *Talbot's Box*, Talbot's spirituality can exist only by eluding religion.

Such an imagination, in which things constantly call their opposites into being, can never rest easy, can never feel a sense of consummation, and Kilroy's imagination remains deeply restless. It is a way of working not conducive to a fixed, solid reputation, but it is also one which is, of its nature, always fascinating and challenging.

Sebastian Barry

The Irish Times, 13 June 1992

The best play I know about the collapse of Communism in Eastern Europe is set on an island off the Irish coast in the 1890s and has nothing whatsoever to do with either Communism or Eastern Europe. Sebastian Barry's *Prayers of Sherkin* is, however, in its re-enactment of the story of Fanny Hawke who must leave her millenarian sect on Sherkin Island in order to marry, a superb metaphor for the necessary death of a community and an ideal so that the individual may live.

This is how theatrical metaphors work: if they are strong and rich and subtle enough they will mean different things at different times. Such plays live on because, every time they are performed they seem to speak in the present tense. I have the feeling that Sebastian Barry's plays, like *White Woman Street* – the Bush Theatre production of which finishes its run at the Peacock tonight – will live.

Sebastian Barry is an original playwright in a field where originality is not that highly valued. Playwrights steal all the time, and the whole history of Western theatre could probably be reduced to a handful of plots and characters. It is much less important to be an original playwright than it is to be an original poet or novelist. Barry is, nevertheless, an original, and his breadth of imagination makes him the most important Irish dramatist to have emerged within the last decade.

As with most originals, the first things you notice, often to your annoyance, are the things that aren't there. Watching any of his three plays, and in particular *White Woman Street* which is his most daring, you are struck by the absences. Where is the drama? Where is the action? Where is the psychology? Where is the suspense? And, in particular, since he is a modern Irish dramatist, where is the conflict?

Modern Irish theatre has been a theatre of conflict, of contradictory world views clashing outwardly and often violently, the whole thing rooted somewhere in the traumatic shifts that happened in Irish culture 30 years ago. Barry, who replaces conflict as the driving force of his theatre, is our first completely post-1960s playwright.

The daring and the triumph of his venture lie in two things. Firstly, that he can discard what we have come to think of as the staples of drama and still create plays that are intensely involving and deeply moving. And secondly, that he moves away from conflict without moving away from politics. On the contrary, his plays are much more clearly public plays than those of many of his predecessors.

They are shaped by history in open and sweeping ways: *Boss Grady's Boys* by the War of Independence, *Sherkin* by the troubled coexistence of Catholic and Protestant in modern Ireland, *White Woman Street* by the long agony of Irish emigration since the Famine. You shouldn't be able to deal with these forces in a way that is calm and often (that most unfashionable of aesthetic terms) beautiful, in a voice that is never raised. Fortunately, nobody has told Sebastian Barry this.

He manages it through language. What he has managed to do is to construct a theatrical language that is so assured, so muscular, that it can afford to yoke together within its own cadences the most heterogeneous images. What you hear when you listen to the lines he puts in his characters' mouths is the King James Bible, that oracular but sturdy rhythm that pronounces a peculiarly earthy kind of divinity. That rhythm is so sure-footed and truly pitched that it can contain starkly conflicting images and yet hold them all within a severe and awesome unity.

Thus he can bring together images of a timeless Ireland and of a post-television Ireland in a way that, without ever denying their contradictions, imposes a linguistic order that is unified and calm and full of dignity.

For instance, two of the recurring images of his plays are those of the natural landscape and of the Wild West. Jesse James comes into *Sherkin*; *Boss Grady's Boys* ends with the old men imagining themselves encircled by Indians; but equally *White Woman Street*, which is actually set in the Wild West, is haunted by the pastoral imagery of rural Sligo.

Images which would be corny or banal in themselves – the joys of nature, cowboys and Indians – are shocked back into life by their imaginative coexistence in Barry's language. The tension between alternative versions of Ireland is not denied, but rather made clearer and stronger by being absorbed within a hauntingly expressive language.

For, such is the pleasure of a Barry play, it is easy to forget that his plays are remorseless and unflinching in their vision of Ireland as broken and fragmented. The love he shows within his circles of characters is matched only by the isolation of those circles from the surrounding world.

The image of people carried on 'a river flood' of history and deposited as detritus on unknown shores occurs in *White Woman Street* but could be in any of his plays. So shattered by history is the world of those plays that only a stringently beautiful and strangely abstract language could allow his characters to occupy the same stage at all. If the language were not poetic, these people, cut off as they are, would have nothing to say to us or to each other,

White Woman Street, though less immediately beautiful in its construction than *Prayers of Sherkin* was, is in some respects a more remarkable achievement. Whereas the previous two plays have kept a deliberately narrow focus, this one is stunning in its breadth, imagining its characters from a range of races and cultures and building a common language which can contain them all. It moves from strangeness to almost unbearable familiarity, becoming, for an Irish audience, a majestic lament for our scattered and our forgotten, for the spawn of the coffin ship and the Virgin Jumbo, for the innocents made guilty by their forced conquest of a new world.

Politics and Theatre

Redmond O'Hanlon

The most common critique of O'Toole as a theatre reviewer is that he is 'too political' and not sufficiently 'theatrical' in his approach. There is no doubt but that he displays a manifest sympathy for oppressed social and political minorities: we can see this in his pieces on poverty and arts access, on Gerry Stembridge's *The Gay Detective*, and in his various pieces on Roddy Doyle's realism as a defamiliarization of the middle-class world. He regularly makes explicit his strong left-wing sympathies and his critics might feel that these often blunt his aesthetic judgement, as, for example, when he wrote that *Peter Pan* embodied 'a colonial image of the colonized'. And his review of the Donal O'Kelly/Kenneth Glenaan play, *The Business of Blood*, might add some fuel to the fire of such critics. Here he clearly approves of the authors' political purpose, their sharply focused attempt to inform, persuade and outrage their audience and induce in it an awareness of Herbert's notion that the poetic task is to salvage justice and truth. At the same time, he is aware that, ultimately, aesthetic criteria must count. In his review of Jimmy Murphy's *A Picture of Paradise* we sense his sympathy for the homeless and for Murphy's 'proper political anger'. He nevertheless notes the limitations of his realism and his lack of metaphorical resonance, stating his clear preference for a play like McGuinness's *Baglady* which is for him a more effective exploration of homelessness because it is more oblique and theatrically innovative.

There's an interesting example of O'Toole's political bias in his review of Marie Jones's *Somewhere Over the Balcony* where he states: 'The pity is that all of this is talked about rather than acted out, that everything remains essentially at the level of reported speech', yet he then goes on to say that it is 'a sharp and captivating show'. Bernard Farrell or Hugh Leonard wouldn't have got the benefit of this doubt! And yet in his review of another Jones play, *A Night in November*, the universally acclaimed theatrical vitality of the performance made little impression on him. Can this have something to do with his very hard-line anti-Republicanism?

In his pieces on Bogdanov's impressive and very 'political' left-wing approach to *Hamlet* at the Abbey (*Sunday Tribune*, 17 April 1983) O'Toole clearly approves of his working methods: his quest for the core of political truth at the centre of a play and his rigorous analysis of the forces at work in its socio-political world. Of course, what has always intrigued him about Shakespeare is the subtle dialectical interplay of the private and public domains, which also fascinated him in the plays of Athol Fugard. Writing of Fugard's *Hello and Goodbye* (*Sunday Tribune*, 20 October 1985) he reacted warmly to those intimate moments 'which seem to be private and self-contained but which turn out to be indelibly marked with the circumstances of time, place and politics. His discussion of *He Left Quietly* (*Irish Times*, 29 November 2002) leads him to propose an exceptional dramatic category – the theatre of witness – which, as he puts it, renders criticism 'impertinent' when we are faced with an actor of great presence who is re-enacting his torture and death sentence as if he were a kind of ghost speaking from the other side of death and extinction.

In a review of Pinter's *Betrayal* (*Irish Times*, 10 May 1994) he extends his notion of the political, seeing, in this history of an affair, personal life as a kind of power politics and the home as a police state: 'His distinctive theatre comes from applying to sex, marriage and domesticity the categories in which thriller writers and left-wingers see repressive political states'.

I hope, then, that a reading of O'Toole's reviews over the years will show that he is far too subtle a critic to be treated as some sort of crude proponent of Marxist reflection theory, though he is politically committed and this puts pressure at times on his aesthetic judgements. Like the rest of us, he is caught in a web of contradictions, but this is no ignoble condition and in O'Toole's case it is a condition which gives depth, perspective and edge to a critical sensibility which is increasingly open to the poetical and performance dimensions of the theatrical experience.

Song of the White Man's Burden, by Peter Weiss

Project Arts Centre
Sunday Tribune, 13 March 1988

[…] *Song of the White Man's Burden* (better known in English as *Song of the Lusitanian Bogey*), currently at the Project Arts Centre in a splendid production by the young Co-Motion company, is about Portugal's colonial war in Angola, a war which ended seven years after the play was written in 1967.

All of [Weiss's] plays are to an extent documentary, even in some cases agitprop, and yet manage to go well beyond the business of merely reflecting events.

The question for a production of *Song of the White Man's Burden* is to what extent a play with avowedly agitational intentions, written as an intervention into a very specific political situation, can survive a change in that situation. Angola has not been at war with Portugal for 14 years now, though it continues to fight a very different battle with South Africa. The story Weiss is telling is an unfinished one: we hear nothing of the MPLA's victory in Angola, of the subsequent civil war, or of South Africa's continuing efforts to end the country's fragile independence.

When we hear stirring descriptions of particular Portuguese practices, our shock or anger is muted by the fact that we know these practices happened in the past. When someone says: 'In Angola nothing has changed whatsoever,' we know that very much has changed. And yet, partly as a result of the sheer power of some of Weiss's writing, partly because of parallels between the events he is describing and what is now going on in South Africa, and largely because of a strikingly vigorous production by Joe O'Byrne, the play lives on.

Co-Motion were clearly aware in tackling the play of the danger of distance, the possibility that the whole thing might seem like past history. To avoid this, they approach the piece with a head-on physicality, a muscular strength of movement that allows no prisoners to be taken.

The play has no characters, no plot, no subtleties of interpretation. Weiss is not here interested in individual psychology or motivation. His concern is with, in both senses, black and white, oppressed and oppressor. Slow build-ups or carefully modulated inflections would be beside the point. Co-Motion take this to heart and offer us a *blitzkrieg* rather than a slow infiltration behind the lines. While retaining elements of Weiss's cabaret style, they streamline everything into a perpetual motion machine.

Which is not to say that the production lacks the essential musicality. Like *The Investigation*, *Song of the White Man's Burden* could be called an oratorio. Much of it is sung, but even where it is not, the performers are more like singers than they are like actors playing a part. An actor is now a black peasant, now a white colonist.

What matters is that the voices build into a formal pattern as they do in music. Side by side with the relentless physical activity is a rich and complex soundtrack of drumbeats, train noises, sirens, birds, all performed by the actors themselves. These elements of movement and sound combine to create an impenetrable wall through which no inappropriately naturalistic musings on character and motive can emerge.

The constant barrage of impressions allows us to put up with a wide diversity of styles and sensations, from the burlesque to the grotesque, from almost unbearable sadness to broad and crude parody.

The production moves through them with deceptive ease, the actors functioning not so much as individuals, but more as a single unit, their track-suit costumes distinguished only by numbers, like football players combined into a team. To do this, and do it successfully, is unusual in the Irish theatre, and underlines Co-Motion's emergence as a vital new force.

Too Much Too Young, by Anto Nolan

Tivoli Theatre
The Irish Times, 4 July 1995

Anto Nolan's first play, *Too Much Too Young*, produced by Passion Machine at the Tivoli in Dublin is essentially the same old story: emigrant returns to old pals, prompting revelations of past conflicts and reminding pals of static nature of own lives. Instead of a naturalistically reproduced country cottage we have a naturalistically reproduced Corporation house bedroom. Instead of a shared folk memory of fairs and crossroads dances, we have a shared folk memory of a Madness concert in Dublin. The surface has changed but the underlying drama is the same. [...] If *Too Much Too Young* doesn't manage to tell that story in an especially fresh way, it does manage to make the general particular, to put flesh and blood on the dusty skeleton in Ireland's cupboard.

What it does have, though, is still considerable. Anto Nolan has learned a lot from [Paul] Mercier's ability to project a visual style into a naturalistic setting, his characteristic grasp of the way self-conscious, stylized performance is not at odds with everyday reality but an integral part of the way ordinary people behave. Nolan captures very well, both in the writing and the direction, the sense that these young men live in a world, not just of burger-flipping and dole cards, but also of television, movies and, above all, pop music. Fantasy is not for them an escape from reality but an integral part of their reality.

This comes across most obviously in the brilliant re-enactments of Madness performances against a backdrop of bunk beds and wardrobes, which are not just funny and exciting but also genuinely poignant. Against a patronizing tendency to view pop idolatry as slavish and infantile, Nolan manages to make a case for it as an assertion of dignity and choice by young men whose choices are limited and whose right to any sense of dignity is constantly denied.

Less obvious, but just as poignant, is the way Nolan shows pop culture as the one thing that gives the characters a sense of personal history. He gives us conversations on a homecoming that are fragmented, disjointed, stories that are continually interrupted and diverted. Buster's emigration means that he and the others no longer share a common history. Instead, they measure out their lives in pop styles – Showaddywaddy succeeded by the Bay City Rollers, succeeded by the Bee Gees, until Madness and the Specials provide moments of shared and secure memory.

Return to the Hill, by Lee Dunne

Eblana Theatre
The Irish Times, 5 September 1995

[…] The interest of *Return to the Hill* lies in […] the way it pictures the relationship between its characters and the world around them. For all the awfulness, Dunne does achieve something quite unique – a sense of a class of people to whom the world happens. While good drama, almost by definition, is about people who think they can shape the world or at least modify its force, Dunne gives us people who never even imagine in the first place that they have any say in the matter.

On the same principle, the play is full of things – prostitution, adultery, alcoholism, addictive gambling, fraud, mental illness – that in any other play would be presented as 'issues' or 'problems'. Here, they are just facts. And the political world above and beyond it all is no less inscrutable.

The very thing that makes the play impossible as a piece of drama – the absence of a controlling authorial eye, watching, weighing, judging – makes it accurate as a picture of the world-view of people for whom the very idea of a coherent, controlling force in life simply doesn't exist. Conversely, if the play were better made, if it had been given the orderly shape that a piece of drama has to have, it would be further from the reality of the lives it depicts.

Art, of course, is about precisely such a distance, but it is because it so accurately reproduces the point-of-view of a section of society that *Return to the Hill* reaches an audience that little else in the theatre can touch. Because there are still many people for whom a play about characters who don't expect to be able to control their own lives seems to be telling it like it is, there is still an audience willing to return to the hill, again and again.

The Business of Blood, by Donal O'Kelly and Kenneth Glenaan

Project Arts Centre
The Irish Times, 26 September 1995

[…] *The Business of Blood* has at its heart a serious Christian, the campaigning pacifist Chris Cole, who has been in and out of prison for his non-violent protests against British Aerospace's supply of Hawk Jets to the Indonesian regime for use in the genocide in East Timor. For another, it draws on the resonance of Christ's trials in its teasing out of the opposition between justice and the law that is implicit in the episode of the woman taken in adultery.

Most importantly, though, *The Business of Blood* is itself an act of writing of the kind that Jesus engaged in to save a life. It is written in the dust, written in the hope of being ephemeral. The authors could have no greater ambition than that their play might be incomprehensible to posterity because its content would have become irrelevant. Its purpose is to induce shame, to help save lives, not to be an aesthetic creation of enduring majesty. Indeed, if it does endure, it will be because it has failed, because it does not help to make the world it describes a barbarous anachronism.

There is a strong tendency to patronize such writing, to see it as at best a lesser form of art, at worst a corruption of aesthetic purity. But actually this kind of art can more truthfully be said to address itself to the necessary precondition for all other kinds – civilization. The Polish poet Zbigniew Herbert has written that the task of the poet in the modern world is 'to salvage out of the catastrophe of history at least two words, without which all poetry is an empty play of meanings and appearances: justice and truth'.

Without civilization, without the ideas of justice and truth, all plays are empty play. The question posed by *The Business of Blood* – whether civilization can be said to exist at all while complicity with mass murder is treated as a legitimate business – is a question that addresses the very possibility of art itself.

This is not, of course, to say that plays with a civilizing political purpose like this one are somehow exempt from all aesthetic criteria. On the contrary, a play that takes to itself the right to teach us something of urgent moral significance actually raises the aesthetic stakes by making the price of failure much heavier than it would otherwise be. A bad play about suburban lust is just a bad play. A bad play about genocide is also bad morality. If it is banal, or trivial, or tedious or patronizing, it actually makes a bad situation worse by discrediting the very moral outrage it seeks to evoke. It may not, in other words, have to be aesthetically superb but it absolutely must not be aesthetically crass. *The Business of Blood* passes this test with great distinction.

It is written with a splendidly clear sense of its own purpose. It is explicitly and unapologetically functional, aiming to inform, to persuade and to outrage, and it gives us the pleasures, if not of a great painting, then of a really good industrial design.

Everything is shaped so as to best serve its purpose, ruthlessly stripped of the superfluous. We learn nothing of Chris Cole's private life, say, or of his deep inner motivations. But within this utilitarian structure there is room for both theatrical invention and intellectual complexity. Unlike most agitprop, *The Business of Blood* is never patronizing. It is didactic but not preachy, passionate but not po-faced, deadly serious but also pleasantly playful. [...] There is no self-indulgence, no lapse into an inappropriate attempt to fill in the details of characters who have to remain as bold images of a moral and political conflict. By lashing on the broad brush strokes of passion, humour and energy, they stop us from hankering after the kind of detailed portraiture that would, in the context, be a distraction.

There has to be room in the theatre for work as instructive, as angry and as well aimed as this. Pointing the finger of blame may not be the most complex, subtle or elegant gesture that can be performed on a stage but if it is done, as it is here, with a steady hand and a keen eye, it will always be a powerful one.

from **Lack of access to arts goes to the heart of poverty trap**

The Irish Times, 11 February 1997

Exclusion from the arts is therefore not a just a side effect of poverty; it is an integral part of what it means to be poor. Combat Poverty, in its report on community arts published last Septmeber, rightly pointed out that 'a lack of access to and participation in arts and culture is part of the experience of poverty'.

So cultural exclusion isn't just about saying it is a pity the unemployed don't use their free time to read *War and Peace*. It is a very significant aspect of what keeps people poor in the first place.

The standard answer to complaints about the exclusivity of the audience for many cultural activities is that great art is of its nature elitist. It is complex, challenging and almost always out of line with the assumptions of everyday life. This is, of course, true, but it is also beside the point. Even if some kinds of art will always be a minority interest, why should it be so easy to define that minority in terms of socio-economic class? Is it mere coincidence that art-lovers are easier to find in homes with two cars in the driveway?

The Arts Council advances the idea, previously mooted by Combat Poverty, of 'developmental community arts'. This kind of work is not about 'bringing art to the people' but about making neglected areas visible to themselves and to others, about using art as a way of understanding the present and imagining the future – the first steps in any process of social change.

A Picture of Paradise, by Jimmy Murphy

Peacock Theatre
The Irish Times, 1 June 1997

The homeless in the modern city present a peculiar paradox. On the one hand they are, by definition, obvious. Living on the streets, they are on public display, and homelessness is, as well as everything else, an absence of privacy. On the other, though, they are also invisible. As individuals, they melt into the streetscape. For various reasons – familiarity, embarrassment, anguish – they cannot really be looked at. Their lives are, for the vast majority, mysterious.

For the theatre, their plight is particularly perplexing, because one of its assumptions is that we believe what we see, that if something is presented to us with sufficient conviction, it will affect us. Yet here, on the theatre of the streets, are stark realities that we see but do not believe in strongly enough to feel or do anything very profound.

Jimmy Murphy's new play at the Peacock, *A Picture of Paradise*, is an attempt to solve the paradox. It sets out to reveal the lives behind the images and to tell the stories which make people suffering individuals, rather than abstract problems. But it is, in the end, more a demonstration of the problem than a solution. For what it shows is, above all, just how difficult it really is to present for the comfortable society that fills theatre seats a convincing image of how and why the homeless become what they are.

This is, unapologetically, a play about a social problem, and the impulse behind it is profoundly realistic. But the difficulty of finding a form within which to contain such an impulse is at least tacitly acknowledged in the opening moments of the play.

For since it was published by Faber last year (in the collection *The Dazzling Dark*) *A Picture of Paradise* has been very radically revised. The published version has a family breaking in to squat in a flat in the first act, then thrown outside in the second. Its tone is that of a flat, documentary-style narrative.

Now, in David Byrne's fine production, the play begins with the expulsion – the mother screaming as mattresses and bags rain down from an unseen balcony above. It is an arresting theatrical image. And with the help of Barbara Bradshaw's superb set – a stylized enclosure of grim towers – Byrne tries to push the piece further and further towards the kind of metaphorical resonance that an effective piece of theatre needs. He makes the family into a kind of Adam and Eve after the expulsion from Paradise, with the added, grotesque twist that the Eden they are desperate to re-enter is a grim kip in a junkie-infested compound.

This is undoubtedly the right way to go, and the surreal effect of having a family's furniture – armchair, table, mattresses – set up around a desultory tree and a garden bench does much to sustain the theatrical life of the piece. The problem, however, is that the writing remains so relentlessly realistic that it does not marry with the style of the production. The dialogue and characterization have been restructured, but not quite re-imagined.

There are good things in the writing. Flashes of the savage wit that made Murphy's *Brothers of the Brush* so exhilarating break through the gloom. The contrast between a city that can afford to put a clock that doesn't work in the Liffey and the reality of those for whom hope is a lottery scratch card or a desperate double at the bookie's, is powerfully drawn.

And one of the strengths of the play is Murphy's refusal, for the most part, to wallow in simplistic sympathy. There is a proper political anger in his writing, but no glib suggestion that everything would be all right if the family had more money. The depiction of the working class is honest enough to include the way Angela (Barbara Brennan) gambles the savings away, the way his old friends turn away from Seán (Paul Bennett) when he is in trouble, and the fact that their tormentor is a baseball-wielding member of the flats' residence committee.

But decency and honesty don't of themselves make for good drama, and there is simply not enough substance to make them live on stage. Realism is just not up to the job of dramatizing fractured lives and broken worlds. Oddly, the more realistic the play becomes, the less convincing it seems. As characters too small-scale for the elemental story in which they are caught, these ordinary decent people stuck in a hopeless situation come to seem almost prim and proper.

Good political intentions are wasted on thin theatrical forms. Conversely, there is no necessary contradiction between form and content – it is possible for a play to be both an exploration of theatre and an exploration of society. A play such as Frank McGuinness's oblique, highly-charged monologue *Baglady*, for instance, is not just a better play but a more effective exploration of homelessness. And it is also worth remembering that the most memorable, most truly realistic image of what it means to be homeless, King Lear on the heath, is also the maddest and strangest sequence in theatrical history.

He Left Quietly, by Duma Kumalo and Yaël Farber

The Helix, DCU
The Irish Times, 29 November 2002

[…] The immense disparity between the suffering to which it bears witness and the privileged position of the critic is such as to render criticism merely impertinent. Here, the sense of witness is literal. *He Left Quietly* is based on the life of Duma Kumalo. It is performed, along with two actors, by Duma Kumalo. We cannot, in other words, separate the dancer from the dance, the experience from the representation.

Duma Kumalo was sentenced to death in 1984 on a false charge of taking part in the murder of a town councillor in Sharpeville, in what was then apartheid South Africa. Along with five other men, he formed the Sharpeville Six – a group analogous to the Birmingham Six, except that they were sentenced to hang.

Kumalo is, in a sense, a ghost, a revenant from the world of the dead. In March 1988, he was measured for his coffin, and for the noose. His last meal of a whole chicken was brought to his cell. He had his final meeting with his heartbroken father. And then, a matter of hours before his execution, he was reprieved as a result of international pressure and, after another four years, finally released.

Kumalo's story is not unique to South Africa. The 'common purpose' laws under which he was convicted were also used in Northern Ireland, most notoriously in the horrific case of the corporals lynched in West Belfast. The racist politics of Death Row under apartheid are still played out every day in the US.

But *He Left Quietly* cannot be a universal metaphor. Kumalo's own presence as narrator and actor takes the piece far beyond the familiar realms of artistic imagery. It is inescapably real. The only other piece I've seen that has this same quality is George

Seremba's extraordinary re-enactment of his own torture and attempted murder by the Ugandan secret police, *Come Good Rain*.

Kumalo's story is told very differently from Seremba's electrifyingly direct performance, however. The writer and director Yaël Farber has given it the deliberation and distance of a ritual. With Lebohang Elephant enacting Kumalo's narrative with mime, movement and laconic utterance, and Yana Sakelaris re-creating Farber's own involvement as a white South African of Jewish extraction, the piece successfully converts raw reality into a cooler, more abstract, performance.

This might be jarring were it not for the nature of Duma Kumalo's own extraordinary presence. He is calm, almost stoical, speaking and moving as if he really is a ghost, looking at his own life from the far side of death. Through this presence and the increasingly eloquent suppleness of Farber's beautifully-judged production, the piece becomes almost literally haunting.

Essays on Criticism

Julia Furay

In addition to his theatre criticism and political commentaries, Fintan O'Toole has occasionally written about criticism as a profession; excerpted here are three of the pieces in which he attempts to clarify his intentions as a critic, and to justify criticism as a form. For the most part, he succeeds. He does so by never letting himself or his fellow critics off the hook in terms of critical responsibility, and by admitting the limitations of the form, while still insisting that criticism is a necessary factor in any democratic society. His arguments are persuasive.

His varying views towards criticism are also evident. 'If this is criticism, I want my old job back' was written while O'Toole was on leave from critical duty, working instead as literary adviser at the Abbey. And here is where he is harshest on critics and criticism: 'If the function of criticism is to enlighten and clarify, then we critics as a bunch are failing mightily'. Compare that with his 1991 Golden Rule article in which he reminds us that criticism typifies the spirit of a democratic culture. Or with a 1996 piece written for *The Economist* (and not reprinted here), when he became further inclined to make grandiose claims: 'At best, albeit at the risk of tears, [criticism] cuts through to the core and allows the work itself to emerge'.

And seeing these arguments here in context with his theatre criticism allows us to see if his arguments are carried through in practice, and how his views on criticism compare to those on theatre. Similar themes certainly crop up: as always, he comments on the fusion of forms and splintering of society that have rocked the arts in Ireland.

from **Putting my prejudices on the table**
The Irish Times, 11 November 1988

[...] I don't believe that criticism has any authority to undermine. I take as a motto the definition by which the playwright Arnold Wesker meant to rubbish theatre critics – 'Criticism is personal opinion magnified by print'.

To me the critic doesn't speak for the public, the newspaper, the audience, tradition, the proletariat, the spirit of the age or civilization as we know it. The critic is a walking, or generally sitting, bunch of prejudices which can be stimulated, met, confirmed, challenged or, occasionally, overturned by the events at which he or she is present.

What the reader needs to know is what those prejudices are, and to what extent they conform to his or her own. If at least some of them do, then the critic may be of some use to the reader.

Here, then, are some of my prejudices.

I believe that theatre is first and foremost a public art form and that this obvious fact has all sorts of consequences for the way we should talk about it. Theatre is public both in its creation and in its reception. Even in its simplest forms it is made by a number of people acting together – and it doesn't exist without its audience.

Theatre, if it happens at all, happens between the audience and the actors. The First Folio of Shakespeare or the Faber edition of *Faith Healer* isn't theatre: nor is a performance of *Hamlet* in Cracow in 1968 the same piece of theatre as a performance of *Hamlet* in the Gaiety in 1988. Theatre, in other words, is not an object (like a book or a photograph or a painting or a U2 record), it is an effect.

And that means that every piece of theatre must address itself at some level to its audience, to a particular time and a particular place. If the critic wants to explain the effect, then he or she has to deal as much with that particular time and place as with the form and content of what is happening on stage.

That, in turn, brings in what in the broadest sense can be called politics: the way in which we understand or interpret our society, our own particular here and now.

Now, it's important to be clear on what I am not saying. I am not saying that a critic has a licence to judge plays by purely political criteria. It is patently idiotic to say that *At the Hawk's Well* is a bad play because Yeats was a proto-fascist and *The Drums of Father Ned* is a good one because O'Casey was on the side of the workers.

Of course we all bring political prejudices to the theatre, and mine make me more inclined to like O'Casey than to like Yeats.

But I still think that *At the Hawk's Well* is an infinitely better play than *Father Ned*, assuming that both are performed with the same clarity and skill, precisely because it seems to me to be far better able to address an audience, to achieve an effect.

For the same reason – that it does not attempt to engage its audience from moment to moment, but rather attempts to present a prepackaged conclusion – I hate most agitprop.

Nor am I saying that I don't like plays if they don't have an overt political content. *The Importance of Being Earnest* or *The Gigli Concert* have little in the way of stated politics, but I would number both among my favourite plays. What I am saying is that the shape of a play can be connected to the shape of the world, and that when it happens the effect is extraordinarily powerful.

Earnest is not a political tract about Victorian values, but its whole movement is to invert those values. *Gigli* isn't a dissection of contemporary Ireland, but its whole force as a piece of theatre comes from its transformation of our world. And if you want to invert or transform or simply describe a world, you have to understand it and make it concrete. That, whether you like it or not, involves politics.

So, what I look for in a play above all else is a sense of clarity, a sense of how an audience is to be addressed and what effect is to be achieved. It seems to me that when things don't work in the Irish theatre it is generally not because of incompetence, at least on the part of the actors.

Far more often it is because not enough thinking has been done, because there is no clear vision of what is to be communicated. Either a play has been chosen with no real sense of what it can be made to say to an audience at this time and in this place, or else that sense has been muddied in rehearsal, leaving the actors with no real notion as to what they are doing and why.

In which case I see it as my job to try to identify the lost opportunities rather than just to abuse the actors for their failures, to put forward some vision of the way a play might have worked (assuming that it could work at all) and measure what actually happened against it.

This clarity of purpose involves questions of form as well as of content. It's not just that the form of a production has to have a coherent relationship to its content, it's that the content is likely to be richer, more open, more effective in making an audience think and feel, if it uses the great advantage which theatre has: its ability to make more than one thing happen at any one time.

I am prejudiced in favour of theatre that uses the fact that we have eyes as well as ears, that we respond to movements as well as words and that words and movements can be used either to contradict or complement each other. I am prejudiced against theatre that is static and one-dimensional – unless, as is the case with much of Beckett's work, the paucity of movement is there to draw attention to every detail of gesture, to every movement that survives.

The really dangerous prejudices in a critic are the ones of which he, and the readers, are unaware. That's where petulance, unfairness and downright perversity come in. Luckily, in the Irish theatre and among its public, there are always those kind and generous enough to point out such failings.

from **The Golden Rule is that there is no Golden Rule**

The Irish Times, 11 June 1991

'How,' asked the great American man of the theatre Harold Clurman, 'can the audience be reached directly without the middleman intervention of these fools?' – meaning the critics whom he described as 'lean dry men who know little or nothing

about the theatre'. Many poets and fiction writers have sent up
the same plea: can we not be allowed to communicate directly
with our readers? Must we always have our work strained
through the hollow colander of criticism? What are critics but
would-be censors, filtering the works of great minds through
their own much smaller ones?

Most of what its detractors say about criticism is true [...] It is
unfair, since no one view is innately more valid than another and
there is no guarantee that a critic's view of a poem or a novel or a
play is held by a majority of its readers.

Indeed, not only is criticism unfair, but it is no good at all
unless it is in some degree unfair. 'A critic,' as Oscar Wilde wrote,
'cannot be fair in the ordinary sense of the word. It is only about
things that do not interest one that one can give a really unbiased
opinion, which is no doubt the reason why an unbiased opinion
is always absolutely valueless. The man who sees both sides of a
question is a man who sees absolutely nothing at all'. And critics
are always in a sense unqualified: either you are a practitioner of
the art you criticize, in which case you many lack the distance
necessary for criticism, or you are not a practitioner of the art
and therefore can never *really* know what it involves.

The crux of criticism is like the crux of Christianity as Bernard
Shaw saw it: the Golden Rule says that 'as you would that men
should do to you, do you also to them in like manner'. But what,
asked Shaw, if they don't have the same taste? Criticism can
come up with as many Golden Rules as it likes, but they will all
run up against differences in taste. The only Golden Rule that
ought to apply is that there is no golden rule. Critics ought to
have discernible criteria. They also ought to be open to the
possibility of those criteria being blown apart or shoved aside by
a work of art that is powerful enough to do so.

And the criteria themselves cannot operate in the way that
rules do, unless, as in Royalist France or Stalinist Russia or
Triumphalist Ireland, critical categories are to become, not a mild
form of censorship, but censorship itself.

The rational categories by which a critic tries to explain a
judgement have to come after and not before that judgement. All
of the apparatus of criticism is nothing more than a way of trying

to communicate as clearly as possible an irrational and incommunicable feeling: 'I liked this, I didn't like that'. If criticism is any good, it is because it honestly reflects that experience. If it isn't, it is because it isn't honest, because the experience offered by a work of art wasn't entered into, or because the critic is too scared, or too polite, or too incompetent, to say what it is that happened when the critic faced into the work.

Still, all of this does nothing to answer the basic question: by what right does criticism interpose itself between the work and the reader or viewer of that work? Is the critic not the eternal gooseberry, refusing to leave the room while the author and the reader get on with consenting spiritual intercourse in private? It doesn't sound like much to ask for: some time alone with the reader to allow what you have written to be accepted or rejected on its merits, on its ability to engage another mind and heart. All works of the imagination are now approached through labyrinths of newsprint. And if we cannot be allowed to approach them directly, let us at least approach them through the words of other creative writers whose imaginative powers will match those of the works 'themselves.

To deal with the second part of this plea first: great creative writers can be as questionable in their judgements about their fellow writers as the worst hack critic can be. Shaw thought that *The Importance of Being Earnest* was not nearly as good as *An Ideal Husband*. [...] The plea for unmediated engagement with the reader is a little disingenuous in most cases. In the case of the theatre, of course, the writer's work has already passed through large numbers of mediations before it reaches its audience.

But the notion of an unmediated relationship between writer and reader is, anyway, a bit hard to take. The modern idea of criticism arises at the same time, and in the same context, as the spread of literacy and the emergence of literature as a product, a commodity which can be bought and sold. Where works of art are continuous with the social processes which they reflect – a Gothic cathedral, a heroic epic declaimed by a bard after a battle, a mediaeval morality play performed by the guilds of a city – the notion of an outside judge of standards, a critic mediating between the work and its audience, doesn't arise. Criticism comes in when you no longer have common, fixed cultural values to which both the artist and the audience refer. But when art becomes something that can be bought and sold then there is already something in the way, standing between the work and the audience for it: money.

You could go further and say that what defines the modern world as opposed to the mediaeval one is that it is an era of opinions rather than of convictions. The mediaeval world is a world of conviction – one in which people know what they are supposed to think. It is consequently also an anti-democratic world, one in which individual views can be judged only by their conformity or otherwise to 'truth', in other words to the accepted convictions about the way the world works. In such a world, you have no real need for criticism, only for censorship.

In the modern world, however, we have replaced convictions with opinions. That, ultimately, is what democracy is about: you have your opinions, I have mine, neither of us claims an absolute monopoly on truth. This is where criticism comes in. [...] What brings criticism into disrepute is that critics sometimes claim the rights of the modern world while behaving as if they were still in a mediaeval one, measuring works of art for their conformity to true convictions, not their effect on individual opinion. Writers and readers have the right to expect that critics display their convictions and opinions with the humility that knows that many of the things of which they are convinced are likely to be wrong.

If criticism exists precisely because of the social changes that have made literature into a product, then the more literature becomes a product, a marketable commodity, the more need there is for criticism. Marketing sets out to sell books and plays by making claims for them, claims which are expressed in a dizzying vocabulary of hyperbole. When every second novel is the book that is going to change your life, in what language can we still discuss *King Lear* or *Ulysses*? The worst of criticism is generally better than the blurbs that adorn even books from respectable publishers.

The question is this: is it better for a choice to be influenced by the ingenuity, spending power and hard neck of marketing people alone, or is it better if that marketing is counterbalanced by honest, independent and intelligent criticism, however flawed? […] The spirit of criticism – making demands, asking questions, expecting the best – is also the spirit of a culture which wants to read and write. If we can't demand to get what we want, we will end up wanting what we get, and there are plenty of hype-merchants around to helps us towards that state of ignorant bliss.

from **If this is criticism, I want my old job back**

The Irish Times, 9 Nov 1991

Great minds may think alike but critics usually differ. Criticism is not a science, and there is no final court of appeal. […] Even in the quicksand of critical judgement in general, though, Irish criticism has been on very unsure ground of late. Fractious and disputatious as the Irish Culture Club has always been, it is hard to remember a time when across a whole range of issues and forms there has been such utter disagreement about fundamentals. It is not a question of the usual range of tastes and enthusiasms, but of, in some cases at least, a choice between absolute rapture on the one hand, and utter revulsion on the other.

If the function of criticism is to enlighten and to clarify, then we critics, as a bunch, are failing mightily. I imagine that for most readers the present sense of things is of criticism as a source of confusion and bafflement rather than of light and clarity.

I have my own highly partisan views on all these issues, and I will dispense them at unconscionable length to any poor passer-by, but it might be worth taking a breather from the battle and try to discern the disposition of forces.

Why is it that criticism, rather than being an enabling force for public discussion and judgement, has become a disabling one, a stalemate of locked horns from which no great conclusion can at present be expected? I think there are at least three different sets of reasons, and if we can unravel them, we might at least be a bit clearer about what is happening and why:

The writers won't keep their places

Fundamental to criticism as it is generally organized is the idea of specialist critics. I know about poetry, you know about fiction, she knows about about cinema, and so on. The forms give security and comfort to the critics. But the forms are breaking down. Most of our writers are now writing in at least two forms [...]

Ten years ago none of this was true. We had novelists, playwrights and poets and they kept their places. Now, the basic handrails of form which critics grasp onto in order to steady themselves are falling away. This is a mean trick on the part of the writers, and one which disorients criticism. It is particularly mean in the theatre, which is the meeting point of most of this subversion of forms. The question of what is a play and how are we to judge it is up for grabs.

The idea of High Art is being desecrated

Once upon a time, there was a division between us and them, the great writers and the great unwashed. There were people who went to serious theatre, listened to serious music and read serious literature, and there were people who liked potboilers, pop music and bodice-rippers. This distinction was continually blown apart by much great art (Dickens, O'Casey, The Boys from the Blackstaff etc.) but it is an intensely important one for critics. What qualifies me to be a critic is that I have read Milton and Shelley, Joyce and Beckett, whereas the poor sods who are going to ignore my judgements and go out and buy Jeffrey Archer novels in their millions haven't. This is what justifies my judgement in the face of the public's ignorance. It is hugely important to my sense of myself as a critic in touch with the Great Tradition.

Then, Irish writers started to mess this up. John McGahern wrote a book called *The Pornographer* which upset many people because of its demolition of the whole notion of the Artist and its deliberate mixture of literary prose and bad pornography. Paul Durcan started making poems that owed as much to Van Morrison as they did to Kavanagh. Roddy Doyle and Paul Mercier started to use football, rock and roll, quiz shows, movie thrillers, soap operas, the whole rag-bag of mass entertainment forms in their work. Not only were realism and fantasy, brutality and lyricism mixed together with alarming promiscuity but the whole fundamental distinction between High Art and Low Art started to fall to pieces.

In the theatre, writers like Tom Murphy and, again, John McGahern, dared to use old sneered-at 'popular' forms like melodrama to make highly serious work. Tom Kilroy wrote a play that had the bloody gall to put together potboiler forms and highly complex intellectual concepts. One of the basic self-assurances of the critic has been mercilessly stripped away.

The fruitful dichotomies of Irish writing, the tensions that have informed the great work of the last 30 years, are no more

Most obviously in the theatre, but in other forms as well, an underlying social tension, between tradition and modernity, between the old Ireland and the forces of change unleashed in the 1960s was the stuff of the great revival in modern Irish writing. But those tensions have lost their shape and dissolved into a fractured, highly complex society. There is no longer one story and one Ireland. There are many Irelands, some of which are literally unrecognizable to the others.

The tensions of the 1960s onwards, which were part of a great clash of forces, led to the possibility of making classical work. You could, for instance, write a tragedy in Ireland in the 1960s when elsewhere the form was said to be dead. Now the great shaped masterpiece, the single metaphor for an entire society, is virtually impossible. Both the work itself and the perspective from which it can be judged, are inevitably becoming more fractured, angular and messy.

The job of criticism is to take stock of what that means and how it is going to be addressed. That will in itself be a messy, angular and sometimes painful process.

In Conversation with Redmond O'Hanlon

ROH *When I look at your theatre reviews, particularly your early ones, I'm struck by how attached you are to the idea of coherence – the centre of the play, what the play is about.*

FOT I do think coherence is a useful critical category: what you are looking for in any production is a coherence of purpose, which may not be the same thing as coherence of effect. On the one side there needs to be an impression that, because this is a collective enterprise, it is functioning along a single track. Now, the single track may not be that there is a simple and true line, but that if it is attempting to have multiple effects, everybody is trying to achieve the same multiple effect.

A piece of theatre is, at a certain level, a reflection of a mind. Now, that mind may be singular or collective, it may be a mind which is born out of the interaction of a number of different minds – the mind of the playwright, the mind of the director, the minds of the actors, but there does need to be a sense that those minds have met, and that what you are getting is some kind of collective approach. It's important not to confuse that with saying there is a preconceived idea of what that should be.

Obviously, the creation of a piece of theatre is a dynamic process, and your reception of a piece of theatre is also dynamic. It's changing as you're sitting there, but very often, when things don't work, it's not because people are incompetent – it's because their different competences have not, in fact, been directed, in a simple sense. So, that is very much one of my concerns. It's just inherent in the nature of theatre itself that it is just as much a form which needs orchestration as a piece of classical music. And if you don't have that, then what you get is a series of individual events, which don't really cohere into a single event.

ROH *In the earlier days, it did appear to me that you were much more sure of what a play was about. That always worries me, particularly in theatre, because the play is never, or rarely, simply about something, it is a set of possibilities for performance.*

FOT Yeah, that's a very valid criticism; you know, I started off as a very clear, quite tough-minded Marxist. There needs to be a map, even if the map is the wrong map. It no longer really matters to me whether I agree with what they're saying with the play. It does matter to me that they have a sense of having a mental map of the journey this play is taking.

ROH *That the director and cast are taking one of the possible journeys together.*

FOT If you think about a play as this set of possibilities, it is not an infinite set of possibilities. And one of the things you realize when you look at a piece of theatre, when you sit in a rehearsal room, is that every second, literally, involves the picking of one from an enormous range of choices, the movement, gesture, the tone of voice, the stress on a particular piece of language, plus everybody else making the same range of decisions; all those who are on stage at the same time, the lighting and design people and everyone else.

But it is a field that does have some walls, and you do need to have a sense as well where the boundaries are in any particular piece of work: this is not simply about content in some sort of crude sense. Form imposes limits – that's what form is, it's a set of limits – and sometimes one of the reasons a piece of theatre doesn't work is because there's not a clear enough sense of what the form is, what the conventions are, and what you're doing with them. I have no problem with somebody saying: 'We're going to play Chekhov in the nude as if it was a piece of Brecht' so long as they have cut a map through the play which actually allows for that to be a coherent possibility. I would doubt it, but I'm open to being convinced.

I guess the other thing that I have learned is that you become less absolute in your sense of what works and what doesn't work. I would no longer ever say about a production that it didn't work because the interpretation was wrong; it's quite possible that the interpretation was completely wrong, but it was a fantastic piece of theatre. Wrong doesn't really come into it in that sense. Again, what matters is the quality in the shaping of imagination which is communicated, not whether they themselves think they have a coherent view; it's whether they have managed to communicate that coherence.

ROH *But you never write: 'I went there last night, this was extraordinary, I don't know why, but this image hit me, that move was amazing, but I can't …' It's as if you need to get some mastery, is that being severe?*

FOT No. But I also don't think that's necessarily a bad thing, because my function is to communicate as well. And I have written reviews which say: 'This image is fantastic'. But, I would hope to be able to put that into some form of context because images are not innocent; we may not be able to decipher them in their entirety, and maybe we shouldn't seek to but they cannot function outside of a context either. A piece of theatre creates a context. And it is part of my job to put it into context – to say that this is how it actually seems to me in that particular context. I would regard myself as having failed if I wrote my piece and said: 'I liked this, but I have no bloody idea whether it means anything, or whether it is any good or not'. Maybe I am a peculiar kind of creature in that the vast majority of pieces of theatre I've seen, I've seen as a critic; so my experience of the theatre, my presence in the theatre is completely shaped by my experience as a critic, so even if I'm not reviewing, I'm trying to join up the dots, somehow.

ROH *I remember some years ago every so often you would do a piece saying: 'These are my prejudices, this is the way I go about my business', and I remember you said that one of the duties of a critic was to be constantly open to a given play redefining your notion of what theatre is. Can you remember those moments in your critical career that really knocked you and made you rethink what theatre might be?*

FOT The first time I saw Footsbarn it was extraordinary, the atmosphere they created, the circus atmosphere was completely unexpected, it was not what you would associate with theatre.

ROH *I got the impression that they loosened you up actually, in relation to what you thought was theatre.*

FOT The sheer power and physicality of their performance style, and the directness of it – the lack of any kind of pretension.

ROH *And the physical exuberance of the play. You said they were on a quest, still wondering, and it seems there was a mysterious world to be wondered at.*

FOT I remember really vividly their production of *Lear*. They had been at one of these Festivals in Northern Italy, where they have very elaborate Festivals of flag-throwing, or flag-waving, and they'd picked up this – it was one of the great things they did – their journey was literal as well as metaphorical; and they'd picked up this idea – they'd integrated it into *Lear*, so that throughout the play you had this very elaborate use of flags, giving them enormous importance, which was an incredibly simple but very brilliant metaphor for the play's reflections on sovereignty, on territory, the idea of: 'Is England one thing, or is it many things?', and the whole idea of it being a play all the time. This play has so much formality in terms of the court scenes, but also then you've got battle scenes – you know, all that sort of stuff going on around us, so you can use it; but what I loved about that was not that they simply used this as an extra element of the play, but that they made a kind of wordless language out of it, which was then connected, like two wires connecting together, at the moments of the play when words have failed – as when Lear has Cordelia in his arms and there is nothing to be said.

They had Lear coming in and the soldiers come in with the flags while he is there – it was just a simple look, then, that Lear gives them. For him, everything is now completely meaningless. His daughter is dead, and that sort of moment where the physical becomes as eloquent as a language was really quite electrifying, but when you talk about those mind-expanding things you realize that really great theatre artists can create significance through what they do, so some thing is given significance, not in itself, but through the course of the play, so that it then, when they want it, is like a battery that is fully charged up and it's the simplicity, but also the extraordinary level of skill which is necessary to be able to make objects magical in that way.

ROH *There are some very powerful examples of this in Chekhov: in* Three Sisters *when Masha finally has to say goodbye, she just says 'goodbye', and the whole thing is moving towards desolation, you know, the band playing, the garrison has to leave town. I'll never forget that moment when Geoff Golden playing Vershinin with his medals was leaving town forever. All Masha could say was 'goodbye' and her entire universe collapsed. Now you or I can write 'goodbye', or Gaev's 'sister, sister, sister' in* Cherry Orchard *when they are leaving the house for the last time, but we could never get that overwhelming sense of desolation in such a simple way.*

FOT Essentially what's happening there is sacramental. And maybe this goes back for me to my search for a replacement for the Mass.

ROH *The elevation, that silence, that transformation.*

FOT There is a form of transformation going on there where physical things cease to be physical and become imaginative objects which have more meaning, but that meaning is not clear.

ROH *That mystery too, you can intuit it but can't grasp it.*

FOT That meaning is not capable of being expressed in words, which is precisely why we are there; why this whole skill has been devoted towards the making of such things; so things like that don't just change your sense of theatre, they change your sense of reality, you know, they actually say to you: 'There are intangible forms of reality that are just as real as more physical things'.

ROH *Can you think of other such moments in Irish theatre?*

FOT Certainly, in great Murphy moments; the first night of *The Gigli Concert*, which of course has the very same sort of structure. The voice of Gigli becomes that thing which transcends reality, and also *Bailegangaire* – the ending of *Bailegangaire*, particularly, with Siobhán McKenna.

ROH *One day when I was ten, Angela Newman said to me: 'Just wait. One of these days we'll do real plays, great plays – Lorca, O'Casey, Brecht'. I didn't know who these people were but I sensed great frustration on her part with the limitations of the Abbey style and repertoire. It's a wonder they* *didn't all become drunks. I remember about eight years later the Abbey suddenly did some Lorca, and Brecht - they did a great Galileo with Mick Hennessy, so Europe was suddenly blowing into the corridors of the Abbey. Then the Abbey suddenly opened their doors to Hugh Hunt, people like that. European classics came in. Any thoughts on what the European classics did to us, what they might do for us?*

FOT I think that the primary influence of the European classics, and indeed of the European *avant-garde*, you know, the stuff coming from Poland and wherever else as well to the Dublin Theatre Festivals was to bring the body back into theatre. It's slightly paradoxical, because we are talking about quite literary works in many cases, but the way in which, say, *Galileo* was written is not what we are used to in Ireland; the structure of the work, the way in which physical movements are given, is actually very different. You know the scene at the start of *Galileo* where he is washing himself – the washing is as important as the words and perhaps Irish actors were not entirely up to it; it was a different way of being on stage. Movement was very minimal, and very predictable, there was very little sense of physical presence on the stage.

ROH *John Kavanagh was the very first Irish actor I remember who, even in smallish parts, acted with his entire being.*

FOT I'll tell you what, when I was starting you had two extraordinary poles, both of whom were incredibly electrifying. One was Kavanagh, who was, I'd say, physically present in a way that was very unusual; he had that sort of activity to him. The other pole was McCann. But the other person close to that pole was Tom Hickey who had a very similar presence. Yet McCann had something quite different, and almost more extraordinary, which was a stillness. It was not lack of movement: his stillness was sort of dynamic, like a black hole that sucked everything into it, so there was an extraordinary sense of movement, a sense of physical presence, even though he didn't jump around the place.

   We've often talked about that great production of *Faith Healer*. I'll just never forget the sensation of feeling that McCann was literally ten feet tall, he did something – and I still don't know what he did but when he was alone on stage, particularly when he was in the last act alone for the second time, he comes out and he moves from the back of the stage towards the front of the stage in that last ten minutes or whatever. You'd swear he was ten feet tall. I'm not saying that as a metaphor. He had actually ceased to be a human being and had actually become this kind of Finn McCumhaill or whatever.

And that was also extraordinary but this was what you were asking me about – I think what the European classics did was to show us that it's impossible to perform any of them without trying to strike a relationship between physicality and language, and if you don't, they are terribly dull. If you do Molière, for example, without a sense of movement, it just doesn't work at all – it's like a soufflé that's gone flat. And Brecht, O'Casey and Synge, if properly directed, have an incredible physicality, but it doesn't automatically leap off the page as it does with Brecht. Brecht, of course, was a great director as well as a great playwright. He's not writing theatrical pages, he's writing theatrical scenes, he's writing a whole kind of physical conception of what it's going to be like on the stage.

ROH *It's interesting that you say that about* Galileo, *because you know when you read accounts of productions, the sort of absolute seriousness with which a tiny event, a physical event, was given its fullness of attention was extraordinary – as opposed to the sloppiness of putting on the rashers and eggs on the Irish stage.*

FOT Absolutely, there was a lack of attention, there was a sense that there was no particular difference between walking in and sitting down on stage and walking in and sitting down in real life. Whereas when Tom Hickey played the Volunteer in *The Hostage*, he articulated the role through such extraordinary precise detail of voice and movement that it became an act of creation in itself.

ROH *He never got a bad review from you!*

FOT I really admire him, because he is a very brave actor as well and he has the Stanislavsky thing in that a role is a role, and you have to do as much work in understanding what it is you are supposed to be doing if you're the Volunteer who is guarding the room as when you're the lead, and that does bring you back to something essential about the theatre: it is an art form in which lots of different things can be happening at the same time. That's a richness of texture that it has.

ROH *Kowzan says that there are, I think, about sixteen different sign systems that are at work in theatre.*

FOT Yeah, and if it's a form that is still valid, it's purely because of that, it's because the cinema remains linear – it doesn't have depths of field, it can have an image on the screen that's incredibly startling and extraordinarily interesting, it's moving away from you while you're watching it; it's because the pace of theatre is slower, and because it's three-dimensional, which cinema isn't.

ROH *It's a kind of a presence.*

FOT It has those layers and layers happening at the same time, and that's what you're looking for as a critic. You're wondering are they just doing it, or are they doing something else and something else as well? And it goes back to the idea of coherence in the sense that what we mean by coherence is not that they've decided on one thing, and they're just giving it to you; it's that there's a coherence of purpose which may often mean complicating things. Adding things to them, but again, the greatest theatre adds in order to be able to come back to incredible simplicity – to just that point in which everything coheres.

ROH *Everything explodes. As in Chekhov and the Greeks. Why is it much more in theatre than in poetry and in the novel that we are haunted by the Greeks? Could this be a way of getting away from – of saying we can't deal with the complexity, and the messiness of contemporary life? Why will the Greeks not lie down and go away? What can they still do for us?*

FOT What you find with the Greeks is that they work all the time on two different levels: they are rooted in narratives.

ROH *They are rooted in song and dance as well.*

FOT As part of the narrative. On the one hand you've got acts of impulse, which is always primitive, there is a sense that the narrative is primitive, that you already know the story. So, it's about narrative itself, it's about them retelling, somehow it's about that energy in a form that demands to be retold.

ROH *But it is a retelling, a re-scrutiny of traditional myths through the new democratic lens. And isn't it also about their extraordinary archetypal power and energy? That dangerous energy?*

FOT In a way, if it was about the archetypes in a simple sense, then they ought to have gone, for the archetypes, for the most part, are religious, seriously religious, I mean. Aeschylus is a seriously religious writer, and in Sophocles there is a really serious sense that the Gods are not just a kind of abstract presence, there is a really serious thing there, and they ought to therefore have lost their function in a secularized modern twenty-first century society. I think it's stronger than that, that it goes beyond religion to the roots of religion.

ROH *But in fifth century Classical Greece the distinction secular/religious is not at all as clear as it is for us, so we have to remind ourselves about that.*

FOT It's sort of pre-religious in a sense. It's asking the questions that religions were formulated to deal with. Why do we not feel at home in the world? Why, no matter what we do, are we incapable of an ultimate happiness? Why do things go wrong? Basically these are the questions, but at a much deeper level.

ROH *A line from Sophocles comes to mind here: 'For mortals greatly to live is greatly to suffer'. That's one of the essential givens.*

FOT That sense of being rooted in a set of questions which are unanswerable, I think, also guarantees a kind of timeless power. We are not likely in the near future to be able to understand why we are here and why we keep screwing up.

ROH *There is a mystery about the daemonic forces, but what theatre needs to do is face these, confront them, so then get rid of them. But it's the getting rid of them is the problem.*

FOT The great gesture of Greek tragedy is looking at them in the face. There is something particular about the fact that we've lived through the most violent century in human history, that more people died in wars in the twentieth century than in all previous wars since the dawn of time put together. That horror is a daily presence for us, but it is present and absent at the same time; we are intensely aware of it but we don't look at it, we can't actually deal with it, nobody in history has ever been in the same situation that we're in: we know pretty much all the horrible things that are happening around the world, and often instantly. So there is a Greek sense of powerlessness which the nineteenth century didn't have, with its faith in progress and the power of humanity to overcome problems; whereas we're faced with this disjunction between our intelligence and our emotions on the one side and our ability to actually change things significantly.

ROH *Talking of theatre and politics, you did a recent piece on* He Left Quietly, *talking about the problem of witness, and of how it bends the usual protocols of criticism. I don't know if you heard the thing I said on the radio about it, but I really was very angry. I felt that I was being manipulated, as a 'Leftie', if you like; put in the position of saying: 'I can't say anything bad about this,' because it's awful to say something bad about somebody who has gone through this terrible suffering and is telling you the story of it. And when they asked us all to get into the shoes of the murdered victims, I nearly threw up – towards the end. But I was told it was going to be theatre. Now you felt it was much more theatrical than I did. And I'm just wondering why was it that I just couldn't buy it. I am wondering was it that I felt that this play had designs on me, and it wasn't theatre. And yet I think I have a pretty flexible notion of what theatre is. Can you relate to that?*

FOT One one level I can, absolutely. You are completely right about the coercive nature of anything like that, but I find that itself quite interesting, which is that you are suddenly shaken out of your perception of your power as a member of the audience, which is: 'I am here to judge this piece of work, I either like it or don't like it'.

ROH *I just want to be seduced by it.*

FOT As a member of an audience, you have a power of non-committal in a sense. So there is something hugely invasive about a piece of theatre that says: 'Look, this is the actual guy here' and it disturbs your assumptions. And you have to ask also what the appropriate response is; because when it's the real person, questions of politeness, for example, come into play. But I suppose one of the reasons I liked it was because I am getting fed up with theatrical events that have no sense of danger at all, that are so beautifully packaged that you can sit there, you can be perfectly entertained for two hours, and you can have no sense at all that anything was at stake. Now, at least with *He Left Quietly* I felt there was something at stake.

ROH *What was at stake?*

FOT What was at stake was this: Can this story be told in this way? It's a really open question. And how am I supposed to respond to this story? Am I supposed to respond aesthetically as a member of a theatre audience, or am I supposed to respond humanly as a human being? It was actually putting that into play, which, it seems to me, has force in itself..

ROH *Could it be that our different responses relate to that mysterious entity 'presence'. For me that actor [Duma Kumalo] hadn't got such a presence, and the enactment was too easy - untroubled, in a way. And yet for you it was very potently theatrical. Why?*

FOT I would go back to – there are questions of connection, which are completely mysterious. And I found the way he moved really interesting in itself, the way he moved like somebody who had been in prison for a long time.

ROH *You felt this sort of 'haunting', that there was some sort of a ghost? The miracle of coming back to tell a story that he mightn't have been able to tell?*

FOT What gathered a certain kind of force for me was that there actually was that theatrical element which was that you got to the point where all those other people were dead and he wasn't, and it was them, it was not him but them – the conjuring of their presence which made it theatrical – something invisible, something intangible was actually being brought into existence. If you didn't have that, then it's not theatrical, you know, it's just somebody telling you about himself. What I liked about it was that there was actually a certain sort of humility about it, that what he really wanted to tell you was not about him. What you saw as formulaic I saw as ritual.

ROH *I actually saw it as having the distance of allegory.*

FOT Yeah, but I saw that distance as a 'ritual' distance. I thought the form was a bit like somebody going through a religious ceremony. Considerably more than just somebody telling a story.

ROH *I've noticed that there is something you seem to love in theatre, especially in both Fugard and Shakespeare – that they seem to be able to make the individual public, political and vice versa.*

FOT Absolutely.

ROH *And the twain were melded. You couldn't separate them.*

FOT Utterly inseparable, and the great example of that is *Hamlet*. One of the things I hate most in theatre is when you go to see *Hamlet* and the ghost is a voice inside Hamlet's head – one of those Freudian interpretations of *Hamlet*. It goes back to what we were saying: 'Is there a right and wrong way of doing a play?' Well, actually, that stuff does seem to me to be wrong – I mean, just completely betraying the nature of the play. It's not that you don't have a million other choices that you can make in terms of how you perform *Hamlet*, but Shakespeare creates a world in which nothing is private - you know, the bedroom is not private, even when he is talking to his mother in the most extraordinary terms Polonius is hiding behind the arras; Hamlet's conversations with Ophelia are overheard all the time.

ROH *Berkoff said there were more spies in* Hamlet *than in MI5!*

FOT Your own father's ghost comes back from the afterlife to tell you something, and everybody else knows about it before you do. That sense that the private is impossible, almost to a pathological degree. But that is the great thing about Shakespeare, he sort of elides these categories of public/private – the political and personal.

ROH *It's a real dialectic of the personal and the public.*

FOT And what you get in Shakespeare all the time is that it is completely dynamic, the story is changing from second to second, but not only the story, the people are changing; it's not just that they are not the same people at the end of the play as they were at the beginning, but they are not the same person from moment to moment almost, it's almost pure reaction – everything that happens changes everybody, it's a dynamic system entirely.

ROH *People have often accused you of being too political. And yet in your reviews of* The Island *you are extremely sensitive to the whole gestural* *structure. After all, the opening of* The Island *has no words at all, for maybe ten minutes. Everything is happening through a little pattern of gesture, and I think if I were going to defend you against a charge of being crassly political, I'd point to the reviews of* The Island *where you were so fascinated by all these ambiguities and the shifts of power and intimacy between the two of them as their situation shifted, one prisoner having to stay on forever, one of them being released. And there was this very painful choreography, almost, of pained movement – sometimes very intense closeness, sometimes great distance.*

FOT You see, it comes back to what do you mean by 'political'. In theatrical terms, I mean 'public' – that it is a public art form.

ROH *It's about power as well, it's about shifts in power. You can't get away from power, can you?*

FOT And the shifting dynamics of relationships in terms of power. I mean, power goes back again to what you asked me about things that had really kind of forced me to rethink about theatre. One of the other ones actually was in the 1981 Festival; I did one of those kind of *omnium gatherum* kind of pieces for a book, but it was this Icelandic guy in *Not I* who haunted me. He would only do the play for one person at a time.

It was in the old Damer, and you went just inside the door, it was dark, he comes out as the hooded figure, you can't really see his face, he just takes you by the hand, just brings you in, puts you in a darkened room, sitting on a chair, it goes just completely dark, and you just sit there in silence for a couple of minutes, and then the lips appear. And it was absolutely terrifying but again, it interested me more as I think about it because it's the only time I have ever been in the theatre when it was not public. It was one of those exceptions that prove the rule. It felt much more like something had happened to you as you were walking home at four o'clock in the morning, in a completely non-aesthetic context altogether – a very disturbing event that happened to you, or something you saw in the street, or whatever.

It felt like that, rather than a piece of theatre. The only reason I am mentioning this is that, in a funny way, this is why it is so haunting: it reminds you very forcibly of the fact that it ceases to be aesthetic in a way; so the aesthetic experience of theatre is absolutely essentially public. It's about being in the presence of other people.

ROH *And it's about a biochemistry; something happens in the circuit between you, the other spectators and the actors.*

FOT It does, yeah, and there is something visceral about that, you know, but it's as much about the crowd as it is about anything else. One of my most vivid memories as a child was going into Croke Park, going down into the tunnel and then coming up.

ROH *Into this surge of human bodies.*

FOT And it is something pre-conscious, you know, it's just physical sensation.

ROH *Maybe theatre overlaps with sport in a certain way?*

FOT It does share something with sport, historically the Greeks invented sport and theatre. But you know if that is true, and I think it is true, how could it not be political in the broad sense, how could it not have the sense that it is doing something in relation to the society in which it exists?

ROH *Why do so many theatre people still say that your criticism is far too political? Now we know that theatre isn't reality, it's about transformation. But what's this resistance all the time? They must have decided that Fintan was this bad conscience, forced, in a sense, on them. In fact what surprised me, reading through your criticism over the years, was that you became more and more sensitive to the theatrical, despite being fairly hard-line in some ways.*

FOT But I also come back to the fact that, again, you are a critic, that your function is to connect this event with everything else that appears in the newspaper. In a sense, you know, it is journalistic, it is part of the experience of reading a newspaper, so I could be different kinds of critic – there are other ways of writing about the theatre.

ROH *And you are still clear nearly all the time that it is not the raw world.*

FOT Absolutely, but it is a transformation of the world, and the world is as important as the transformation

ROH *There's a term that you have been using systematically in your criticism that surprised me: stylized. Would you just talk to me about that? It might seem trivial, but it seems to me it's a term that says everything and yet relatively little; for you seem to mean 'non-naturalistic'. And you use it a lot, but normally you make very fine distinctions.*

FOT I'm aware that I've used it; it's a term which I would defend to some extent. It's obviously the case that in every production, if it's in any way coherent at all, is consciously using a set of conventions, and playing with that set of conventions. Beyond that, there's a level at which it's drawing attention to the conventions, which is what I would regard as stylized. It's not simply using them and shaping itself around them, it's also going to the other level of that, which is essentially presenting itself as an exercise in style. […] I don't think it's entirely a problematic term.

ROH *I'm not actually saying that it's problematic. I'm saying that it's a term that one would want to be very wary of using, because it often requires quite a bit of qualification: because it comes all the time, and in very different contexts.*

FOT You do have to bear two things in mind. One is that you're writing for an audience whose grasp of technical presentations of convention is not necessarily terribly strong. So you're trying to get a common language, which might describe something which is going on in a way that makes some sense to a general audience. And also you have to bear in mind that this is journalism. There's a hell of a lot of lazy language, it's written under very extreme deadlines in terms of the pressure of time, and we all have clichés and terms that we fall back on, and that may well be one of them.

ROH *The dominant values for you as critic would seem to be: order, coherence, clarity, rigour, sometimes severity. But there's another little sub-personality Fintan O'Toole who loves getting out to play every so often, and loves sheer fun, but that doesn't get out as often as it might. And it can be absolutely terrific when it does – very funny and very perspicacious.* The Bearded Lady *comes to mind. You were trying to make sense of this extraordinary play, you reacted very powerfully to a lot of moments, you had difficulty with the coherence, and yet at the same time you responded to the inventiveness.*

FOT You have to remember that there are two levels of translation going on. There's the normal level, which is where you're translating an experience into your own terms, as an individual watching it. And there's the other level, where you're translating that experience into prose. Which is a very different language. I always come back to this, that it's very like translating Urdu into English, or Uzbek, or even a stranger language. That all you can do is try to put some system and order on your own experiences of the theatre. And that, inevitably, just in the nature of it, privileges the coherent elements of the experience to which you can respond, and which you can put into words, and that you can create at least some kind of argument, some kind of coherent piece. You know, my main task is not to inform the people who are there as to what they are doing; it's to write a readable piece of prose, which actually hangs together and makes some sense to the reader. And so there's that element of it. Then there's also the fact that yes, different sides of my own personality would be continually in play when I'm at the theatre. I mean there's a part of all of us, which is fuelled by ideas and is looking for some kind of content in the broadest sense. And then there's also a part of you which responds purely to form, which is about play, is just about the danger of the experience.

ROH *Yes, people forget that. Play is both exhilarating and dangerous. You never quite know where it's going to lead.*

FOT Absolutely not. And as I go to the theatre now, I'm increasingly disappointed in work that doesn't have a sense of danger. Maybe as I get older, I'm more in search of something that has an element of pushing the boundaries, and an element of unpredictability, and a sense that something is at stake. That if I were to now simply define what I think is a good piece of theatre, it's one in which there's a lot at stake. What may be at stake may be pure anarchy, may be pure enjoyment, may be pure play. Or it may be a very serious political reflection. And of course, it may not work. But it's interesting that you pick up those things, because perhaps over a period of time, that's an accurate reflection of the process itself, of the way in which you try to respond. But there is an epistemological question, which is about the extent to which a theatre review actually relates to the experience of theatre itself, and how much does it relate to what you've brought to bear on it?

ROH *You mean it has to put it in aspic to some extent, or even freeze it?*

FOT Yeah. And it's very much, of course, against the nature of the piece of art that you're engaged in …

ROH *I think it's the difficulty of writing about music and theatre. It's in flow. It's partially a time art.*

FOT And it's a performance. A work of music doesn't exist unless it's being performed, and theatre even more so because a recording is not even an approximation. So because of all that, there's a set of tensions around trying to look for the things in a piece which will allow you to write intelligently about it, which may not in fact be the same things as the core of the piece itself. And in a very enigmatic piece of work, like some of those Mac Intyre pieces, because you're a professional theatre critic, half of you is sitting there, saying, what the hell am I going to write about? How do I do this? Because you don't have the benefit of reflection. And there probably is an inbuilt bias, to be fair, against work which does not allow itself to be expressed in terms of concrete prose. […]

ROH *As you know, we have disagreed in print over this issue but I do feel you are prone to falling into the trap of the intentional fallacy. Do you think I'm being unfair in saying that you have a very soft spot for the core of a work, the purpose of a work, the intention? Because you come back to it a lot.*

FOT Yeah, I do. I'm not entirely persuaded by deconstructionism, the idea that there is no centre. There is a centre. It's not a fixed centre. I certainly don't naively propose that there is a little nugget that if you can dig far enough, you can pick up. But there is a centre to the experience, if a piece of theatre is engaged with its time – and it has to be, of its very nature, because it is fundamentally an act of communication.

ROH *Are you saying it's the piece of theatre at that moment? In that moment of the flow of history where certain pressures are working then, and that that core might be different ten years ago?*

FOT Yes. Or rather, that the meaning of the core may certainly change over time. And of course does change, has to be continually reinvented. But what you can get with a piece of theatre is that the core is actually the bit of the text which is superfluous to the conditions of its creation. *King Lear* is about all sorts of things going on in Shakespearean England. There are huge elements of reality captured within it. But the essence of the play is what surpasses the story, what surpasses its own creation, its own time, its own circumstances.

ROH *So, the essence is outside of time, then?*

FOT The essence is not outside of time, but it's timeless in a way which continually changes, if that doesn't seem to be too much of a contradiction. Timeless doesn't mean static. Timeless means, if you like, that there is a mystery which, precisely because it is mysterious, will speak to us in any number of given circumstances, or any number of given times. What it will say to us may be very, very different. But the capacity of a text to communicate over time has to be rooted in some sense that there is a part of it which cannot be simply subsumed into a Marxist analysis.

While I agree with you that the intention is not something where we could simply say that we found a piece of paper where

Shakespeare tells us the way in which things should be done. We're talking about a very large area of aesthetics, that if works of art in general could be subsumed into whatever particular crossroads the artist stood at in a particular time, they would be incommunicable outside of that frame. And the fact is, they're not. The fact is, we are capable of being moved, being stimulated, being disturbed, by work that goes back as far as we can trace human history. So what happens when you see Lear coming out onstage in the last scene, howling, does have some kind of absolute core to it. Because it's rooted into the mystery of human experience.

ROH *Are you saying that is a moment outside history? No matter what you do with that, no matter how forces are changing, King Lear's 'never, never, never, never, never' must be the most awful single word repeated in all of drama.*

FOT And they are irreducible. In a way, you can't go behind them or beyond them. And it's about the fact that theatre works towards moments. That one of the things that's characteristic of the form is that a three-hour piece of theatre can justify itself entirely in two seconds. It's not like a painting. As a member of an audience, you forgive everything, because all the elements came together, and because you've been through all the other frustrations like 'This isn't going anywhere, I'm bored,' which can actually push you toward a moment. I suppose it's related to the spiritual angle of theatre for me. Which is that the moment is beyond us, in some sense. It cannot be transcendent if there is no core, if there is no point which is almost impregnable and invulnerable.

ROH *But what about the notion that in a piece of theatre different audiences will point up other big moments around which the play will turn for them, because they are living a different sort of drama at that moment that the play reaches to? And it may not be that moment that reaches us in* Lear, *for instance, that devastates a given group, if the audience is splintered, divided, contradictory, with different tensions within it, different points of view – you've made this argument yourself in relation to Roddy Doyle. There isn't an Ireland; there are fundamentally different and opposing Irelands. Given* *there's a splintered audience, how then do you marry that with the notion of a core?*

FOT Because – and this may be where I again seek refuge in spirituality – what makes theatre a communal event, in spite of the splintered audience is that when it really works, there is at least a sense of communal presence. There is a feeling that we are actually all there at that moment. The Murphy formulation, I think, is the simplest – that in *The Gigli Concert*, he continually goes back to 'You and I are alive in time, at the same time'. That's what theatre is about. And it's actually a very good formulation, because it deals with this business of time and timelessness. That to be alive in time acknowledges that time is shifting and continually changing. But to be alive in time at the same time, also acknowledges that there is a possibility to freeze time, to stop time. And because theatre is such a temporal experience, in those moments of intensity you completely lose the sense of time. What great art does is actually move outside its own time, in the sense that it is expressing what is impossible in the conditions of its own society.

ROH *You mean intuiting something that is hardly expressible until the artists come along. For historians, it's too early.*

FOT In a really radical sense artists are not of their own time at all. Or at least, the bad ones are, but the good ones aren't. And you could say that with Irish theatre. One of the things that's extraordinary when you look back at the plays of 1958, 1959, 1960: they are completely prefiguring an Ireland which does not yet exist. Out of the rage, and the sense of despair, and the sense of loss that this whole construct hasn't worked, they are actually implying the existence of another Ireland, another place that will come into being in some way.

I suppose what I'm trying to say is that something is contained within the structure of a play which has been captured at a certain moment by a certain mind. In order to actually be faithful to that intention, you have to change almost everything. So rather than this idea of faithfulness to intention being a license for static theatre, it's in fact the very opposite. It's that you have to rethink your way back into that core.

Even if it's wrong, even if it is based on a fallacy, it produces much more interesting work than ignoring the idea of intention altogether. Because if you ignore intention altogether, you lose a sense of urgency. You stop thinking about, what is the relationship between the play and the audience now? And how does that compare with the relationship of the initial intended audience and the work itself at that time? If you ignore the history of the piece, if you simply say: well we can never get the intentions anyway, so therefore all we've got is this text, it seems to me that you lose some of the essential tension. There is a huge act of translation to be done. What you get is the sense that we don't know. Maybe Shakespeare didn't know what *King Lear* was about, or why it was written. Therefore, what you have is the intention of the work, rather than the intention of the author.

ROH *Absolutely. The intention of the author is a hopeless quest.*

FOT And I think, when I generally use the term intention, what I'm talking about is the intention of the piece, rather than the intention of the work.

ROH *You're very interested in the movement of history, and also in the primal forces that appear to be outside time. And it seems to me, quite often, what you respond to, even in a socially committed, left-wing play, is when it resonates, often beyond its time, to very deep and very dark forces. Any comment on the relation of history to archetype?*

FOT I suppose it goes back to what we've just been talking about, to some extent. It is clear, the more you read, and the more you look at text, or rituals, or performances that we can reconstruct at all, that there is something primal about the business of performance. That it is actually rooted in something about what it means to be human. And it would seem to me that it's rooted in the problem of humanity, the problem of how do we recognize each other as human? One of the ways that emerges, of course, is compassion. And that, in turn, is based on empathy. And actually, that is at the core of politics. It's at the core of human interaction in general, perhaps. It is why, I think, performance has an element to it which is deeper than just play. It is an education, and a sharpening, and a rehearsal. It's a laboratory. That ability to empathize does imply that we have a capacity to create archetypes in our heads, which we then use as reference points for what, at any one time, we think of as fundamental to the process of empathy.

It is an experience which is utterly tied up in compassion and empathy. The archetype, maybe, is one of the ways in which we express not just our sense of empathy of one human being for another, but also the development of that, which is our extraordinary capacity to empathize with work which comes from extraordinarily different times and places. For it to be communicable, there must be something there which still speaks the same language.

ROH *Usually, the language of pain, which needs the body, implicates the body.*

FOT Yes – the constant, throughout history, is oppression, is failure, is pain, is torture. It's not mysterious that those things should speak to us, because they don't go away. It is possible, at least in the abstract, to imagine a world in which much of our theatre would be incomprehensible.

ROH *That brings me to a point about writing history, and writing about revisionist historians. You wrote about them, and seemed to suggest something like this: revisionist historians' so-called objectivity have ironed out the trauma, haven't entered into the pain, and their story has no imagination any more. And that's why we need the great artists like Friel: they're the new historians with passion, and the power of imagination to open up new myths. The historians have opted out of their duty. Is that to some extent the way you'd feel about revisionists?*

FOT Certainly, there was a period in which this whole idea of history as a science – which seems to me inherently absurd – was claiming the high ground, and was ironing out history. And certainly theatre. One of its attractions as a historical art form is that it does, in fact, engage us in the mentalities of different historical periods. And it does remind us that our superiority towards the past is misplaced. It also allows the past to engage us. The fact is that the text of *Antigone* does go back a very long time. Its continuing power is chastening. It can be depressing, in a sense, because you often feel –

ROH *That they understood the basics? The fundamentals?*

FOT And we haven't. Neither artistically nor socially. We haven't gone beyond those problems. And I suppose the other concern with flattening out history is that it leaves this huge emotional need for narrative, which can be filled by crap. By distorted, highly politicized, tendentious versions of history.

ROH *Those stories need to be revised, obviously. But you seem to be suggesting that we need historians that somehow have the imaginative power to create a more compelling, imaginatively rich and empathetic story. And meanwhile, the best artists are doing it.*

FOT Suppose the artists do end up doing that. And it's not unproblematic. *Translations* is a very good example. There's no doubt about the fact that *Translations* on one level is a terrible travesty of the history of the Ordnance survey. But nevertheless, what may be more important than that is that the play revivifies our capacity for historical analogy – which is basically what it is. It's not a play, in fact, about the 1830s; it's a play about the 1970s. And one of the bracing things about good historical drama is that it opens us up again to the idea of metaphor. It uses the past as a metaphor for the present.

ROH *Ultimately, though, you hate agitprop, which may surprise a lot of people. But you will always respond, when the real is well articulated but points elsewhere, when it resonates to deep, bigger things. That seems to be what you want.*

FOT Very much so. What you're looking for is an engagement with the metaphorical imagination. And what's wrong with agitprop is that it's not metaphorical, it is hugely reductive in terms of the power of the form itself, and pretends that it can affect things directly. It's based on a misunderstanding of the way art works. Poetry makes nothing happen. But to say that it doesn't make anything happen is only the beginning, really, because then you say, well, what does it do? It can hold open a space, if nothing else. At least you can say it does that. But perhaps more importantly it retains the sense of possibility that theatre is very much engaged in the idea of what's possible, rather than what is or what will be.

Although I'm very much against agitprop, I also see nothing wrong at all with the use of theatre for specific purposes at specific times with no pretension that it's doing something else. I'm also opposed to a snooty idea that work – say politically motivated community theatre which aims to teach people to read and write, or aims to retell a community its own history – that none of that is art. There is still an extraordinary prejudice towards what is actually a very nineteenth century, bourgeois ideal: that art is only about posterity, somehow. That if it won't last, it isn't art.

ROH *So there is a place for ephemeral art, yes?*

FOT Completely. And it's maybe just as important. We do have a right to say: 'Look, this will probably not be of the slightest interest to anybody in twenty years' time, but at this moment in time, it's possible it could be a great work of art'. You know, the idea of great art is not static, either. And in the theatre, that could be quite extreme. It could be a great work of art this year, and not next year. But I think what happened in the twentieth century is that we're all looking over our shoulder all the time, saying – especially with new work – will I go down in history as the guy who couldn't understand a great new play? Will I be laughed at? Will there be footnotes about me in the history books? And this operates to me at a very direct level. I've had experience of fellow theatre critics saying to me: 'I got that play wrong, because everybody else liked it, and I didn't'. Or vice versa.

ROH *And what do you say to that?*

FOT What I say is that the idea is completely absurd. There is no right and wrong. The only right, in terms of criticism, is, is this as honest and accurate a translation of your own experience as you can make it? That's all you can do. And looking over your shoulder, either at posterity, or at other critics, or even at the audience is absurd.

ROH *Now the connection between theatre and politics is complicated. Very early on, you wrote something about a play called* Pledges *and* Promises. *Do you see it all starting there? Looking from there, where would your line* *be on really interesting political drama in Ireland. The big moments, you might say?*

FOT The first movement of political theatre that I would have been aware of and watching was really the Project, and the Sheridans in the Project. [...] The Project was very exciting in that it had a very clear, left-wing sense of mission. So there was actually quite a structured attempt to create a theatre that dealt with both political ideas and with immediate politics – political figures, and you had stuff like this coming out of it. So that would have been my first immersion in it.

ROH *Did 7:84 make a big impression?*

FOT Well, it made a big impression both ways, actually. I remember seeing *The Cheviot, The Stag and The Black, Black Oil* which was a fantastic show. Really groundbreaking stuff. But then, a couple of years later, I remember being in Glasgow and seeing a show they were doing. I can't remember what it was called. But it was dire. I mean, it was agitprop. And it actually hugely disappointed me and annoyed me. Because it was in a working-class community, in a community hall. It was actually patronizing. I was quite shocked. So it also made me think about the limits of agitprop.

ROH *And the other big moments: would Passion Machine be the next?*

FOT The Project thing broke up in a relatively short amount of time. It sort of went nowhere. And there was quite a hiatus, really, in terms of Irish political theatre until Passion Machine.

ROH *Why do you think that was? Was it the conservatism of the Eighties?*

FOT No, I actually think it was more to do with two factors. One was the conditions of production – it actually takes an incredible amount of energy and commitment to keep a company together to do political work over a period of time. The Sheridans just got tired and stopped. So it almost, then, needs something else to happen – it's a young person's game. But I would have been aware of Paul Mercier from UCD. Most of what Paul was doing was in the Irish language. I went to see them because I knew Paul, and I liked him a lot, and I remember seeing a show that he did about emigration, using ballads. It was very powerful. You could see he was developing styles of theatre there which were very sophisticated. And they were much better than DramSoc. So I would have been aware of that. I also would have known Roddy and John Sutton who were also involved in Passion Machine.

ROH *So how do you explain that extraordinary Passion Machine phenomenon which has been relatively strong for so long? How do you explain its arrival and its continued strength, and what are those strengths?*

FOT One of the interesting things about it is that if you flew somebody in from England, and they looked at it, they'd say that some of it was quite derivative, in that it was the kind of stuff English left-wing theatre companies had been doing. But in fact it wasn't derivative at all, it was very much *sui generis* in terms of the way it happened. And the key to its success was the unity of writing and direction. Because Paul was so central to it, both as writer and director, you actually had a check and balance operating: the director wasn't interested in the writer producing work which was too crude. There was a huge theatrical impulse there going hand in hand with the political one. There was a nice balance being kept all the time.

It can be a disastrous combination, as we all know. Someone like Friel directing his own work has never quite worked. But for the particular nature of the enterprise it was perfect because you had a very strong sense that the form was as important as the content. Not just because Paul was trying to direct it in innovative ways. But I think also what was really interesting about Paul's work was that there was a layer that went beyond that. Intellectually, what he was interested in was fantasy, the way that people's fantasies reflect on their lives.

ROH *Whatever you do in political theatre, there is the Scylla on the one hand, which is agitprop, and the Charybdis is boulevard theatre, just putting bums on seats. And between that, what you have to take into account is the forms of working-class theatre. Paul seemed to have a sense that you needed to engage with the forms that grab younger audiences. There are certain forms you have to engage with if theatre is to remain meaningful.*

FOT It's an interesting business about Passion Machine, that it effectively came from teachers. And it's not accidental to it. Teachers learn very quickly about the texture of working-class mentalities, because they're trying to get through to those mentalities. They're trying to get attention; they're trying to hold attention.

ROH *You have to do some seduction, and some leading, and some pushing.*

FOT Particularly if the theatre audience is going to be – and theirs was – the same audience that there would be in the classroom.

ROH *And they do appear to have built, very definitely, a new audience. Over nearly twenty years.*

FOT With incredible difficulty. And of course it never made sense as an economic proposition. I don't know how they kept the show on the road. It's one thing I've never been quite comfortable about as a critic. That on the one hand your job is not to be aware of the difficulties of getting stuff on – the other side is you can't completely ignore it. The last few years there have been few companies which have been able to more or less do what they want, but it's terribly unfair because the pressure on individual productions becomes almost unbearable. If they don't do reasonably well either at the box office or get a very good critical response, which in turn maybe encourages the Arts Council to give them money, then they're gone. And that's where there's an immoral side to reviewing.

ROH *But how does theatre take on board the channel-hopping, the mobile phones – infinite low-quality communication. How is theatre going to reach an audience which wants buzz and action?*

FOT I have strong feelings on this. There are actually two ways you can go. One is that you can say this is now the culture. It is

visual. It has a short attention span. It demands excitement, it
demands change, it demands noise. Therefore we'll do theatre
which is noisy, which is visual, which accepts all that and tries to
operate within it. That seems to me to be doomed, because it will
never be as exciting as a video game, if that's what you're looking
for. So it seems to me that one of the interesting arcs in terms of
my period as a theatre critic was going from anti-text, visual
theatre – which was completely necessary, and I would utterly
defend it as a necessary corrective, back towards text more, and
more, and more. Because you feel that the antithetical nature of
theatre is tied up in text. Text is the most bloody, radical, strange,
angular thing you can possibly have now in our culture.

ROH *It is now subversive.*

FOT It is. And that doesn't mean that we go back to bad
naturalism. But it does mean that there is a subversive quality to
rich verbal language.

ROH *Is that because it resonates at different levels. And for it to resonate,
you have to attend fully.*

FOT Precisely. And quietness – the experience of going into a
theatre and it being quiet and dark – the different pace that
theatre operates at, probably means that it will be a less popular
art form. But it actually might be a more potent one, because it's
becoming increasingly redundant in mechanistic terms. It doesn't
really function any more; it's at odds with the general culture. But
you can't take a completely mechanistic view of audiences either.
The fact is that what tends to happen is that people often go to
art looking for what they don't get in their daily lives, or in the
world around them. They're interested in strangeness. The
narrow idea of relevance, of tailoring ourselves to whatever cloth
we can actually buy doesn't make sense, ultimately.

ROH *Is the trick that we have to engage with the forms of the young people,
but we don't have to engage in that rhythm? By virtue of the presence of the
actor, and the actor-audience chemistry and the mystery of that contact, you
may be able to get people to stay in depth with an experience?*

FOT It is. There is no one way of doing it. It depends very much
on what you're trying to achieve. It seems to me that it isn't

either/or. Theatre has always been a range of forms anyway. The very least we can say is that text has become interesting again – that the idea of a relatively dense language which is also comprehensible is very interesting. What I'm saying is that you don't have to respond to the prevailing culture only by responding to its violence and its speed. You can also respond to it by creating a dense language which at the same time has an immediacy. Which, I think, is Sebastian Barry's great achievement. One of the reasons I'm really interested in his work is because of what he's done in narrative, dramatic and linguistic terms.

ROH *I think of him as a musical writer.*

FOT Very much so. And his language is formally poetic, and yet utterly comprehensible in a theatrical context. So you don't have to read the words to understand them while they're being spoken. You can work out what the characters are saying. He's struck a balance between using a theatrical form which is of the moment, and does actually engage the audience in a really direct way, and at the same time, having that layer of strangeness.

The other response you can make to the contemporary world is neither of those things, but is post-modernist. It is the sort of pastiche of older forms, which is what Martin McDonagh does so wonderfully well.

ROH *Yes, but you seem to have a visceral resistance to intertextual play in theatre, yet you like McDonagh.*

FOT I suppose the difference is that McDonagh isn't inter-textual. He's not referring to specific texts.

ROH *Then take* Northern Star, *the Stewart Parker play. You seemed to quite like that in spite of the intertextual play.*

FOT There is a difference, I think. What *Northern Star* does is use the textuality politically, formally in a really serious way. What he's interested in doing is creating a metaphor. An historical metaphor where he's moving forward in time. What I don't like is the idea of writers writing about writers. It's just unsuitable to the public form of theatre. It works in a novel because a novel happens in your own head. For the form of theatre, it always

seems to me to be strained. Which isn't to say that someone
might not do it magnificently. There's not a problem in principle,
I just haven't seen it work very well.

ROH *What would you say to this: I came across a criticism where you were
talking about* Somewhere Over the Balcony, *by Marie Jones. And on
the one hand, you said: 'The pity is that all of this is talked about rather
than acted, everything is reported speech'. And two sentences later: 'the actors
rollicking energy makes for a sharp and captivating show'. The implications
of those two things coming together are potentially huge.*

FOT I would have no trouble with the idea that something can
be captivating by virtue of the energy of the actors. But there is a
broader issue. This raises something which has occurred here: the
dominance of the monologue form, which is reported speech.
And I'm very uncomfortable with its predominance among the
younger Irish playwrights. (Nevertheless, most of the Conor
McPherson shows I've seen have been compelling.) It's not that
they're bad, or that they don't engage your attention. It's what we
were talking about earlier – a lack of the sense of danger. If you
start out from the premise that this is a narrative, it's therefore a
report on something that has already happened. It's a matter of
taste, I suppose, but what I go to the theatre for is a sense that
we are on a journey.

Looking back on it, from this distance, one of the huge
absences, actually, is a sort of contemporary Irish naturalism. For
formal reasons, we all had to campaign against naturalism so
much.

ROH *Absolutely. And it's the most difficult territory to be in, as a
playwright. It hampers you.*

FOT Yeah, but it's not an ignoble condition. It's one form
among many forms, and there shouldn't be a prejudice.

ROH *So what might the new Irish naturalism offer us? Why might it be so
necessary? Because you were very hard on naturalism a lot of the time.*

FOT Very much so. One of the things that interests me now is
saying, 'Look, there's been a revolution in interpersonal
relationships, and naturalism is very good at describing
interpersonal relationships'. You know, it's very good at the

texture of conversation between men and women, for example. It's very good at – oh, you know – what's it like going on a date, what's it like having a dinner party, all that stuff.

If you think of naturalism as the arrival of modernity in the theatre – in a general sense, nineteenth century modernity. In the same sense, then, as a society we seem to have gone from pre-modern to post-modern with nothing – and uncompleted modernism – in between. I think also theatrically, when you look back on it, we've kind of gone from a sort of pre-naturalistic, or certainly non-naturalistic phase– the initial Yeats/Synge mould – whatever else it is, it's not naturalism, to a sort of plurality of forms, without ever having actually gone through the naturalistic stage. And that's interesting now, if you think about the extraordinary explosion of sexuality in Ireland, which is almost completely unrepresented in the theatre. I mean, even simple stuff about what's it like now between men and women. There's a huge theatrical area where you almost don't have a theatrical language to explore, because the most obvious language would be naturalistic. Now, I'm not saying it will be naturalistic in the same sense that *Hedda Gabler* is, but it would be in that territory somewhere. And if I feel slightly guilty about anything, it may be that.

ROH *You've been too hard on naturalism, is it?*

FOT Yes and for very good reasons. I would actually now say that I was wrong to identify a lot of what we were seeing as naturalism, because it was sub-naturalism, in a way. I remember seeing a Peter Stein production of *The Cherry Orchard*, which was utterly naturalistic in the sense of detail, and in the perspective of cause and effect, which of course has its limitations, but it is part of that scientific view of the world. When done to the nth degree, which that Peter Stein production did, it's extraordinarily powerful.

ROH *The detail in the production allowed the resonances to speak, instead of keeping it out?*

FOT Very much so. It wasn't crude naturalism. But all I'm saying is that it is wrong to use naturalism as a term of abuse, which I would certainly be guilty of having done at various points.

ROH *Would the example of* A Whistle in the Dark *be useful here? There's a level at which it is rigorously naturalistic, and yet the reason that I think it works is because it is beautifully detailed, but yet the primal forces aren't too far away. Would that play be the sort of naturalism you're talking about?*

FOT It's the sort of naturalism you might aim for. But, look, it doesn't all have to be great. It seems to me that most theatre is just what it is. It's fine. But it doesn't have to be absolutely outstanding, earth-shattering, all the time. And I think it was Eric Bentley who said that the mark of a theatre culture is not the good things, it's the ordinary things. How good is the ordinary, bog-standard stuff? And when I came into writing about the theatre at first, the bog-standard stuff was absolutely appalling. And it was sub-naturalistic, as I would now say. And acting was naturalistic in the most narrow sense, which is that it was only about performing actions which pretended to be real, and to be holding up a mirror to the way in which people would actually move and speak, and all that.

ROH *So the criterion might have been something like how real it was, not whether it might have been pointing up yawning chasms or opening up to other dimensions.*

FOT Precisely. Whereas what Garry Hynes did, she's a brilliant naturalistic director in that sense, in that she uses naturalism to build a platform. She uses its conventions. And you're absolutely right about *A Whistle in the Dark*. There is a simple sense in which it is an imitation of real life, but the convention pushes up the drama.

So what seems to me to be the case is that because we pushed naturalism aside, perhaps prematurely, all we've got now, about whole areas of Irish life, are bad chick-lit novels and bad television adaptations of them. So if you want to see how people behave in interpersonal relations in Dublin, you either look at soaps, or the occasional adaptation of a chick-lit novel, and that's it. You don't find it in the theatre. It's just remarkable if you think back on the last thirty years – where are the naturalistic plays? There really aren't any.

ROH *This brings the other question, which you've exercised your pen a lot on – what about the middle classes? They ought to be able to write drama.*

FOT It's a very good question, because there is an inverted snobbery, undoubtedly, and I would have been guilty of it, perhaps as much as anyone else. Certainly I would now say that the middle classes have just as much a right to be represented on the stage, to present themselves, to laugh at themselves, as anybody else has and there's not some innate virtue in the fact that the working classes are doing it for themselves rather than the middle classes. So I would accept that. But actually one of the things that is really interesting about Irish middle-class drama is that it's actually relatively confined. Because again, the Abbey was not like a typical national theatre, which would be a bourgeois institution trying to represent the middle classes. By and large it didn't. You started off with poetic drama, you had O'Casey's representations of the working classes, and then you had a very long period in which it was dominated by the small-town shopkeeper classes. Very little in terms of the actual urban middle class, as they began to take off in the 1960s here.

Clearly, there are two people who have done it: one is Hugh Leonard and the other is Bernard Farrell. And they've both done it occasionally with extraordinary success. Especially when you get into the dark territory a sense of something happening is really present, because it ceases to be just a confirmation of the audience. It actually becomes something of a confrontation with the audience, which is probably more powerful coming from within than it is from without.

ROH *A playwright recently said to me: 'If you're popular, they'll get you,' – meaning the critics. What is going on there? Because you're a middle-class dramatist, you have to do an awful lot extra?*

FOT There's no doubt about the fact that certainly at the period when I came into it, the centre of gravity in criticism was left wing. And if it wasn't left wing, it was patrician. And the one thing the patricians and the lefties will always agree on is the stupidity of the middle classes, because they're looked down upon by the patricians, and they're held in contempt by the Left. There's no doubt about it, the critical culture has been largely antipathetic. It wasn't true in Ireland – if you look at the Gate, at the *Irish Times* reviewing going back a long time, it's always been very sympathetic to Alan Ayckbourn, to Hugh Leonard, to Bernard Farrell, and I was probably the odd one out.

But first of all, I don't set out to get anybody because they're popular, and secondly, much of what I've reviewed with incredible enthusiasm has turned out to be incredibly popular. I would even have the other accusation thrown at me, in relation to Martin McDonagh, of going soft on stuff which was popular. So I get it from the other side, as well. But the fact is that there is no relationship between commercial popularity and quality. And I know this better than most people in Ireland because I've sat through feckin' Broadway for three years.

The fact is that you can sell a show on marketing, on a kind of comfortable familiarity. You can sell it on the idea of a few laughs. There's nothing wrong with that. People will pay good money to go out and have a very undemanding evening in which they get a laugh. And maybe they're laughing mostly because they're in the mood to laugh, rather than being stimulated to do so. It's a night out that happens to be in the theatre. I just don't think we should confuse that with theatrical quality. Because it is an art form whose quality is bound up with unpredictability, with danger, and risk.

ROH *So what advice would you give to a young, middle-class Irish writer who wants to write that experience, to make a strong theatre?*

FOT All I would say is that first of all, remember that actually this is a great time to write about the middle classes. For the first time in our history we have become a middle-class society. We've been through an economic boom in the course of which the solid majority of the population is now employed in relatively well-paying jobs, and that is something which has never actually been the case before in our history.

ROH *But it doesn't solve fundamental, psychic, deep problems.*

FOT It certainly doesn't. But it does mean that what you can now do, which you couldn't do twenty years ago, is write about middle-class experience in a way which has the potential to be a metaphor for the society as a whole. Just as Synge could write about relatively poor country people and credibly make them a metaphor for society, you can actually now do that with urban middle-class experience. So I wouldn't be at all worried about writing it. The question, then, is the formal question. Can you represent that reality in a way which is metaphorical? And that is a question of form.

ROH *And that breaks the old forms. Your argument seems to run something like this: up to about the mid-1970s, you had the new Ireland versus the old Ireland. But then, towards the Eighties, Ireland started breaking up, and became very fragmented. So you couldn't talk of old Ireland and new Ireland. The agons became much more diverse, complex and chaotic. Therefore, the formal questions have to be confronted. It's a real problem for form. Would it be something like that?*

FOT Very much so. What distinguishes Irish theatre is that there has never been, throughout the twentieth century, a workable distinction between mainstream and avant-garde. Because the general mainstream impulse, which tried to represent daily life in a realistic way, is one which, in the Irish context, inevitably involves fantasy, dream, surrealism, discontinuity. There isn't a story you could simply tell.

ROH *But you seem to suggest there was.*

FOT Yeah – for a long time, playwrights could deal with that by saying there isn't a story, but there is a conflict between two stories. And that conflict can give a sort of shape to the work that we do in a way that makes it metaphorical. That ceases to be the case in what I see now as an emblematic play, *Boss Grady's Boys*, which was Sebastian Barry's first big play. Suddenly, you get rural Ireland onstage as soft, as broken, with a sense of elegy about these old men who have a history with Michael Collins. They're no longer slightly threatening. If you think of Bull McCabe, and of Boss Grady's Boys, that's the arc. McCabe is capable of killing you, Boss Grady's Boys are the nicest fellas you could ever possibly meet. So the sense of double narrative is now gone. There's one narrative, but it's a narrative of a very strange, discontinuous society which has emerged, and its relationship with the past is sometimes very difficult. So what you can do, then, is try to look at the bits that are left over, look at different worlds within it. Which is very much what younger Irish playwrights start doing. But then you are, again, forced to confront the question of form, because those fragments don't cohere with anything else, much. You're trying to construct a whole society out of a few pieces of pottery.

ROH *As in* Volunteers. *Which is a very interesting metaphor – that stage set with all those bits and pieces, and no continuity at all. You have tenth century, fifteenth, Stone Age stuff …*

FOT In visual terms, *Volunteers* is probably the right Friel play. But *Faith Healer* is the locus of contemporary Irish playwriting. Everybody's rewriting *Faith Healer*. Conor McPherson is rewriting it, Mark O'Rowe is rewriting it.

ROH *And* Molly Sweeney, *there's an awful lot of rewriting* Faith Healer *there, as well.*

FOT Very much so. And what *Faith Healer* is about is the impossibility of narrative. The problem I have now is that because *Faith Healer* has been done, and was an incredibly dangerous piece of work at the time, you can't just rewrite it and keep the same sense of risk.

ROH *Very bleak. At the time I would have bet that Friel would never have written another play.*

FOT It had that feeling of an endgame to it. But what you now have is the model. So whereas Friel was confronting genuine cultural and political disarray, very often the temptation right now is to just confront *Faith Healer*, to think that the monologue is a form which is available because you don't have to imagine a coherent world.

ROH *Doesn't* Faith Healer *also open up that terrible spiritual abyss? A lot of people wouldn't realize that you are terribly interested in spirituality in the Irish theatre. What is your view on the spiritual quest in contemporary Irish theatre?*

FOT In a way, theatre has been a kind of school of spirituality for me. What you get very strongly, particularly from the best of contemporary Irish work, when I look back on the period I've been reviewing, is an absolute quest for transcendence. Time, and time, and time again, when you come back to the emotion that's generated in these plays, it is a desire to transcend the given. *Faith Healer* and *Portia Coughlan* are both plays which are set on the liminal borderline between life and death. You can't be much more engaged in the idea of transcendence, and the search for the question of what continues and what doesn't, of how life itself is shaped and defined. It remains a very philosophical theatre, in a lot of ways.

ROH *And yet the great thing about* Portia Coughlan *is that it's so visceral as well.*

FOT Mentioning *Portia Coughlan,* one of the reasons I have such admiration for Derbhle Crotty is that she's someone who almost embodies this sense of walking this very dangerous line all the time. You always feel that she is mapping out the journey every time she takes it. People like Tom Hickey, as well. He can be easily caricatured, but there is a huge integrity to every Hickey performance I've seen, whether it works or not. That sense of commitment to the edge, to seeing where it's going to take you. There's never a sense that this is a completed performance. And that's why it's worth going to, isn't it? If you don't have the sense that this gives you something that isn't available otherwise, then it really isn't worth seeing.

Afterword

Fintan O'Toole

Dear Fintan,

You're wrong about [my play]. The problem with any theory, such as yours about contemporary Irish drama, is that it needs to modify itself when faced with individual plays, not try to modify the plays to fit the theory. If you had done that, you might have noticed a rather more complicated, stylistically and thematically heterogeneous play than you were prepared to see. [...]

What I'm trying to do is, ironically, what you accuse me of as if it is a problem: merge social comedy or comedy of manners with philosophic or spiritual tragedy. [...]. Maybe you think it can't be done. [...] But here's the thing: you can't judge it by latching on to whatever style (comedy of manners) you first recognize, and then disallowing all the other diverse elements. You have to allow for the juxtaposition of styles and themes, for the impurities and vulgarities. You have to watch it with an open mind. Judging from your review, I don't think you did. [...]

And the actors (and director) had a hollow laugh at your suggestion that they were never stretched: this was an immensely gruelling rehearsal period, and it's an incredibly demanding play to perform. [...] And if the cast make it look easy, well, that's because they're brilliant.

Mostly though, what pissed me off was the dismissive tone: even if I were to hold myself at your judgement of me, as a kind of facile wit, a sardonic, satirical entertainer — are we actually so overwhelmed with those virtues in the Irish theatre that you can afford to be so mean-spirited and begrudging? And as I don't, as I'm clearly trying to do something way larger, well, maybe you think I don't succeed, but is there no virtue in trying to write a State of the Nation, Way We Live Now play, one that embraces religious and philosophical and political ideas? Or are you so consumed by your theory that that kind of synthesis can't be achieved any more that you're unable to see what's actually before your eyes? Or that it might be achievable, just not by me?

The least I feel I'm entitled to from the Theatre Critic of Record is a fair viewing: I don't believe you gave me one. You used to write a column called Second Opinion; in this case, I think you should have one. Because, first time round, you were wrong.

These are extracts from a letter I received from a distinguished Irish playwright whose latest work I had just reviewed. It is fairly typical of such correspondence. Having unfavourable things said about you in print is an unpleasant experience. (I know this because I am attacked in print far more often and far more harshly than any playwright, actor or director.) The psychic immune system responds to this invasion of nasty thoughts with the insistence that the criticism is evidence, not of one's own failings, but of the prejudices, inadequacies and perversions of the critic. The reply is written and I suspect in most cases torn up and put in the bin. The desire not to give the bastard the satisfaction usually outweighs the desire to give him a piece of your mind. Sometimes, though, especially since the invention of e-mail, the angry epistle is fired off before the forces of restraint can interfere. The wounds are exposed and the cry of pain is heard.

I could be smart and point to my long experience of the paradox whereby the same people who reassure themselves of your complete idiocy when you don't like one piece of their work are suddenly reminded of your brilliance and perspicacity when you are enraptured by another. I could point out that for every complaint of excessive harshness from a playwright, actor or director I get ten complaints of excessive kindness from disgruntled theatregoers. I could also suggest, again from experience, that what I write, even at my most intemperate is mildness itself compared to the things theatre folk say about each other.

But in fact I have a great deal of sympathy with such complaints. Theatre is an inherently ephemeral form. Neither a script nor even a high-quality video recording preserves the event in any real sense. Even the same production of the same play encompasses performances that vary widely from night to night. To see a production at the end of its run is – for better or for worse – to witness a very different spectacle from the one that took its first steps on opening night. And what is left to history? The musings and impressions of a handful of observers who are, merely by virtue of their profession, entirely untypical of the audience. Theatre history itself, moreover, is shaped by these people: a new play that is slaughtered by the critics may not have an afterlife at all.

From the point of view of those involved in a production, moreover, there is the added infuriation that these observers are outsiders who do not understand the intentions of the artists. In fact, it is even worse than this. It is not just that I, as a critic, do not understand their intentions. It is – and this is where the greatest gulf of misapprehension between the practitioner and the critic yawns – none of my business to understand. I am not interested in what they want to say, but in what they actually succeed in saying. The critic's interest is not in intention but effect. And the appalling truth is that the only effect that the critic can measure is that on him or herself. In that sense, criticism is essentially a kind of self-analysis. The critic is asking the simple but rather solipsistic question: 'What effect did this have on me?'

And here's where the real trouble starts. For although this question is capable of being answered honestly and with integrity, no one but the critic can testify to that honesty. The standards of accountability that apply to other kinds of journalism are rendered almost entirely redundant when it comes to criticism. If I write that Politician C took a bribe from Businessman B, I have to prove it objectively with documents, witnesses or other evidence. Other people can establish whether or not I'm telling lies. But if I claim that my correspondent's 'stylistically and thematically heterogeneous play' actually struck me as a bit of a mess, no one can tell whether I'm giving a truthful account of how I felt when I came out of the theatre or pursuing some stupid ideological or personal agenda. It is quite possible that every single review in this book is a lie, that I really loved the shows I panned and hated the ones I raved about. The only person who actually knows for sure is me.

For the plaintiff, this is rough justice. My correspondent who demands a Second Opinion must know that this court of appeal would be just as arbitrary. If I were to review the play a second time, and come to a different conclusion, the praise would be meaningless, coming, as it would do, from a critic who has proved to be so untrustworthy the first time. If someone else reviews it in my place, the view is theirs, not mine, and it is part of my professional ethic not to be swayed by other people's opinions. And even if the second view contradicts the first, who is to say that it is more honest, more insightful and more sensitive? Unless we are to say that gushing praise is innately more truthful than murmurings of disapproval, the question cannot be answered.

This works both ways, of course. Just as my correspondent can't prove that I watched his play with a closed mind, I can't prove that my mind was open. I can point to some reasonably obvious factors. I can say that I genuinely want to like everything I go to see, not because I am Mister Bountiful, but because there are few things on earth more boring, more dispiriting and more tortuous than a bad piece of theatre. I am, it is true, paid to write reviews, but I can make a living without doing so, and frankly the money isn't worth the hours of excruciating torment that a run of bad plays inflicts on the viewer. (Remember that the torture is actually worse for critics. The ordinary playgoer is having a night out, and can deaden the pain with drink or, at worst, leave at the interval.) I can say, too, that a quick look over these reviews should confirm that I do, as my correspondent demands, modify my general views in the face of the particular experience of a particular piece of theatre.

But these claims, too, are impossible to test. If, as Karl Popper has shown, the essence of a scientific statement is that it is capable of being falsified, then criticism is resolutely unscientific. And this means that it is also essentially unaccountable. As someone who spends many of his waking hours as a journalist demanding accountability of people who occupy positions of public power, I cannot be unaware of the irony of occupying a position of minor but essentially unaccountable power myself. If a politician accused of bad faith were to say: 'Trust me', I would be the first to attack. Yet when my correspondent accuses me of bad faith, what can I reply? 'Trust me, I did my best to enjoy your play'.

The truth is that the word that rings out like a knell in the first and last sentences of my correspondent's letter – wrong – is simply misplaced. There is of course a simple sense in which a critic can be wrong – one of my predecessors at *In Dublin* who reviewed *Hamlet* under the impression that Gertrude is the prince's aunt, for example, was clearly wrong. Reviews which refer to Richard Brinsley Sheridan as a Restoration playwright are wrong. Calling *Waiting for Godot* a naturalistic play would be wrong. But 'wrong' in the sense that my correspondent means it – mistaking his wonderful play for a less-than-wonderful one – does not compute. Critics are honest or dishonest, not right or wrong. They either express what they thought or felt or they distort it. And even if they distort it for nice reasons – they admire the playwright's other work, they know how hard the cast has worked and how much a good review would mean to them, they want the theatre to do good business – they are liars.

No one in the theatre complains about these nice lies, of course. Given the capricious nature of the business and the often arbitrary nature of criticism, theatres can hardly be blamed for using quotes from critics they regard as fools or knaves to sell their shows. Theatre people are, besides, inured to the social necessities of their small world in which 'You were marvellous, darling' serves as the currency of mundane politeness in much the same way that 'How are you?' does among the civilians. But for those of us who do this unaccountable job, there is nothing to hold on to but honesty. Since no one can really check whether or not we are telling the truth about our reactions, the only handrail is the critic's own integrity.

It seems to me that this is true even in the most extreme of cases. If we look back, for example, on the eighteenth century critics who thought that *King Lear* was unplayable as Shakespeare wrote it or that Ibsen was vile or, conversely, that Richard

Cumberland was a theatrical genius, it seems easy to say that they were wrong. But this is to forget that they were not writing for us. Their reviews were not missives to posterity. They were telling their readers how it seemed to them in the here-and-now that they all occupied. And in fact the notion that the last act of *King Lear* is unstageable, which may seem almost incomprehensible to us, has the integrity of its time and place. The fact that someone might genuinely have felt it is surely a powerful indication of a particular mentality. It still tells us something, not about Shakespeare but about the critics and about the culture in which their views did not seem absurd.

I know, of course, that this is a deeply unsatisfactory state of affairs. The notion that critics can be neither right nor wrong renders theatre people powerless, since there really is no arguing about taste. But, if it's any consolation, it also renders the critic powerless. It does so in a double sense. I actually can't help liking or disliking a show. I can't decide to be impressed or to be bored. All I can do is describe as accurately as possible what I felt. And this sense of powerlessness should be balanced by another. The power of the critic to dictate what is good and bad, to be the arbiter of value, has to be broken. If the review is merely a record of the critic's feelings, it should not bear the weight of great authority.

The only people who can break that power, though, are the readers. It is for them to take the review for what it is – one person's impressions which may be worth taking into account in deciding what to see and may be worth considering as a foil to the reader's own thoughts and feelings after the play has been seen. So if this book of reviews which were not written for posterity is worth reading at all it is not as a history provided by what my correspondent calls The Theatre Critic of Record. All that is recorded here is the fluctuating reactions of an individual with unconscious prejudices and blind spots, with likes and dislikes for which he cannot account, stuck with a particular set perceptions because they are the only ones he has. It is, I hope, sufficiently fragmentary, episodic, annoying, incomplete and contradictory to remind readers of its glaringly obvious limitations.

Index

Plays listed under author, director or theatre company refer only to the pages in which they are reviewed. In all other instances plays are listed separately.

CARYSFORT PRESS

The Press aims to produce high quality publications which, though written and/or edited by academics, will be made accessible to a general readership. The organisation would also like to provide a forum for critical thinking in the Arts in Ireland, again keeping the needs and interests of the general public in view.

Carysfort Press was formed in the summer of 1998. It receives annual funding from the Arts Council.

The directors believe that drama is playing an ever-increasing role in today's society and that enjoyment of the theatre, both professional and amateur, currently plays a central part in Irish culture.

The company publishes contemporary Irish writing for and about the theatre.

Editorial and publishing inquiries to:

CARYSFORT PRESS

58 Woodfield, Scholarstown Road,
Rathfarnham, Dublin 16,
Republic of Ireland
T (353 1) 493 7383 F (353 1) 406 9815
e: info@carysfortpress.com
www.carysfortpress.com

NEW TITLES

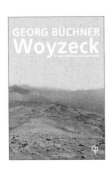

GEORG BÜCHNER: WOYZECK
A NEW TRANSLATION
BY DAN FARRELLY

The most up-to-date German scholarship of Thomas Michael Mayer and Burghard Dedner has finally made it possible to establish an authentic sequence of scenes. The wide-spread view that this play is a prime example of loose, open theatre is no longer sustainable. Directors and teachers are challenged to "read it again".

ISBN 1-904505-02-3
€8

THE THEATRE OF FRANK MCGUINNESS
STAGES OF MUTABILITY
BY HELEN LOJEK

The first edited collection of essays about internationally renowned Irish playwright Frank McGuinness focuses on both performance and text. Interpreters come to diverse conclusions, creating a vigorous dialogue that enriches understanding and reflects a strong consensus about the value of McGuinness's complex work.

ISBN 1-904505-01-5
€15

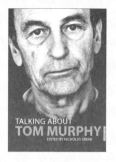

THE THEATRE OF MARINA CARR

"BEFORE RULES WAS MADE"

EDITED BY ANNA MCMULLAN
& CATHY LEENEY

As the first published collection of articles on the theatre of Marina Carr, this volume explores the world of Carr's theatrical imagination, the place of her plays in comtemporary theatre in Ireland and abroad and the significance of her highly individual voice.

ISBN 0-9534-2577-0
€20

TALKING ABOUT TOM MURPHY

EDITED BY NICHOLAS GRENE

Talking About Tom Murphy is shaped around the six plays in the landmark Abbey Theatre Murphy Season of 2001, assembling some of the best-known commentators on his work: Fintan O'Toole, Chris Morash, Lionel Pilkington, Alexandra Poulain, Shaun Richards, Nicholas Grene and Declan Kiberd.

ISBN 0-9534-2579-7
€10

HAMLET

THE SHAKESPEAREAN DIRECTOR

BY MIKE WILCOCK

"This study of the Shakespearean director as viewed through various interpretations of HAMLET is a welcome addition to our understanding of how essential it is for a director to have a clear vision of a great play. It is an important study from which all of us who love Shakespeare and who understand the importance of continuing contemporary exploration may gain new insights."

From the Foreword, by Joe Dowling, Artistic Director, The Guthrie Theater, Minneapolis, MN

ISBN 1-904505-00-7
€18

THEATRE OF SOUND

RADIO AND THE
DRAMATIC IMAGINATION

BY DERMOT RATTIGAN

An innovative study of the challenges that radio drama poses to the creative imagination of the writer, the production team, and the listener.

"A remarkably fine study of radio drama – everywhere informed by the writer's professional experience of such drama in the making...A new theoretical and analytical approach – informative, illuminating and at all times readable."

Richard Allen Cave

ISBN 0-9534-2575-4
€20

THEATRE TALK

VOICES OF IRISH THEATRE PRACTITIONERS

EDITED BY LILIAN CHAMBERS, GER
FITZGIBBON & EAMONN JORDAN

"This book is the right approach - asking
practitioners what they feel."
Sebastian Barry, Playwright.

"... an invaluable and informative collection
of interviews with those who make and
shape the landscape of Irish Theatre."
Ben Barnes, Artistic Director of the Abbey Theatre

ISBN 0-9534-2576-2
€20

IN SEARCH OF THE SOUTH AFRICAN IPHIGENIE

BY ERIKA VON WIETERSHEIM
AND DAN FARRELLY

Discussions of Goethe's "Iphigenie auf
Tauris" (Under the Curse) as relevant to
women's issues in modern South Africa:
women in family and public life; the force of
women's spirituality; experience of personal
relationships; attitudes to parents and
ancestors; involvement with religion.

ISBN 0-9534-2578-9
€10

THE STARVING AND OCTOBER SONG

TWO CONTEMPORARY IRISH PLAYS

BY ANDREW HINDS

The Starving, set during and after the
siege of Derry in 1689, is a moving and
engrossing drama of the emotional journey
of two men.

October Song, a superbly written family
drama set in real time in pre-ceasefire
Derry.

ISBN 0-9534-2574-6
€10

SEEN AND HEARD (REPRINT)

SIX NEW PLAYS BY IRISH WOMEN

EDITED WITH AN INTRODUCTION BY
CATHY LEENEY

A rich and funny, moving and theatrically
exciting collection of plays by Mary
Elizabeth Burke-Kennedy, Síofra Campbell,
Emma Donoghue, Anne Le Marquand
Hartigan, Michelle Read and Dolores
Walshe.

ISBN 0-9534-2573-8
€20

THEATRE STUFF (REPRINT)
CRITICAL ESSAYS ON CONTEMPORARY
IRISH THEATRE
EDITED BY EAMONN JORDAN

Best selling essays on the successes and
debates of contemporary Irish theatre at
home and abroad.

Contributors include: Thomas Kilroy, Declan
Hughes, Anna McMullan, Declan Kiberd,
Deirdre Mulrooney, Fintan O'Toole,
Christopher Murray, Caoimhe McAvinchey
and Terry Eagleton.

ISBN 0-9534-2571-1
€19

URFAUST
A NEW VERSION OF GOETHE'S EARLY
"FAUST" IN BRECHTIAN MODE
BY DAN FARRELLY

This version is based on Brecht's irreverent
and daring re-interpretation of the German
classic.

"Urfaust is a kind of well-spring for German
theatre… The love-story is the most daring
and the most profound in German
dramatic literature." *Brecht*

ISBN 0-9534257-0-3
€7.60

UNDER THE CURSE
GOETHE'S "IPHIGENIE AUF TAURIS",
IN A NEW VERSION
BY DAN FARRELLY

The Greek myth of Iphigenie grappling
with the curse on the house of Atreus is
brought vividly to life. This version is
currently being used in Johannesburg to
explore problems of ancestry, religion, and
Black African women's spirituality.

ISBN 0-9534-2572-X
€8.25

HOW TO ORDER
TRADE ORDERS DIRECTLY TO

CMD
Columba Mercier Distribution
55A Spruce Avenue
Stillorgan Industrial Park
Blackrock
Co. Dublin

T (353 1) 294 2560
F (353 1) 294 2564
E cmd@columba.ie

or contact
SALES@BROOKSIDE.IE